two writers Buffett admired: Sidney Weinberg and John Weinberg of
man Sachs. It is stunning how relevant the advice and the examples from
t 100 years ago will seem to any director today."

onald Graham, Chairman Emeritus, Graham Holdings Co.

droom Legacy is a fascinating and engaging read that brings the history
ard leadership to life while illuminating its continuing relevance. This
htful examination reminds us that the values at the heart of effective
nance—judgment, integrity, and stewardship—are as important
as ever."

ary Francis, Corporate Secretary and Chief Governance Officer, Chevron
oration

day's chaotic times for corporate boards, *Boardroom Legacy* goes back to
with wisdom from Sidney Weinberg and John Weinberg of Goldman
fame and board success. Lawrence Cunningham and several other
nance experts bring to life a director's role as steward, questioner, and
ian of long-term value. A must-read for directors and those interested in
rate governance."

lenn Hubbard, Russell L. Carson Professor of Economics and Finance,
nbia University; former Chairman of the President's Council of Economic
ers; Chair, MetLife; Chair, BlackRock Fixed-Income Funds; Independent
tor, TotalEnergies

sterful assembly of governance principles. Lawrence Cunningham reminds
t exceptional boards are built not simply on governance structures, but
dership, integrity, and sound judgment. *Boardroom Legacy* is a timely
oughtful reminder that directors create lasting value through character,
rdship, and the courage to ask the discerning questions that matter most."

erman E. Bulls, Vice Chairman, Americas, and International Director,
Chair, Fluence Energy; Vice Chair, USAA; Director, Host Hotels &
ts and Comfort Systems USA; 2024 NACD Public Company Director
Year; retired Colonel, US Army Reserve

droom Legacy brings together among the earliest perspectives on the
nd responsibilities of corporate directors in John L. Weinberg's 1948
ton thesis and two shorter pieces by his father, Sidney J. Weinberg. With

Praise for *Boardroom Legacy*

"An insightful and revealing look inside the corporate boar

— **David M. Rubenstein**, Co-Founder and Co-Chairman, T
bestselling author, *How to Lead* and *How to Invest*

"Businesses change, but people do not. Lawrence Cunningha
book—a timeless, wise, and readable study of governance th
those who have seen it up close."

— **Morgan Housel**, bestselling author, *The Psychology of Mo*

"An unexpected gem of a book. As someone who spent years
of Goldman Sachs, I was delighted to see that Lawrence C
discovered documents I never found: a 1933 essay by Sidney
the responsibilities of a corporate director, and John Weinberg
senior thesis on a similar topic. Corporate governance enthusia
the Weinbergs, but will stay for the poignant essays by Leo St
Rogers, Richard Gephardt, and others."

— **William D. Cohan**, bestselling author, *Money and Power*
Sachs Came to Rule the World

"Lawrence Cunningham, widely regarded for distilling the mo
ethics of Warren Buffett, takes us back to the source: John
remarkable Princeton thesis, written in 1948 when he was ju
writings and experience of his equally distinguished father, Si
the Weinbergs helped revolutionize the boardroom, advancin
directors were obligated to supervise, not blindly rubber-stamp, a
shareholders' best long-term interests. Cunningham has unearthe
documents that—graced with his beautiful introduction—pres
and urgent questions of what we now call corporate governance

— **Roger Lowenstein**, bestselling author, *Buffett*

"Lawrence Cunningham is the curator of the legacy of Warren B
edited what Buffett has written in his annual reports into adv
including the function of boards and of directors. This volume con

commentaries by leading voices in modern corporate governance, Lawrence Cunningham has created a must-read for corporate directors, corporate lawyers, and all who counsel public companies and corporate boards."

— **David A. Katz**, Corporate Partner, Wachtell, Lipton, Rosen & Katz; Adjunct Professor of Law, NYU School of Law

"As corporate governance faces renewed scrutiny, there is no better time to revisit John L. Weinberg's remarkably prescient thesis. *Boardroom Legacy* is indispensable reading for directors, governance professionals, and thoughtful observers of the boardroom."

— **Amanda M. Rose**, Cornelius Vanderbilt Chair in Law, Professor of Law, and Co-Director of the Law & Business Program, Vanderbilt University

"Boards are a central element in corporate governance. This volume will be valuable to all interested in what makes boards work and how boards, and the thinking about them, has evolved over time."

— **Lucian A. Bebchuk**, James Barr Ames Professor of Law, Economics, and Finance and Director, Program on Corporate Governance, Harvard Law School

"America's greatest companies have earned respect not only through performance, but through leadership grounded in judgment, integrity, and stewardship. These values were espoused and lived by John L. Weinberg, and they remain essential to effective corporate governance today."

— **Jay Clayton**, Senior Policy Advisor and Of Counsel, Sullivan & Cromwell; former Chairman, US Securities and Exchange Commission; former US Attorney for the Southern District of New York; former Chair, Apollo Global Management; former Director, American Express

"Sidney and John Weinberg were ahead of their time in their views on the proper role of corporate directors. By situating the Weinbergs' analysis in historical context, and relating their prescriptions to current corporate challenges, *Boardroom Legacy* provides a timely, incisive reminder of core governance principles at a moment of upheaval in US corporate governance."

— **Renée M. Jones**, Professor of Law and Dr. Thomas F. Carney Distinguished Scholar, Boston College Law School

Boardroom Legacy

The Weinbergs of Goldman Sachs and the Evolution of Corporate Governance

Foreword by John F. W. Rogers

Preface by Richard A. Gephardt

Afterword by Leo E. Strine, Jr.

Edited by Lawrence A. Cunningham

Hh Harriman House

Harriman House

Harriman House
www.harriman-house.com

First published in 2026 by Harriman House, an imprint of Pan Macmillan
Associated companies throughout the world
www.panmacmillan.com

Hardback ISBN: 978-1-80409-501-0
Ebook ISBN: 978-1-03742-373-4

01

Printed in the United States of America.

Cover design by Charlotte Smith. Adobe Stock images used.

Contents

For Stephanie Cuba

sine qua non

Acknowledgments

I am grateful to all who made this project possible. My deepest thanks go to my wife, Stephanie Cuba, who first encouraged me to search for John L. Weinberg's long-forgotten Princeton thesis and whose insights shaped the book from the outset. I am indebted to Tiffany Robson, research librarian at The George Washington University, whose tenacity enabled us to track down the thesis in the Princeton library.

I thank the Weinberg Center and its Advisory Board for embracing the project, with special thanks to Andy Bouchard, Simon Lorne, Bill Rock, and especially Bev O'Toole, whose enthusiasm and Princeton–Goldman Sachs connection helped open many doors. For extraordinary support, I thank John Rogers and Goldman Sachs.

For research support throughout the project, I thank the Weinberg Center's Steele Fellows—Brooke Burkhardt, Robby Erikson, Joey LaForte, Dante Pavan, and Alex White—along with the Center's Operations Manager and Assistant to the Director, Nicole Rich, whose outstanding assistance in managing the Weinberg Center holds everything together.

I am also grateful to the distinguished group of scholars and practitioners who contributed to this volume. Their thoughtful engagement with the Weinberg materials has enriched the project immeasurably. I extend thanks as well to the moderators and participants in the symposium associated with this book, whose insights added meaningfully to its development.

Finally, on behalf of the University of Delaware, I express our appreciation to John L. and Sue Ann Weinberg, and to their children John S. Weinberg and Jeannie Weinberg Rose, for enduring support of the Center that bears John L. Weinberg's name.

Lawrence A. Cunningham
July 10, 2026

Style Note

This volume presents Sidney J. Weinberg's 1933 memorandum and 1949 speech and John L. Weinberg's 1948 thesis largely as they were written, with limited stylistic adjustments to enhance readability. The substance has been preserved for historical accuracy. Endnotes and annotations supply context or perspective.

For clarity, some long paragraphs have been divided, we added commas to aid flow, and we use asterisks (*) for footnote markers to distinguish them from the endnotes we added. Minor grammatical or composition issues have been corrected. The thesis's table of contents included outline-style headings (e.g., I.A.2) that did not appear in the body; we have inserted those designations where appropriate.

The thesis and its bibliography retain their original citation style; the remainder of the book follows *The Chicago Manual of Style* (18th ed.). The thesis is structured into seven chapters, numbered I through VII, which are distinct from the book's chapters, numbered 1 through 14.

All three works originally employed exclusively male pronouns, reflecting the demographics of corporate leadership in the mid-20th century. To balance historical fidelity with contemporary usage, we retain the original pronouns in Sidney Weinberg's memorandum and speech, which have been published previously and are brief. In the thesis, we have adopted gender-neutral language using the least intrusive method suited to each sentence.

Finally, this book discusses two individuals with the same surname. To distinguish the two, we invited individual chapter authors to refer to them by first and last name or simply use first names, without any intent to diminish formality or respect.

Contributors

Mary K. Bush – Former US Representative to the IMF Board; President, Bush International; corporate director

Brian R. Cheffins – S.J. Berwin Professor of Corporate Law, University of Cambridge

Lawrence A. Cunningham – Presiding Director, John L. Weinberg Center for Corporate Governance, University of Delaware; Henry St. George Tucker III Research Professor of Law Emeritus, The George Washington University; corporate director

Richard A. Gephardt – Former Majority and Minority Leader of the US House of Representatives; CEO, Gephardt Government Affairs; corporate director

Joan MacLeod Heminway – Rick Rose Distinguished Professor of Law and Director of the Clayton Center for Entrepreneurial Law, The University of Tennessee Winston College of Law

Andrew Jones – Principal Researcher, Governance & Sustainability Center, The Conference Board

David F. Larcker – James Irvin Miller Professor Emeritus of Accounting and Director, Corporate Governance Research Initiative, Stanford Graduate School of Business

Simon M. Lorne – Adjunct Professor of Law, University of Texas School of Law; former SEC General Counsel; corporate director

Dalia T. Mitchell – Louis Harkey Mayo Research Professor of Law & Professor of Law and History, The George Washington University

Michael Montelongo – Former CFO and 19th Assistant Secretary of the US Air Force for Financial Management & Comptroller; Executive Fellow, Harvard Business School; corporate director

John F. W. Rogers – Executive Vice President and Secretary to the Board, Goldman Sachs & Co.

Leo E. Strine, Jr. – Of Counsel, Wachtell, Lipton, Rosen & Katz; Michael L. Wachter Distinguished Fellow in Law & Policy, University of Pennsylvania Carey Law School; former Chief Justice of the Delaware Supreme Court and Chancellor of its Court of Chancery

Brian Tayan – Researcher, Corporate Governance Research Initiative, Stanford Graduate School of Business

Paul F. Washington – President & CEO, Society for Corporate Governance

Harwell Wells – Richard H. Walker '75 Chair in Law, Temple University Beasley School of Law

Amy Deen Westbrook – Norman R. Pozez Chair in Business & Transactional Law and Director, Business & Transactional Law Center, Washburn University School of Law

David A. Westbrook – Louis A. Del Cotto Professor of Law; Director, NYC Program in Business & Law, University at Buffalo School of Law

Foreword

The Measure of a Director
John F. W. Rogers

I recently listened to an oral-history interview with John L. Weinberg, conducted at our firm in 2002 by John Cohen, his longtime chief of staff—a conversation I had the privilege of attending. I was struck anew by its timing. The interview took place the same year the Weinberg Center for Corporate Governance was founded, just a few years before its namesake passed away. Listening again was a powerful reminder of what an extraordinary life he lived—what a lion of a man he was—and of the unshakable character that defined him.

John's sense of duty and character was forged early. He left Deerfield Academy during his senior year to serve as a second lieutenant in the US Marine Corps during World War II. Still a teenager, he led men into combat in the Pacific. He learned to listen to battle-tested noncommissioned officers, to carry himself with humility, and to lead with quiet authority. Those lessons stayed with him. Years later, he took a leave of absence from Goldman Sachs to rejoin the Marines during the Korean War, eventually advancing to the rank of captain.

That sensibility—the subordination of oneself to a greater good—became the foundation for how John lived his life and how he later led Goldman Sachs as a senior partner and cultural carrier. During the conversation that afternoon, he spoke about the firm's early history and its improbable rise into the top tier of investment banking. In the 1950s, Goldman Sachs was competing against entrenched firms such as Morgan Stanley and Dillon, Read. There was a great deal of pitching, he recalled, but not much business at first. Over time, however, through a relentless focus on earning trust and cultivating deep relationships, the firm strengthened its acumen and resilience—helping clients work through challenges rather than merely transact around them.

Transparency and constructive, respectful engagement are more important than ever. As we reflect on John Weinberg's leadership and legacy, it is worth recalling that he never viewed work in the private sector as separate from the public interest. He believed the role of the director was to enhance the long-term value of the corporation for its shareholders—and, in doing so, to advance the public good.

Like his father, Sidney, before him, John believed that companies operate under an implicit social contract: an obligation to remain continually mindful of the human consequences of boardroom decisions. Even as a student, John expanded on the role of corporate directors and boards, emphasizing that companies must contend not only with economic realities but also with social and governmental priorities. As he wrote in 1948, "The key to national prosperity and welfare, perhaps national survival, may well hinge upon the ability of directors to solve the intricate economic problems confronting them." He added that a director must not only be willing to direct, but—more importantly—must know enough to direct.

Looking ahead, as corporate governance continues to evolve in response to the needs of companies, shareholders, and regulators alike, the foundational principles John Weinberg articulated remain timeless. He believed governance should be anchored in prudence and long-term stewardship—resisting short-term pressures and remaining faithful to enduring values. Boards, in his view, were not paper institutions, but bodies of accountability and strategic guidance, balancing rigorous oversight with room for innovation.

Above all, John believed in character and integrity. My friend, the late Senator Alan Simpson of Wyoming, once said, "If you have integrity, nothing else matters. If you don't have integrity, nothing else matters." John understood culture itself as a form of built-in accountability—a governing force that binds institutions together and aligns the interests of clients, shareholders, and society at large.

He believed that well-run companies are engines of economic prosperity, whose benefits extend broadly. And he believed that boards play an essential and enduring role in providing oversight and direction to promote long-term corporate value—not only in the interests of investors, but in support of the vitality, dynamism, and prosperity of the American economy.

Read alongside the thesis that follows, these reflections illuminate why a document written by a 23-year-old undergraduate has endured. John Weinberg's early articulation of the director's role—as steward, questioner, and guardian of long-term value—was not a youthful abstraction. It was a blueprint he carried into the boardroom and into the institutions he served. The chapters that follow examine, test, and extend those ideas, but they begin here.

Preface

The Human Stuff in Board Service Through the Ages
Richard A. Gephardt

I had the privilege of being a public servant in the St. Louis Board of Aldermen for five years and a member of the US House of Representatives for 28 years. Since leaving public service in 2004, I have had more than 20 years of service in the private sector, with two different efforts.

First, I have accepted assignments to assist many different corporations in having a more successful and productive relationship with their workforces. This included Goldman Sachs in the years just after John L. Weinberg served as lead partner. Second, I have served on five public boards: U.S. Steel, Ford, Spirit AeroSystems, Centene, and CenturyLink. My service on the Ford board followed John Weinberg's years of service on that board, which in turn followed his father's and preceded those of his son.

What has always guided me in all of my public and private work and service is the most important advice that I received from my mother, Loreen Gephardt, when I was five years old. She would get down on her knees and look me in the eye and say:

> Dick—always treat people the way you would like to be treated. Before you say anything to anyone, think about how you would like it said to you. Before you do anything to anyone, think about how you would like it done to you. And always be humble, because you deserve to be.

Later, when I was a little older, she would say, "Most of the time you are going to get back what you give out. So, if you treat people badly, you are going to get bad treatment back. Why would you want that?"

This advice provided the North Star for the rest of my life. And what I have discovered is that the Golden Rule and humility are behavior habits that can bring you success and a happy, fulfilled life with your family and any human organization or entity you are ever part of.

When I was Leader of the Democrats in the US House for 14 years, I tried to follow those rules to help get Congress to achieve compromises to solve difficult, controversial issues and problems that faced our country.

In 1999, we finally achieved the goal of balancing the federal budget: the result of nine years of hard, patient, painstaking work with 535 members of Congress and two different presidents from two different political parties. In those nine years, enough of us used the Golden Rule enough of the time to achieve controversial compromises that solved an important problem for the first time in 50 years.

Stepping back from that nine-year experience, I conclude that it is a vivid example of how basic human relations are at the heart of progress and success in human history. John Weinberg's thesis stresses the importance of many of these same basic human relations in the corporate boardroom.

How did humans come to dominate the earth, in place of much larger and more powerful species? Humans possessed a bigger brain—and, importantly, they invented language, which allowed them to communicate.

That, in turn, allowed them to *work together*, so that they could solve common challenges or problems. Early humans were hunter–gatherers, so communication and planning allowed them to get the best results from their hunting and gathering activities. At the heart of that experience was their ability to trust one another—and eventually to understand that treating one another as they wanted to be treated achieved optimal results for everyone. Individuals who were not trusted were selfish, and those who treated others badly were outcasts.

John Weinberg makes two points that are relevant to these basic practices. First, he highlights the importance of keeping directors informed through various methods. This parallels my point about communication being crucial for early humans. John mentions, "The basic purpose underlying a consistent flow of information to the board is the maximum and most efficient utilization of the mechanism for the greatest benefit to the corporation."[1]

John also emphasizes the importance of mutual understanding and cooperation in top management, which aligns with my point about early humans working together to solve common challenges. John states, "Only through teamwork can this mechanism function smoothly and efficiently."[2]

With all of this as background, let me tell you how I have seen this "human stuff" impact corporations positively through the years.

My consistent experience is that corporate leaders and boards who pay close attention to the human stuff—among themselves and with all of their employees—always get the best results for *everyone*. The corporation, its leaders, its board, all of the employees, and all of their customers win.

The Ford Motor Company

Ford has been the foundation of the American automotive industry for over 100 years. When I was in Congress, I had all of the Big Three's auto plants in my district. When I traveled the country, I would routinely visit auto plants, and before arriving I would always ask to meet the plant leadership and the UAW workers together.

Chrysler's and GM's plant leaders would always refuse to meet with me at the same time as their employees. I would then refuse to come, and usually the leaders would relent and have a meeting with me and the workers together. When I arrived at the meeting, all of the leaders were on one side of the room and all of the workers were on the opposite side of the room. It was like they came from two different worlds.

When I called ahead to Ford plants, the leaders said my request was unnecessary; they always took meetings with the leaders and workers together. When I arrived at the Ford meeting, the workers and leaders were all in the middle of the room, and it was obvious that they were used to communicating. They liked one another, and they were used to *working together*.

Through the years, I quizzed UAW members everywhere about which of the Big Three companies was the best to work for. Without exception, and whomever they worked for, they would say Ford. I would say, "Why?" The answer was always the same: Ford treated everyone like they were part of the Ford family. This was proof positive to me that Ford leadership and boards treated all of their employees the way they wanted to be treated. And guess what? They were getting back what they gave out—not complicated, but very powerful.

When Ford Motor went public, it tapped Goldman Sachs and Sidney Weinberg, John's father, to advise the company. Sidney and John, in addition to leading Goldman Sachs for most of the 20th century, also served long tenures on Ford's board. In my observations of the two companies, I found that both emphasized teamwork and partnership with employees. This comparison reflects the shared values of collaboration and mutual respect that drive success in both organizations.

Springfield ReManufacturing Corp. in Springfield, Missouri

I met Jack Stack early during my congressional career. Early in my career, people in Missouri told me he had created over 20 companies in Springfield that were all very successful because of the way he treated his employees.

Jack explained to me that, originally, he was plant manager at a John Deere manufacturing facility that had fallen on hard times. He was told to close the plant, but instead he got the local bank to lend him enough money to buy the plant from Deere, based on pledging his house as collateral.

He returned to the plant from his bank-loan meeting and gathered the 100 or so employees together to tell them what he had done. He said, "I just hocked my house to buy our plant, and I need your help to save the plant so that I don't lose my house. So, we are now all partners, and I am going to give all of you shares of stock in this new company."

He said that every Monday morning, he called all the employees together for a "huddle" to share ideas on how to solve problems and bottlenecks in the plant. The meetings included the salesman who was now marketing the tractor parts that they were making to the outside world. This allowed the manufacturing workers to get input from the customers that they needed to buy their products. The meeting also allowed the maintenance team and the janitor crew to understand how their roles were very important to the financial results of the company.

They had the CFO report to all of the employees every week about the financial position of the company, and he commented on the vital importance of inventory control and other issues that, before, no one ever addressed. The workers also had a weekly understanding of the value of their own shares of stock in the company.

Jack always told me that the main responsibility of a CEO or leader of any corporation is to engage with every employee, so that you are getting 100% of everyone's discretionary effort, including the janitor's. And never forget that Sidney Weinberg, ultimately a titan of finance along with his son, began his career at Goldman Sachs as the assistant to the janitor.

Over the last 50 years, Springfield ReManufacturing Corp. has blossomed into 20 or so different successful companies and has produced many millionaires in Springfield. Jack calls it "the great game of business," and his strategy is founded on the simple principle of getting people to *work together* for common success. I have always believed that Jack understands and uses the power of the Golden Rule.

John Weinberg's thesis speaks to how these are important values for the corporate boardroom as well. For example, John discusses the need for directors to have integrity, loyalty, and a broad social viewpoint. This dovetails with my emphasis on trust and treating others well to achieve optimal results. John notes, "Not only must their characters be above reproach, but they should also be [people] with a broad social viewpoint and public spirit."[3]

John also discusses the significance of selecting a chief executive who can lead effectively, similar to my examples of corporate leaders engaging with employees. John states, "The one administrative function unanimously accomplished by the board of directors is the selection of the chief executive."[4]

Private Equity Firm KKR

For some time, KKR has worked with competitors to get their portfolio companies to adopt a program they call "Ownership Works." The program advocates that any company give a meaningful share of workers compensation in the form of stock in the company. Thus far, they have gotten 14 of their portfolio companies to try the program, and the financial results of those companies have consistently been superior to those of their competitors.

Takeaways

At the heart of these three different examples is the practice of treating all of their employees the way the leadership of the company would like to be treated. In all three examples, their employees share in the profits and financial performance of the company. They see themselves as full partners, not just "employees" or "workers." They feel respected and valued by the leadership. Isn't that the way we all want to be treated?

Again, it is fitting to relate my experiences in this book about the Weinberg family. That is the way they provided leadership in the financial industry. In the end, families, businesses, communities, and nations are just made up of people—human beings. If they are led right, included, listened to, and treated fairly, they will achieve incredibly positive results.

In his thesis, John explores the evolving social responsibility of corporations, a discussion that complements my examples of companies treating employees well and achieving positive results. He writes, "The social conception of the corporation has gone beyond the mere protection of stockholder interests."[5]

If you think about it, America's founders established the country on four simple ideas: democracy, freedom, rule of law, and capitalism. All four ideas, to me, are an articulation of the Golden Rule.

And I believe that is why America is, and has been for 250 years, the "shining city on a hill." In boardrooms, as in democracies, enduring success rests on timeless human values—none more so than the simple yet powerful ethic at the heart of John Weinberg's legacy and this book.

Introduction

From Thesis to Testament

Lawrence A. Cunningham

Today's debates over corporate purpose, social responsibility, and director functions may seem unprecedented and unresolvable. However, fruitful discussions of such topics were occurring 80 years ago in the aftermath of the Great Depression and two world wars. Astute voices from that era included the father-and-son pair of Sidney J. Weinberg and John L. Weinberg. The two served as directors of scores of public companies and as the legendary leaders of Goldman Sachs for most of the 20th century: Sidney from 1930 to 1969, and John from 1976 to 1990.[6] A decade later, John endowed the John L. Weinberg Center for Corporate Governance at the University of Delaware.

Sidney J. Weinberg (1891–1969) grew up in Brooklyn as one of 11 children of poor Jewish immigrants. He began his career at Goldman Sachs as a janitor's assistant.[7] After dropping out of junior high school, his diligence and determination propelled him through the firm's mailroom and onto a trading desk, ultimately leading to his role as senior partner.

Sidney took the helm of Goldman Sachs in the wake of the Great Crash of 1929, after the collapse of the Goldman Sachs Trading Corporation (GSTC). A highly leveraged subsidiary like today's hedge funds, GSTC was the brainchild and downfall of Goldman's incumbent head, Waddill Catchings.[8] In 1930, Sidney joined the boards of several major American companies, including General Foods (which encompassed today's Post Brands), B.F. Goodrich (now part of Michelin), National Dairy (later Kraft), and Sears, Roebuck. (For a list of Sidney's board service, visit the Weinberg Center website.[9])

In 1933, inspired by lawsuits against distinguished directors of the period for failing to prevent fraud, Sidney wrote a memorandum outlining 11 principles of board oversight. These principles are durable and were expanded upon in Sidney's influential 1949 speech to the Harvard Business School Club of Cleveland, entitled "The Functions of a Corporate Director."[10] During his career, Sidney was a director of at least two dozen public companies and a prominent corporate leader. His obituary appeared on the front page of *The New York Times*, calling him "Mr. Wall Street" and "a director's director."[11]

John L. Weinberg (1925–2006), raised in Scarsdale, New York, attended Deerfield Academy. He enlisted in the US Marine Corps during his senior year, and led troops in World War II while still a teenager.[12] After his service, Weinberg enrolled in Princeton University, along with a large cohort of fellow veterans, all possessing unusually worldly experience for undergraduates.[13] At Princeton, John's senior thesis, *Status and Functions of Corporate Directors*, clearly drew on Sidney's speech as well as his circle of corporate directors and business leaders.[14]

After graduating from Princeton with honors, John attended Harvard Business School before joining Goldman Sachs in 1950. From there, he took a leave of absence to rejoin the Marines to fight in the Korean War, advancing to the rank of captain. Finally, he returned to Goldman as an investment banker. He spent the rest of his career there, while also serving on at least 20 boards, including those of Goldman Sachs, Knight Ridder, Providian Financial and Yum! Brands. (For a full list of John's board service, visit the Weinberg Center website.[15])

All three of the Weinberg works—Sidney's memorandum, his speech, and John's thesis—are among the earliest treatments of the functions, status, and responsibilities of directors, marking the beginning of what would later evolve into the field of corporate governance.[16] The Weinberg works, and the thesis most vividly, reflect the zeitgeist of their era while also capturing themes that resonate today. The enduring value of the Weinbergs' writings lies in how they transcend the specifics of their time. Revisiting this work offers a grounding perspective on the core values and principles that underpin corporate governance today.

The Weinbergs' work was innovative because it unsettled prevailing assumptions about corporate governance in their era—and it leaves open questions that remain contested today. Sidney's insistence on informed, engaged directors challenged the then-dominant view of boards as largely ceremonial bodies composed of eminent figures whose primary value lay in prestige rather than oversight. John's thesis, while grounded in practical boardroom realities, departed from both managerialism and pure shareholder primacy by treating directors as an independent governing institution—neither passive agents of management nor mere conduits for shareholder will.

That conception raised tensions that persist: how active directors should be without usurping management, how far boards may consider social consequences without diluting accountability to shareholders, and whether professionalized directors risk becoming detached from operating realities. The Weinbergs did not resolve these tensions so much as illuminate them, offering a framework that was ahead of its time but intentionally incomplete—inviting judgment, discretion, and continual reassessment rather than fixed rules. It is this combination of innovation and unresolved challenge that gives their work enduring relevance.

Sidney's boardroom memorandum "The Responsibility of Directors" was inspired by the fallout from the infamous fraudulent scheming of Ivar Kreuger. Known as the "Match King,"[17] Kreuger amassed a fortune by lending money to European governments in exchange for matchstick monopolies. Between 1913 and 1932, Kreuger built his family-owned company, Swedish Match, into a $600 million empire (some $15 billion in today's dollars). Operating in 36 countries, he controlled 40% of the world's match production.[18] It wasn't until after his suicide in 1932 that the empire was revealed to be a massive deception of pyramid schemes, forged documents, and inflated earnings.

The fallout included lawsuits against the directors of Kreuger's companies, one of which, in particular, inspired Sidney's memorandum. The board was a who's who of corporate America at the time, featuring prominent lawyers and bankers (including the founder of Allen & Company, a partner in J.P. Morgan & Co., and a Boston Brahmin), leading industrialists (such as a railroad executive, a sugar tycoon, and a real estate magnate), and a scion of the Rockefeller dynasty. The board sought to have the lawsuit dismissed, but the court denied its request in an opinion dated June 4, 1933.

Sidney wrote his memorandum, dated June 21, 1933, for the CEOs of the companies whose boards he served, as well as fellow directors. He highlighted the importance of directors being well informed and actively engaged in the oversight of corporate affairs. He proposed a balanced approach, advocating that directors receive regular, comprehensive updates on company operations while ensuring that executive officers retain the ability to manage day-to-day activities efficiently. The memo underscored the need for a cooperative relationship between directors and executives, aiming to establish a code of procedure that would enhance accountability and governance within corporations.

Ironically, Sidney's 1949 speech was inspired by his own experience serving on the board of McKesson & Robbins amid a notorious fraud.[19] The storied wholesale drug company, with roots dating to 1833, was sold in 1926 to Frank D. Coster, whose real name was Philip Musica. Musica's family were corrupt food importers who bribed dockworkers to inflate the weight of shipments. From 1909 to 1916, Philip and other family members were repeatedly arrested and jailed. After a stint working undercover for the district attorney, Musica returned to crime, including posing as the president of a pharmaceutical company that fronted for a bootlegging operation. By 1926, with his name and identity changed, he seemed a respectable businessman and acquired control of McKesson & Robbins.

During the ensuing 13 years—while Sidney was on the board—Musica/Coster looted the company, stealing some $3 million by creating elaborate fictitious accounts. When the company treasurer finally smelled the rat, an SEC investigation resulted, finding a galactic failure not only of financial reporting but also of corporate governance. In 1939, Musica/Coster killed himself. The scandal prompted reforms, beginning with the SEC's requirement of shareholder election of auditors, and eventually led to board oversight through the audit committee.

Sidney's 1949 speech aimed to educate his fellow directors and improve board service across corporate America. Repeating and expanding on the 11 principles from his 1933 memorandum, Sidney added two more: have a company's chief accounting officer attend every board meeting, and form a board audit committee comprised solely of outside directors to interact with the company's independent auditor. Sidney's advice was spot-on: independent audit committees were eventually required for listed companies by the New York Stock Exchange (NYSE) from 1977 and for all public companies by the Sarbanes–Oxley Act of 2002.

Sidney published that speech the year after John submitted his thesis, which elucidates on themes of the speech and Sidney's memorandum. John's thesis provides an overall assessment of company directorship and contemporary corporate governance. It is structured into six main chapters that address such topics as corporate social responsibility and the foundations of corporate administration (including board authority, the distinction between directors' and managers' roles, board composition, director liability, and the profile of an ideal director).

While the thesis focuses on practical aspects of boardroom life, it also engages with fundamental debates on the purpose of a corporation and the resulting role of directors. It explains that American industry in 1948 faced a critical test, addressing severe challenges to the system of free enterprise. The business corporation, as a cornerstone of democratic capitalism, held a dominant position, and the board of directors played a crucial role in its performance. Yet there was a lively debate over the purpose of corporations, veering from solely protecting stockholder interests (advocated by Adolf Berle), to reconciling private enterprise with the social needs of a democratic system (advocated by Merrick Dodd).

The Berle–Dodd debate and the transcendent issues it raised remain of central relevance today, as people disagree about whether corporations should prioritize shareholder value or promote social objectives. Equally resonant are the more mundane topics the thesis addresses, such as director selection, board size, and shareholder engagement. While contexts have shifted, including the rise of institutional investors and the complexities of proxy voting, the underlying challenges persist.

The Weinbergs anticipated other developments, such as the importance of occupational diversity on boards, John asserting that "the wider the variety of occupations and experience, the greater will be the benefit to the corporation."[20] Although their use of masculine pronouns reflects the norms of the era, the emphasis on diversity—now including gender and racial diversity—was ahead of its time. Sidney's 1949 endorsement of board gender diversity reflected his years of experience serving alongside the remarkable Marjorie Merriweather Post on the General Foods board.[21]

Another prescient argument concerned director compensation, which has changed significantly since the 1940s. Directors were often unpaid at that time, but they now receive substantial remuneration, with NYSE company directors averaging $300,000 annually. John and Sidney appreciated this, arguing for well-compensated directors to meet the growing demands of the role—an argument that remains highly relevant.

The Weinbergs' analysis of the legal underpinnings of corporate governance also holds true today, with only minor updates. Discussion of the board's statutory authority, the business judgment rule, and the role of directors as a collective rather than individuals reflect principles that continue to shape governance. Above all, Sidney's repeated emphasis on the importance of information flows and John's mention of an "implicit" duty for directors to stay fully informed are foundational. The latter was codified in the landmark 1985 *Smith v. Van Gorkom* case.[22]

Modern readers will also appreciate the emphasis throughout the Weinberg works on functions rather than features: both John's thesis and Sidney's speech use the word "Functions" in their titles. They focus on substance and purpose, not symbol or ritual. For example, John's thesis details the chairman's role and context, while today many advocate splitting the chair and CEO roles without a similar probe; the thesis focuses on functional skills, backgrounds, and traits of ideal directors (the "desiderata"), while today's governance often prioritizes skills matrices, meeting length, and recordkeeping. His partial solution was a professional cadre of directors, serving multiple non-competing organizations and earning their living from board service. The proposal mirrors the current trend toward professional board members.

The thesis stresses the value of the "discerning question." According to a contemporary scholar the thesis cites, Harvard Business School Professor John Baker, "the most effective directors … are those who ask the most discerning questions."[23] That belief persists, as prominent critics, led by Harvard Business School Professor Myles Mace in his 1971 book *Directors: Myth and Reality*, skewer boards for failing to pose discerning questions.[24] Responses to this deficiency have tended to focus on formalities rather than functions—from director independence to corporate compliance.[25] In the process, while the discerning question remains a staple of business management thought, its importance to corporate governance may be underappreciated.

The foundational role of the board in corporate governance explains why the thesis and speech refer to the board as the corporation's "supreme" authority, akin to what scholars today might dub "director primacy."[26] On the other hand, the Weinberg works stress that directors are ultimately beholden to stockholders, reflecting an enduring "shareholder primacy" norm, while allowing consideration of other constituencies. That is, the shape and function of the board of directors, in turn, influence the roles, functions, and status of all other elements in the broader corporate governance ecosystem, beyond directors and shareholders. While the Weinberg works touch on many elements of this broad stage, their primary interest, as the titles underscore, is the board of directors.

* * * * *

Over his career, John Weinberg was a boardroom denizen, serving on the boards of many corporations and civic organizations, as well as leading Goldman Sachs. The Goldman Sachs that he and his father built over the 20th century was renowned for a culture of partnership, ethics, and honor.[27] As a director, John lived up to the aspirational desiderata of his thesis—and then some—being not only discerning but independent, decisive, and pragmatic.

In the early 1970s, for example, John served on the board of U.S. Financial, a California-based homebuilder. The company had a motto: building homes the way Ford built cars.[28] U.S. Financial, led by CEO Robert H. Walter, was riding high during the era's real estate boom. As John perused the financials, however, he grew increasingly skeptical of the company's reporting, with concerns about accounting for certain transactions. As the board pressed for answers, Walter made a presentation attempting to explain, but gaps appeared.

When the answers were not forthcoming, John led the board, on November 23, 1972, to request Walter's resignation as CEO. This was promptly tendered.[29] A subsequent federal investigation revealed criminal behavior,[30] leading to charges against Walter and several other executives, including his son, for conspiracy and filing false reports. Walter pled no contest and received a prison sentence. U.S. Financial's stock collapsed, and the company ultimately filed for bankruptcy. John's leadership in firing the CEO was a critical turning point, demonstrating a discerning and decisive exercise of board power in corporate governance.

In the 1980s, John was serving on the board of the United States Golf Association (USGA) when it was sued. Polara Enterprises had patented a self-correcting golf ball that adjusted hooks and slices in flight. The USGA, the entity that writes the rules of golf, declared that the ball did not comply with the rules and would harm the game. Polara responded by suing, accusing the USGA of conspiring with the Professional Golf Association (PGA) in violation of antitrust laws. The case went to trial, with a jury verdict for Polara. Notwithstanding that verdict, the judge dismissed the case, handing the USGA a clear win.

While Polara threatened to appeal, a settlement proposal emerged: the USGA would pay $1.5 million to resolve the matter, buying Polara's patents on the self-correcting golf balls in order to, in effect, bury them. As the board considered the proposal, another USGA director, who was also the USGA's general counsel, Bill Williams, argued that the USGA was right in its decision and should win an appeal.[31] But John Weinberg countered that the risk of losing an appeal was not worth taking. He said the better bet for the USGA was to pay the settlement amount and bury the patents, which is what they did—offering a pragmatic resolution.

In 1981, John joined the board of Seagram, the Canadian spirits company led by Edgar Bronfman. John and Bronfman had known each other since their early days in New York, when they lived in the same building while courting their wives.[32] That personal familiarity helped when Seagram—seeking to diversify beyond beverages—acquired a substantial stake in Conoco during the oil company's dramatic struggle to fend off T. Boone Pickens. The resulting takeover battle, then the largest in history, ended with Conoco being acquired by DuPont, Delaware's storied chemical company.

Seagram's new position as DuPont's largest shareholder produced a complicated relationship. The two firms differed markedly in products, governance styles, and corporate cultures. It fell to John Weinberg to ease the friction. Over the next several years, he served as a trusted intermediary, carrying messages, clarifying expectations, and helping both sides manage an unusual ownership structure. His steady, diplomatic role in this period led DuPont, in 1986, to invite him to join its board, on which he served until 1995.

Those were consequential years for DuPont. The board was unusually large, including several former executives and members of the DuPont family, and the company navigated significant strategic decisions. In 1989, the board selected Edgar S. Woolard, Jr., as CEO, beginning a partnership between Woolard and John that proved constructive and influential during their overlapping terms.[33]

* * * * *

It was while researching John's career that I first encountered his long-forgotten Princeton thesis. In preparing to deliver the Weinberg Center's 2024 Distinguished Lecture, I looked for his views on whether business leaders should speak out on political issues. The public record was sparse; he was famously media-averse, reportedly even hiring someone at Goldman Sachs to help keep his and the firm's name out of the press. His Princeton thesis is therefore one of the few public sources revealing his thinking—expressed when he was young but, according to multiple people I consulted who knew him at Goldman Sachs and in the boardroom, consistent with the principles he practiced throughout his career.

John's thesis therefore stands as one of the few public statements of the values he carried into his professional life, and it provides the backbone of this book. The volume opens with the two short but foundational works by Sidney Weinberg, followed by John Weinberg's thesis, all accompanied by annotations commenting on historical context and continuing relevance.

Part II places the Weinberg works in their historical setting by exploring the foundations of corporate governance. Highlighted are both shareholder activism and director independence (concepts that took root in the period when the Weinbergs wrote), along with corporate purpose—in particular, what John's thesis contributes to ongoing debate. These historical perspectives are richly woven by three of today's most influential writers in the field: Brian Cheffins, Dalia Mitchell and Harwell Wells.

Part III moves on to the craft of corporate governance, as distinguished directors and public servants Mary Bush, Simon Lorne, and Michael Montelongo explore the continued value and relevance of the Weinberg works for boards. They discuss timeless principles such as culture, integrity, diligence, and profit, revisiting John Weinberg's insights on external threats through a modern geopolitical lens in a new conception of patriotic capitalism.

Part IV explores more aspirational aspects of directorship evident in the Weinberg works and today—along with practical limitations. Joan Heminway examines board leadership issues such as separating or combining the roles of board chair and CEO. Amy and David (Bert) Westbrook probe the "discerning question" that John's thesis emphasizes. Both chapters confront the challenges associated with such admirable aspirations and share thoughtful perspectives on how to optimize.

Part V presents empirical research and context on more than a dozen specific topics, all as important and debated today as they were when the Weinbergs wrote. Topics include the familiar but vexing challenges of board composition, size, leadership, and evaluation, as well as executive succession planning, compensation, and shareholder voting rights. Implications range from the importance of context when assessing such practices—that one size has never fit all, as the Weinbergs emphasized—to the value of data in benchmarking them. The contributors are David Larcker and Brian Tayan, along with Andrew Jones from The Conference Board and Paul Washington from the Society for Corporate Governance.

A conclusion and afterword juxtapose gaps in current thought with a sense of continuity despite change, in pieces by Leo Strine and me.

* * * * *

Undergraduate theses do not typically aim to contribute original knowledge in the way doctoral dissertations do. Their purpose is to demonstrate mastery of ideas and to cultivate intellectual discipline. Yet the strongest undergraduate theses do more than restate existing thought—they clarify it. At Princeton, the senior thesis has long held a distinctive place, one that generations of alumni have described as the most valuable academic experience of their undergraduate years. John L. Weinberg's thesis fits comfortably within that tradition: deeply researched, intellectually serious, and reflective of the values that would later define his career.

There are notable precedents for publishing or revisiting undergraduate theses when they illuminate a later life. Princeton examples include F. Scott Fitzgerald's *This Side of Paradise* (originating from undergraduate work) and John C. Bogle's thesis, which later became the conceptual foundation for the index fund. Work by Justice Samuel Alito and Michelle Obama has likewise drawn sustained public attention decades after graduation. Beyond Princeton, David Foster Wallace's Amherst thesis was published by Columbia University Press, and John F. Kennedy's senior thesis was reworked into *Why England Slept*—a book that drew renewed praise when republished during his presidency.

John Weinberg's thesis invites comparison with that of John F. Kennedy. Like Kennedy, he was the son of a prominent leader; his undergraduate work shows both the perspective of a young scholar and the early articulation of principles that would shape a consequential professional life. Publishing it today—80 years after its completion—recovers not only a historical document but a source of continuing insight.

A few anomalies surround the original submission. John dated the thesis April 1948, nearly a year after completing his coursework with the class of 1947, and his research appears to have extended into that additional year. Princeton's records identify no faculty advisor, suggesting that his father played an informal advisory role.

Readers may reasonably ask whether an undergraduate thesis deserves publication. Our answer rests not on nostalgia or family lineage, but on the work itself and the relevance of the questions it raises. The thesis stands on its merits, and its interest is only deepened by the reflections of the thoughtful scholars and practitioners who engage with it in the chapters that follow.

I. The Weinberg Director: Duties, Status, and Functions

Chapter 1

The Responsibility of Directors
Sidney J. Weinberg

Memorandum

Regarding: The responsibility of directors and an outline of the program suggested as the basis of cooperation between officers and directors of a corporation.

By Sidney J. Weinberg (June 21, 1933)

Recently there was handed down an opinion by Justice Black of the Supreme Court of the State of New York[34] emphasizing very strongly the responsibility of directors to corporations for all matters in connection with the management of their affairs.[35] Moreover, the recently enacted Federal Securities Act imposes very stringent liabilities upon directors of corporations in connection with the issuance of new securities.

The coincidence of both these things happening about the same time has served to focus public attention on the question of a director's liability, and similarly it has given food for thought to men like myself who are directors of several companies as to whether or not we are discharging our duties as directors in a manner in keeping with the spirit and letter of the law and in conformance with what stockholders have come to expect of directors.

Without desiring to make this memorandum legalistic, I quote a few extracts from the legal opinion referred to above, merely to give the reader the gist of such opinion:

> "Directors should direct."

> "[T]he directors of the corporation are charged with the duties of trustees and bound to care for its property and manage its affairs in good faith, and for a violation of that duty resulting in waste of its assets, injury to its property … they are liable to account in equity the same as ordinary trustees."
>
> "The law of this state is that to avoid liability for misfeasance or non-feasance, directors are bound to exercise the same degree of care in their office that men of common prudence generally show in their own affairs."
>
> "[W]here they [directors] accept these positions of trust they are expected and required to give them the care and attention that a prudent man should exercise in like circumstances and charged with a like duty, usually the care that he shows in the conduct of his own affairs of a similar kind."
>
> "The law has no place for dummy directors."

The problem comes down to the question of the extent and quantity of information which a corporation ought to provide each director regularly and in a satisfactory manner in order to enable him to exercise the reasonable care of a prudent man in the discharge of his duties.

To go to extremes in either direction may be equally as unsound to the best interests of all concerned. It obviously would be a short-sighted policy to set up a working arrangement between the executives of a business and the board of directors which prevented the ordinary and administrative business of the corporation from being handled expeditiously by such officers, or by an executive committee, rather than by the board of directors itself.

A saner approach to the problem is the determination of the amount of, and kind of, information which a director ought reasonably to be given periodically as well as the extent to which directors ought to be consulted at meetings of the board as to questions of broad policies to be pursued by the executive officers.

With this thought in mind, I have worked up a program which I believe can serve as the basis of cooperation between the executive officers of a corporation and its directors, particularly those directors who are not connected with its active management. This suggested program is offered as nothing more than a starting point for discussion, as I realize well that not all the suggestions are applicable in their entirety to every corporation just as I realize that I may have omitted certain suggestions which are most important in the case of other corporations. Subject to the foregoing, I submit the following as the essentials of a code of procedure:

1. Boards of directors should hold regular meetings monthly at a fixed time and place.
2. In advance of such a meeting, directors should receive an agenda of the matters to be brought up for consideration at the meeting. Directly after a meeting, they should receive a copy of the minutes of that meeting. Such a procedure would be of great value as it would give a director an opportunity in advance to give some thought to matters to be brought up for discussion at the meeting and would also post a director who was absent from a meeting as to what had transpired at such meeting.
3. I believe the corporation's counsel should be present at every meeting of the board, irrespective of whether or not he is a director, in order to give directors the benefit of his advice on the legal aspects of any proposition being considered.
4. At, say, the first meeting of the board of directors after the annual stockholders' meeting, the board ought to have presented to it for approval the salaries of all executive officers for the ensuing year where not covered by existing written employment contracts already approved by the board, as well as approval of directors' fees, if any.
5. In the case of companies having executive committees, such committees are to have the right to transact the "ordinary and administrative" business of the corporation during the interval between meetings of the board. Their acts should be ratified by the directors in each case at the next subsequent meeting of the board. Decisions of the executive committee on problems and policies not in the ordinary course of business are to be approved by directors either at a regular or special meeting before being carried out. In law the executive committee has no powers except those which are delegated to it from time to time by the board of directors, which continues fully responsible for any action taken by the executive committee by virtue of such delegated powers.
6. I believe that each month directors should receive monthly figures of sales, profits, balance sheet changes, etc. I realize there may be companies where for one reason or another it may not be possible to give to directors as complete figures as in the case of other companies; however, too often in the past the objections on the part of the executive officers to giving all or part of such information have been based on reasons which did not adequately take into consideration the liabilities and duties of directors and the necessity of furnishing directors with the data necessary to enable them to discharge such liabilities. If a man has assumed such responsibilities, I think it reasonable to assume that he can be trusted to keep such information confidential.

There are some companies which have followed the practice of giving no, or practically no, information to directors currently. Others supply directors with such information for use only after directors' meetings but which they cannot take with them. Still other companies follow the practice of supplying such figures, etc., to directors, permitting them to take such statements away with them, and making copies thereof to all directors who were not present at such meeting. I strongly recommend the latter course and believe it to be the soundest for the company as it enables directors, who are supposed to "direct," to acquire a clear picture of the trend of the business and therefore enables them the better to be of value to the management in the determination of policies, etc. This is particularly true of the "outside" directors who can bring to the discussion of a problem an "outside" independent point of view that can be very helpful at times.

7. In addition to the data referred to in 6, all directors should receive copies of all reports and statements prepared by the outside auditors. I refer to the detailed reports submitted by such auditors and not merely to the condensed statements released to stockholders.
8. All profit-sharing plans should be approved, not only by the board of directors, but by the stockholders as well.
9. Options to purchase stock should be approved by the board of directors, and by the stockholders as well, and mention thereof should be made in all published balance sheets thereafter until either exercised or terminated.
10. A corporation should make no loans to officers, directors, and/or stockholders, except after approval by the board of directors—and even then obviously only if such action is legal.
11. Questions of bonuses and profit-sharing should be discussed and approved by the board with only those directors voting who do not share in such bonuses or profit-sharing.

* * * * *

Chapter 2

The Functions of a Corporate Director[36]

Sidney J. Weinberg

A century ago, most corporations were local and dominated by one man. Corporate law required a board of directors, but one man generally controlled the board, which, as a rule, was composed of subordinates or relatives. As corporations grew in size and scope and in number of stockholders and became public companies, it became evident that it was necessary to have more diversity in the board of directors.

Stockholders insisted on representation on the board aside from the active executive management, and outside directors proved of help to the company in bringing fresh points of view. As a result, in most widely owned public companies today, some of the directors are executives of the corporation; others are elected from the outside. I am an outside director on the boards of several corporations, and [below] I am speaking primarily about the functions of an outside director.

There seems to be some mystery about being an outside director of a public company. A great many people do not seem to understand just what it entails, what the responsibilities of such a director are, the field in which he operates, and how he functions.

Language of the Law

The laws of many states say that it is the responsibility of the board of directors to manage the corporation. As a practical matter, the directors cannot manage a corporation. In the narrow sense of this definition, the law is a relic of the past, when corporations were small and local. Under the law, the director has no power except during a directors' meeting at which a quorum is present.

For the rest of the time, he must fulfill his duties to the corporation through the influence he is able to develop by means of the work he has done and is doing for the corporation. His relations with the internal management as to the operations of the corporation are for the most part advisory.[37] The management of the corporation—that is, its day-by-day executive management—must be in the hands of the officers, who are elected by the directors. The officers' powers are derived either from the by-laws or from resolutions of the board. The board of directors is the supreme body of the corporation.

The law imposes upon a director fiduciary obligations and also the duty of giving to the affairs of the corporation that same degree of care and judgment that a man would exercise in connection with his own affairs; but, in addition to that, there are statutory obligations such as imposed by the Securities and Exchange Act, whereby a director of a corporation with securities listed on a stock exchange has to report his purchases and sales to the SEC and the stock exchange, and must also surrender to the corporation any profit he makes arising from purchases and sales within a six months' period.

A director who habitually does not attend board meetings may well run a serious risk of liability; if he attends and votes on matters that subsequently go wrong, he can urge that he used his best judgment, but a man who stays away does not have that defense. Also, if the figures put out by a corporation turn out to be wrong, the directors may be liable to stockholders who relied on them to their detriment.

The director has obligations to all stockholders. Beyond his legal duties, he must recognize the broad social responsibilities he has to the general public and to the country.

Composition of the Board

The effectiveness with which the director can meet these obligations is influenced by many things, among them the composition of the board itself.

I believe that the ideal board should have a majority of its members chosen from outside of the management and a minority from the executive officers group, although I am on many boards that do not have this ratio. I also know there are many large corporations, including the Standard Oil group, which have no outside directors. There are in my opinion, however, many real reasons why it is desirable to have the majority from the outside.

In the first place, the outside director, with his experience in other fields, brings perspective and a fresh point of view to the board's deliberations. He stands in a sense as an interpreter between the outside world and the internal operations of the company. His view is the broad extensive view compared with the intensive view which is natural for the operating officers.

As an example, in 1948, the problem arose in a company of which I am a director, as to whether it should raise its prices because of increased costs or whether it should retain its former prices and take it on the nose. Although this was a management problem, the president called a special meeting of the board particularly for the purpose of getting advice on this problem from the outside directors, which he knew would be of a special value to the management because of their experience in the affairs of many other companies in varied fields of business. The decision was not to raise prices.

In the second place, the outside directors in a special sense represent the stockholders. The outside directors must see that the officers operate the company for the benefit of the stockholders, and must review the work of the officers as well as advise them.

Another reason for having only a minority of the board chosen from management is that the board of directors must fix the compensation of the officers, and on that subject the officers themselves, of course, should not vote. In many corporations, when the officers are a majority of the board, the salaries are proposed to the board by a committee of directors excluding officers, so that in effect the minority of the board determines the salaries. If the salary of an officer is challenged at a stockholders' meeting, I believe it is the duty of the salary committee, or a member of it—and not the duty of the officer—to justify the salary.

Boards sometimes have an executive committee which has the power of the board between meetings. The advantage in having executive officers a minority on the board will in part be lost unless they are a minority also on the executive committee.

I believe a board of 12 or 15 members is the ideal size in that it is large enough to provide diverse points of view and yet small enough to act intimately and efficiently.

The composition of the board—aside from the proportions between officers and outside directors—has developed a good deal of controversy in recent years. Recently there has been an organized campaign to elect women to boards—apparently just because they are women.[38] Also there are groups advocating cumulative voting by stockholders to elect directors.

As to electing women to a board, I see no reason why a competent woman should not be elected to a board, as I think it would be desirable to get a woman's point of view, especially in the case of corporations dealing directly with women as customers, particularly when some companies have more women than men as stockholders. But the important point is to be sure that you get an able board member, whether it is a man or a woman.

As to cumulative voting, there are reasons in favor of it and, I believe, at least equally strong reasons against it. This subject should be given objective study by some institution, which could weigh judicially the advantages and disadvantages of cumulative voting and make public a report to help clarify the situation.[39] I am hopeful that such a study will soon be undertaken by the Harvard Business School.

A Basis of Cooperation

In order for a director to function effectively, the officers must provide certain tools the directors must have to be informed. Sixteen years ago, when I was being elected to a number of directorates, I drew up a memorandum on the duties and responsibilities of directors, setting out in some detail the basis of cooperation between officers and directors of a corporation, and sent it to the head of each company of which I was a director.

Not many years afterwards came the historic episode of McKesson & Robbins, in which company I was and am a director, and in the investigation that followed, when I was a witness, the attorney brought this memorandum forward and asked me why I had not operated as a director of that company in accordance with the standards I had set up in the memorandum. I pointed out to him that Moses had brought down the Ten Commandments from Mount Sinai, that we all believe in them, but that unfortunately few of us live in accordance with all of them.

Perhaps you would be interested to know the chief points I made in that memorandum, dated June 21, 1933—a time when not so much general thought had been given to this subject as has been since. The points, in brief, were these:

1. Boards of directors should hold regular meetings monthly at a fixed time and place.
2. The directors should receive in advance of such meeting an agenda on matters to be brought up for consideration and, after such meeting, a copy of the minutes of that meeting.

3. Corporation's counsel should be present at every meeting, whether or not he is a director.
4. At the first meeting after the annual stockholders' meeting, the board should have presented to it for approval the salaries of all executive officers for the ensuing year.
5. Executive committee minutes should be submitted to the directors in each case at the next subsequent meeting of the board.
6. Directors should receive monthly figures of sales, profits, balance sheet changes, etc.
7. In addition, all directors should receive copies of all reports and statements prepared by the outside auditors.
8. All profit-sharing plans should be approved by the board and by the stockholders.
9. Options to purchase stock should be approved by the board of directors and by the stockholders, and mention thereof should be made in all published balance sheets thereafter unless exercised or terminated.
10. A corporation should make no loan to officers, directors, or stockholders except after approval by the board of directors—and then obviously only if such action is legal.
11. Questions of bonuses and profit-sharing should be discussed and approved by the board with only those directors voting who do not share in such bonuses or profit-sharing.

In the light of the experience I have had since drawing up these points, I would add another one: that the comptroller be present at all directors' meetings, and that every board have a committee on audit composed entirely of outside directors and, thereby, have direct contact with the independent auditors.

Tools for the Director

Many of these proposals have since become standard practice and a number of them have been enacted into law. Here again, all the companies whose boards I am on do not follow all of these commandments in full—but I still believe in these principles as goals toward which I work.

Some of these points involve data that the directors must receive from executive management and others involve what the director should contribute on his own. Although all of these matters are of vital importance to directors, in many of them it is the duty of the executives, as a first step, to bring the material before the directors.

There are other tools which the officers should provide for the director if he is to function effectively. In broad terms, the officers must give the director cooperation all along the line. The director must be informed of what policies and problems are under consideration by the officers, together with the facts and figures necessary for him to form an opinion on the subject. New plans and policies should be presented not as something in effect or about to be put in effect, but as something in contemplation.

If the chief executive officer bears in mind that the board is created to consult together rather than to contend with each other, he will go over new proposals with the directors individually beforehand, and in this way he may find that some modification of his original plan may be wisest and can be brought about without the embarrassment to the board which may occur if the modifications had to be made at a board meeting. I remember one instance when a board was presented unexpectedly with a plan for the corporation to enter a new business quite foreign to its usual line of activity. The board turned the plan down, but less blood pressure would have been engendered all around if the officers had brought it up with the various directors individually before the meeting. The directors should never be presented with a surprise at a board meeting.

The director should be given the opportunity to meet and talk with the younger, coming executives who are not on the board. Only in this way can he get the knowledge which is necessary in choosing top executives from within the organization and form a judgment as to the organization underneath the top management. The director should watch especially for younger men who have possibilities for development.

I think it is a good idea for a president of a corporation, after the annual stockholders' meeting, to give a dinner for the directors and the top officers and to have at that dinner what might be called the "sub-cabinet" of officers. This gives a boost to the younger men's morale and an opportunity for the members of the board to become better acquainted with the men who, in addition to the top officers, are operating the company from day to day. It is the custom of Mr. Wilson, president of General Electric—a great and very enlightened businessman—to give such a dinner, after each annual meeting, and I believe they are helpful in every way.[40]

The Most Important Function

One of the most important functions of the board of directors—probably its most important function—is selecting the chief officers. The board should get a good operating management and then back it up. It is certainly true that a corporation is just as good as its management.

The board passes on the salaries of the management, and on other forms of compensation management receives. In addition, the board should make decisions on major policies which are out of the ordinary routine of daily business. They should see that policies determined upon are carried out and watch what the results are. They should continuously check on the effectiveness of the executive group.

In my opinion, an outside director has a difficult task. He must be a diplomat in all his relations. He is dealing continuously with personalities, and I suppose I am revealing no secret in saying that in a directors' meeting you are likely to find a prima donna from time to time. By comparison, being an investment banker is easy. I have long said that corporations should reasonably compensate an outside director for the services he renders the corporation as a director, although it is impossible fully to compensate him for the responsibilities he assumes.

A conscientious director must work at it—and not only during the directors' meetings. It is fairly common for boards to have standing or special committees (in addition to executive committees) to look into matters on behalf of the board and report, with recommendations for board action. Sometimes the most important and the most time-consuming activities of an outside director consist of his services on these committees. I consider being a director in a widely owned company a semi-public service, and directors should look at it in that way or not serve.

The Business of Directing

Now, how does a director go about directing? Judges have said, "Directors must direct."[41] This is perfectly true, but it doesn't seem to me to throw much light on the subject, because it isn't words that count, but work and action.

In carrying out his functions, the director must take the long view in decisions and bear in mind the public interest. He must have a social sense and must be continually aware of the human problems involved in decisions of the board. Board decisions affect human beings. For example, a corporation of which I am a director owns several plants.[42] Business dropped to the point where it became necessary to reduce production, and the natural decision was to close the highest-cost plant. That plant, however, was in a small community, chiefly dependent upon the plant's operations, so that it was necessary to consider the effect on the community and to work out our decision in such a human way as to disrupt the community's life as little as possible, as well as to protect the company's interest.

Controversial matters often come before a board and there are times when a director who is any good must be willing to stand up and be counted. The day of the stuffed-shirt director, elected because he is in the Blue Book, has come to an end. It is better if a controversial issue is not sprung on a board unexpectedly. If at a board meeting there is presented some new plan I don't know about, I will say what I think about the plan or ask more time for study.

However, if the chief officers of the corporation do not want me to speak my mind, they should not have invited me to be a director. If they insist on a policy of my silence, I will resign and publicly say why. Above all, directors must be independent. The better way, I have found from experience, is, as I have said, for the president to take up controversial questions individually with the directors beforehand, and that is what most able executives do.

Do Your Homework

I have mentioned that a director must do homework. No active man on many boards can find time during office hours to study and digest the information that he should have before attending a directors' meeting. Some men make a hobby of stamp collecting. My interest is reading reports from corporations, reports on plans in prospect, reports on the results of plans adopted, and figures on operations, which I usually do on weekends, and at nights.

If management gives a director the information he should have before decisions are made at directors' meetings, the director must then give conscientious work and take time to prepare for the meeting itself. The directors should spend time also in developing informal contacts with the executives of the company and the other directors. In the case of many of my directorships, I spend as much time on the company's affairs outside meetings as in meetings.

The board meetings themselves usually involve general discussion of the affairs of the company and the adoption of formal decisions. An important function of the board member during a meeting is asking constructive, challenging questions, which will bring out not only the weaknesses but at times the strength of the corporation and of its officers. But he will not know the right questions to ask if he doesn't know the company and hasn't taken the time beforehand to study the matters coming up at the meeting. Experience in being a director on other boards, I find, is very helpful.

The outside directors must not get involved in day-to-day management. I do not feel that I am capable of operating a corporation just because I am a director. I have refused to be chairman of the board or of the executive committee several times because I have felt those are management positions. The job of the outside director is to be an advisor to management, but he should not get entangled in the operations.

Re Stock Ownership

A director establishes his influence in the corporation through his service to the corporation, rather than through stock ownership. It is not, I think, an important question how much stock a director owns, although I own some stock in each of the corporations of which I am a director. There are some able men on boards of directors who, as a matter of principle, won't own any stock in the corporation, but personally I believe it is desirable for a director to own some stock, within his means. His ability to act as a director depends on the man himself, not on his stock ownership. Every director represents all the stockholders.

The question arises from time to time as to the position of an outside director who—himself or his company—in some way is doing business with the corporation. If their dealings are fully disclosed and fair and reasonable, I see no objection to such a relationship. It should be remembered that all directors must pass on the fairness of any contract and on the amount of compensation to be received and that the director involved does not vote on it, and should not be present when it is voted on.

As in all affairs, problems confronting directors and officers of a corporation change. I find that in every decade corporations have new sets of problems. In addition, every company, like every child, is different, and each presents different problems.

As one example of the relations of the board of directors to a specific problem, actual labor negotiations must be left to the experts on that subject among the officers, but the board should be kept fully informed and from time to time may give useful counsel on policies and helpful support to the executives.

The Effective Director

Now, in closing, I would like to summarize a few of the points I have been talking about.

First, I believe the outside directors should be in the majority in a publicly owned corporation and that they can make an important contribution by choosing able top management and supporting that management, and through bringing to the company's policy problems the perspective and broad views which come from experience as a director in other companies. In meeting company problems, the director must always bear in mind the public interest. One must remember that every time a national corporation takes a step which is, or appears to be, against the public interest, it reacts on all corporations and is detrimental to our whole system of private enterprise.

Second, to be effective, a director must work at his job—and it is a hard job. The outside director must give top priority to his schedule of board and committee meetings. (I have 22 regularly scheduled meetings monthly—boards and committees of boards—and make all of them unless out of town.) The director must conscientiously do his homework to prepare himself for board meetings, and outside of board meetings he must be ready to respond, when requested, to the day-by-day calls for counsel and advice from the executives of the companies he serves. He should be careful to keep out of the internal management of the corporation.

Third, I am convinced, from many years of observing boards of directors, that the influence of a director comes from his faithful, competent, and diplomatic performance of his duties and from his abilities and experience—not from his stock ownership.

Fourth, the board can function most effectively only when executives cooperate with the outside directors. The best way to bring about that cooperation is for management to try and meet what I refer to as the Ten Commandments for cooperation between executives and directors.

Many corporations, I know, have had trouble in getting good directors. The way to get and keep such directors is, I believe, to work with them and keep them informed. Through this mutual cooperation, good teamwork will develop, and that is important for the stockholders and for all concerned.

In conclusion, I wish to emphasize that a director of a company must keep a broad outlook, high hopes, and believe in the future of this country. He must keep his feet on the ground but this need not keep him from looking off to the horizon.

* * * * *

Chapter 3

Status and Functions of Corporate Directors

John L. Weinberg

STATUS AND FUNCTIONS OF CORPORATE DIRECTORS

By

John L. Weinberg, '47

*

* *

* * *

* *

*

Submitted to

Princeton University

Department of Economics and Social Institutions

In Partial Fulfillment of Requirements for the
Degree of Bachelor of Arts
April, 1948

TABLE OF CONTENTS

Chapter I: Background and Characteristics of the Corporate Environment Affecting Directors Today

American industry is today, in many ways, facing the most critical period in all its history. The system of free enterprise is under severe attack. Abroad it has suffered defeat in many lands, submerged by the force of totalitarian principles of economics. At home our system's right to survive is challenged by its frequent inability to maintain a stable equilibrium in the face of rapidly changing economic and political conditions.

In our system of democratic capitalism, the business corporation holds a dominating position. In the performance of these business corporations, the board of directors assumes an especially significant role. It is toward this phase of the free enterprise system, namely, the status and functions of corporate directors of industrial, nonregulated corporations, that this thesis will direct attention. The feeling that proper operation of this corporate mechanism will determine in large measure the fate of our existing economic way of life permeates this thesis.

A. The Background for the Board of Directors[43]

Problems involving director relationships are far from novel situations. Even in the infancy of the corporate form, directors were regarded skeptically. Adam Smith, often regarded as the father of the modern free enterprise system, recognized one phase in 1776:

> The directors of such companies … being managers rather of other people's money than their own, it cannot well be expected that they should watch over [it] with the same anxious vigilance with which the partnership in a private co-partnery frequently watch over their own. … Negligence and profusion, therefore, must always prevail more or less.*

Following the American Revolution, the state legislatures inherited the charter-granting power from the royal governors, proprietors, and colonial legislatures who had formerly exercised it. Each charter was individually enacted by the legislature. Picture the corporation of that era. It consisted of a small number of stockholders who elected a board of directors from their own number. This board of directors, delegating powers of management, was protected by a series of fixed rules under which the management had a relatively limited play.

*Adam Smith, *The Wealth of Nations.* (Everyman's Library Edition, Vol. II, 1947), p. 229.

In this period, until the latter half of the 19th century, not only was the number of stockholders per corporation small, but also the corporations themselves were diminutive. Although some of the stockholders were probably not active [businesspeople], they usually knew what was happening in the corporation, and actively participated to protect their investment. The management of the corporation, indeed, was thought to be a set of agents running the business for a number of owners. While they had greater power than agents as a rule enjoyed, they were held strictly accountable and were in a position to be governed in all matters of general policy by their directors.

The Industrial Revolution, with its increase in large-scale production and consequent need for more capital, changed the American economic environment considerably. Because the corporate form supplied the needs of this new economic trend, much pressure arose for easier incorporation.

General incorporation laws in most states resulted, under which the advantages of the corporate form were made available to the community. We see the elimination of the legislature from negotiations attending the granting of the charter of incorporation. In place of the body which had scrutinized and possibly prescribed arrangements, there was substituted a state official, usually the secretary of state, whose primary duty was to see that the document filed complied with the state law.

Always an important factor in these early charters was the desire to secure the greatest freedom of action possible, in the type of business endeavor as well as in the manner of operation. Such legal devices as pyramiding, use of non-voting stock, and voting trusts further concentrated control. Due to this facility of incorporation and the growing industrialization of the country, the number and size of corporations increased immeasurably.

B. The Separation of Ownership from Management[44]

This change in the economic environment was especially significant and far-reaching to the board of directors. Where in the early 19th century the presence of an active, coherent electorate alleviated the pressure on the board in many ways, we see a changed situation, causing tension within the corporate mechanism. No longer are the stockholders generally informed; no longer do the stockholders generally attend meetings.

Legal and economic doctrine pertaining to corporations has been built upon the theory of representative government. It was accepted that active managers were appointed by directors who, in turn, were elected by a cognizant ownership group. These managers were to seek to combine capital, labor, and materials in the most economic proportions in their efforts to obtain maximum profits. The active ownership group and a management sensitivity to this group were integral parts of the overall doctrine.

We note two major obstacles to this ideal situation in modern corporations: (1) The diffusion of ownership into large, diversified groups of individuals who, for the most part, are ignorant of the intricacies of modern industry. (2) The concentration of control both into larger economic units and in the trend for management to grasp the reins of the enterprise and to rule without stockholder aid.

The increase in the number of stockholders in corporations has been extraordinary. The growth of stockholders reflects, in part, the tremendous increase in size and complexity of American industry, but such expansion was only made possible by wider participation of the public in corporate securities. To be more specific, a study of 1,572 corporations with total stockholdings of 11,432,492 showed that 9,884,962 (or 85.5%) were holdings of a hundred shares or less.*

In commenting on the American Telephone and Telegraph Company, the National Resources Committee stated: "In this largest of all corporations, stock ownership is so widely disbursed that no one person or small group is in a position to dominate the corporation as a result of stock ownership. Neither are stockholders as a group in a position to exercise significant control."** In the same study the committee found that in many cases the legal devices used to divest the stockholders of control were insignificant in the light of the trend toward greater dispersion. Not only is the increase in members of the stockholders a restraint to action (the organization of the 659,000 shareholders in the American Telephone and Telegraph Company for efficient action would be practically a political miracle), but also the average stockholder neither has the background and experience nor the will to participate intelligently in company affairs.

The increased complexity of industry and the difficult economic, political, and social problems which arise are beyond the scope of the thesis, yet one must realize their existence in considering why stockholders are not able to participate effectively in managing large modern corporations. This new type of stockholder is no longer an entrepreneur, but in reality … must be considered an investor.

*US Temporary National Economic Committee, "Bureaucracy and Trusteeship in Large Corporations," *Investigation of Concentration of Economic Power*, Monograph No. 11 (Washington: US Government Printing Office, 1940), p. 65.

**US National Resources Committee, *Structure of the American Economy*, Part I (Washington: US Government Printing Office, 1939), p. 156.

[The] purchase of stock in one of the large corporations today is a mere loan of funds: no intervention in management is even considered, as a rule.

We must also consider the second obstacle to the idea that the government of the corporation is accomplished through the not infrequent participation of the ownership group, namely the concentration of control.

"A few men controlling a few banks control a majority of the corporate wealth of the nation, if not a majority of the entire wealth of the nation."* This statement is far from being a myth. Of 3,544 directorships on the boards of the 200 largest nonfinancial corporations and 50 largest financial corporations in 1939, 400 men held approximately a third of these important positions.** There is not only a concentration of wealth in a few large units in the nation, but also concentration has taken place in the different industries. The war has accentuated the concentration movement. Since 1940, 18 of the largest corporations in the country with assets over $50 million each have merged with 242 smaller concerns.***

With this concentration into a few powerful units we note a few men serving on many boards. Some have carried this to ridiculous extremes. There are instances of men having served on as many as 70 to 80 boards at the same time. When we consider the proper functions and heavy liabilities of a director, this fact will become almost unbelievable. When confronted by this situation, [businesspeople] point to the scarcity of men capable of doing the job and declare that a few minutes with an able man of quick perception and sound judgment is of greater value than much more time with the less able man. Due to this increased size and complexity, we also note a trend (see Chapter IV) in which professional managers have become the dominating factor in corporate functions.

The increased strain on the board of directors resulting from the separation of ownership and management is more readily discernible when we consider that, when stripped of all embellishments, the board becomes the legal and managerial locus of responsibility in the corporation. To carry this new load successfully, maximum utilization must be made of the existing mechanism. The board must be renovated into a working unit with the functions specified and efficiently integrated into the corporation unit.

* Hon. Wright Patman, *Congressional Record*, 75th Cong., First Sess., Vol. 81, p. 5777.
** US Temporary National Economic Committee, *op. cit.*, p. 7.
*** John Fischer, "The Lost Liberals," *Harper's Magazine* (May, 1947), p. 387.

C. Abuses by Directors[45]

In times of prosperity with rising profits and rising business activity there is little interest in who runs the corporation or how they are managed. One can always sell [a] stock. However, since 1929, when business activity dropped and depression gripped the country, stockholders have held their stock and blamed management. Many shady practices and abuses have been exposed. The abuses which concern this thesis involve the failure of boards to function: the presence of "rubber stamp" directors, multiple directorships, management domination and self-dealing, and the improper use of inside information.

A simple solution in discussing the inadequacy of boards of directors is to spend much time and space flaying the "financial gigolos" and "economic decay" in our system. It seems just to the writer that suspicion has been cast upon boards of directors in the light of past abuses, but a general condemnation of the entire system because of these abuses appears to be a negative approach to the solution of the problem. The chief explanation for these violations may be found not so much in the individuals, but more in terms of the faulty education of directors and executives and a failure to define the functions and powers of the directorate.

D. The Development of Social Responsibility[46]

In a study of this type, one cannot travel far without being struck by the shifting attitude of business. A definite change is taking place. The social conception of the corporation has gone beyond the mere protection of stockholder interests. The complex and unsolved problem now existing is the reconciliation of private enterprise and freedom of action with the smooth functioning of a democratic society including justice for all groups—stockholders, executives, employees, creditors, and the public at large. This broad concept is, however, not only often overlooked, but it is scarcely recognized by the courts who officially still hold the board of directors to the narrow path of securing maximum profits for the stockholders.

Absolute power is necessary in building an organization. Slower, yet equally sure, is the development of social pressure demanding that the power be used for the benefit of all concerned. Despite the confusion caused by the legal institutions and some [businesspeople] who are unwilling to recognize the inevitable, responsibility to the public is gaining greater recognition. An example of this new attitude: "[N]o longer can industry plow a single furrow toward a strictly economic objective; instead, it must manage its affairs with due regard to the whole field of human relations."*

*Address by Edward R. Stettinius, Jr., Chairman of the Board of the U.S. Steel Corporation at the annual convention of the Association of Life Insurance Presidents 1939.

The need for a socioeconomic philosophy for American industry, aimed at benefiting the whole economy, cannot be overemphasized. The crux of the problem lies in the fact that business is encouraged by law primarily because it is a service to the community rather than because it is a source of profit to its owners. The function of enterprise is the production and provision of goods and services for the public. The incentive to produce as cheaply as possible is profit. In other words, the most efficient *means* to accomplishing cheap production of goods for the general public is private enterprise with profits.

If this means will not provide the proper end, the system is faulty in some way. For example, the prices, wages, and production of the U.S. Steel Corporation are much more important to the United States than those of an ordinary private enterprise. The economic welfare of the entire country depends to a great extent upon the position of U.S. Steel. Obviously, if the corporation is to maintain its freedom from government control, responsible capitalism is demanded.

How will this social responsibility fit into the existing environment? Again, the crucial position of the board of directors must be noted. Although the directors are selected by the stockholders of the corporation, their task is to manage the business in the interest of the investors, employees, customers, and consumers of the company's products or services and in accordance with public policy as expressed in the laws of the land. To make a profit is basic. There can be no joint benefit if the corporation fails. However, after survival, the harmony of interests must occur.

It seems that the only way boards of directors can best meet the needs of the American people, most nearly supply their wants, maintain profits, handle problems of unemployment, and face the Russian challenge, is through outstanding leadership, which accepts social responsibility. Such leadership will seek to frame constructive plans based not on the interest of capital or capitalism alone, but in the interest of the American people as a whole.

This can be summarized by considering the twofold nature of life in a democracy, where every [person] is two [people]—a worker and a citizen. So far as [businesspeople are] concerned, [they are] responsible on the one hand to the particular enterprise of which [they are] a part, and on the other hand, to the community. It is never true of a good business[person] to say that the profit motive is secondary, yet the [person] who has lived through the ordeal of the last two decades knows that … profits are not unrelated to other people's profits, including profits for labor and the consumer.

E. The Significance of Directors[47]

The importance of the corporate form in American business is irrefutable and constantly increasing. Taking all industrial groups together, Gordon* found very roughly that from 60% to 65% of the total volume of business in the United States in 1937 was performed by corporations. Although these figures may be very rough indeed, we can safely conclude that in terms of business volume, the corporation is by far the most important form of business organization in this country. This strategic position and importance of corporate directors in our economy is easily recognized when we consider that they are held responsible for setting the major policies and selecting the operating management for this major portion of the country's productive mechanism.

Further significance is given to their position when we note the increasing inactivity of the large stockholder group. Upon boards of directors, to a certain extent, rests the responsibility for American industry and therefore the welfare of the whole country. The decisions of [business leaders] are important today as never before. We can even declare that the fate of private enterprise, as we know it, may well depend upon the success or failure of directors to solve such knotty problems as stability of employment and production, inflation, and management–labor disputes. Eloquent orators and full-page advertisements may extol democratic capitalism endlessly, yet if this system loses the confidence of the people, collapse is only a matter of time.

The urgency for educating directors and executives concerning the true duties and responsibilities of the board, and showing these members of the business community the advantages obtained as a result of proper utilization of this mechanism, cannot be overemphasized.

Chapter II: The Legal Foundations and Significant Factors Affecting Proper Performance of Corporate Boards

Before attacking the problems and dilemmas relating to the board of directors, it is necessary to observe the legal foundation and the general conduct of this intricate mechanism.

*R. A. Gordon, *Business Leadership in the Large Corporation* (Washington: The Brookings Institution, 1945), p. 14.

A. The Legal Status of the Board

In the modern business corporation, the locus of responsibility has been placed by the law in the board of directors. "The business of every corporation organized under the provisions of this chapter shall be managed by the board of directors."* Boards become the device which provides management of the corporation with the necessary authorization to function. They do not exist merely because corporations are nonphysical legal entities, incapable of activity except through this human agency, nor because the statutory requirement necessitating boards of directors is dictated by the interest of the state in the matter. Boards of directors exist because of statutory recognition that the efficient and economical management of the corporate business is promoted by centralization of management in a small group.

By management, we mean that body of [people] who, according to law, have formally assumed the duties of exercising [dominion] over the corporation's business and assets. Universally under the American system of law, management consists of a board of directors and the senior officers of the corporation. The board commonly secures its title to office through election by the stockholders. The board has the power to transact any regular business which the corporation itself can transact; in fact, it is through the directors that the enterprise does transact its business. In the absence of bad faith, fraud, or negligence, and acting within the corporate charter and the laws of the land, the power of the board is supreme; the courts will not interfere with corporate management.

The courts further recognize the value of group discussion and action by proclaiming in most cases that an action by the board of directors is legal only when taken at a properly called and convened meeting.

> The stockholders of a corporation have a right to expect from their directors a conscientious consideration of every proposition which is presented which involves any interest of the company, in conforming to the oath which they have subscribed. They have a right to have the individual viewpoint of the several directors expressed at a conference. ... It is fundamental that officers of boards can only act as constituted boards when assembled as such, and by deliberate and considered action dispose of the issue under consideration, and that they cannot act in an individual capacity outside of a formal meeting, and a majority of the

* General Corporation Law of the State of Delaware, as revised on April 9, 1941, Art. I., Chap. 65, Section 9. [Editor's note: This provision today appears at 8 Del. C. § 141(a) and reads as follows: "The business and affairs of every corporation organized under this chapter shall be managed by or under the direction of the board of directors, except as may be otherwise provided in this chapter or in its certificate of incorporation."]

> individual expressions be the action of the board. The law believes that the greatest wisdom results from conference and exchange of individual views, and it is for that reason that the law requires the united wisdom of a majority of the several members of the board in determining the business of a corporation.*

There is unquestioned value to outside, informal talk as we shall see, but decisions must be voted at meetings.

The board has the power to delegate to officers, agents, and committees authority to carry out the will of the majority and to transact the ordinary affairs of the corporation, but it may not delegate to others the power to discharge duties specifically imposed on the board by the state statute, the by-laws, or charter that involve the exercise of discretion and judgment.

The variety of judicial opinion as to what is the proper status of corporation directors presents a truly bewildering picture. Many have called the director an agent; others have called him a trustee. The truth of the matter appears to be neither concept. The position of a director is a distinct legal relationship and the duties and obligations only become more confusing if too frequent references to the laws of trust and agency are used. In some of the more recent decisions there is a decided tendency to refrain from labeling a director categorically as being either an agent, on the one hand, or, on the other hand, a trustee in a narrow technical sense. Rather, the tendency is to characterize [a director] as a quasi-trustee or one who has, in a general sense, responsibilities of a fiduciary character. In reality, a director is a representative of the shareholders in the top management of the corporation, and is entrusted to conduct the business for the benefit of the shareholders as a body, and as such, … has responsibilities of a fiduciary nature.

The law holds top management to certain standards of conduct. This is the legal link between ownership and management. As the separation of ownership from management becomes greater or is more thoroughly accomplished by legal devices, this legal protection becomes increasingly more important to the security owner. If the situation ever arises in which there is a management, in fact, not chosen by the corporation's security holders and having no duties toward them that are recognized at law or enforceable through legal means, then the security holder has a piece of paper representing a capital contribution,

* *Ames v. Goldfield Merger Mines Co.*, 227 Fed. 292, 301-302 (1915). Some exceptions to the rule, followed by a minority of the courts are: (a) Directors may choose their own mode of doing business. *Buckley v. Jennings*, 95 Vt. 205, 114 A.40 (1921). (b) Directors may act without a meeting if the shareholders know this practice and do not object. *Berman v. Minneapolis Photo Engraving Co.*, 144 Minn. 146, 174 N.W. 735 (1919).

which is valuable only as the good nature, good faith, or economic advantage of the [people] actually in charge of the company's affairs lead them to make it so. We are thus led to conclude that the strength of the law in this regard is the major enforceable safeguard for proper performance of directors that the security holder has.

B. Legal Qualifications for Directors[48]

Because corporations are chartered by the states, the state statutes govern to a major degree [the] eligibility and qualifications of directors. However, in certain types of corporations, the federal government has placed restrictions on who may serve as a director.

The general tendency of the state laws has been to leave eligibility and qualifications of directors to the certificate of incorporation or by-laws. Some states have set broad limits, such as New Jersey,* where the law provides each director shall be a bona fide shareholder in the corporation or a bona fide shareholder in the corporation holding 25% or more of capita stock in [the] company. The New York statute** provides that at least one of the directors of the corporation be a citizen of the United States and a resident of the state.

Since this thesis is limited to directors of industrial, nonregulated corporations, most federal statutes will not affect us here. Where the federal government's influence has been felt most with regard to directors' qualifications is in the field of interlocking directorships. The fight against these interlocking financial controls has raged with varying degrees of intensity since before the turn of the century. The major weapon used by the government since Woodrow Wilson's time has been Section 8 of the Clayton Act, which states:

> [N]o person at the same time shall be a director in any two or more corporations, any one of which has capital, surplus and individual profits aggregating more than $1,000,000, engaged in whole or in part in commerce … if such corporations are or shall have been theretofore, by virtue of their business and location of operation, competitors, so that the elimination of competition by agreement between them would constitute a violation of any provisions of any of the anti-trust laws.

*New Jersey: General Corporation Act Rev. Stat. § 14: 7-1.
**New York, General Corporation Law, § 27.

C. Elections of Directors[49]

The election of directors has been one of the most controversial points in the whole problem. The sole control of stockholders over directors is the election process. In substance, however, the selection of directors does not conform to the intended democratic process. The fact is that stockholders elect directors, but do not choose them. They are, in reality, chosen by the chief executive and the board itself. During ordinary times the board becomes a self-perpetuating body.

The occasional crisis situation may be disregarded as an integral part of the election system since the organizations mobilized in these crucial times are usually so crude that they are a travesty on the "democratic" procedures they report to be. The stockholder vote for directors as an effective instrument has evolved into a residual power reserved for crisis (see Chapter IV). Dissatisfaction with the management will more frequently result in sale of stock, than action to remove the directors.

Stockholders cannot choose directors for three main reasons: (1) They are not organized as a political body in such a way as to make their franchise effective; (2) Real choice of directors by stockholders would be an extremely costly and disruptive procedure, causing damage to efficient management and therefore to the stockholders themselves; and (3) The average stockholder has neither the background nor experience to make an effective choice of directors.

The real question is how to obtain high-caliber [directors] and promote efficient boards. To the writer such methods as cumulative voting to give minorities greater representation on the board and greater publicity by the corporation in notifying the stockholders of the types of [people] to be elected are extremely useful safeguards. However, the major reform to be undertaken seems to be the self-renovation of the board by industry. Because it has become a self-perpetuating body, a greater need has risen for active, responsible boards of directors.

D. Stock Ownership of Directors[50]

Although the common law rule states that unless required by statute, articles of incorporation, or by-laws, a director need not be a shareholder in the corporation, state laws in the past have generally stipulated the need for directors owning "qualifying shares." Recently, however, the revisions of the laws show a tendency to eliminate this requirement, and leave the decision in the hands of the corporation itself. Furthermore, where a requirement that directors must be shareholders does exist, its practical effectiveness has been weakened by the rule, followed by an overwhelming majority of the courts, that the person who holds the legal title to the stock on the books of the corporation is qualified to act as a director, even though the beneficial ownership of the stock may actually be in another person.

Two opposite schools exist on the subject. One side argues that the primary consideration is to obtain the best directors possible. They feel that ownership for its own sake is a meaningless ritual and if these qualifying shares prevent the securing of the best qualified [people], the loss speaks for itself. Others, more extreme, urge that lack of ownership is more beneficial to the corporation, as [such directors] will act with less selfish interest.

The other side of the argument feels that unless a director has a personal stake in the success of the enterprise, [his or her] performance will be more or less perfunctory. The National Industrial Conference Board* found that although desirable, the holding of stock equity was a secondary qualification for the ideal director. Of 97 answers to the question presented to business executives, only two felt that a large equity was indispensable for a good board member; on the other hand, only nine answers felt that it made no difference.

Corporations either with or without large personal stock ownership by directors may succeed or fail—no general rule is applicable.

E. Directors' Functions[51]

The job of evaluating the functions of the board of directors is indeed a complex one. The appraisal of the functions in a single corporation is no uninvolved task, but to generalize for industry is practically a fantasy. We are confronted by different products and services, different competitive situations, different company traditions, and most important of all, different capacities and personalities. No two corporations handle their top-management problems alike.

Not only are the raw materials different in each case, but also the philosophies deviate to a great extent. The concepts of directors' functions vary from those who feel the board should obtain the best possible chief executive and support [that person] as long as [they] continue [to be] successful, to those who believe that the board should enter in many ways the day-to-day operations of the business.

Despite this great variance, however, the board mechanism, defined by law, exists as the building block. From this base it is the duty of the corporation to provide a program for the board's maximum utilization toward the most

*National Industrial Conference Board, "Compensation and Duties of Corporate Directors," *Studies in Business Policy*, No. 16 (New York, 1946), p. 4.

beneficial end. From this locus of supreme power come the rules, instructions, and delegation of specific responsibility—the provision of means and the outline of ways.

In the overall evaluation of the properly functioning board of directors, we note the board's work is concentrated in four major areas: selection of the chief executive, efficient delegation of power and responsibility, both development and approval of broad policy, and the supervision and check-up on the performance of the corporation as a whole. In the next chapter, we shall investigate more fully the administrative aspects of the board.

Directors are the representatives of the owners in management, but are not so much a part of that that they should involve themselves in everyday operations. Their duties and responsibilities are to sit with management, observe its procedures and methods, and advise the operating executives in such a way that the policies and conduct of the corporation coincide with the directors' interpretations of the most advantageous long- and short-run interests of the owners.

Although a majority of the work accomplished is through the medium of delegated authority, this does not mean a transfer of responsibility; rather it is a correlation. The one to whom a task or job is delegated becomes responsible for doing the job, but the superior who delegates this authority remains responsible for getting the job done correctly. Within the sphere of the board lies the task of utilizing the best possible talent wisely, boldly, and honestly.

One of the most challenging problems of management is to give authority to those capable of exercising it and yet retain control in the hands of those ultimately responsible. If management is to function effectively, devoting its major attention to planning, directing, and coordinating activities, it must efficiently place at each level the proper authority and power. Usurpation by the board of too much power is as harmful as the retention of too little power. The situation requires a delicate balance and proper perspective as to the functions of each factor.

F. Teamwork in Top Management

A primary requisite for a properly functioning board is mutual understanding and cooperation. Through delegation of power, a machine is instituted. Only through teamwork can this mechanism function smoothly and efficiently.

The legal authority exists, but the real strength of the board lies in its ability to integrate all groups and carry out a common program. The implications are far-reaching: enlisting cooperation from the stockholders, operating executives, separate committees, and … the entire organization. The vitality of a corporation lies in this ability. A policy of "enlightened self-interest" would seem proper. This would include reconciliation of stockholder interests and the corporation's continuity of existence plus comprehension of the public interest. The supreme test of corporate management is the ability to run the corporation at a profit and recognize, at the same time, in a broad sense, the public interest.

Teamwork between the board of directors and active management is also vital. While the executives should respect the ability and status of a director pertaining to [his or her] fiduciary capacity, so the directors should recognize the executives' position with the necessity for freedom of action to meet administrative hurdles. Executives should consider the board a useful stabilizing influence. The fact that active management must be fortified with reasoned answers to anticipated questions will create an incentive in the chief executive to present every proposal so well premeditated that the board will never refuse an executive recommendation.

This preparation and challenge are the healthiest of conditions provided they are accomplished in a spirit of teamwork and cooperation. As we shall see, policy-making is a joint product of the board and the operating executives. Participation of the active staff does not lessen the responsibility of the board; it merely facilitates action.

Another important aspect of board teamwork is the cultivation and integration of committees. Despite their alleged shortcomings, they are an important administrative device and provide an effective means of coordinating activities and points of view. Most directors will agree that the spirit of the board making it a cohesive group is of prime importance in the smooth functioning of the mechanism.

G. The Mechanics and Size of the Board

Observation overwhelmingly exposes the advantages of clearly defined functions and workable size, with membership properly representative and confined to those able to visualize the needs and able to make major contributions toward the success of the company as a whole.

The general rule states that meetings be called monthly either by the chairman of the board or the president. The place of meeting is usually the principal office of the corporation in the state of its creation; however, the charter, by-laws, or the board itself may authorize the meeting to take place anywhere unless limited by the state corporation law. A quorum is not necessary for a meeting to take place, but it is needed for the legal transaction of business.

Usually, a rather meticulous adherence to parliamentary procedure seems to characterize the conduct of board meetings, despite informality in some cases. The chairman of the meeting occupies a very important position. It is [the chairman's] responsibility to obtain the maximum use of the time and abilities of the [directors] present. This is usually accomplished by previous organization of the agenda and information submitted to the directors.

There are many different plans used to facilitate discussions at meetings. These include strict adherence to an agenda, preparation of a brief synopsis of all subjects to be discussed, and the requirement in some corporations that all business must first be submitted to the finance or executive committees for sifting before presentation to the board. As important as the standards of procedures at the meetings is the need for mutual regard and enquiry.

To obtain a proper perspective with regard to board meetings, we must recognize the informal work done by directors outside the boardroom. Although recognized by comparatively few people, these luncheons, telephone calls, and private conversations should not be ignored. Board meetings often serve merely to ratify hours of informal discussions, numerous telephone calls, and exhaustive memoranda, which cover all phases of problems with which directors must deal. Through such processes, far-reaching decisions are crystallized which may take less than a dozen lines in the minutes of a meeting.

Another important aspect of the board mechanism is the information given to directors. Obviously, the contribution of non-officer directors is directly dependent upon the type and amount of information they receive from the operating executives. Although there exists a great diversity in practice, the basic purpose of all companies in this regard should remain the same: namely, to maintain the flow of essential facts in readily absorbable form to provide an adequate background for the directors, permitting informed action on the matters to be considered.

[People] who by position, ability, and achievement qualify as corporation directors have, or should have, the ability to analyze and interpret quickly a substantial body of operating data. The sense of trusteeship which they should feel as representatives of the owners would suggest a sustained desire for an accurate picture of the corporation in all pertinent areas.

The size of corporate boards varies to a great extent; however, the National Industrial Conference Board* found in 1946 that for companies with assets of less than $1 million, the typical board numbers from five to seven members. The boards of corporations with assets of $50 million or more tend to range from nine to fifteen members, the average around twelve. There is always a tendency for boards to increase in size either through mergers and consolidations or by having older executives "kicked upstairs."

One can often trace the history of a corporation by looking at its board of directors. The National Dairy Products Corporation has 22 directors. Its history is characterized by the purchase of many companies. The Gulf Oil Corporation, on the other hand, with assets approximately two and a half times those of National Dairy, has only eight directors.**

Two criteria should decide the size of the board: (1) essential representation (i.e., a balanced board), (2) workable size. One authority compares the size of the board to Sally Rand's fan—not so large as to be unwieldy, but large enough to cover the subject—efficient management.[52] When the board becomes too large in size, usually the executive committee becomes more prominent. The SEC has repeatedly advocated small, active, and integrated boards.

H. Three Dilemmas Confronting Boards of Directors[53]

When analyzed, the problem of the board of directors appears to crystallize into three major dilemmas, which will receive consideration in later chapters [and are summarized here].

The first dilemma emerges as an aspect of the administrative versus fiduciary interpretation of the directors' functions. If the directors' primary duty is to preserve the assets and protect the stockholders' interests, which is primarily a trusteeship function, how will the corporation be able to expand, make an adequate profit, and preserve the vitality and vigor necessary for its survival in our competitive economic environment?

On the other hand, is it true that the directors' primary duty is an administrative one? Should they actually enter into the corporation's operations? If the board of directors becomes an administrative force which animates the business, formulates long-range policies, and engages in economic risks; if it performs the duties of a true entrepreneur, how will it preserve the wealth and assets of

*National Industrial Conference Board, "Compensation and Duties of Corporate Directors," *Studies in Business Policy*, No. 16 (New York, 1946), p. 4.
**Moody's Investors' Service, *Moody's Manual of Investments—Industrial Securities* (New York, 1947), pp. 2732, 2811.

the corporation? How will the members of such a board fulfill their obligations to the stockholders who have entrusted to this board their capital through the medium of investment in the corporation?

The horns of the second dilemma, which concerns the directors' relationships with the active managerial group, are equally sharp and dangerous. How can directors comply with the legal requirement of "managing the corporation" without directly trespassing upon executive functions—a condition which would cause confusion, jealousy, and low morale? However, if the majority of functions, administrative details, and decisions are within the executive sphere, how can directors avoid becoming "window dressing," "rubber stamps," and useless management-dominated appendages to the corporate structure? Granted, active executives need freedom of action, but how may we prevent an excess of this freedom from causing directors to become passive tools of management? The issue has gone beyond getting directors who *will* direct; the question has become how to obtain directors who *know enough* to direct.

The third dilemma slashes into the heart of the problem: manpower. How may corporations expect to obtain the able, intelligent [people] of high caliber so necessary for this exacting, time-consuming job, if the legal liability is so great and the reward so nominal? No matter how well organized the board's mechanism, no matter how capable the chief executive, the efficiency and productivity of the board vary directly with the ability of the [directors] composing the directorate. Contrariwise, if the liability is decreased and the pay increased, how can accountability be enforced to check the improper fulfillment of their fiduciary responsibility? If there is no superior force to set limits to the standards of conduct, where will be found a force strong enough to compel directors properly to assume and discharge their duties and responsibilities?

Chapter III: Administration Versus Trusteeship

The question of administration versus trusteeship with respect to the board of directors becomes very complex because of the varied definitions given the two terms and the far-reaching implications for different courses of action. A recent study* has divided the functions of top management into three basic zones: (1) Trusteeship, (2) General Management or Administrative, and (3) Divisional.

The board is obviously concerned primarily with the first zone. The question is, how far into the second should and can it venture? Before going further, we must ask ourselves two questions.

*P. E. Holden, et al., *Top-Management Organization and Control* (Palo Alto, Calif.: Stanford University Press, 1941), pp. 15–17.

Exactly what is meant by the directors' trusteeship function? Because a director stands in a fiduciary relationship to the stockholders, [he or she] is responsible for preserving and safeguarding the interests of the owners. This includes a competent review and appraisal of overall results. However, since the director is also charged with the management of the corporation, [the] trusteeship function is broadened. [The director] is ... motivated [not only] to protect the stockholders' interests but also to further these interests and increase the corporate wealth through an aggressive spirit of enterprise and the most effective use of the company's assets.

The second question is: How far can a director go in carrying out this trusteeship function? It may be argued that all transactions of the business are, or should be, for the interest of the stockholders. At what point, therefore, should the trusteeship for the stockholders' interests, as such, cease, and the more direct forms of management begin?

In other words, how far should the directors enter into the actual management of the business in order to properly discharge this trusteeship function? Although limited by the possibility of becoming a hindrance to management and not having sufficient time from their other business obligations to devote to the company, directors should generally provide management, advise management, and supervise management.

The importance of a clear expectation of ... the board's functions ... cannot be overemphasized. The powers which are retained by the board should be set forth in the by-laws. Only when both executives and directors thoroughly understand their respective parts in the big picture are they able to devote their full energies toward the effective discharge of their proper functions, thus avoiding confusion and friction.

In the modern corporation, there is an urgent necessity for both administration and trusteeship. Survival and the drive for profits place sufficient emphasis upon the administrative aspect of a director's job. The protective aspect of a director's task can never be overstressed provided a proper perspective is secured. With the increasing inactivity of stockholders, the need for a responsible representative in top management becomes obvious. However, a violent "watch-dog" or "do nothing" attitude will be quite as harmful as a reckless position. The situation calls for a delicate balance between these two important functions of directors.

A. Administration[54]

We must reiterate at this time the difficulty encountered in attempting to generalize methods of administration used by boards of directors. It is basic, however, that the board's prime administrative functions are delegation and coordination. From the bare corporate foundation, the directors must construct an administrative mechanism and through the medium of policies provide lubrication for its smooth and continuous operation. The crux of the problem lies in the amount of authority and power the board may properly delegate and still retain enough control in the hands of those ultimately responsible. Most of the directors' administrative duties can generally be delegated to officers or committees. No legal liability is likely to follow such deputation. But trusteeship duties, it would seem, must actually be performed by directors, and it is out of this type of function that legal difficulties often arise.

The implication to the board of directors of "administering" differs greatly from the application it has to others in the corporation. Donham* defines administration as "the determination and execution of policies involving action. Such policies must be conceived by [people]. Such actions must be affected by human organization." Obviously, the board cannot administer in the strict sense of the term. It can, however, aid in the determination of policies and can delegate certain types of responsibility to the operating executives, whom it appoints.

Baker** points out four different methods of board action. A board can *decide*—selects the chief executive. It can *confirm*—probes executive proposals for weakness and impracticality. It can *counsel*—advises and encourages executives. It can *review*—inspects and investigates existing policies and programs. We must again stress the value of teamwork and mutual interaction between the board and the active executives. The relationship is often distorted by two misconceptions which do untold damage. They are both the result of inadequate comprehension of the proper functions of the board.

Some quarters feel that directors should be *experts* in some field. Because industry has become so technical, they say that directors should be obtained primarily because of a special skill. This attempt to obtain expert advice for the nominal fee of a director is wrong. It neglects the true functions of the board. The director as an *individual* derives no rights or duties, with respect to management, from [a] position on the board. The goal of management, to be sure, is to obtain the widest possible background on the board because all official action is the result of *group* effort. It is often a healthy condition if the

*W. B. Donham, "The Theory and Practice of Administration," *Harvard Business Review*, Vol. 14 (Summer, 1936), p. 405.

**J. C. Baker, *Directors and Their Functions—A Preliminary Study* (Boston, Mass.: Harvard Business School, Division of Research, 1945), pp. 16–18.

executives must explain and justify policies concerning technology to non-technical [people].

Copeland and Towl,* in their survey, found that the outstanding omissions of actions and the undesirable steps taken showed a far greater lacking in the fields of public relations, human problems, and broad questions involving business judgment, than in the technical field. Technical skill may be an asset to a director, but a [person] is not a good director because of this skill; other qualities are much more important.

The other erroneous idea which interferes with the proper functioning of the corporate mechanism is the attempt by a director to impede upon executive functions without becoming an executive. The analogy between corporate and political government is helpful in discerning the separation of the legislative or policy function from the executive duties.** The board is considered a legislative body and specializes in the formulation of basic policies. When the policy is adopted, the chief executive and operating staff integrate these precepts into the operations of the corporation.

This trespassing into the executive field leads to confusion in policy, conflicting sources of action, and divided loyalties. Disaster is inevitable when there is no single individual in the enterprise strong enough to achieve and accept leadership. Any attempt by a director to bolster a weak chief executive is an illusion. When a director attempts to give "official" instructions to any member of the operating staff, [the director] is either meddling or has a misconception of [their] duties. The legal doctrine and practical application are complementary in saying that a director has no special authority outside the boardroom of a properly called and convened meeting.

1. Keeping Directors Informed[55]

One cannot consider any aspect of director participation in administration without considering their education. A director must not only be willing to direct, but more important, … must *know enough* to direct. The basic purpose underlying a consistent flow of information to the board is the maximum and most efficient utilization of the mechanism for the greatest benefit to the corporation. The amount and type of information plus the methods used require a high degree of teamwork and mutual understanding.

* M. T. Copeland and A. R. Towl, *The Board of Directors and Business Management* (Andover, Mass.: The Andover Press, 1947), p. 138.
** B. Ruml, *Tomorrow's Business* (New York: Farrar and Rhinehart, Inc., 1945).

It is difficult to overemphasize the importance of the chief executive in this area. It is quite possible for [the CEO] to keep the directors ignorant of the corporation's true condition. The outstanding example of this is the infamous McKesson & Robbins scandal. On the other hand, the director has a responsibility to devote the time necessary before meetings, so that [he or she] may provide [the] maximum contribution. [A director] has implied obligations to study and comprehend reports submitted …, request explanation and further information when necessary, and participate actively in board discussions.

There is a pronounced tendency among some outside board members to be overcautious. The general statutes are vague, even negative, in defining the duties of a director. Also, as part-time workers they often have an inferiority complex in dealing with full-time executives. The inclination of many directors who attend a meeting, listen to the discussions, and usually vote "no" because they know little or nothing about the proposal, is pernicious and destructive.

There are two aspects to the informed board of directors: the type and amount of data supplied in the media used to supply this information.

The type and amount of information vary a great deal. It depends on the part played by the board in running the corporation, the composition of the board, the company's size and complexity, and the judgment and decisions of the operating executives. If the board is simply an advisory group or if the board is predominantly composed of outside [directors] who can give only limited time, the information supplied will be affected. The information presented to outside directors must be brief, easily absorbed, and consist[] only of the most important issues. The chairman of the board should handle this classification and presentation of information.

Another cause for the great variety of types of information presented to directors is individual preference. Some [directors] desire narrative summaries and charts, while others desire statistics and operating data. The whole question of data supplied is intimately connected with the actual board meeting. Legal recognition that the greatest wisdom results from conference and the exchange of individual views has strengthened the conception that the official meeting is the foundation of board functions. The exposure of directors to the facts is designed for the proper and most efficient utilization of the monthly board meeting where business is actually transacted.

The methods used to supply the board with information vary quite as much as the types of information supplied. The National Industrial Conference Board listed some media for supplying the board:

Summary of the principal methods and media employed by management to keep directors informed:*

1. Board meetings.
2. Advance agenda.
3. Reports of the board's committees.
4. Regular reports on finances and operating results.
5. Special reports on matters of current importance.
6. Budgets and forecasts.
7. Reports of management committees.
8. Participation in the meetings of management committees.
9. Daily, weekly, and monthly newsletters.
10. Regular luncheon meetings.
11. Visits to plant properties.
12. Informal personal contacts.
13. Phone calls, telegrams, and letters.

It is important to note from the above list that the board meeting and other formal media employed to supply the board with information fail to indicate the true story of a director's participation in the board's activities. Informal talks, luncheons, and visits are important not only as ways of exchanging information, but also as means of direct participation by advising and consulting with the chief executive.

The formal methods, such as minutes, budgets, etc., to be used effectively, should be integrated into the corporate structure by a well-organized plan. The Standard Oil Company of New Jersey illustrates a unique method of informing the board. That company uses full-time directors, each of whom is responsible (*not* in an executive capacity) for a certain aspect of the company's business. It is the individual director's duty, both by formal and informal means, to keep the whole board informed as to the conditions in [that director's] specified department of the company.

Through the provision of pertinent information by the chief executive well before the meetings and with proper consideration of this data by the directors, the corporation will obtain a more intelligent participation from its board and the benefits resulting will be extremely worthwhile.

* National Industrial Conference Board, "Keeping Corporation Directors Informed," *Studies in Business Policy*, No. 24 (New York, 1947), p. 4.

2. Policy Formulation and the Board of Directors[56]

From the standpoint of top management, an administrative policy is a course of procedure formulated or established for the members of an organization in making decisions on problems as they arise. They are probably the primary instrument of coordination and control for the board. Without the consistency of action provided by policies, current operation is ineffective and desired, ultimate objectives are not likely to be attained. Because they become laws for the conduct of business, the methods of formulation and promulgation are extremely important.

Although some policy-making is delegated to the various committees, the board is the ultimate judge. It is fundamental that policy-making should be a joint product of the combined efforts and ideas of the operating staff and the board. Through full and free discussion between executives and the board, both individually and as a group, a sound policy will evolve.

The process is neither slow nor simple. It requires time, effort, and a real skill. The use of subordinate executives and informal discussions between the chief executive and the various board members will aid in the formulation of a policy, utilizing the widest range of experience possible. To what extent directors as a group usually initiate policy proposals, and to what extent they act as a body of review for policies developed by officers is not clear and presumably varies from corporation to corporation. In many of the large corporations today, however, the tendency of boards to be greatly dominated by executives with regard to policy formation is a threat to the entire corporate structure. Proper functioning with regard to policies does not demand of the board constant initiation, but it does call for strong consideration and review.

A policy becomes effective only when it is thoroughly understood, accepted, respected, and followed by all executives and other employees affected by it. It is a good practice to promulgate major policies in writing. This will insure the same interpretation for all, prevent obscurity after a period of time, facilitate checks for proper compliance, and alleviate difficulties in reviewing these policies from time to time for the purpose of changing them to meet current conditions.

Simply because a policy has been properly formulated is no guarantee that it is operating successfully. Improper compliance may be due to friction within the organization or changed conditions. Because of these possibilities, the board should reexamine basic policies at stated intervals. This potential challenge to management is an extremely healthy condition.

The most effective method used is the discerning question which will be discussed below under trusteeship. The check-up is an intricate process requiring much study and an implicit awareness of the changing conditions in the economic, political, and social environment.

Although the directors can delegate authority for the execution of policies, they cannot divest themselves of the ultimate responsibility for getting the job done. This check-up does not in any way imply lack of confidence in management; rather it is a recognition of the teamwork so essential to the success of the corporate undertaking, for this investigation tests the board as well as executive management.

3. Selecting a Chief Executive[57]

The one administrative function unanimously accomplished by the board of directors is the selection of the chief executive. In many ways it is simply the institution of a policy. As the chief administrative officer in the corporation, the long-range implications of [the] choice are great. An outstanding example of this was the election of Justin Dart to the presidency of the United–Rexall Drug, Incorporated, in 1945.

The move was accompanied by a good deal of publicity concerning the innovations that Mr. Dart was insisting upon as a condition to his acceptance of the position. In electing Mr. Dart, the board of directors in a very real sense made a major policy decision affecting the location of the company headquarters, the emphasis on company-owned stores, and an extension of lines to cover a wide range of products other than those customarily sold in drug stores.

Although the job of selecting an executive is infrequently undertaken, when the need for a chief executive arises, the task must be accomplished efficiently.

Since continuity of existence is a primary aspect of the corporate form, the question of future chief executives is a consistent problem. It is the duty and responsibility of the board not only to attend the management, but also to encourage development of a new generation of ability and leadership capable of maintaining the successful conduct of the business in the future. One cannot belittle the wisdom of developing a competent understudy for the chief executive within the organization. The board should make a real effort to canvas all possible executive timber within the organization.

Very often no acceptable candidates appear and the board must make plans either to bring a [person] in immediately as a "crown prince" or make preparations to obtain the proper [person] from the business community when the need arises. Informal talks and negotiations are valuable in that they allow the directors to air their antipathies in confidence. With constant thought in preparation, the job will be accomplished with fewer repercussions and greater efficiency.

When the situation must be met, it is generally true that the better job the board has done in the past, the easier task it will have in negotiations with the new executive. The prestige, reputation, and condition of the corporation are of great import. An ailing corporation will have to compensate for its condition by granting more favorable [terms] and compensation to any new president.

If no executive has been chosen when the vacancy occurs, the board mechanics must carry the lead during the interim period. It cannot be emphasized too greatly that it is the responsibility of the board to select the chief executive. Even if the chief executive has designated [a] successor, the board must take positive action when the vacancy occurs.

When the new [CEO] takes office, [the executive] deserves the board's wholehearted support. If any rivalries exist, or if the retiring executive remains on the scene, it is the duty of the board to clear the air and support the new executive.

4. Some Additional Obligations

It has been said that all a board of directors can do today is supply management and supervise management. At second glance, however, this entails a surprisingly wide range of duties. We have seen the scope of choosing the chief executive, and some of the intricacies of policy-making. While the directors may not [bulk] large as factors in initiation and formulation of policies, their approval and veto power with the opportunity to challenge and ask discerning questions should not be underemphasized. The board can never overstress the function of coordination. Lubrication of the corporate mechanism is never completed. This includes improvement of the board itself.

Directors, from time to time, should instigate a self-appraisal of the board situation with regard to the way they are producing for the corporation. Strengthening the board should be a constant process, since the average turnover on boards is approximately one director a year per board.

Another function of the board is cultivation of the stockholders and the investing public. The frequently mentioned lack of risk capital can be partially alleviated through better public relations and development of stockholder confidence.

Willingness to answer questions of stockholders, better annual meetings, letters welcoming new stockholders, and understandable annual reports will aid in receiving this shareholder confidence.

The matter of dividends is also within the scope of the board. Although in practice the chief executive proposes and the board approves the dividend policy, the veto is especially important here because the board is held legally liable that the dividends be paid only from available earnings or surplus profits and [do] not in any way impair the capital of the corporation.

5. The Board Committees[58]

A director's membership on a committee is an important aspect of [their] administrative function. Often this membership provides a mechanism whereby the individual director can grasp a problem and make active contributions. The purpose of committees is to secure prompt, decisive action and obviate the necessity for frequent board meetings. The basic committees, such as the executive or finance committees, serve in two major capacities: they substitute for the board in approving and often formulating some of the more important short-term decisions; they act as a "filter" for the board with respect to recommendations to be offered at future board meetings.

The true function of a committee is to deliberate upon previously developed facts, to exchange viewpoints, and, through collective judgment, to recommend action and endorse conclusions. From the similarity to the functions of the board itself arises the danger of overemphasizing committees. The need is evident for distinct organization and integration of committees. In most companies, there is a logical position within the management plan for well-defined committees. However, the functions, relationships, limits of authority, and composition should be as clearly defined as those for any other unit in the organization.

These committees can be of real value in providing management with additional advisory, coordinative, and control agencies. Through proper use, such criticisms as wasting time, slowing action, stifling individual initiative, producing compromises rather than clear-cut decisions, and lessening the sense of individual responsibility can be avoided. The types of committees vary from corporation to corporation; however, the most important seem to be the executive, finance, salary, and audit committees.

The executive committee is by far the most significant of the top-management committees, since, according to the by-laws of many corporations, it is often empowered to direct all the affairs of the corporation during the interval between meetings of the board. As early as 1859* the courts recognized the principle that the board could delegate some of its power for the purpose of permitting intermediate board action between the regular board meetings. The courts carried this doctrine further in 1897,** when they permitted the board to delegate power requiring discretion and judgment. In addition, there is general statutory recognition of these principles in the state corporation laws. Large corporations, especially, utilize the executive committee.

The National Industrial Conference Board*** found that over 60% of the corporations studied, with assets of $50 million or more, have executive committees. In corporations with assets under one million dollars, only 7% use this mechanism. They found the membership to range from three to ten members, with the average around five.

The composition varies. In most cases, the outside directors are represented but outnumbered by the operating executives. When a finance committee exists as well as an executive committee, often the executive committee is mostly executive and the finance committee is predominantly outside [directors]. These two committees often are significant factors in shaping the corporation's overall policy.

When a large directorate exists, usually as a result of the company's size, the executive committee should be on a full-time basis, or nearly so. If wisely chosen and adequately compensated, such a committee would enable the board to reduce many of the slow and cumbersome aspects of large business organizations to fast-moving, dynamic business procedures, and provide a final source of authority instantly available. The boards that refuse to appoint an executive committee penalize their company by forcing speedily required action through the ofttimes sluggish board mechanism. We must, however, remember where the ultimate responsibility lies, and act accordingly.

Another committee of importance is the salary committee. Obviously, an equitable and rational plan for paying the executives is needed to obtain and maintain a high-caliber group of [executives]. An important point to note is that this committee must be controlled by outside directors. The duties are variously reported as being the submission of recommendations, the approval or the actual establishment of salaries, up and down the scale.

* *Hoyt v. Thompson's [Executor]*, 19 N.Y. 207, 216 (1859).
** *Jones v. Missouri*, 139 Mo. 25, 40 S.W. 353 (1897).
*** National Industrial Conference Board, "Prevailing Practices Regarding Corporate Directors," *Studies in Administrative Control*, No. 2 (New York, 1939), p. 16.

Another committee whose importance has recently received national attention is the audit committee. As shown in the McKesson & Robbins case, the importance of a thorough, efficiently handled audit cannot be overemphasized. The SEC, in one of its conclusions to the case advocates "establishment of a committee to be selected from non-officer members of the board which shall make all company or management nominations of auditors and shall be charged with the duty of arranging the details of the engagement."*

In other words, the purpose of the committee is to see that a complete audit is taken and that the auditors have complete freedom and cooperation throughout the job. These auditors should be directly responsible to the board. Three criteria will aid in the establishment of a more efficient audit procedure: (1) The audit committee should be completely independent of management—all outside directors. (2) The audit committee should be a standing committee. This will give the members experience and a general "feel" of the situation. (3) The auditing firm should be appointed early in the year, thus affording it time to become acquainted with the corporation's accounting procedures.

In its investigation, the SEC found adequate auditing procedures sadly lacking in the fundamental principles. In the majority of companies, the audit is handled by the chief executive or some other officer. The final report usually goes to the president, who then presents it to the board. The situation demands reform to the point where the procedure harmonizes with the intended trusteeship function [that] an audit should accomplish.

We have just dealt with the more important committees. As the committee becomes more specialized, such as a profit-sharing committee, it frequently participates more actively in the field allocated to it. However, the real significance of committees lies in the sum total of their contributions in developing the board policies and objectives for the corporation as a whole.

To conclude this administrative section, we note that the board participates in many different ways. The important point, however, is that a board must function in some manner aimed in the general direction indicated. Failure of the board to function has been held to constitute mismanagement and the courts have authorized the appointment of a receiver in that situation.

* *United States of America before the Securities and Exchange Commission in the matter of McKesson & Robbins, Inc.* (Washington: US Government Printing Office, 1940), p. 5.

B. Trusteeship

In our consideration of trusteeship, so far, we have noted two aspects of the function: (1) the narrow meaning of mere preservation and protection, and (2) the duty to further the stockholders' interests by increasing the wealth of the corporation through the most fruitful use of its assets. Upon closer examination, a new concept emerges, conflicting in many ways with the existing legal theory, which broadens the scope of the problem to envelop the entire system of democratic capitalism.

The accepted legal concept of the corporation states that the sole purpose of its existence is to provide profits for the owners. Recently, however, public opinion, which ultimately makes law, is making substantial strides in the direction of a view that the business corporation exists as an economic institution, which has a social service to perform as well as a profit-making function. Although this conflict of doctrine encompasses the whole private enterprise system, it is of special significance to directors since the present legal view limits their fiduciary duty to promoting the welfare of the body of stockholders.

Our discussion of the trusteeship function is divided into three parts: (1) the need for, and rise of, the trusteeship concept, (2) evaluation of the social aspect of director trusteeship, and (3) methods and media for affecting trusteeship.

1. The Increasing Need for Trusteeship

Narrowing our attention to the stockholder phase of the problem for a moment, the necessity for a strong trusteeship attitude on the part of directors cannot be denied. The increasing separation of ownership from management and the development of the corporate structure so as to vest in small groups control over the invested capital of great numbers of small, uninformed investors make imperative for directors a fresh and active devotion to their trusteeship function.

If directors are to meet their increasing responsibility, it seems clear that they must devote more thought and planning to developing a distinct philosophy of action. With the advent of the modern era there has been a steady movement toward a more exacting trusteeship in the courts, where more precise standards of conduct are demanded, and in the statutes where directors are required to obtain adequate knowledge of the corporation and are held liable accordingly.

Indeed, the acceptance of funds by the corporation from the public at large places the directors in a fiduciary position. Such utterances may sound platitudinous, but in the long run they are warranted in the light of cold business-like decisions. Large-scale business today is vitally dependent upon the flow of capital from millions of small investors whose willingness to invest will depend in large measure upon the treatment they are accorded. Abuses by directors of their trust, imposition on the shareholders' rights of ownership, or unwarranted assumption of power by a few will serve to break the lifeline of confidence which is essential to investor support.

2. Conflicting Thoughts on Trusteeship[59]

The problem confronting us is essentially a social question. In essence, the query asks whether a director's responsibility rests simply within the corporate entity, or whether it includes the customers, consumers, suppliers, and public at large. The social philosophy in this case has evolved much faster than the legal doctrine. Essentially, the conflict is between two different concepts of trusteeship.

One side* advocates an increased emphasis on the doctrine that managerial powers are held in trust for stockholders as sole beneficiaries of the corporate enterprise. The proponents believe that greater stockholder protection will result from this policy. Corporate powers, they feel, are exercisable only for the benefit of the body of shareholders as their interest appears. Use of these powers should be restricted when they are used to the detriment of any shareholder, no matter how absolute the grant of power was or how technically correct the use of this power will be.

In other words, every corporate action must be twice tested: (1) with the technical rules having to do with the existence and proper exercise of corporate power, and (2) with the equitable rules somewhat similar to those imposed upon trustees by the instrument which grants them broad powers and makes them fiduciaries. The overall result of this doctrine will be increased flexibility in corporate actions, since, according to this doctrine, a board of directors may do things, if beneficial, which are now hampered by technical rules. Contrariwise, where no benefit may be shown and where one group will be sacrificed for another, action can be prevented.

The opposing attitude** recognizes the need for protecting the stockholders against irresponsible actions of management, but this group perceives, as more important, the evolution of public opinion with regard to the social functions

*A. A. Berle, Jr., "Corporate Powers as Powers in Trust," *Harvard Law Review*, Vol. 44, No. 7 (May, 1931), pp. 1049–74; also, "For Whom Corporate Managers *Are* Trustees," *Harvard Law Review*, Vol. 45, No. 8 (June, 1932), pp. 1365–72.

** E. M. Dodd, Jr., "For Whom Are Corporate Managers Trustees?" *Harvard Law Review*, Vol. 45, No. 7 (June, 1932), pp. 1145–63.

corporations should perform. Not only has the public become conscious of this new ideal, but many industrial leaders have also awakened to the new concept.

A pioneer in this recognition was Owen D. Young, who stated: "One no longer feels the obligation to take from labor for the benefit of capital, nor to take from the public for the benefit of both, but rather to administer wisely and fairly for all concerned."** Recognizing that laws eventually coincide with public opinion, this school feels that a great mistake will be made if an increased emphasis is placed upon the rights of stockholders. They point to recent writing which indicates a demand for a substantial increase in the obligations of business to the community. The new concept of responsible capitalism is a great challenge and its reconciliation to our free enterprise system is far from a solution.

There is no doubt that capitalism must adapt itself to this new philosophy if it is to survive: the real question appears to be—will the readjustment be accomplished fast enough and in the right direction? There are many legal obstacles to this readjustment. We cannot abandon emphasis on the view that business corporations exist for the sole purpose of making profits for their stockholders until such time as we are prepared to offer a clear, reasonable, and enforceable scheme of responsibilities to somebody else. Another even knottier problem is the whole question of private ownership of property and freedom of contract. For the time being, however, the healthiest attitude seems to be that although corporate powers have steadily increased, with each additional right also goes added responsibility.

3. Methods and Media for Effecting Trusteeship[60]

As representatives of the stockholders in top management, the board of directors has a definite obligation to appraise the overall results of the corporation. The director, in protecting the interests of the stockholders, checks on the operations with the fundamental belief that the stability and continuity of the enterprise are the prime considerations. For instance, the board declares a dividend which benefits the stockholders, but the long-run result of the action jeopardizes the future status of the corporation. This is not trusteeship in its true sense.

The various checks and balances employed by different corporations include budgets, reports, inspections, and outside audits. In the General Foods Corporation, for instance, the Salary Committee is composed entirely of outside directors in order to avoid self-dealing. Also, in considering new financing, disinterested directors are placed on the executive committee in place of

*The Life of Owen D. Young, *Fortune*, Vol. 3 (March, 1931), p. 94.

commercial or investment bankers. In general, directors with a personal interest in the proposal do not vote.

Without doubt the most effective instrument to the director in carrying out [the] trusteeship function is the discerning question. However, by its definition ("a really discerning question typically opens up a situation where action or at least a thorough review of policy is called for"),* its scope goes far beyond trusteeship. If properly utilized, a discerning question may also be an effective administrative tool. The value of this instrument to a director cannot be overemphasized.

Its worth is recognized by many chief executives. "The most valuable directors we have are those who challenge most intelligently and frequently."** [T]he most valuable directors are those with the ability to question frequently and pertinently yet not derogatorily. The question is of further value as a two-way method of education. The executives' thinking is clarified as well as supplying information to the directors. A good director will not only give advice and counsel, but … will listen and provide the means whereby the executive … can reach the decision.

Through these conversations a director can appraise the management's ability—an extremely important aspect of trusteeship. Another extremely valuable quality of the discerning question is that a worthy result is achieved, yet the director in no way becomes involved in management. A director is excluded from everyday operations and his thoughts are concentrated toward broad policies and objectives.

Although a discerning question is invaluable, its import is lost unless utilized in the most efficient way. The manner of inquiry is very important. The question should be asked pleasantly, discreetly but firmly. It is definitely not a cross-examination, because the director is a participant seeking to guide and evaluate results.

In [the] attempt to be vigilant regarding the welfare of the corporation, the director may make excellent use of discerning questions if [asked] from an independent, outside point of view. This constant challenge will promote sound reasoning on the part of the chief executive because, as a result of an explanation and defense of his [or her] policy, the faults and weak spots are exposed. A common pitfall of directors is frequent failure to go beyond the initial reply to the underlying reality. Unless directors follow through on the

*Copeland and Towl, *op. cit.*, p. 95.

**Clarence Francis, Chairman of the Board, General Foods Corporation. Interview, January 3, 1948.

leads opened, by utilizing and evaluating the answers, the questions become impractical intellectual exercise.

Similar to most mechanisms, the use of discerning questions can be overdone and abused. Boards may be reduced to the level of juries, selected by opposing counsel, exercising an unlimited power of challenge. An overcritical view may discourage new ideas and the spirit of enterprise.

It is very simple to write fluently about the value of discerning questions, yet we must remember the obstacles to their proper use. First of all, they place a heavy burden upon directors. Preparation requires much time and thought. They call for breadth of experience, tact, and sound judgment. Very often, the posing of a necessary question requires courage. It is generally agreed, however, that despite the scarcity of good questioners, and the difficulties entailed in the process, the result is well worth the efforts since the strength and vitality of the board are greatly dependent upon the amount and type of questions asked.

When analyzed, the highly publicized conflict between the administrative and trusteeship functions is greatly alleviated if both directors and executives realize and practice their separate functions, remembering at all times their common goal—prosperity for the corporation. The line between the two areas is often unintelligible. Many acts of a trusteeship nature, such as a policy check-up or the discerning questions, may be considered administrative, while many so-called administrative functions, such as supervising the audit procedure, may be considered trusteeship actions.

Chapter IV. Status of the Board as Affected by the Executive Management and Outside Interests

A prime requisite for the proper evaluation of functioning directors is a discussion of the board's relations with executive management and the effects of certain interest groups on the working board's mechanism. These aspects are integral parts of the environment within which directors must function. Although the influence of these factors varies from corporation to corporation, depending on the setup and type of business, the traditions of the corporation, and the personalities involved, they present problems in some form for all corporations.

A. Management Domination of the Board

When the Temporary National Economic Committee in 1939 reported that boards of directors to a great extent had become self-perpetuating bodies controlled by executive management, many people were considerably dismayed. Few realized the degree to which centralization of control had taken place within the modern corporation. Although we might have expected, due to its legal status, that the board would fight this infringement and try to secure its proper position, in reality boards in many cases actually contributed to this management domination. The problems of absentee ownership and the relationship of the board with the active management group have become increasingly critical.

1. The Pathological Situation[61]

This domination of the board of directors by executive management in many cases has led to pathological situations. Justice W. O. Douglas, Chairman of the Securities and Exchange Commission in 1939, said:

> What we frequently have today is a large majority of directors who are dominated by a few management [people] representing special interests. These directors have abdicated. It is not enough to describe them as directors who do not direct. Too often they do not even *influence*! They have become little more than ratifiers. They ratify decisions which they have not reached based on arguments and evidence which they cannot appraise. What was designed as a position of great responsibility is in danger of denigrating into a position of mere routine.*

Disregarding the variable human elements of the individual directors for a moment, the system which shows a marked tendency for executives to predominate on the board is a paradox. To have the board, which according to the law is the supreme locus of responsibility and the representative of the stockholders in top management, composed of active executives who virtually approve their own actions is a violation of a basic trusteeship principle. This preponderance of executives has destroyed the condition in many corporations of the board existing as a body independent [of] and superior to the active management group.

Another factor within the system which leads to pathological situations is the complete dependence of the board of directors upon management for any and all information. Using the McKesson & Robbins case again, we see the ability of a chief executive to hide the true condition of a corporation from an honest board of directors.

*W. O. Douglas, Speech before the Fort Worth, Texas, Clearing House, January 9, 1939.

At every regular board meeting, directors are normally supplied with reports and summaries indicating the results of recent operations and the current financial position. Very often, scrutiny and evaluation of this data is lacking, and the board yields, to the chief executive, the authority and responsibility it is supposed to exercise. The situation demands that a director should spend the time necessary to become familiar with the affairs of the company and attend the meetings or … resign.

Upon the corporation's conception, the means of insuring proper representation of stockholders was the election of directors. However, the growth of corporations, the dispersion of shareholders, and the manifest impossibility for the vast majority of stockholders to attend meetings, have made the right to vote, in reality, a right to delegate the voting power to someone else. The proxy machinery has thus become one of the principal instruments, not by which a stockholder exercises power over management of the enterprise, but by which power is separated from him.

It is clear that in most large corporations, no small group of individuals has sufficient stockholdings to dominate through stockholdings. Note the importance of control over the proxy mechanism. In the election of a director, a stockholder has three alternatives: (1) … refrain from voting, (2) … attend the annual meeting and vote personally, and (3) … sign a proxy transferring [the] vote to certain individuals selected by the management of the corporation. Practically speaking, then, a stockholder may either refrain from voting or vote for the existing management.

[The] vote becomes an authorization for management to do what it desires. The effect of this manner of electing directors is to perpetuate existing company control and to strengthen the elements of power in a company that are already dominant. While extremely inefficient or dishonest management will probably be removed, mediocre management can be perpetuated indefinitely.[62]

Despite an increasing sense of responsibility among company executives, they should not be left to determine their objectives and responsibility as they see fit. At best, the result would be benevolent paternalism; at worst, exploitation of the weaker interest groups in favor of the stronger ones and management itself.

2. The Proper Relationship between the Board and Active Management[63]

Any sound plan of management might well begin with a determination and definition, preferably in writing, of the functions, responsibilities, and limits of the authority to be reserved for the board, and those to be delegated to management. It is only by a clear delineation of functions that each group will know exactly what part it is to play in the management of the corporation as a whole.

Efficient cooperation requires directors and executives to think through their relations in all phases of the management process. By this effort, they will obtain mutual understanding in which free and critical discussion can take place on all important issues. Achievement of cooperation and free discussion necessitates mutual recognition of status. The executives must recognize the directors' abilities and fiduciary position and the directors should respect the importance of executive freedom to meet administrative hurdles. In this way conflicts will be lessened.

Opinions regarding the status of the chief executive vary a great deal. There is a tendency among many authorities to stress [the CEO's] importance as a professional manager and note the inevitability of a dominant chief executive in our modern complex corporations. This group feels that leadership must be exercised by full-time executives rather than infrequently meeting, unpaid directors having only a superficial knowledge of the business. The writer agrees to this doctrine in that a leader in some capacity must be placed at the pinnacle of corporate authority to maintain the corporation on a steady course. There should be no conflicting personalities at the highest executive level.

In addition, when the directors function properly and choose a new chief executive, they make a long-term commitment to follow a certain course. This was part of the selection process. If the board has chosen wisely and the [person selected] is a strong, dynamic leader, [that person] undoubtedly will come to exercise an increasing influence over the corporation, not because of any nefarious purpose, but because of [the] capable execution of the leadership function. Basic to the whole question lies the concept that directors must trust and support management with a firm but critical backing.

While in agreement with the doctrine of a strong chief executive, the writer feels that the board's superior status must be preserved. The director's problem is primarily one of maintaining a strong *potential* in the relationships with the chief executive. It is very difficult to watch the business operate "from a distance" and yet maintain not only one's alertness to the need for change, but also preserve one's ability to act. The hands of the board should be free to replace the chief executive at any time. A director should always remember [their] position as the locus of legal and managerial responsibility. The old problem of delegating authority to those capable of exercising it yet retaining control in the hands of those ultimately responsible must be emphasized.

In the field of director elections, constructive attempts have been made to develop an equitable relationship [among] the stockholders, management, and the board. The Securities Exchange Act of 1934 attempted to restrict the abuses in the proxy mechanism by requiring certain disclosures, relative to the solicitor and the proxyholders, of any corporation using the mail, agencies of interstate commerce, or any facility of any national security exchange. This use of publicity is valuable because the knowledge that disclosure and explanation must be effected sometime in the future will, in itself, prevent management from taking certain questionable actions.

It will also be necessary, in establishing a more equitable election system, to place control of the proxy mechanism within the jurisdiction of the board itself, preferably through the medium of a special committee. It is worthy of note, however, that a recent survey* found an overemphasis on stockholder participation in the proxy mechanism.

> [I]t appears to us that in many widely owned corporations the directors are performing their function more effectively than are directors in numerous closely held corporations. This merely suggests that stockholder participation in the selection of directors is not enough in itself to assure competency of the directorate.

A more practical solution to this management domination would seem to lie in the improvement of the board mechanism and increasing efforts to obtain and keep capable directors than in attempts to break the control of the chief executive.

B. The Status of the Chairman of the Board[64]

The office of chairman of the board, because of its potential leadership over the directorate, is an extremely important position in the corporation. Its utilization for the benefit of the corporation has only been partially recognized. In 1946 the National Industrial Conference Board found that only about half of the corporations studied had chairmen of the board.** The larger corporations use the office more frequently.

There has often arisen confusion as to the differences between the chairman, the chief executive, and the president. This perplexity may be very harmful. The chief executive is the top administrative officer of the company and … may

* Copeland and Towl, *op. cit.*, p. 178.

** National Industrial Conference Board, "Compensation and Duties of Corporate Directors," *Studies in Business Policy*, No. 16 (New York, 1946), p. 10.

be the president or the chairman of the board. If the chief executive and the chairman are the same [person, there is] a dual responsibility—executive duties and board leadership. If there are two [people] in these capacities, a constructive relationship between them must be established—each with his [or her] own clear-cut duties and responsibilities. One way or the other, however, there is a definite need in a specific place in the corporate structure for someone to handle board leadership.

The duties of the chairman may be divided into two categories: functions at the board meeting and duties outside the board meeting pertaining to the most advantageous organization and utilization of the directors. Because comparatively few corporations have taken the trouble to define the functions, very often the job reflects the personality of [its holder].

A chairman performs an invaluable service at board meetings. A group of directors needs leadership during discussion in order to obtain the maximum benefits from their time and abilities. In controversial situations, there is a need for a chairman who can take an active part in guiding the directors and helping them resolve their differences into a unified, constructive program. Another aspect of a chairman to the corporation is that he [or she] can focus the directors' attention on policy questions rather than operating problems.

The chairman's value is greatly enhanced by his [or her] attempts to provide ways of organizing the board for more effective action. This includes the preparation and refinement of the agenda (which should be given to the directors well before the meeting to allow time for study and consideration of the problems), improving methods of board procedure, promotion of more harmonious relations between the executives and directors, and aiding the board in fulfilling its trusteeship obligations. As titular head of the board, the chairman may be considered the instigator and organizer of board action—the catalyst in the board mechanism.

C. The Makeup of Corporate Boards

The controversy over the merits of inside or outside directors has raged continuously for many years. Often forgotten in the argument, however, is the object and reason for a board of directors. The real criterion of the board is how may it manage the corporation with the greatest efficiency and best results. This should be considered in the makeup of the directorate. In 1946 the National Industrial Conference Board* revealed that in corporations of less

*National Industrial Conference Board, "Compensation and Duties of Corporate Directors," *Studies in Business Policy*, No. 16 (New York, 1946), p. 4.

than $10 million in assets, inside directors predominate. In corporations with assets of $10 million and over, outside directors have a majority. The Conference Board found an increasing trend toward the use of outside directors. Obviously, there can be no rigid standard. The relationship really depends upon such features as tradition, size, business policy, and the type of business. It will be beneficial to evaluate the various schools of thought for and against both types of organization.

1. Inside Boards

Those favoring boards composed of executives have several cogent arguments. First of all, they argue that executives bring to the board a thorough knowledge of current operations and factors affecting these operations. Not only are the most important functions of the company represented on the board, but also these [people] have the "feel" of the business which enables them to make effective policy decisions. Because of their employment status and their central location within the corporation, these executives are in a more realistic position to protect, for instance, the worker or the public as a whole than the average outside director who at best is somewhat remote from the corporation and may even represent a narrow ownership interest.

Those representing the opposite viewpoint to the policies of the inside board ... argue that a board of directors should be a representative of the stockholders *over* management. It is difficult to imagine an all-executive board as a group *supervising* management. Not only will "backscratching" and "logrolling" probably exist, but also we are confronted by a management reporting to, supervised by, and responsible to *itself*—definitely a distortion of the intended system. In addition, there is always the danger, in boards consisting exclusively of executives, of being afflicted with myopia and lack of perspective.

2. Outside Boards[65]

The value to a directorate of [people] not connected with the corporation in any executive capacity is becoming increasingly recognized, as seen by the trend toward the use of outside [people] on boards.* Since a director's true status entails broad supervisory duties rather than executive functions in a strict sense, outside [people] can have an especially noteworthy value to the corporation. By observing the corporation with an attitude of friendly and interested remoteness, they can discern weaknesses in corporate policy which are sometimes invisible

*National Industrial Conference Board, "Compensation and Duties of Corporate Directors," *Studies in Business Policy*, No. 16 (New York, 1946), p. 4.

from the inside. Another important asset brought to the corporation by outside [directors] is general business experience and, more important, experience in the formulation and promulgation of policies. An outside independent viewpoint, broad experience in industry, and an interest and willing attitude in directors are also invaluable assets to corporations.

A survey in 1946*** revealed that the principal occupation of outside directors was industrial, followed by banking and finance, then by law. These facts are interesting because, when compared with statistics taken in 1939, bankers were the primary source of outside directors, with industrial and lawyers following. The wider the variety of occupations and experience, the greater will be the benefit to the corporation. Corporations must remember, however, that if one corporation is to get the benefit of another's executives as directors, there must be a mutual exchange of personnel for this purpose.

Critics of utilizing outside … directors maintain that these individuals often prevent the attainment of corporate unity, thus forestalling decisive action. There is often an absence of strong informed opinion, since many of the directors are unfamiliar with the corporation's business and are unable or unwilling to spend the necessary time to learn it. There are also many directors serving on boards today whose primary goal is not the maximum benefit of the corporation. Either as representatives of a specific interest group or serving for individual benefit, these [people] do much harm in discrediting the system and the directors who work hard and function properly.

3. "Dummy" Boards[66]

There are two major instances when the so-called "dummy" board may develop: the expansion of a [sole] proprietorship and the presence on corporate boards of "window dressing" and big names.

In the case of a successful proprietorship which desires to expand, the original owner goes through the necessary legal process of incorporation in order to obtain additional capital through the sale of stock. However, in forming the board of directors [the proprietor] feels a natural reluctance to use individuals who may cramp [the proprietor's] proven method of business. [The proprietor] therefore selects members of his [or her] immediate family, etc., to serve as a "yes group." The [proprietor] does not realize the proper use of the board, nor how the mechanism can aid [the business]. As a business grows, it outgrows the capacity of one [person]. The combined wisdom of an able group of directors is called for.

* Ibid., p. 5.

The use of big names to pad the directorate is an abuse of the board mechanism which we have referred to, and will pass simply by saying that the use of prominent [people] is not condemned in itself; however, these [people] must not only be competent, but they must also spend sufficient time to perform their duties properly.

4. Proper Criteria for Board Membership[67]

In any attempt to evaluate the criteria for membership on corporate boards, the primary factor to be considered is the most efficient use of the mechanism. In other words, what is desired from the [directors] and in what manner can this knowledge be obtained most effectively? Writers differ in their attempts to solve the problem.

Dr. Baker,* representing one school, has concluded that by far the most significant factor is the type of [person] serving on the board. Others, such as Justice W. O. Douglas** and the Temporary National Economic Committee*** reports in 1939, have stressed the importance of outside directors. The writer must agree to a certain extent with both schools of thought.

While the importance of obtaining and maintaining high-caliber [people] on the board cannot be denied, one may not ignore the method of organization. The qualities desired and incentives necessary to secure good board members are discussed in Chapter VI.

A proper balance on the board with respect to the ratio of inside to outside [directors] is important. Some dismiss this ratio lightly, but due to present conditions in which there is a serious shortage of capable directors, weaknesses in personnel and unhealthy management domination are bound to occur from time to time. The stronger the foundation of the board mechanism, the greater will be the ability of the corporate structure to withstand the vacuum created by mediocre directors.

A 50% to 75% representation of outside, experienced [people] drawn from other fields will give the board a wider horizon and tend to increase the chances of preventing some of the unhealthy aspects of this managerial domination. Executives drawn from within the organization will supply the much-needed knowledge of the company and will help carry the load due to the shortage of directors. This ratio should have flexibility with specified limits since the

* Baker, *op. cit.*, p. 172.
** Douglas, "Directors Who Do Not Direct," *Harvard Law Review*, Vol. 47, No. 8 (June, 1934), pp. 1305–34.
*** [Temporary National Economic Committee], *op. cit.*, pp. 124–25.

deciding factor in selecting an outside [director] should be [the] capabilities and not a legal technicality. By securing a proper balance in this manner and obtaining [people] of high caliber, the board's effectiveness will be increased [manifold].

D. Outside Interests Influence the Board

The status of the board is not only affected by the executive management, but it is also influenced by the various outside interest groups such as government, powerful stockholders, labor, and the public. In our study of the functions of directors, it is important to obtain a proper perspective as to the weight of these groups. For our discussion, we will narrow the consideration of interest groups to the direct effect they have upon the board and its functions. Because the board of directors must perform in a very complex and constantly changing environment, these groups must be equitably dealt with practically all the time.

1. General Advantages and Disadvantages of Outside Interest Groups

In certain instances this constant exposure to outside interest groups may be beneficial to the board. The election by some companies of educators to their boards is a constructive use of the public's influence. In the instances noted these [people] appear to be of great value, not only as good directors with wide vision and broad experience, but also as sensitive feelers within the whole environment, giving boards a more substantial picture of basic conditions. Another advantage of using representatives of the public is that indirectly the people are given an insight into the problems which management faces.

The acquisition of a balanced membership, consisting of bankers, lawyers, and industrialists is also invaluable, provided the interest does not become too powerful. Obviously, representation of the ownership group is also an asset: ownership representation is favored, ownership domination censured. In other words, outside interest groups are desired insofar as they provide a healthy balance of interest, which will benefit the corporation.

The destructive aspects of interest groups with respect to the board of directors are much too numerous to cover thoroughly in this thesis. Often, some of these groups become selfish vested interests. American economic history is filled with instances of the "robber barons" who literally destroyed corporations for the benefit of a very small group. While the power of banker interests has declined in the last two decades, there still exists the danger from vested interests.

When we hear of plans to include representatives of labor, consumers, suppliers, and government on boards of directors, our consideration must again revert to the basic purpose behind the existence of the board—to promote the welfare of the corporation. After we ensure continuity of existence and stability for the company, plus an equitable return for the stockholders, we may consider social responsibility and provision for the various interest groups. These representatives of specific groups may be valuable members of the board, but their value is completely derived from their functions and qualifications as regular directors and not as agents for a particular group.

2. Government Influence on the Board

By far the most powerful interest group today is the federal government. It has unlimited potential power even in our political system based on private property, relative freedom of business enterprise, and universal franchise. Its economic activities have steadily increased due to the depression and the two world wars. Gradually the government is becoming far more than an environmental influence. It is, in fact, performing many of the leadership functions in our corporations.

There exists practically universal opposition to government directors. Mr. G. A. Sloan crystallized the thought on the subject in a report which was unanimously accepted by the Business Advisory Council:**

> It would be inherently difficult for an active, aggressive governmental director not to step over into the field of governmental inspection and regulation and from just the fact that he had been appointed by government attempt to exercise a domination over administration and policy. It would tempt some person to use such a position to promote ambitions in political and other fields. A poor selection would readily wreck sound administrative and directional sense of responsibility in such a company. Further, there would be created the fundamental anomaly, if such appointed government director stuck to his proper functions, of having a company at issue with a government regulatory body over a question of rates, service or other matters. One arm of the government would be opposing another. There would also be constant situations where a government appointed director acting on behalf of the stockholders would be in a position of opposed interest to government agencies with which his company was contracting.

* "Richard C. Patterson, Jr. Urges 'Working Directors'," *Commercial and Financial Chronicle*, Vol. 148 (March 18, 1939), p. 1573.

Direct governmental participation on corporate boards would, in effect, hurdle the existing administrative machinery previously set up over the years. Instead of having the SEC with specific purposes and policies delegated by Congress and subject to some judicial supervision, government would short circuit this elaborate mechanism in favor of direct action governed by no known standards of control. Another danger would be arbitrary political appointments. We must remember that directors make mistakes in or out of government for they are only [people], but the mistakes of government directors would be infinitely harder to rectify than those of private directors.

The answer to this increased power of the government is not active antagonism but ... self-renovation. By improving their boards and functioning competently, corporations will eliminate the need for increased government intervention. The proverbial chips are down: either corporations institute self-reform regarding their boards or the government will be forced by political pressure to attempt the job.

E. The Reconciliation of Conflicts

Few will deny the need for securing understanding and harmony in top management without sacrificing operating efficiency. The primary method of eliminating management domination is education, whereby both executives and directors become familiar with their duties regarding the board of directors. When both factions realize the benefits to be obtained through proper use of the board, the battle will be partially won.

The next step is improved cooperation. Obviously, the board depends heavily on the chief executive for information. The chief executive, on the other hand, can derive no benefit from the board if they do not absorb and evaluate the information supplied them. With regard to this management domination, we should remember the idea which emerges from our second dilemma: a director must enter into the operations sufficiently to *know enough* to direct.

In considering the outside interests we note that certain aspects can be developed and utilized to good advantage, while others are destructive. The board's future as an independent (from government) body depends in large measure upon the extent to which it can attain and maintain a high standard of operation within the environment, consisting of complex forces and powerful interest groups.

Chapter V: The Legal Liability of Directors

Thus far we have appraised a director's functions and some obstacles to [their] proper performance. Consideration of director liability is necessary in order to obtain a proper perspective of the subject, since the standards of conduct demanded and the risk the position entails will not only significantly affect the execution of functions, but it will also affect the personnel who undertake the job. Throughout this discussion, two major factors should be remembered: the increasing size, importance, and absentee ownership of the corporations, and the possible effect the liability will have in discouraging able [people] from taking the responsibility.

A. The Director's Status in Relation to the Corporation and the Stockholders[68]

We briefly mentioned (Chapter II), the confusion arising from consideration of directors as agents or trustees. The relationship of a director to the corporation and the stockholders has also caused perplexity in many quarters. An excellent clarification of the director's position on both these points urges:*

> Directors and other officers while not trustees in the technical sense in which the term is used, occupy a fiduciary relation to the corporation and the stockholders [as] a body. ... But whether or not directors and other corporate officers are strictly trustees, there can be no doubt that their character is that of a fiduciary so far as the corporation and the stockholders as a body are concerned. In other words, it is unquestionably true that, as agents [entrusted] with the management of the corporation for the benefit of the stockholders collectively, they occupy a fiduciary relation, and in this sense the relation is one of trust.

The significance of the above lies in "fiduciary relation" and "stockholders as a body." The question is whether directors stand in the same position of trust with regard to the *individual* stockholders as they do to the *body* of stockholders. The conflict is seen by regarding, as an example, the transaction concerning a director's purchase of stock from a stockholder when [the director] has inside information that the price will rise (disregarding recent legislation for a moment and taking for granted that the corporation is unaffected).

The majority of the courts (predominantly in the large industrial states) feel that the director has a fiduciary relationship with the corporate entity, including the

* Fletcher, W. M., *Cyclopedia of the Law of Private Corporations* (Chicago: Callaghan & Co., 1931), Perm. Ed., Vol. 3, § 838.

body of shareholders and not with the individual shareholders. [T]herefore the director is under no obligation to divulge this information. The minority group (primarily the courts in the southern and western agricultural states) propound the view that the director must reveal this inside information because it is held by [the director] solely as a trustee for *all* the shareholders.

Although, at first impression, the majority appears unfair to the individual, the doctrine becomes harmonious with corporate tradition when we realize that because of its constant efforts to secure stability and continuous existence for corporations, the dogma must necessarily be larger, more profound, and of larger range than the individual.

B. The Common Law Liability of Directors[69]

In general, the rules of conduct applicable to the management of corporations were developed out of common law, not through the statutes. This explains to most observers why these rules appear more satisfactory than do those of the statutes. In many cases the common law is more flexible and realistic than the statute; however, it is definitely laggard in grasping new trends, as we shall see.

Wrongs arising from a breach of trust by the directors are divisible into three major classes: those resulting from fraudulent acts, those resulting from *ultra vires* acts, and those resulting from negligence. It must be borne in mind that these injustices harm the corporation, and the stockholders are affected only insofar as their investment in the business is diminished. In addition, the beneficiary of all suits to recover damages is the corporation and stockholders only receive the indirect benefits of a strengthened corporation.

1. The Liability of Directors for Fraudulent and *Ultra Vires* Acts[70]

Because this thesis is not a legal paper and the emphasis is upon the duties and functions of directors, fraudulent and *ultra vires* acts will be dealt with rather summarily.

At common law directors are liable to the corporation for any losses resulting to it from their fraudulent acts. Not only are they liable to the corporation for their fraudulent acts, but they are also liable to any person who sustained damages as a result of relying on their fraudulent or misleading conduct. In addition, they are liable for the misappropriation of corporate funds, the giving away of corporate property and the issuing of stock to themselves for inadequate or valueless consideration. The statutes of most states make it a criminal offense for directors to commit fraud.

The power of directors in the transaction of corporate business is limited to those actions that are necessary or proper in the carrying out of the "purpose clause" of the corporate charter. In no case are the directors ever permitted to go beyond the stated or implied powers of the corporation. For the doing of any act which is in excess of the purposes for which the corporation was formed, the directors are liable to the corporation. However, the courts generally agree that directors are not liable for *ultra vires* acts when they have acted in good faith, derived no personal benefit, and acted, to the best of their knowledge, for the greatest interest of the corporation.

2. The Standards of Conduct Required of Directors[71]

Throughout our corporate history, the courts have demanded certain standards of conduct from directors in effecting their functions. The crux of the problem has been the ever-changing legal concept of what constitutes *negligence* for a director. There is perhaps no branch of law governing corporate directors which has produced greater differences in opinion than that dealing with the nature of a director's liability for negligence.

The courts have been in agreement that directors occupy a fiduciary position and therefore they are bound to conform to a certain standard of care and diligence. A departure from this standard constitutes negligence and the directors are liable to the corporation for losses sustained.

Note the wide divergence in phrases used by the various courts at different times to define this standard: business discretion; care, caution, and prudence; fidelity and reasonable diligence; ordinary care; ordinary care and prudence; ordinary care and skill and diligence; ordinary skill, vigilance, judgment, and diligence; the customs and methods of the community in which business is done; reasonable care and business judgment; reasonable intelligence, etc.

It appears to the writer that the concept has evolved through three basic stages. The first stage, as depicted in the case of *Spering's Appeal*,* held the directors for very little. This opinion felt directors to be merely gratuitous mandatories and therefore they should be held responsible to the corporation only where their breach of trust was of such a character as to warrant imputation of fraud or gross negligence amounting to fraud. In other words, the courts excused directors, except in the case of flagrant misconduct, who pledged honesty and good faith yet hopeless incapacity.

*71 Pa. 11 (1872).

The second stage held the directors to a more rigid standard of conduct. As represented by the case of *Briggs v. Spaulding*,* this opinion felt that directors should be held to exercise that degree of care which ordinarily prudent and diligent [people] would exercise under similar circumstances. This doctrine recognizes that a director must delegate much of his [or her] power; yet in this delegation and throughout the following check-up, [the director] must exercise ordinary diligence and prudence. In addition, the court recognized the different amount of care required under various circumstances. For instance, a director of a grocery store would be required to exercise less care and diligence than a director of a bank where much of the public's personal wealth is deposited.

The third stage, although it was conceived in 1880, is gaining wide recognition today and is a further development of a more rigorous standard of conduct. This stage is represented by the case of *Hun v. Cary*.** Directors are required to discharge the duties of their office in good faith and with that diligent care and skill "that [people] prompted by self-interest generally exercise in their own affairs." This doctrine takes for granted that one who voluntarily takes the position of director possesses at least ordinary knowledge and skill and must bring them to bear in the discharge of his [or her] duties.

The whole problem is complicated by the impossibility of the courts to measure ability in business matters. Each case concerning standards of conduct and negligence must be decided upon through an examination of the existing factors. However, we may generalize by saying that there has recently been a definite trend in the courts to hold directors to a more rigid standard of performance.

3. Director Liability for Bad Judgment and Lack of Knowledge About the Corporation[72]

As fiduciaries, directors must give a conscientious consideration to every question involving the interest of the company[.] [H]owever, if they act without corrupt motive and in good faith with reasonable care, diligence, and prudence, they are not liable for errors in judgment resulting in loss to the corporation. In addition, the courts feel that directors in no way guarantee above-average skill and business acumen by acceptance of the job; therefore, they are not liable for lack of experience.

The knowledge of the corporation demanded of directors also rests upon the standard of conduct required. The director is not only charged with the knowledge actually required [but is] presumed to know everything that …

* 141 U.S. 132, 11 Sup. Ct. 924 (1891).
** 82 N.Y. 65, 71 (1880).

might have [been] found out by exercising reasonable care and making inquiries consistent with the proper performance of [their] duty. The courts, however, do recognize the need for a director's dependence upon data supplied by the operating management.

4. A Director's Transactions with the Corporation and the Stockholders[73]

A discussion of a director's personal business transactions with respect to any aspect of the corporate entity must be divided into two separate categories: a director's personal dealings with the corporate management regarding its business, and the personal transaction of individual directors as affected by their official status yet not affecting the corporation.

The courts have developed several well-settled rules which define the director's duties and responsibilities to the corporation arising from their fiduciary relation. Directors must exercise the utmost honesty and fidelity in all transactions touching their duties to the corporation and its property. All their dealings with or for the corporation must show the highest degree of good faith and fair dealing. The directors must act at all times for the benefit of the corporation and may not, directly or indirectly, derive any personal advantage or profit which is not enjoyed in common by all the shareholders. Also, all secret profits made by directors in any dealings concerning the corporate enterprise must be accounted for to the corporation.

However, the above does not make it impossible for directors to deal with the corporation. There are many cases where mutual benefits can result. Before such transactions, the courts generally look favorably upon full and complete disclosure, good faith, and abstinence from voting on the part of the interested party. Because of their fiduciary position, directors should avoid at all times any position in which their personal interest is adverse to that of the corporation. If that situation arises frequently, they should resign.

As we have noted above, with regard to a director's personal transactions not affecting the corporation, the majority of the courts have persistently refused to impose any obligation on a director to divulge inside information affecting the value of the company's stock since they hold that no fiduciary obligation exists between the individual director and the individual shareholder. Two factors have recently had a steadily increasing effect on this problem: the statutes (discussed below) and business ethics. Although not infallible or enforceable, the profession of business is always awakening to the need for cultivating the small stockholders.

In drawing conclusions to the common law liability of directors, we must note that the rules of conduct and exactly what constitutes negligence or proper performance vary. These are questions of fact which must be determined in case of circumstances such as: the character of the business, the condition of the business, the usual methods of managing such companies, and other relevant data. In addition, we must realize that the courts' scope is limited. They are ill-equipped to solve or even grapple with entangled economic problems; rather the courts are concerned that corporations be honestly and fairly operated by their directors within the law.

C. The Statutory Liability of Directors

An examination of the state corporation laws reveals a universal lack of a substantial progress covering director functions or liabilities. As we noted above, the major dogma in this field has evolved through the common law. The statutes, however, do deal with the problem in certain fields. We may generalize by saying that directors are liable for the doing of certain acts according to the statutes of almost all states. Those differ among the various states but the following are included in such state laws:

1. The payment of dividends except from surplus (impairment of capital).
2. The signing of a statement, report, or public notice which is known to be false.
3. Causing or permitting false entries to be made on the books of the corporation.
4. Refusing to allow stockholders their proper right of examining the corporation's books and records.
5. Failure or refusal to make certain reports.
6. Making transfers of property when the corporation is insolvent for the purpose of defrauding or giving preference to creditors.
7. Embezzlement, larceny, conversion, and misapplication of corporate property.*

The federal government has recently entered into the field of director liability in industrial, nonregulated corporations through the media of the Securities Act of 1933 and the Securities Exchange Act of 1934. Although the federal government had been concerned with the interlocking relationships of directors previously, these acts were its first attempt at imposing standards of conduct upon directors.

*E. F. Donaldson, *Business Organization and Procedure* (New York: McGraw-Hill Book Co., Inc., 1938), p. 374.

The main responsibility and liability of directors under the Securities Act of 1933 arises out of their managerial position and the requirement that the registration statement be signed by certain members of the board of directors of the corporation issuing the new securities. They are liable for misstatement of material facts or omission to state any material facts in connection with the sale of securities to the public, unless they had reasonable ground for belief that the statements were true.

The Securities Exchange Act of 1934 is significant to the problem since it attempts to eliminate the benefit derived by directors from the use of inside information. Section 16 of the Act requires all directors of corporations registered on the national security exchanges to file with the SEC a statement of their holdings in the corporation and file a supplementary statement within ten days after the close of any month in which there has been a change in [such] holdings. In addition, any profits which they may make by sale or purchase of securities held less than six months belongs to the corporation, and if the corporation does not sue to recover, any stockholder may institute a suit to recover in the name of the corporation.

D. Derivative Suits Against Directors[74]

In the light of the steadily increasing liability of directors, in the statutes as well as the common law decisions, there has necessarily been an increase in the number of derivative suits against directors. Where, by reason of the negligence of directors, the corporation['s] funds, property, or rights have been decreased, the injury practically and ultimately affects the stockholders. In the eyes of the law, however, the injury affects the corporation and it is here that the responsibility for recovery rests. It is only if the corporation refuses or is unable to institute legal proceedings that the stockholders are allowed to enter. Even then, the suit is generally *on behalf of* the corporation.

The need for this medium of recovery is obvious from the history of our economy, where the gains and profits of industry have not always been honestly preserved and administered for the benefit of those who are entitled to them. The expense, the difficulty and delays of litigation, the power and wealth of the guilty parties, and the secrecy and skill of their methods have tended to complicate the process for the stockholder.

From the other side of the fence, however, there is also a history of abusive use of the derivative suit on the part of the stockholders. There are all too frequent instances of derivative actions brought by stockholders owning an infinitesimal proportion of the company stock, very largely for the benefit of their attorneys, whose fees, in the event of success, are disproportionate. Very often these "strike suits" are initiated with the hope of being bought off. The courts have generally followed the "business judgment rule" in cases of dissatisfaction with the policies of the board.

The courts feel that the determination of such matters lies in the realm of the board and may not be disturbed in the absence of fraud, illegality, or negligence. Legal authorities generally agree that the majority of the cases brought to court where a loss resulted from the inaccuracy of a corporate policy are simply mistakes of business judgment, and directors are therefore not held liable. The derivative suit is definitely necessary as a check, but the director must be protected in some manner from its abuses.

1. Some Attempts to Alleviate Directors from Expenses in Successfully Defended Suits[75]

As a result of these increasing suits there has been a steady movement to relieve directors from the heavy potential expense of defending … against "strike suits." Through the 1930s many able [people] developed a reluctance to risk not only their wealth, but also their personal reputations in accepting directorships. The business community, realizing the danger, advocated reimbursement of directors out of the corporate funds for successful defense against derivative suits. The solution appears fair and equitable from the stockholder's point of view, as well as from the director's, since ability to induce high-caliber [people] to serve as directors will benefit the corporation and thereby promote stockholder welfare.

Since the late 1930s these indemnification articles have been placed in the by-laws of most corporations. There has been general acceptance of this doctrine. New York State, for instance, in 1941 took steps in this direction. It not only passed a statute authorizing the voluntary indemnification of directors by their corporations, but it also granted judicial authority to reimburse directors for their litigation expenses in the event of successful defense against derivative suits. The SEC, watchdog in these matters, has supported indemnification with the limitation that if carried to extremes by insuring directors against their liabilities, the doctrine would be against public policy and unenforceable. As the situation stands at this time, the doctrine of indemnification is generally accepted, but it has not been properly tested by adjudication in the courts.

E. Some Thoughts on Director Liability[76]

We have observed the steady sharpening [of] responsibility, both in the common law and the statutes. Although nominally the courts have not changed their standards of conduct for directors in half a century, it is evident from a study of the decisions that the courts are today, in fact, holding directors accountable for a higher degree of care, diligence, and judgment than did the courts which first announced the rules that are being applied today. The trend, as we have seen, is toward the much stronger doctrine of *Hun v. Cary*. Realization of this fact indicates the danger that a [person] risks by accepting multiple directorships and failing to function properly in any or all of them. [People] should definitely limit themselves to the number of positions they can properly fill.

Any consideration of the legal status and conduct required by the law is confronted by the rising social responsibility of corporations and their directors. Although previously mentioned in Chapter III, it is necessary to stress at this time the sluggish response of both statutory and common law to changed economic conditions and ... liberal social philosophies.

Statutory lethargy in meeting the challenge of the changing economic environment becomes evident when we consider that a board physically cannot accomplish the tasks it is theoretically held for (that is, "to manage the corporation"). Although the courts recognize the directors' ineptitude and make allowances, nevertheless the system itself is resting upon an unrealistic foundation.

We have already discussed the common law sluggishness coping with changing social philosophy. The courts sooner or later must recognize the interests of the general public, as well as those of the stockholders. This doctrine is gaining wider acceptance in the business community; the courts must evolve legal dogma to match it.

The future, in the light of this rising social philosophy and changed economic environment, offers two alternatives. Either the present mechanism of the board of directors can absorb the strain created, through reconciliation of the basic conflict (despite this increased liability to provide necessary accountability, maintaining the ability of boards to attract the high-caliber [people] required), or the system will change, holding those [people] liable who are realistically able to handle it. For instance, the creation of two boards of directors, an outside board composed of [people] of affairs (the Advisory Board of Directors) with a very limited liability, and a second board composed of active executives (the Managing Board of Directors) with much greater liability, may provide an answer.

To the writer, however, the primary effort must be to revitalize the present system. Although the liability is unrealistic at present, the best possible method of avoiding difficulty and maintaining a smoothly functioning board is the acquisition, by providing the proper incentives and conditions of work, of competent [people]—a question of personnel.

Chapter VI: The Board of Directors and the Problem of Personnel

Recognition of the true scope of a director's functions not only accentuates the need for sound board organization (Chapter IV), but it also emphasizes the need for capable and responsible [people]. As we noted in our third dilemma (Chapter II), the question of manpower slashes into the crux of board problem[s]. It is fundamental that no matter how perfectly the board is organized or how competent the chief executive may be, the qualifications of the board members themselves are the deciding factors in effecting proper participation of the board in corporate administration.

The increased liability with such nominal compensation (discussed below) has caused a truly critical situation because there has developed a reluctance in many able [people] to undertake the responsibility of the job. The increased demands upon directors seem valid from a public standpoint, yet they magnify the problem of securing the competent manpower necessary to accomplish the job of directing our corporations. In other words, our basic problem is to promote incentives great enough to obtain the type of [people] needed in this position, despite the increasing liability—in brief, a problem of personnel.

A. Desiderata of Directors

Our first consideration in attempting to solve this problem is an examination of the raw materials. Exactly what are the requisites for a good board member in today's industrial corporations? These requisites may be divided into two categories of equal weight: the human attributes and the components of business competence.

1. Human Attributes Desired in Directors

Mere recognition of the significant position directors occupy demands that they be [people] of the highest integrity and loyalty. Not only must their characters be above reproach, but they should also be [people] with a broad social viewpoint and public spirit. An outstanding code of ethics, both business and moral, also stands high on the list of necessities.

In addition to the character and code of ethics of directors, we must also stress their attitude and interest in the welfare of the corporation. Since much of the directors' contribution to the company occurs through their own initiative, they must be conscientious, vigorous, alert, and willing to cooperate. A pitfall of many corporations in taking retired executives on the board is that although the corporation gains the experience of [such people], very often these individuals lack vigor and initiative.

Other significant factors associated with these important human attributes are the director's overall intelligence and personality. These qualities include the maintenance of an independent viewpoint, the courage to challenge management, the personality to criticize without heckling, and in general, the capability to become a useful member of a cohesive group. A good director must also have the talent for judging [people] and the ability to maintain a long-range foresight as distinguished from a dependence upon expediency. Irrespective of rules, regulations, and organization, the personality and thinking of the [board put] indelible imprints on all corporate policies and practices.

2. General Business Background Competence

Since the primary duty of corporate directors is to promote the general welfare of the corporation, it would be difficult to overemphasize the value of obtaining directors with the broadest possible business experience and greatest competence. It is essential that a director must comprehend the basic functions of business.

If one quality may be considered more important than others, it will be experience. One cannot be "taught" experience. There is no substitute for personal subjection to the direct impressions. We shall divide experience into the specialized kind and the more expansive type.

[People] with specialized knowledge and experience in the fields of finance, law, or some function of industry are often desired. As we noted above, these [people] should not be used in a consultant capacity, but the specialized knowledge can be utilized valuably to broaden the horizon of the board. Because of recent trends, an understanding of the roles which government and labor play has becoming a necessity. Knowledge of the influence these two interest groups have upon the modern corporation often affects the chances of a company's healthy existence. An additional area where directors should have an understanding is in the whole field of world affairs and its potential influence upon American industry.

In the category of broader experience, we see a need on corporate boards for [people] of experience in different industries. This wide experience will give them not only an enlarged view of the company's business, but it will also furnish a knowledge of procedure enabling directors to become skilled in the formulation and promulgation of effective policies. Another result of this wide experience will be an increased ability to ask discerning questions.

Directors will not only learn which are the important factors to watch in a company, but they will also ascertain more efficient methods of checking these factors. In addition, they will be in a better position to evaluate changing conditions and appraise important trends. Today it is especially important for directors to have a competent understanding of the important inter-relationships between the economic, political, and social phases of the national development.

Any conclusion about the desiderata of directors must realize that obviously no board will be able to secure all the above qualities either in one [person] or within the whole unit, but there must be consistent efforts to obtain [people] who represent the widest range of the above qualities, keeping in mind that not only are [people] desired who are *willing* to direct, but also [people] are needed who *know enough* to direct.

B. Inducements to Become a Director

The previous section indicated the type of [people] desired on a board of directors; now let us investigate the different types of motives which would lead this type of individual to accept board membership. The whole question of inducing [people] to accept directorships applies to the procurement of outside directors. If a [person] within the company organization is offered board membership, … acceptance is practically assured since not only will [the person feel duty-bound] as an executive to take the job, but also elevation to the board from within the corporation is a much-desired honor.

Noting the universal shortage of directors, our task is to evaluate the various motivations of [people] to accept directorships and discuss means of increasing the pressure of these incentives with the end in mind of obtaining the most competent personnel. The problem of inducements logically divides itself into the financial and non-financial aspects.

1. Financial Compensation for Directors[77]

It is fundamental in our law that directors are not entitled to compensation for their services rendered within the scope of their duties as directors.* Special compensation may be authorized by the articles of incorporation, the by-laws,

* For the legal foundation of this concept see: R. S. Stevens, *Handbook on the Law of Private Corporations* (St. Paul: West Publishing Co., 1936), § 157.

a vote of the stockholders, or by a vote of directors themselves under authority conferred, but without some special provision, remuneration for services is not given. The rule is founded upon the presumption that each director will have a stock interest sufficiently large to justify his [or her] devotion.

The usual method of payment is the fee per meeting. A recent survey* revealed the average payment to be about $50 in 1946 as compared with $20 in 1938. The larger corporations (over $50 million in assets) pay more, about $64, and the smaller corporations (under $1 million in assets) pay about $20. Payment of directors through normal dividends and appreciation in the value of shares owned are other methods regarded favorably by many because of the incentive involved. Other media of compensating directors used every so often are: bonus payments, salaries, discounts, expense allowances, profit-sharing, and participation in new issues.

From the standpoint of a substantial incentive to serve as a director, the present system seems wholly inadequate. However, there has been a significant trend in the last ten years to pay directors salaries more in line with their duties and liabilities. Many suggestions for computing the amount have been presented. The most equitable and practical appears to be the Johns–Manville method,** which determines the sum according to the actual amount of service rendered.

Increased remuneration seems advisable, since not only will it add justification to the chief executive's requests for frequent consultation and discussions over and above attendance at board meetings, but also a reasonable compensation will act as an incentive for directors to contribute more of their time and effort to the corporation. To a certain extent, salary is not only a payment for talent but it is also a means to the access of talent. As the burdens of a directorship become greater, a substantial financial inducement must be utilized in order to obtain capable [people]. However, the pecuniary motive is not the only incentive. It is also important to recognize the influence of altruistic endeavor in motivating [people] to accept directorships.

2. Non-Financial Compensation for Directors[78]

At such nominal compensation as mentioned above, it is apparent that other motives must exist which induce [people] to risk their wealth and reputations in this job. Many [people] are influenced to accept a directorship because of the power and prestige it entails. Others sincerely have a sense of obligation

* National Industrial Conference Board, "Compensation and Duties of Corporate Directors," *Studies in Business Policy*, No. 16 (New York, 1946), p. 6.

** R. W. Lea, "The Director's Job in Management," *Management Review* (May, 1940), p. 164.

to serve the public with the business community. [People] frequently become directors because of loyalty or friendship to the chief executive.

An important incentive in many [people] is the opportunity to associate with outstanding business and financial leaders. Another influential incentive is the challenge inherent in the problems that confront the board. Some individuals receive an intense personal satisfaction from the intellectual exercise necessary for proper solution of the intricate problems involved.

An important aspect of this incentive, however, is the atmosphere and working conditions on the board. Obviously, this type of [person] will not long remain a member of the board where he [or she] is merely a "rubber stamp" with little opportunity to make constructive contributions.

An additional inducement to accepting board membership is the opportunity to obtain experience for one's own business. Many [people] utilize the education acquired on one board to aid them under similar circumstances in their own organizations.

In conclusion, it is important to realize the significance of both types of incentives. In securing the proper personnel, not only will pecuniary incentives be necessary, but we must also recognize the extremely important non-financial inducements. As a supplement to these important factors, the environment of the board must be such that able [people] can efficiently participate.

C. Recruiting the Personnel

Before the job of recruiting directors can be effectively accomplished, the foundation must be prepared. Proper utilization of the board mechanism must be recognized. The task is primarily an educational one. Not only must present and potential directors be taught the scope of their duties and responsibilities, but executives of the corporations must also be schooled in the advantages of a properly functioning board. … After the atmosphere is cleared and wholesome working conditions are secured, the attempts to furnish the board with capable and responsible [people] can begin. Through the proper use of inducements, [people] of the desired qualities will be attracted to the job.

1. A Partial Solution—The Professional Director[79]

The title "professional director" is generally a red flag in the business community, since corporate executives universally distrust the potential government influence, the lack of business experience, and the academic abstraction implied in the term. The meaning of the term for this thesis is the presence on boards of well-paid directors serving several non-competing organizations holding no executive position and representing no particular group.

The basic criteria of this group must be a broad background and extensive experience in business affairs. Because these individuals earn their livelihood chiefly by serving on several boards, not only will they be qualified to supply a fresh, outside viewpoint, but they will also be able to devote a large part of their time to becoming adequately familiar with the corporation's business to permit intelligent participation.

There are significant weaknesses in the concept, such as establishing the dividing line between director and executive functions, adding an expense with no guarantee of a commensurate gain, providing a dumping ground for [people] of influence, and the practical difficulty of finding [people] in this category. Because of these difficulties, it would be unrealistic to depend upon this type of director exclusively; therefore, we consider the professional director a partial solution to our personal problem. In other words, if the increased inducements create a group of this type—so much better.

The opportunity for solution of this personnel problem exists since the turnover of directors is fairly great (the average being approximately one director per year, per corporation). However, success in the acquisition of the desired type of personnel by means of establishing constructive working conditions on boards and augmenting incentives is a difficult task and presents a great challenge to industry.

Chapter VII: Conclusion

It is only in the conclusion that the status and functions of corporate directors assume their true degree of complexity. Because of its central location within the corporation, multiple factors are constantly acting upon the board of directors to complicate its environment. A true picture of the status and functions of directors will not only be influenced by economic, political, social, and legal forces, but it will also be affected by the extremely influential and variable human elements.

The present problems and dilemmas confronting directors are direct results of the almost unbelievable growth of our economy and the increased importance of the corporate form within this industrial expansion. The growth of the absentee ownership, becoming more detached from management all the time, and the increasing centralization, both into a few large units per industry and in the trend for the executive group in a corporation to grasp the reins of management, have changed the economic conditions under which corporations, and therefore boards of directors, must operate.

As a result of the increased size and complexity of corporations, we see a general inconsistency arising: the board of directors is *practically* unable to carry out the tasks it is *theoretically* supposed to. This incongruity affects both the functions demanded and the liabilities imposed. Because directors physically could not "manage" the corporation, the common law evolved certain standards of conduct expected of directors which we divided into three increasingly strict stages.

Also, due to this changed economic environment, we see the need for an increasing devotion to general trusteeship. Despite this, however, we noted the sluggish response of the courts to an increasingly recognized social responsibility (a trusteeship allegiance of a broader scope than mere stockholder protection). The idea is slowly gaining acceptance in the business community that the corporation receives its ultimate sanction from usefulness to society.

Although resting upon a somewhat unrealistic foundation regarding both the functions to be performed and the liabilities imposed, and probably in need of a realistic redefinition in both areas eventually, very likely the most feasible initial efforts toward reforming the board of directors lie in attempting to revitalize the board within the present system. This renovation must take place within the framework of slowly evolving statutory and common law doctrines with appreciative regard for the forces, such as the changing economic environment, and the emergence of a new socioeconomic philosophy, which caused the present disequilibria in the board mechanism.

The primary step to be taken is a comprehensive educational program. Both corporate directors and executives throughout the business community must be made to realize what the true functions of the board are and what advantages will accrue to the corporation which utilizes its directors properly. There must be an overall clarification and development of existing doctrines concerning the powers, functions, and responsibilities of directors.

The program for accomplishing this renovation of the board should include three courses of action:

1. *Strengthen the foundation* of the mechanism by developing a sound and workable plan of organization with clearly defined duties, powers, and responsibilities, which will enable the board to perform its true functions.
2. *Increase the efficiency* of the directorate by promoting workable size, integrated committees, and proper balance (both varied experience and in the inside–outside relationship).

3. *Acquire the personnel* capable of performing the task by increasing the inducement to accept a directorship.

A significant point to be emphasized is that this reform movement must be accomplished by industry itself. The incentive is not measured in dollars and cents, or in conformity to government demands for boards that are responsible. [It] is the incentive of strengthening the whole American system of economics so that it can withstand, repulse, and overcome the various attacks on it, which are in existence and are sure to increase in the future. The present-day doubts concerning not only the ability but also [the] *right* of our system to survive can only be eliminated by proper performance.

The significance of the board emerges if we regard the problem within the context of our economy as a whole. When we realize that the board of directors, as the central agency of corporate power, is in a position to provide and supervise management for a major proportion of our country's productive mechanism, the necessity for discovering a valid solution to the problem becomes obvious. The key to national prosperity and welfare, perhaps national survival, may well hinge upon the ability of directors to solve the intricate economic problems confronting them today.

BIBLIOGRAPHY[80]

1. Books and pamphlets

Baker, J. C., *Directors and their Functions—A Preliminary Study*. Boston, Mass., Harvard Business School, Division of Research, 1945.

———, *Executive Salaries and Bonus Plans*. New York, McGraw-Hill Book Co., 1938.

Barnard, C. I., *Functions of the Executive*. Cambridge, Mass., Harvard University Press, 1946.

Berle, A. A., Jr., and G. C. Means, *The Modern Corporation and Private Property*. New York, The Macmillan Company, 1933.

Conyngton, T., R. J. Bennett, P. W. Pinkerton, *Corporation Procedure*. New York, Ronald Press Company, 1922.

Conyngton, T., *A Manual of Corporation Management*. New York, Ronald Press Company, 1911.

Cook, W. W., *The Principles of Corporation Law*. Norwood, Mass., Norwood Press, 1925.

Copeland, M. T., and A. R. Towl, *The Board of Directors and Business Management*. Andover, Mass., The Andover Press, 1947.

Couse, H. A., *Organization and Management of Business Corporations in Ohio.* Cincinnati, Ohio, W. H. Anderson Company, 1915.

Donald, W. J., *Handbook of Business Administration.* New York, McGraw-Hill Book Company, 1931.

Donaldson, E. F., *Business Organization and Procedure.* New York, McGraw-Hill Book Co., Inc., 1938.

Fletcher, W. M., *Cyclopedia of the Law of Private Corporations.* Chicago, Callaghan & Company, Perm. Ed., Vol. 3., 1931.

Gordon, H. A., *Business Leadership in the Large Corporation.* Washington, D. C., The Brookings Institution, 1945.

Gulick, L., and L. Urwick, *Papers on the Science of Administration.* New York, Institute of Public Administration, 1937.

Guthman, H. G., and H. E. Dougall, *Corporate Financial Policy.* New York, Prentice-Hall, Inc., 1940.

Holden, P. E., L. S. Fish, and H. L. Smith, *Top-Management Organization and Control.* Palo Alto, California, Stanford University Press, 1941.

Husband, W. H., and J. C. Dockeray, *Modern Corporation Finance.* Chicago, R. D. Irwin, Inc., 1946.

Johnson, J. F., *Modern Business,* Vols. I, II, III. New York, Alexander Hamilton Institute, 1917.

Morgan, Stanley and Company, *Prospectus.* J. P. Stevens and Company, Inc., Capital Stock, August 6, 1947

National Industrial Conference Board, "Prevailing Practices Regarding Corporate Directors," *Studies in Administrative Control,* No. 2. New York, 1939.

———, "Compensation and Duties of Corporate Directors," *Studies in Business Policy,* No. 16. New York, 1946.

———, "Keeping Corporation Directors Informed," *Studies in Business Policy,* No. 24. New York, 1947.

Noyes, C. E., *Responsibilities of Corporation Directors,* Editorial Research Reports, Vol. I. 1939, pp. 251–264.

Parker, J. S., *The Corporation Manual.* New York, United States Corporation, 1948.

Pecora, F., *Wall Street Under Oath.* New York, Simon Schuster and Company, 1939.

Regulation X-14—S.E.C. Rules Relating to the Solicitations of Proxies. New York, Lincoln Engraving and Printing Corp., February, 1946.

Ruml, B., *Tomorrow's Business.* New York, Farrar and Rhinehart, Inc., 1945.

Smith, Adam, *The Wealth of Nations.* (Everyman's Library Edition, Vol. II, 1947).

Stevens, R. S., *Handbook on the Law of Private Corporations*. St. Paul, West Publishing Co., 1936.

Stockder, A. H., *Business Ownership Organization*. New York, Henry Holt & Company, 1922.

2. Newspapers and periodicals

"A Director of Directors Defines a Director's Job," *Business Week*, April 29, 1931, pp. 24–25.

"A Director on Directors," *Business Week*, March 29, 1941, p. 63.

Arsht, S. S., "Liability of Directors for Negligent Mismanagement," *University of Pennsylvania Law Review*, Vol. 82, 1934, pp. 364–71.

Atwood, A. W., "No Formula for Choosing Good Corporation Directors," *Public Utilities Fortnightly*, Vol. 24, November 19, 1939, pp. 595–605.

"Auditors as Directors," *Journal of Accountancy*, Vol. 63, April, 1937, pp. 243–46.

Baker, J. C., "The Board of Directors," *Dun's Review*, February, 1946, pp. 11–15.

Ballantine, H. W., "California's 1943 Statute as to Directors' Litigation Expenses," *California Law Review*, Vol. 31, No. 5, [1943,] pp. 515–29.

Bates, G. E., "The Board of Directors," *Harvard Business Review*, Vol. 19, Autumn, 1940, pp. 73–87.

Bates, G. E., and E. M. Zuckert, "Directors' Indemnity: Corporate Policy or Public Policy," *Harvard Business Review*, Vol. 20, Winter, 1942, pp. 244–64.

Berle, A. A., Jr., "Corporate Powers as Powers in Trust," *Harvard Law Review*, Vol. 44, No. 7, May, 1931, pp. 1049–74.

———, "For Whom Corporate Managers *Are* Trustees," *Harvard Law Review*, Vol. 45, No. 8, June, 1932, pp. 1365–72.

Bower, M., "Becoming a Director—A Business Honor or a Financial Boomerang?", *Harvard Business Review*, Vol. 9, April, 1931, pp. 371–82.

Bowes, H. E. and L. A. DeBow, "Cumulative Voting at Elections of Directors of Corporations," *Minnesota Law Review*, Vol. 21, March, 1937, pp. 351–70.

"Business and Government," *Fortune*, Vol. 21, March, 1940, pp. 38–40.

Calkins, H. W., "Directors' Status Changing Rapidly," *New York Times*, May 4, 1941, p. 31.

Carlisle, P. M., "Insurance Limited for Directorships," *New York Times*, April 23, 1939, p. 32.

———, "New Type Insurance to Protect Company Directors Proposed," *New York Times*, April 9, 1939, p. 29.

———, "Professional Type of Directors Urged," *New York Times*, January 17, 1939, p. 28.

Carson, R. M., "[Current Phases of] Derivative Actions Against Directors," *Michigan Law Review*, Vol. 40, No. 8, June, 1942, pp. 1125–60.

———, "Further Phases of Derivative Actions Against Directors," *Cornell Law Review*, Vol. 29, June, 1944, p. 431.
"Concerns Ponder Work Directors," *New York Times*, December 10, 1939, p. 31.
Corporation Service, Prentice-Hall, Inc., Vol. 2, Sections 3000–3400, 1947.
"Directors Face Anti-Trust Suits," *New York Times*, October 11, 1947, p. 20.
"Directors' Fees," *Fortune*, Vol. 8, December, 1933, p. 10.
"Directors Who Direct," *Business Week*, February 15, 1941, pp. 22–29.
"Directors Who Direct," *Management Review*, March, 1941, p. 79.
Dodd, E. M., Jr., "For Whom Are Corporate Managers Trustees?", *Harvard Law Review*, Vol. 45, No. 7, May, 1932, pp. 1145–63.
Donham, W. B., "The Theory and Practice of Administration," *Harvard Business Review*, Vol. 14, Summer, 1936, pp. 405–10.
Dortch, J. S., "Qualifications and Eligibility of Corporate Directors," *Virginia Law Review*, Vol. 28, No. 2, December, 1941, pp. 292–305.
Douglas, W. O., "Decline of American Directorates," *Management Review*, February, 1939, pp. 43–44.
———, "Directors Who Do Not Direct," *Harvard Law Review*, Vol. 47, No. 8, June, 1934, pp. 1305–34.
"Favor Paid Directors," *Business Week*, May 6, 1939, p. 41.
"Fee Splitters," *Fortune*, Vol. 17, April, 1938, p. 14.
Fischer, J., "The Lost Liberals," *Harper's Magazine*, May, 1947, pp. 387–93.
Gould, L., "Justice Department's Latest 1948 Move—War on Directors," *New York Journal-American*, September 30, 1947, p. 20.
Hardy, R. C., and R. D. Youle, "The Power and Responsibilities of Corporate Directors," *Journal of Accountancy*, Vol. 82, October, 1946, pp. 280–96.
Heimann, H. H., "Urges Corporation Directors Based on Ability," *Commercial and Financial Chronicle*, Vol. 164, July 18, 1946, p. 397.
Hendershot, R., "Director Status," *New York World-Telegram*, August 26, 1947, p. 20.
"How Can Directors Earn Their Salt?", *Kiplinger Magazine*, December, 1947, pp. 17–20.
Howe, A. M., "Directors Must Direct," *Printers Ink*, Vol. 154, February 5, 1931, pp. 17–20.
"Industry Turning to Paid Directors," *New York Times*, March 31, 1940, p. 28.
Jervis, H., "Corporate Agreements to Pay Directors' Expenses in Stockholder Suits," *Columbia Law Review*, Vol. 40, No. 7, November, 1940, pp. 1192–205.
"Johns–Manville and Its Workers," *Business Week*, July 16, 1938, pp. 30–31.
Kane, K. B., "Interlocking Directorates," *Cornell Law Quarterly*, Vol. 23, April, 1931, pp. 445–51.

Lea, R. W., "The Director's Job in Management," *Management Review*, May, 1940, p. 164.
"The Life of Owen D. Young," *Fortune*, Vol. 3, March, 1931, p. 94.
Murphy, J. A., "The Board of Directors That's Loaded with Deadheads," *Sales Management*, May 15, 1939, pp. 18–20.
Nathanson, M. H., "Legal Safeguards about Transactions Between a Director and His Corporation," *University of Pennsylvania Law Review*, Vol. 83, 1935, pp. 55–66.
"Need for Directors' Liability Insurance," *Management Review*, January, 1941, p. 30.
"New Jobs for Directors," *Management Review*, February, 1940, p. 45.
"Odds and Ends," *Kiplinger Magazine*, January, 1948, p. 17.
Patterson, R. C., Jr., "Creed for Directors," *Management Review*, May, 1940, p. 163.
———, "The Responsibilities of Directors," *Advanced Management*, Vol. 5, No. 1, pp. 57–62.
———, "Wanted: Directors Who Direct," *New York Times Magazine*, January 21, 1940, p. 6.
"Pay for Directors Urged by Douglas," *New York Times*, January 10, 1939, p. 26.
Plaut, E., "Needed: Real Directors," *Printers Ink*, Vol. 159, May 20, 1937, pp. 17–19.
Porter, R., "New Rating Given Intellectuals," *New York Times*, October 26, 1947, p. 25.
"Power of the S.E.C. to Limit Directors' Purchases of Stock," *Harvard Law Review*, Vol. 56, No. 1, September, 1942, pp. 126–30.
"Practices Regarding Corporate Directors," *Management Review*, October, 1939, pp. 336–37.
Raymond, W. T., "Fewer Bankers on Corporate Boards," *Barron's*, Vol. 15, August, 1935, p. 24.
Rhoads, C. B., "Personal Liability of Directors for Corporate Mismanagement," *University of Pennsylvania Law Review*, Vol. 65, 1916, pp. 128–44.
"Richard C. Patterson, Jr. Urges 'Working Directors,'" *Commercial and Financial Chronicle*, Vol. 148, March 18, 1939, p. 1573.
Rohrlich, C., and E. Rohrlich, "Psychological Foundations for the Fiduciary Concept in Corporation Law," *Columbia Law Review*, Vol. 38, No. 3, March, 1938, pp. 433–52.
Rukeyser, M., "On Choice of Directors," *New York Journal-American*, August 18, 1947, p. 10.
"Salaried Corporation Directors Advocated by W. O. Douglas," *Commercial and Financial Chronicle*, Vol. 148, January 14, 1939, p. 216.

"Salaried Directors," *Business Week*, January 14, 1939, p. 44.
"Salaries Paid Directors," *Journal of Accountancy*, Vol. 82, December, 1946, p. 519.
Saunders, D. M., "The Executive Committee in Corporate Organization—Scope and Powers," *Michigan Law Review*, Vol. 42, August, 1943, pp. 133–47.
"S.E.C. Proxy Rules and Shareholder Participation in Management," *Harvard Law Review*, Vol. 53, No. 7, May, 1940, pp. 1165–73.
Sloan, G. A., "The Corporate Board of Directors," *Conference Board Economic Record*, Vol. 3, July 24, 1941, pp. 319–24.
———, "The Corporate Board of Directors," *Management Review*, August, 1941, pp. 303–5.
"Standing Target," *Business Week*, May 25, 1946, pp. 19–21.
Sullivan, J. F., "Indemnification," *Cornell Law Review*, Vol. 30, November, 1944, pp. 249–55.
Swope, G., "Some Aspects of Corporation Management," *Harvard Business Review*, Vol. 23, No. 3, pp. 314–22.
Taylor, E. H., "The Board of Directors That Is Streamlined," *Public Utility Fortnightly*, Vol. 39, May 8, 1947, pp. 644–45.
"These Advertising Agents Are on Boards of Directors," *Printers Ink*, Vol. 162, February 23, 1933, pp. 41–42.
"These Directors Toe the Line," *Management Review*, April, 1941, p. 145.
"The 30,000 Managers," *Fortune*, Vol. 21, February, 1940, p. 108.
Tracy, J. E., and A. B. MacChesney, "The Securities Exchange Act of 1934," *Michigan Law Review*, Vol. 32, June, 1934, pp. 1025–68.
Walker, R., "Duty of Director by a Director Purchasing Stock from His Stockholders," *Yale Law Journal*, Vol. 32, No. 7, May, 1923, pp. 637–44.
Washington, G. T., "Litigation Expenses of Corporation Directors in Stockholders' Suits," *Columbia Law Review*, Vol. 40, March, 1940, p. 431.
———, "The S.E.C. and Directors' Indemnity: Recent Developments," *Columbia Law Review*, Vol. 40, November, 1940, pp. 1207–8.
Williams, J. S., "Directors Should Share Risks of Ownership," *Magazine of Wall Street*, Vol. 64, July 1, 1939, pp. 282–83.
Yerrall, W. W., "Common Law Duties of Directors of Corporations and Remedies for Breaches Thereof in Massachusetts," *Massachusetts Law Quarterly*, Vol. 21, No. 3, April, 1936, pp. 50–55.

3. Government Publications

Lewis, E. A., *Laws Relating to the Securities Commission*. Washington, US Government Printing Office, 1944.
Notice of Proposal to Revise Proxy Rules. Securities Exchange Act. SEC Release No. 3998, 1934.

United States of America before the Securities and Exchange Commission in the Matter of McKesson & Robbins, Inc. Washington, US Government Printing Office, 1940.

U.S. National Resources Committee, *Structure of the American Economy*, Part I, Basic Characteristics. Washington, US Government Printing Office, June, 1939.

U.S. Temporary National Economic Committee, "Bureaucracy and Trusteeship in Large Corporations," *Investigation of Concentration of Economic Power*, Monograph No. 11. Washington, US Government Printing Office, 1940.

4. Judicial Decisions

Ames v. Goldfield Merger Mines Co., 227 Fed. 292, 301-302 (1915).
Briggs v. Spaulding, 141 U.S. 132, 11 Sup. Ct., 924 (1891).
Hoyt v. Thompson's Executor, 19 N.Y. 207, 216 (1859).
Hun v. Carey, 82 N.Y. 65, 71 (1880).
Jones v. Missouri, 139 Mo. 25, 40 S.W. 353 (1897).
Spering's Appeal, 71 Pa. 11 (1872).

5. Interviews

Clarence Francis, Chairman of the Board, General Foods Corporation, New York City, NY, January, 1948.

Edward Green, Law Partner, Sullivan and Cromwell, New York City, NY, January, 1948.

II. Roots: Shareholder Activism, Director Independence, and Corporate Purpose

Chapter 4

Boards and Shareholders: A Historical Perspective
Brian R. Cheffins

John L. Weinberg's 1948 senior thesis,[81] Sidney J. Weinberg's 1933 memorandum,[82] and Sidney's 1949 speech[83] focus on directors. Sidney barely referred to shareholders in his 1933 memo. Shareholders, in contrast, are significant supporting players in both John's thesis and Sidney's speech (they used the term stockholders with greater frequency). This chapter supplements and contextualizes what John and Sidney said about shareholders, focusing in so doing on John's 1948 thesis and Sidney's 1949 speech.

The chapter puts into perspective what John and Sidney had to say about stockholders in two ways. First, the chapter engages with John's and Sidney's analyses of what is now often referred to as "corporate purpose." It identifies and explains in so doing the emphasis John and Sidney simultaneously placed on directors serving shareholders' interests while acknowledging a readjustment of board priorities might be in order. Second, the chapter discusses the potency of shareholder pressure on boards during the period when John and Sidney were discussing directors. The analysis focuses on contested shareholder votes and attempts to obtain corporate control that incumbents opposed.

The chapter proceeds as follows. First, there will be a precis of the analysis of shareholders in John's 1948 senior thesis and Sidney's 1949 speech. Second, the chapter engages with John's and Sidney's characterizations of corporate purpose, with particular reference to shareholders. Third, and finally, the chapter assesses the extent to which the possibility of contested shareholder votes and what Henry Manne famously referred to as the market for corporate control[84] might have motivated directors to prioritize shareholders at the time John and Sidney wrote.

With the chapter's analysis of shareholder pressure on boards, a key departure point is a hand-collected dataset of "proxy" contests compiled through searches of major daily newspapers. The "proxy" terminology arises from the fact that a shareholder who wants to vote their shares when they do not attend a shareholder meeting in person will most often delegate the task to an agent referred to as a "proxy." The chapter concludes by suggesting John and Sidney offered a realistic assessment with what they had to say about mid-20th-century shareholders.

The Weinbergs and Shareholders

When corporate governance initially emerged as a widely debated topic as the 20th century drew to a close, the analysis was oriented primarily around shareholders and managers.[85] Assessments of corporate governance factoring in non-shareholder corporate constituencies ("stakeholders") have grown in prominence more recently.[86] Still, with respect to corporate governance amongst corporate constituents, shareholders likely remain first among equals.[87] Various shareholder-friendly aspects of corporate law reinforce the pattern.

In the United States, as distinguished Delaware-based jurist Leo Strine has said, "only stockholders get to elect directors, vote on corporate transactions and charter amendments."[88] Also, while no state corporation code imposes an explicit duty on directors to prioritize shareholders,[89] to quote Strine again, if a director "admits that he is treating an interest other than stockholder wealth as an end in itself, rather than an instrument to stockholder wealth, he is committing a breach of fiduciary duty."[90]

The shareholder orientation of corporate law implies that while John was writing about boards in his senior thesis and Sidney was talking about boards in his speech, shareholders would also have had pride of place in their analysis of corporate arrangements. John and Sidney both assumed that in the past shareholders had indeed been at the center of the action. Sidney said in his 1949 speech, "A century ago, most corporations were local and dominated by one man. Corporate law required a board of directors, but one man generally controlled the board, which, as a rule, was composed of subordinates or relatives."[91]

According to John, from the late 18th century through to the latter half of the 19th century, corporations "consisted of a small number of stockholders who elected a board of directors from their own number" and while "some of the stockholders were probably not active [businesspeople], they usually knew what was happening in the corporation, and actively participated to protect their investment."[92] Managers were "thought to be a set of agents running the business for a number of owners [shareholders]" who "were held strictly accountable."[93]

Sidney and John both indicated the mid-20th-century corporations they were focusing on differed considerably from the 19th-century firms where the stockholders were ostensibly pivotal players. Sidney noted in his 1949 speech that corporations had grown "in size and scope and in number of stockholders and became public companies."[94] He said this meant boards needed "more diversity" and indicated that "[s]tockholders insisted on representation on the board aside from the active executive management" but did not elaborate on how stockholders might have changed.[95] John, in contrast, took advantage of the substantially greater expositive latitude that writing a thesis afforded him and described the then current status of stockholders, implicitly characterizing them as a corporate sideshow in so doing.

John said that since the 19th century there had been a "tremendous increase in size and complexity of American industry … made possible by wider participation of the public in corporate securities."[96] A downside, John suggested, was "the increasing inactivity of the large stockholder group."[97] According to John, "This new type of stockholder is no longer an entrepreneur, but in reality … must be considered an investor."[98] This followed on from the fact that "No longer are the stockholders generally informed; no longer do the stockholders generally attend meetings."[99] Correspondingly, the trend was "for management to grasp the reins of the enterprise and to rule without stockholder aid,"[100] a pattern reinforced by the fact "the average stockholder neither has the background and experience nor the will to participate intelligently in company affairs."[101] This all had significant implications for boards. Shareholders elect directors, John acknowledged, but shareholders "do not choose [the directors]. They are, in reality, chosen by the chief executive and the board itself. During ordinary times the board becomes a self-perpetuating body."[102]

While John expressed doubts regarding the veracity of shareholder election of directors, both he and Sidney used rhetoric consistent with what is referred to presently as shareholder primacy, which has been defined as being in place when "the only legitimate purpose of the corporation [is] to maximize shareholder value."[103] According to Sidney's 1949 speech, "[t]he director has obligations to all stockholders."[104] He added that outside directors, whom he defined as directors other than active executive management, "in a special sense represent the stockholders."[105]

John concurred that the board served as "the representative of the stockholders in top management."[106] He elaborated when he referred to "the directors' trusteeship function," saying, "Because a director stands in a fiduciary relationship to the stockholders [he or she] is responsible for preserving and safeguarding the interests of the owners."[107] It followed that "the directors' primary duty is to preserve the assets and protect the stockholders' interests,"[108] and that "[t]he supreme test of corporate management is the ability to run the corporation at a profit."[109]

While John and Sidney described the law in a manner that accorded with shareholder primacy, they envisaged a role for directors more substantial than merely serving the interests of shareholders. Sidney, in his speech, said of a director, "Beyond his legal duties, he must recognize the broad social responsibilities he has to the general public and to the country."[110]

As for John, he intimated that in practical if not legal terms directors' obligations may extend further than stockholders, saying that "their task is to manage the business in the interest of the investors, employees, customers, and consumers of the company's products or services."[111] This aligned with public opinion as John saw it, which he said was moving in the direction that "the business corporation exists as an economic institution, which has a social service to perform as well as a profit-making function."[112] John acknowledged this characterization did not correspond with then current corporate law doctrine, attributing this to "common law sluggishness coping with changing social philosophy."[113] He suggested, though, "[t]he courts sooner or later must recognize the interests of the general public" because "[t]his doctrine is gaining wider acceptance in the business community; the courts must evolve legal dogma to match it."[114]

How did what the Weinbergs had to say about shareholders tally with shareholders' actual mid-20th-century status? We will consider next corporate purpose and will see that John and Sidney not only correctly observed that directors' duties were shareholder focused but also identified a soon-to-be-dominant sentiment that boardroom priorities should not be so narrowly oriented. After this we will assess whether John's verdict that management had grasped "the reins of the enterprise" and were ruling "without stockholder aid"[115] underestimates at least to some degree the pressure late 1940s shareholders could bring to bear on how companies were run.

Corporate Purpose

John Weinberg, when he offered his assessment of what corporate directors should prioritize, acknowledged other commentators had staked out previously the positions he identified. He referenced by footnotes what has been described as "a great debate over the nature and purpose of the public company"[116] between corporate-law scholars Adolf Berle and E. Merrick Dodd. John did so when recognizing there were conflicting views on "whether a director's responsibility rests simply within the corporate entity, or whether it includes the customers, consumers, suppliers, and public at large."[117] He cited a 1931 *Harvard Law Review* article by Berle[118] when saying, "One side advocates an increased emphasis on the doctrine that managerial powers are held in trust for stockholders as sole beneficiaries of the corporate enterprise."[119] John referred to a 1932 article by Dodd[120] when describing "[t]he opposing attitude," which emphasized "the social functions corporations should perform."[121]

Based on the synopsis of John's views in the previous section that indicated he believed companies had "a social service to perform",[122] one might infer that he subscribed to Dodd's point of view. In fact, his assessment ultimately aligned substantially with the position that Berle staked out in a 1932 response to Dodd's piece that John also cited.[123] Berle, in his 1932 article, acknowledged that "[a]s a matter of economics and social theory" the argument Dodd advanced was "sound" as well as "familiar."[124] From a legal perspective, however, the logic was misguided. According to Berle, in the absence of "a clear and reasonably enforceable scheme of responsibilities to someone" other than the shareholders, abandoning "emphasis on 'the view that business corporations exist for the sole purpose of making profits for their stockholders'" amounted to handing "economic power … over, weakly, to the present administrators with a pious wish that something nice will come out of it all."[125]

John's take was very similar to Berle's. John said there was for directors "the duty to further the stockholders' interests by increasing the wealth of the corporation through the most fruitful use of its assets."[126] This was normatively appropriate because "[w]e cannot abandon emphasis on the view that business corporations exist for the sole purpose of making profits for their stockholders until such time as we are prepared to offer a clear, reasonable, and enforceable scheme of responsibilities to somebody else."[127] That aligned in turn with the views of Sidney Weinberg, who again indicated that directors' duties were shareholder oriented even if directors should be aware of social responsibilities.[128]

How do John's and Sidney's assessments of directors' responsibilities square up with mid-20th-century jurisprudence and academic opinion? In Dodd they had a somewhat surprising ally. Again, what John and Sidney said corresponded with the views Berle expressed regarding what the law obliged those running companies to prioritize, and Berle in his 1931 and 1932 pieces staked out a normative point of view with which Dodd disagreed in his 1932 article. Nevertheless, with respect to the nature of the duties directors owed as a matter of law, Dodd advanced propositions that anticipated what John and Sidney would subsequently say.

Dodd acknowledged in his 1932 article "lawyers have commonly assumed that the managers must conduct the institution with single-minded devotion to stockholder profit."[129] In a 1935 piece he indicated he concurred with this assessment, saying that "[p]rofit-making for absentee owners [shareholders]" was "the legal standard by which we measure [managers'] conduct until some other legal standard has been evolved."[130] Dodd additionally went a long way toward conceding Berle (and by extension John and Sidney) was correct normatively as well as doctrinally. Dodd said in his 1935 article that because the law offered no guidance to those running large corporations on how they might act as trustees for their corporations rather than just for shareholders, "as Mr. Berle tells us, the courts and the legal profession cannot relinquish the idea of treating managers as trustees for security holders without freeing the managers from substantial control of any kind."[131]

Were John, Sidney, and Dodd correct regarding the interests corporate law obliged directors to prioritize? The point cannot be taken for granted. According to political theorist David Ciepley, "[b]y the 1930s, the dominant view in legal circles was that directors were trustees for the corporation, but also for the community at large."[132] Since Sidney was giving a speech, he unsurprisingly did not cite any authority in favor of his claim regarding the stockholder-oriented obligations a director had. John referenced a number of law-review articles and a few cases in his bibliography, but when discussing directors' duties he cited specifically only a single corporate-law treatise.[133] It correspondingly is possible that their shareholder-focused assessment of director priorities was erroneous.

As for Dodd, the only case he cited in relation to the law on corporate purpose was the Michigan Supreme Court's 1919 decision in *Dodge v. Ford Motor Co.*[134] According to Dodd, the case offered "a vigorous assertion" of the proposition that "[t]he sole function of the corporation is … conceived to be the making of profit for its stockholder-members, so that they are the ultimate beneficiaries of the business."[135] What the Michigan Supreme Court said on point—"A business corporation is organized and carried on primarily for the profit of the stockholders. The powers of the directors are to be employed for that end"[136]—currently "is familiar to just about anyone who has sat through a survey course in corporate law."[137]

While *Dodge* became an "iconic citation" with respect to corporate purpose,[138] various commentators have sought to discredit it as case-law authority. It has been said, for instance, "the Michigan court cited no statute or case law for [its] decisive statement of … corporate governance law."[139] Moreover, *Dodge* skeptics say, the case is old, and much water has gone under the corporate-law bridge since it was decided.[140] Also, the Michigan court's pronouncement on corporate purpose was "dicta,"[141] with "the holding of the case [having] nothing to do with acting primarily for the profit of the shareholders."[142]

Despite the doubts that have been cast upon *Dodge v. Ford Motor Co.* as shareholder-oriented case-law authority in relation to corporate purpose, the views John, Sidney, and Dodd expressed regarding interests directors should prioritize under corporate law likely accurately reflected the prevailing view at the time John and Sidney wrote. With the Michigan Supreme Court, its "articulation of its theory in the *Ford* case was typical of the time."[143] It appears additionally that from when the Michigan Supreme Court ruled in 1919 through until when John and Sidney discussed corporate purpose, it was well accepted that as a matter of corporate law this was oriented around profits and shareholders.

A 1940 guide to corporate law for directors quoted a 1919 decision of the New York Court of Appeals where the court said "the stockholders are the proprietors of the corporate interests and are ultimately the only beneficiaries thereof,"[144] saying of the passage that the fiduciary obligation of directors had been "well described."[145] Henry Ballantine, in the 1946 edition of his corporate-law treatise, maintained, "A business corporation is regarded as being carried on primarily for the profit of its shareholders. The discretion of the directors does not, in general, extend to humanitarian purposes … or even its employees, at the expense of the shareholders."[146] He cited *Dodge v. Ford Motor Co.* as authority for this proposition.[147]

While John and Sidney likely were correct in emphasizing stockholders when discussing corporate purpose, they also accurately anticipated a shift in how those running companies thought of what they were doing. Again, John and Sidney both cited the broad social responsibilities those in charge of corporations had. This foreshadowed corporate purpose trends. During the 1950s, 1960s, and 1970s it was widely assumed that in practical terms shareholders were merely one constituency among a number of those running public companies would take into account. Donald Langevoort has said of this "managerial capitalism" era and corporate purpose, "[t]he usual historical narrative posits that managerialism held sway for a few decades during the middle part of the last century, enabling managers to share some of the rents with employees, communities, and the government ('benevolent managerialism')."[148]

Views editors of *Fortune* expressed in 1951 were indicative of what was destined to become an increasingly prevalent "managerial" view of corporate purpose. They said, "One of the most pressing concerns of almost every large company today is what people are going to think about it," with management "no longer occupied exclusively with the interests of the stockholder" and exhibiting "a sense of responsibility toward its employees."[149] In a 1954 essay on managerial responsibilities, management theorist Peter Drucker identified a "trend among managers to think of themselves almost as public servants, not as men driven by a ruthless craving for profits."[150] *Business Week* said of a 1957 symposium on directors with a "brass-studded roster of participants," including Berle, "the consensus seemed to be that the corporation now has to be as much a citizen as a money-making enterprise—and the board has to make sure it does both."[151]

Berle himself noted the substantial change in thinking with respect to corporate purpose, indicating in 1954 that because of the shift in approach, with respect to his debate with Dodd in the early 1930s, "[t]he argument has been settled … squarely in favor of Professor Dodd's contention."[152] Again, Dodd acknowledged soon after he published his 1932 article the correctness of Berle's position on the law and expressed substantial agreement with Berle's assessment of the normative implications.[153] Nevertheless, commentators tend to treat Berle's stakeholder-friendly revised stance as the final word, with Berle "conceding the battle"[154] and thus proving Dodd "the winner."[155]

How did those running mid-20th-century corporations have the scope to pursue a stakeholder-friendly managerialist agenda, given that *Dodge v. Ford Motor Co.* and related jurisprudence indicated that corporate-law principles precluded directors from advancing the interests of corporate constituencies other than shareholders at shareholders' expense? Recall that John maintained that "legal dogma" needed to evolve to reflect the fact that the business community was seeking to protect interests in addition to those of the stockholders.[156] This did not happen. Instead, "[t]he statutes and rules governing the organization of the corporation … changed little between the 1930s and the 1960s. Nor were the presuppositions of corporate law transformed."[157]

Contemporaries were aware that with respect to corporate purpose and corporate law the shareholder-oriented status quo continued to prevail. For instance, according to a 1964 analysis of the Berle–Dodd debate, "[t]he thesis … that corporate powers are held in trust for stockholders … would hardly be contradicted today."[158] While the core premises of corporate law did not change in the mid-20th century, it did become increasingly evident during this era that those running companies had substantial scope practically to cater to constituencies other than stockholders. This was most obvious with corporate charitable contributions. During the opening decades of the 20th century, they were vulnerable to challenge on *ultra vires* grounds because the public was benefitting rather than the incorporators.[159] By virtue of statutory reform and case-law developments, however, by the end of the 1950s charitable giving in which boards engaged had been fully legitimized.[160]

A key corporate-law doctrine further enhanced the scope mid-20th-century boards had to engage in corporate altruism. By virtue of the business judgment rule, the judiciary was giving boards a wide latitude to manage companies for the purposes the directors saw fit, so long as their judgment was reasonably exercised on an honest, unbiased basis.[161] This meant, David Ruder argued in a 1965 article, that "there is ample opportunity for expenditure of corporate funds upon worthwhile public welfare measures. The only limitation is that corporate policy must be reasonably related to long term corporate benefit."[162] Through to the end of the 1960s there had been little academic commentary on the business judgment rule.[163] Nevertheless, with courts having applied it for decades by that point in time,[164] those running mid-20th-century public companies no doubt would have been aware of the substantial discretion courts afforded them to forsake delivering immediate benefits to the shareholders.

A dearth of litigation likely reinforced the message for mid-20th-century directors that while, as John and Sidney indicated, directors' duties put boards under an onus to exercise managerial authority in shareholders' interests, directors had little reason to fear a failure to prioritize shareholders would be adjudged a breach of duty. Once *Dodge* had been decided, there apparently was no subsequent 20th-century case where a court struck down a board decision on the basis that the directors had sacrificed shareholder interests to benefit stakeholders or in the public interest.[165] Likewise, challenges of charitable contributions were extremely rare even as corporate philanthropy become much more prevalent.[166]

The foregoing analysis indicates that, for various reasons, directors' duties—regardless of a formal pro-shareholder formulation—likely did little to motivate those running mid-20th-century corporations to prioritize shareholders. This state of affairs helped to provide a congenial setting for managerialism that pre-dominated until the mid-1980s. The next, and final, substantive section of the chapter turns to a different potential incentive directors might have had to prioritize shareholder interests, this being shareholder pressure arising when stockholders expressed their collective will.

Shareholder Pressure

During the managerial capitalism era that was nascent when John and Sidney offered their views regarding boards, those running public companies often sought to balance the interests of various corporate constituencies rather than prioritize shareholders.[167] In the 1980s, a surge in hostile takeover activity pushed shareholders up the priority list of public company executives.[168] In the 2000s, robust activism by a subset of hedge funds reinforced shareholder primacy in American boardrooms.[169]

To what extent might similar forces have motivated directors to prioritize shareholders at the time John and Sidney were discussing boards? We consider this point now. We will see that while neither shareholder activism nor takeovers would shape managerial priorities to the extent they would in subsequent decades, they likely did prompt those running publicly traded companies to take shareholder interests into account to some degree.

Investigating sources of shareholder pressure on those running companies at the time John and Sidney offered their views regarding boards in the late 1940s might seem like something of a fool's errand, given that numerous contemporary commentators were remarking on the passivity of shareholders. The 1940 guide to corporate law for directors cited earlier said, "The average stockholder in a large corporation is … effectively shut out from any participation in its control or management."[170] *Business Week*, in a 1941 editorial entitled "The Stockholder—Forgotten Man," said, "For years now, the American stockholder has been an outsider looking into the affairs of his corporation. He is the legal owner, but not the practical owner."[171] *Forbes* concurred in a 1944 editorial, saying, "One very grave weakness in our present economic order is the actual (though not theoretical) impotency of stockholders. Rarely can they force redress of grievances against management, directorates."[172]

With respect to annual stockholder meetings which shareholders had the right to have held and at which they could formally exercise the powers they had,[173] John said "[w]illingness to answer questions of stockholders" and "better annual meetings" could help to foster stockholder confidence, which could help companies to raise capital.[174] Nevertheless, in 1949, *Forbes* described annual meetings as "[l]ike the North Pole" in that they "are known about by everyone, but seldom visited."[175] Fredrick Lewis Allen remarked in a chapter on corporations in a 1952 history of the United States in the first half of the 20th century that the "annual meeting is ordinarily a farce."[176] As for changes in corporate control arising from the voting power of shareholders, the 1940 guide to corporate law for directors cited above said, "To gain control of a great corporation by outright purchase of stock is beyond the resources of even the very wealthy."[177] *Business Week*, in its 1941 editorial on stockholders, added "attempts to remove managements are rarely undertaken."[178]

Shareholders, however, were not entirely quiescent when John and Sidney were offering their 1940s take on boards. In 1940, *Forbes* indicated there were executives who were "far-sighted enough" to seek to build up loyalty amongst shareholders that could be invaluable in "the frenzied midst of a proxy fight,"[179] which involves, in the context of shareholder meetings, "a campaign to get the shareholders to turn over their votes."[180] Economist Robert Gordon said in his 1945 study *Business Leadership in the Large Corporation* "[f]ear of unfavorable publicity" associated with shareholder meetings where opposition developed "led corporation executives to grant some stockholder demands."[181] *Forbes* noted in 1947, "Stockholders have been known to exert pressure on management through group effort and even have been instrumental in bringing in new management."[182] The same newspaper referred in 1949 to "a hurricane of stockholder discontent."[183] *Barron's* suggested in a 1950 article on proxy contests that "a growing army of stockholders is waging guerrilla warfare against company management."[184]

Shareholder meetings were also not always non-events. In 1940, the *Wall Street Journal* said about Missouri–Kansas Pipeline Co., "[t]he usual stormy performance was put on at the annual meeting," and the counting of proxy votes did not conclude until 5 a.m.[185] In 1942, 300 Electric Bond and Share Company stockholders attended "one of the most acrimonious annual meetings recorded in corporate history," which lasted nearly five hours.[186] A 1947 stockholder meeting of Hudson & Manhattan Railroad Co. "was thrown into turmoil ... when a fistfight broke out between management and opposition supporters."[187] The *Wall Street Journal* acknowledged in a 1949 article on annual stockholder meetings "they were usually cut-and-dried affairs" but said "[f]ireworks have been more frequent this year," with a by-product being that management had become "increasingly conscious of stockholder relations."[188]

Given the conflicting contemporary views regarding the extent to which shareholder pressure was a factor in corporate boardrooms when John and Sidney were commenting on boards in the late 1940s, empirical evidence is potentially instructive. A promising source is a hand-collected proxy-contest dataset based on newspaper searches the author has relied upon in certain respects in previous research and has revisited in drafting this chapter.[189]

The dataset was constructed by searching the *New York Times* and *Wall Street Journal* using the *ProQuest Historical Newspapers* database. This was done for each year from 1900 to 1949 by searching for stories including one of the phrases "proxy fight," "proxy battle," "proxy contest," "proxy solicitation," "consent solicitation," "solicit proxies," "soliciting proxies," or "solicitation of proxies."[190] The newspaper reports thus identified were analyzed to ascertain whether shareholder insurgents sought support from their fellow shareholders in the form of proxies. When this apparently occurred, details were gathered using the *New York Times* and *Wall Street Journal* and other newspapers in the *ProQuest Historical Newspapers* database on the name of the target company, the nature of the issues involved, and the identity and organizational affiliation (if any) of the leading activists.

The proxy contests that were identified from searches of the *New York Times* and *Wall Street Journal* were categorized on the basis of what was at stake. A possibility here was that control of the board of the company involved was in play, with this being the case where shareholder insurgents sought to capture a majority of a company's board seats. Those instances where the dissidents were not seeking board control were subdivided based on whether the dissident shareholders targeted board representation or passed entirely on securing directorships.

Account was also taken of success, or lack thereof. The departure point was shareholder activist objectives revealed by the newspaper reports. If dissident shareholders achieved their stated objectives, this was treated as success. If they failed, this was categorized as an unsuccessful intervention. Finally, if the insurgents achieved their goals to some degree, this was tagged as partial success. For instance, if a dissident shareholder was aiming to control the board and failed, but did secure board representation, this was treated as partial success.

The full 1900–1949 dataset, as deployed for this paper, is comprised of 279 proxy contests. In relation to shareholder engagement that took place in publicly traded companies during these years, SEC data indicate the dataset is underinclusive to some degree. Section 14(a) of the 1934 Securities and Exchange Act authorized the SEC to prescribe regulations concerning the solicitation of proxies.[191] The SEC followed up by promulgating rules on point that required those engaging in this activity to file with the SEC.[192] Until 1955, the nature of SEC proxy solicitation filing arrangements meant it was not feasible to find out readily how often proxies were solicited, to identify which companies had been involved, or to discover who was soliciting proxies.[193] Still, the SEC, in its 1947 annual report, set out the results of a staff study that indicated how many proxy solicitation statements had been filed in 1943, 1944, 1945, and 1946.[194] During these four years, on 93 occasions, or 23.3 per year, there was a filing not made by management. These likely were instances where shareholder insurgents were seeking support as part of a proxy contest. Numbers were lower in the dataset derived from the *ProQuest Historical Newspapers* database deployed here: 46 instances from the same four years, or 11.5 per year.

The shortfall as compared with the SEC data is unsurprising. It is hard to imagine that each and every proxy solicitation associated with a filing by someone other than management would be sufficiently newsworthy to be written up in the *New York Times* or the *Wall Street Journal*. Despite this caveat, the dataset drawn upon here offers apparently unique insights regarding the types of shareholder activism occurring when John and Sidney were discussing boards and the changes such activism might have been eliciting.

Again, the proxy-contest dataset this paper draws upon comprises 279 instances of shareholder activism occurring between 1900 and 1949. The 1940s, when John and Sidney offered their views, was the decade when activism was most prevalent, with 113 instances, or just over two-fifths of the total. Conceivably, newspaper coverage of companies was substantially more comprehensive in the 1940s than previously, but there is no evidence to support such a conjecture. Another potential explanation for the 1940s surge is that there were more publicly traded companies than in previous decades, with the logic being that, all else being equal, more companies will yield more activism incidents. The number of publicly traded companies did indeed increase significantly from 1900 through to 1930,[195] but declined modestly during the latter half of the 1930s and the 1940s.[196]

With respect to the nature of the activism undertaken, nearly three-fifths (159 of 279) of shareholder activism incidents in the full 1900–1949 dataset involved attempts to obtain board control by garnering the support of shareholders for board nominees the insurgents put forward. Insurgents doing this were seeking to carry out a takeover by way of a "transfer by vote," as opposed to "a transfer by sale," where the objective is to acquire enough shares to secure voting control.[197] With one-quarter of the activism incidents, the insurgents were seeking board representation but there was no evidence board control was in play. As for the remainder, just under a fifth of the proxy-contest dataset, the shareholder activists were focusing on a topic other than directorships.

Proxy battles with a board dimension typically would have offered greater drama for newspapers than shareholder activism lacking a board representation angle. Correspondingly, board contests, and particularly de facto takeover attempts, likely are over-represented in the proxy-contest dataset as compared with proxy battles where directorships were not at stake. Regardless of board-control over-representation compared with other types of proxy contest, the dataset indicates that transfers by vote were, during the first half of the 20th century, the primary foundation for the market for corporate control.

With transfers by sale, tender offers extended directly to shareholders—a major corporate governance phenomenon in the second half of the 20th century—were virtually unknown during the first half of the century.[198] Transfers by sale instead occurred by way of an "open-market bid", which involves an attempt to buy sufficient shares on the open market to acquire control of a public company without consent or encouragement from the target company's board.[199] Transfer-by-vote proxy contests were a considerably more popular takeover technique than open-market bids during the first half of the 20th century.[200] Open-market bids indeed had fallen fully out of fashion by the time John and Sidney were writing about boards in the late 1940s.[201]

In contrast with open-market bids, proxy-contest incidents were more prevalent when John and Sidney were writing about boards than at other points in time the proxy-contest dataset covers. Not only was the 1940s the decade when the most proxy contests occurred, but such incidents also increased in frequency as the decade drew to a close. The proxy-contest dataset includes 46 instances from 1947, 1948, and 1949, an average of 15.3 per year, as compared with an average of just over nine per year earlier in the 1940s.

Those familiar with the history of Securities and Exchange Act Rule 14a-8,[202] which currently provides the platform for hundreds of shareholder proposals every year,[203] might assume that developments affecting forerunners to Rule 14a-8 contributed to the late 1940s surge in activism incidents in the proxy-contest dataset. In 1942, the SEC promulgated the forerunner to Rule 14a-8 and required a publicly traded company to include in documentation sent to shareholders when soliciting proxies for a forthcoming annual meeting proposals by individual shareholders that were a "proper subject for action" if prescribed procedural requirements were fulfilled.[204] This right did not extend, however, to director elections.[205] Correspondingly, if the SEC regulations were the catalyst for the increase in the number of instances in the dataset in the late 1940s, the proportion of proxy contests where there was no attempt to secure a board seat should have been higher than it was for the full dataset. This was not the case. Among the 46 activism incidents in the dataset for 1947, 1948, and 1949, only seven involved no attempt to secure a board seat, a slightly smaller proportion than for the entire dataset.

Why didn't the 1942 change to SEC proxy regulations reorient the nature of the proxy contests in the proxy-contest dataset when John and Sidney were writing? A key factor was that the vast majority of proxy solicitation statements filed during this era involved an election of directors.[206] This occurred despite individual shareholders lacking scope under federal securities law to make proposals regarding director elections because most often it was companies rather than individual shareholders that were soliciting proxies.[207] Moreover, since proposals individual shareholders made necessarily lacked board-selection drama, proxy contests arising from such proposals were unlikely to attract press attention and thus appear in the proxy-contest dataset. The fact that shareholder proposals were usually defeated convincingly when a vote occurred would also have reduced their newsworthiness.[208]

While the 1942 change to SEC proxy regulations did not substantially reconfigure the composition of the proxy-contest dataset, shareholder proposals were by no means irrelevant when John and Sidney offered their views. As the 1940s drew to a close, Lewis Gilbert, who made extensive use of the shareholder proposal mechanism (he and his brother filed nearly half of all shareholder proposals made between 1948 and 1951),[209] was referred to in the press as "The Country's Most Celebrated Minority Stockholder."[210] Gilbert's activism was unlikely to result, however, in the sort of intense battle for shareholder support that would attract press attention. This was because, when he made proposals, his practice was not to solicit proxies from shareholders of the companies involved.[211] It correspondingly is not surprising that Gilbert only features in one proxy contest in the proxy-contest dataset, this being where Bethlehem Steel stockholders voted down three resolutions he put forward in 1949.[212]

If Lewis Gilbert, as the mid-20th-century "Conscience of American Big Business,"[213] did not dominate the proxy contests that attracted press attention when John and Sidney were writing about boards in the late 1940s, who were the headliners? One was Graham–Newman Corporation, an investment trust cofounded by famed "value investor" Benjamin Graham, which focused on "special situations" involving smaller companies that were cheap on the numbers.[214] Graham–Newman participated in a 1947 campaign to obtain Bell Aircraft board seats; the investment trust came up short but secured enough support "to scare Bell into finding friendlier hands to hold its stock."[215] Graham–Newman followed up in 1948 by soliciting proxies from shareholders of New Amsterdam Casualty Co. to gain backing for a resolution in favor of more generous dividends.[216]

Louis Wolfson, another participant in a late 1940s proxy contest in the *ProQuest Historical Newspapers* dataset, achieved notoriety in other ways. Wolfson was perhaps best known for being at the center of a scandal that prompted Abe Fortas's 1969 resignation from the US Supreme Court.[217] Wolfson was also the protagonist in an unsuccessful mid-1950s proxy contest for control of the retailer Montgomery Ward, labeled "one of the fiercest battles in the history of corporate finance."[218]

Wolfson is in the proxy-contest dataset in relation to Merritt–Chapman, an engineering and construction firm with a New York Stock Exchange listing that was thought of as a "blue-chip" investment.[219] In the wake of "vigorous proxy contests," Wolfson was one of the 13 directors linked to the dissident cohort named in May 1949 to Merritt–Chapman's 21-member board.[220] In 1951, Wolfson became chair of the board.[221]

Charlie Green is another noted mid-20th-century "proxyteer" who appears in the proxy-contest dataset.[222] He is included due to his first proxy fight in 1949, when in "an ugly campaign" he secured three of nine seats available on the board of Twin City Rapid Transit, a "slow and stodgy" company that provided public transport service to Minneapolis and St. Paul.[223] In 1951, having gained and then lost full control of the Twin City board, he launched a successful proxy contest to secure control of United Cigar–Whelan Stores Corporation, which ran a nationally prominent chain of drugstores and cigar shops.[224] He met with less success with a 1953 proxy contest involving the motion-picture giant Twentieth Century–Fox that was "perfectly scripted to further fascinate and alarm the general public."[225]

The mixed success Green and Wolfson experienced reflects the broader trend with late 1940s incidents in the proxy-contest dataset. Thirty of the 46 proxy battles in the dataset from 1947, 1948, and 1949 involved attempts to secure board control. With these 30, the protagonists obtained board control on 13 occasions. In five instances they achieved partial success, and in 12 they came up empty.

The success rate was considerably better with attempts to secure board control than with other types of proxy contests. Amongst the nine proxy contests from 1947, 1948, and 1949 where the activists sought to obtain board seats without aiming for board control, the protagonist was successful on one occasion and achieved partial success twice. As for the seven proxy contests where no board representation was sought, the activist was only successful once. The pattern may well explain why *Barron's* told readers in 1950 that management had "been able to take in stride the rash of opposition proposals" but had been "jarred … by a growing predilection of shareholders to by-pass ineffective sparring at annual meetings and play for keeps."[226] In turn, "[n]ervously, some companies have been making some gestures of appeasement toward their shareholders."[227]

The challenges to boardroom control which the proxy-contest dataset takes into account indicate why various commentators in the late 1940s and early 1950s were flagging up shareholder activism as a meaningful phenomenon in American corporate life. According to the dataset, boardroom challenges were never more prevalent during the first half of the 20th century than they were as the 1940s drew to a close. Nevertheless, it is also understandable why various contemporaries were emphasizing instead the passivity of shareholders. There were well over 4,000 issuers with shares listed for trading on national exchanges during the late 1940s.[228] Despite the surge in proxy contests during these years, the odds remained very much against a particular company becoming embroiled in a proxy battle sufficiently prominent to be written up in a major daily newspaper. Correspondingly, for John and Sidney, writing as the 1940s drew to a close, not putting shareholder engagement front and center when talking about boards was a defensible choice.

Conclusion

When analyzing boards, John in his 1948 thesis and Sidney in his 1949 speech dealt with shareholders as a sideshow even though stockholders elected directors and corporate-law doctrine precluded directors from forsaking shareholder interests. Was their treatment of shareholders unfair or misguided? No, given the status of shareholders at the time.

John and Sidney both indicated that corporate law put directors under an onus to run companies in the interests of shareholders, and this accurately stated the law at the time they were writing. At the same time, they both envisaged a role for directors that extended beyond serving the interests of shareholders, and in so doing they accurately anticipated what would soon become three decades' worth of corporate "managerialism" in corporate America, where directors had substantial regard for constituencies other than shareholders.

As for shareholder engagement in corporate affairs, Sidney said nothing about this in his 1948 speech, and John referred to the board as a self-perpetuating body in his thesis, despite shareholders formally choosing directors. Their take would be too simplistic if the task they had set themselves was offering a definitive analysis of mid-20th-century corporate governance. Instead, though, the board of directors was their focal point. Accordingly, their choices with respect to stockholders are fully explicable, given that shareholder pressure, while it did occur, was hardly a universal phenomenon. Those specifically interested in the position of shareholders in mid-20th-century corporate America should look beyond what Sidney and John said to find out what was happening, but their treatment of shareholders does not detract meaningfully from their insightful analysis of late 1940s boards.

Chapter 5

The Independent Board of Directors: A Brief History

Dalia T. Mitchell

In the common corporate-law narrative, the independent board of directors is a product of the 1970s, a decade of social, political, and economic upheaval that brought the corporate board to the forefront of public and academic attention. Until then, the narrative goes, independent directors (as distinct from directors who also served as executives) received little attention from jurists. But in the 1970s, debates ensued among lawyers and businessmen about the appropriate role of corporate directors, culminating in the publication of the American Law Institute's (ALI) *Principles of Corporate Governance.*[229]

The ALI *Principles* endorsed the business community's vision of corporate directors as monitors of corporate executives and recommended that boards should be composed of a majority of outside or independent directors. Since the 1980s, and well into the 21st century, the Delaware courts have wholeheartedly endorsed the monitoring model of the board as appropriate for the governance of corporations, even though "the presence of independent directors" has not necessarily correlated with "the firm's economic performance."[230]

The discovery of John Weinberg's thesis challenges this narrative by calling attention to mid-century discussions addressing the potential role that outside directors could play within the corporation. As this chapter further suggests, by complicating the traditional narrative, these mid-century discussions might help explain Delaware's persistence in its embrace of a board model centering on independent directors, despite a growing volume of literature that suggests 21st-century boards have a different conception of their role.[231]

Specifically, the history this chapter explores reveals that changing understandings of the board's role and status throughout the past century correlated with changing definitions of corporate purpose. In the early 20th century, jurists described directors as trustees; in the mid-century, the term changed to representatives; and at the century's end, directors became agents of the shareholders. Directors as trustees and even representatives were tasked with mediating the subjective interests of different corporate constituencies and the community at large, while the description of directors as agents was associated with the more limited corporate purpose of shareholder wealth maximization.

At the same time, the history reveals that, at least since the mid-century, discussions focusing on the independent or outside directors consistently emphasized the latter's role of monitoring the executives for the benefit of the firm's presumed owners, the shareholders.

Indeed, that John Weinberg wrote about independent directors in the 1940s, a time typically described as the height of managerialism, suggests that the legal community has always been of two minds about the question of corporate purpose. While mid-century courts empowered corporate managements to act to benefit the different corporate constituencies, practitioners seemed particularly concerned about the executives' ability to appropriate profit for themselves (or for the controlling shareholders) at the expense of individual investors. These concerns reached their peak in the 1970s, ultimately leading the courts to change course and endorse the monitoring model of the board, with its shareholder-focused vision of corporate purpose.

Why, though, did courts resist the shareholder-centered vision of the corporation until the 1980s? This chapter suggests that, throughout the 20th century, a broader purpose for the corporation played an important role in helping sustain a democratic image of the large publicly held corporation: what we have come to label the Berle & Means corporation, where disperse shareholders were presumed to elect directors, who then appointed executives to manage the corporation for the benefit of its many constituencies.

This democratic image of the corporation, while not necessarily reflecting the complex realties of corporate America, helped assuage concerns that corporations were an anathema to the country's liberal ideals (at the turn of the 20th century), or that the United States might succumb to totalitarianism (at the mid-century). Only in the 1980s, as fears about the fate of American democracy subsided and jurists' attention turned to the securities markets, did the courts endorse the monitoring model of the board and the purpose of shareholder wealth maximization.

The chapter proceeds as follows: the first part, *The Board of Directors at a Century's Turn*, focuses on the early decades of the 20th century. As Progressives sounded the alarm about the power of the rapidly growing corporations, jurists described directors as trustees for the corporation, its shareholders, and the community, so as to alleviate concerns that corporations were a threat to individual freedom and American democracy.

The second part, *Mid-century Managerialism and the Emergence of the Independent Board*, explores how in the mid-century, amidst growing fears about the advance of totalitarianism in Europe, the courts' attention shifted to managers as administrators of the corporate system and defenders of American democratic institutions. Jurists analogized directors to elected representatives while ensuring that, as representatives, they could act without interference from their constituencies. It was in this context that John Weinberg and others emphasized that the duties of the board ran specifically to the shareholders and that, to fulfill them, directors had to be independent from the executives.

Finally, the third part, *Proceduralism and the Independent Director*, turns to the 1980s. Amidst a blitz of hostile takeovers and growing critiques of executive power, directors were, again, called to the rescue. By then, however, corporations were no longer analogized to democratic governments. Rather, the Delaware courts described corporations as merely economic institutions and embraced proceduralism—that is, the idea that certain governance procedures ensure maximization of value for the shareholders. Independent directors became important not because of their expertise or effective management but because they could perform the presumably wealth-maximizing procedures prescribed by the Delaware courts.[232]

The Board of Directors at a Century's Turn

Boards of directors have existed for centuries, but until the turn of the 20th century, they were not considered a significant body and received little, if any, attention from jurists. Antebellum corporate law vested managerial power in the corporation's shareholders, while the corporation's directors could only exercise powers that the shareholders explicitly delegated to them.[233] Directors, if different from the owners, served merely "for the prestige associated with the position."[234] Directors were expected to exercise due care and diligence in managing the affairs of the corporation. But, for the most part, the role of the board was symbolic, and directors were described as "gratuitous mandatories."[235]

After the Civil War, amidst a rise of large corporate combinations, corporate governance structures began to change, as conflicts arose between "technical and financial managers" (especially in the railroad industry). Those who had the financial means to be elected to boards were often unfamiliar with the management of the business or had little time to engage in it. Gradually, "paramount executive authority had emerged."[236]

Changes to corporate ownership helped solidify executive power. Until the 1880s, there was no important class of small individual or institutional investors in securities, but, beginning then, a rapid industrial and business growth increased demand for capital and "stimulated the use of security financing as the most flexible and productive method of supplying capital needs."[237] Soon, American corporations were able to convince the public to invest not only in bonds and preferred stock, but also in common stock.[238] In turn, having a market for securities allowed founders of successful enterprises to sell the company, "leaving intact [its] managerial organization."[239]

Corporate lawyers eagerly supported the new corporate colossi and their managers. As rising consumer demand, increasing numbers of workers, an expanding pool of capital, and the developing national railroads and telegraph networks enabled the creation of large enterprises, corporate lawyers devised different legal tools to allow their clients to increase the scope of their operations so as to avoid destructive competition among large businesses.[240]

Before long, state legislatures, often at the behest of corporate lawyers, rushed to accommodate the needs of business. Beginning with New Jersey, states rewrote their corporations statutes to "eliminate[] restrictions on ... capitalization and assets, mergers and consolidation, the issuance of voting stock, the purpose(s) of incorporation, and the duration and locale of business."[241] The 19th-century corporation, which was subject to strict constraints on its powers, as well as limitations on its capital structure, was replaced by larger and larger units.[242] And these giant units required expert executives at their helms.

Significantly, the new statutes limited the ability of the individual shareholder to participate in corporate governance. Proxy voting, which was banned in the early 19th century, became the norm; corporations could issue stock with unequal voting power; and a majority of the shareholders could effect fundamental corporate changes (eroding the 19th-century requirement of unanimous consent). Shareholders' ability to remove directors at will was eliminated, and charters could also abolish shareholders' pre-emptive rights and their rights to dividends.[243]

At the same time, the new codes granted nearly absolute power to corporate managers, albeit without clearly differentiating between inside and outside directors. For one, Delaware's 1899 revision included a "self-determination" provision, allowing incorporators to include in the charter any provision they deemed fit "for the management of the business ... [and for] creating, defining, limiting, and regulating the powers of the corporation, the directors and stockholders."[244] Instead of having to comply with powers granted by the state in its charter of incorporation, a corporation could now determine its own powers so long as the state did not explicitly prohibit it.[245] As Harwell Wells put it, these modern statutes suggested that "the only way to efficiently run a large corporation was to lodge power in full-time managers, and to limit shareholders' ability to directly influence corporate management to the periodic election of directors."[246]

Reformers were alarmed. Populists and Progressives alike feared that the concentration of power in large corporate units was a threat to individual liberty. And the separation of ownership from control that the new corporations statutes enshrined only exacerbated their concerns.[247] Many believed that the corporation's ownership structure undermined 19th-century economic and democratic ideals—that is, the power of markets equally to "distribute the rewards of individual industry" and to help "conform individual liberty" to socially beneficial ends. As Lawrence Zacharias noted, giant corporations obfuscated "the traditional relationships between individual liberty, competition, and social utility" and made impossible assessment of the national wealth based on aggregations of individual valuations.[248]

Informed by such concerns, some reformers wanted to subject large corporations to national regulation, while others preferred controlling business units locally.[249] Yet, the most enduring response was focused on the unique role that corporate directors could play in ensuring that corporations did not put American values in jeopardy. Seeking to portray a vision of the corporation that resonated with American ideals, Progressives reimagined the rapidly growing business corporation as a form of representative democracy, with dispersed ownership and centralized management; the latter was empowered to attend to the affairs of the corporation and the needs of the community.

In 1932, Adolf Berle and Gardiner Means memorialized this image of the democratic corporation in *The Modern Corporation and Private Property*. As Berle and Means explained, due to the separation of ownership from control in the large publicly held corporation, "neither the claims of ownership nor those of control can stand against the paramount interests of the community. … It remains only for the claims of the community to be put forward with clarity and force."[250]

Sixteen years later, John Weinberg echoed:

> Legal and economic doctrine pertaining to corporations has been built upon the theory of representative government. It was accepted that active

> managers were appointed by directors, who, in turn, were elected by a cognizant ownership group. These managers were to seek to combine capital, labor, and materials in the most economic proportions in their efforts to obtain maximum profits.[251]

As Edward Herman explained, management emerged as a new class, "separate from capital and the owning class" and expected to "rise above class conflict and direct capitalism from a disinterested trustee perspective."[252]

State courts reinforced the democratic vision of the corporation by allowing managers to act to benefit the community at large. Early 20th-century courts reintroduced the idea that the power of the board of directors was "original and undelegated" rather than delegated from the shareholders, and eroded the traditional *ultra vires* doctrine, which limited corporate activities to prescribed charter powers, so as to allow directors to exercise a variety of incidental powers for the benefit of different corporate constituencies.[253]

Specifically, amidst growing labor agitation, courts allowed corporations to attend to the needs of their employees. Courts described "[e]xpenditures resulting in stimulating the employees to better work, and promoting faithfulness and loyalty to the employer" as "tributary to the promotion of corporate objects."[254] Corporations could engage in different actions to promote "the comfort, health, safety and well-being of the employee," and could pay bonuses to keep up employee "morale" and encourage more "energetic efforts."[255] In 1931, an article in the *Columbia Law Review* concluded that courts were "more ready to adjudge gratuitous corporate contributions *intra vires* where the immediate benefit is received by employees than in any other situation."[256]

Corporations were allowed to take actions to benefit community goals, and they were quick to proclaim their desire to do so. "The business corporation ... takes millions of dollars each year and spends the money for the benefit of its workmen," Raynal Bolling wrote on behalf of the U.S. Steel Corporation, counting among such benefits employee stock subscription plans, accident prevention and relief, medical care, and pensions, as well as general community welfare.[257] Similarly, Owen D. Young, chairman of General Electric during the 1920s and 1930s, stressed that business managers were trustees for the public who needed little if any supervision from the states or the federal government.[258]

Business leaders did not necessarily live up to the trusteeship ideal, but they took advantage of the rhetoric. As Roland Marchand explained in his study of corporations' public relations, large corporations exhibited "compassionate concern for [their] employees" as a means of demonstrating that they "possessed human feeling."[259]

The idea that directors were trustees for the community suggested that corporations had duties beyond the maximization of value for their shareholders, but it is important to remember that the concept of corporate purpose remained fluid in the early 20th century. If Berle's and Means's *The Modern Corporation and Private Property* concluded that corporate powers were powers in trust for the community,[260] in a famous article, "Corporate Powers as Powers in Trust," which was published a year prior to the book, Berle proclaimed that corporate powers were held in trust for the benefit of the shareholders.[261]

Concerned, on the one hand, about the power that corporations could exercise over the community and, on the other hand, about potential manipulation of the stock market by those in control of corporations, Progressive jurists oscillated between describing corporate powers as held in trust for the community and arguing that such powers should be exercised to benefit the shareholders. Specifically, Progressives wanted to constrain the control group's ability to harm, through its participation in corporate management or through market manipulation, both the community at large and the individual shareholder. Today, we often describe the interests of the individual shareholder and the community as divergent. But because early 20th-century scholars were concerned about the external and internal dimensions of corporate power, they viewed them as complementary.[262]

At any rate, the Progressives' definition of corporate powers as powers in trust created a role for directors that reached beyond managing their corporations' affairs. By emphasizing that directors were trustees, these jurists made directors the face of corporate America and those responsible, within the corporate structure, for aligning corporate purpose with American ideals. As the following section explores, in the mid-century, as concerns about corporate power dissipated, jurists moved away from the idea that corporate powers were held in trust. Soon, a managerialist ideology came to dominate corporate law. As the following section further elaborates, in this context, John Weinberg's thesis stood out, emphasizing the role of directors as trustees for the shareholders.

Mid-century Managerialism and the Emergence of the Independent Board

Throughout the 1920s, many celebrated the rise of professional management as creating increased corporate gains and profits. Management was described as "the prime mover of business—the veritable fountainhead of economic security for the bulk of the population."[263]

But the rise of the managerial class was not without drawbacks. Due to the absence of federal laws requiring and regulating corporate disclosure and inadequate self-regulation by the exchanges, executives were able to benefit at the expense of the shareholders. As one editorial put it, "Many managements, swollen with power, came to believe that their enterprises had ceased to be reservoirs of trust funds for stockholders and creditors but had become agencies for their own private immediate gain."[264] Huge salaries and bonuses, management's participation in its own underwriting, using corporate funds to manipulate the market, and other forms of self-dealing became common.[265]

After the market's collapse in October 1929, revelations of investment bankers' and management's conflicts of interest and the consequential fraud on the market helped direct policymakers' and scholars' attention not only toward the securities markets, but also toward the corporation's internal structure.[266] In 1933, the Pecora investigation of banking and securities practices led to the passage of the Glass–Steagall Act, which "prohibited bank affiliates from owning and dealing in securities, thereby severing commercial banks from investment banks."[267] And in 1940, the Investment Company Act achieved a similar severance in the mutual-funds industry by requiring mutual funds to be highly diversified (hence have no control over their portfolio companies) and by discouraging directors and officers of mutual funds from sitting on boards of their portfolio companies.

It was in this political milieu that William O. Douglas advocated that corporations be required to have an independent board. Douglas's "Directors Who Do Not Direct" was published in 1934, shortly after the enactment of the securities acts, and three years before Douglas was to become chairman of the SEC.[268] The article argued that corporations should have an independent board that would represent the interests of the shareholders.[269]

Focusing on the "abuses and malpractices" that characterized the 1920s, including many self-dealing transactions, Douglas argued that businessmen lost sight of their public role. To encourage "the development of a social mindedness ... among businessmen and their legal advisers," Douglas wanted to see a board that would not be "called in by the managers," drawn from the managers, or subordinate to the managers in any way.[270] While Progressive legal scholars such as Berle and Means focused on corporate power, Douglas's main concern was the executives' control of the board, which, he believed, was at the root of the problems that led to the 1929 crash.

Significantly, according to Douglas, only an independent board could adequately protect the shareholders' interests (in fact, he believed shareholders should serve as independent directors). As he concluded, independent directors, "the representatives of the stockholders, would be there, not for the purpose of managing the enterprise, but with the object of supervising those who do and of formulating the general commercial and financial policies under which the business is to be conducted."[271]

Lest he be misunderstood, Douglas emphasized that corporate powers were powers in trust for the community. As he put it, "directors are trustees by virtue of business ethics as well as law, and the powers which they exercise are powers in trust."[272] In an address delivered five years after the publication of "Directors Who Do Not Direct," Douglas emphasized that paid professional directors would represent "not only the present but the potential stockholder, and representing the general public as well."[273] In other words, like Berle, Douglas saw no contradiction between the directors' role as trustees for the community and their role as representatives of the shareholders. Like Berle, Douglas focused on the need to tame and constrain those in control, whether large investors or executives. In his view, corporations could act as trustees for the community, while the directors would ensure protection of the interests of the minority shareholders.

Douglas wanted to see the development of professional directors, "skilled in the technique of business, the art of law, and the skill of government." Such a class, he believed, could monitor corporations so as to align the interests of the shareholders with the interests of the public—"so that the profit motive will be articulated with the public good" and the investor assured "more protection against the malpractices of management."[274]

According to the traditional narrative, Douglas's arguments did not stimulate a continuing scholarly debate about the role or legal status of the board of directors. The policies of the New Deal seriously circumscribed the corporation's powers. The securities acts regulated the corporation's dealings with its shareholders as well as its creditors, new federal labor laws regulated the corporation's relations with its employees, and antitrust laws affected the corporation's behavior toward consumers and suppliers.[275] Concerns about the corporation's external power, the story goes, rapidly dissipated, while legal scholarship about corporate internal hierarchies focused mostly on the fiduciary duties of corporate managers, without distinguishing insider from outsider directors.[276]

The discovery of John Weinberg's thesis challenges this traditional narrative, suggesting that Douglas was not a lone warrior. For one, in 1940, Richard C. Patterson, who from 1938 to 1939 served as assistant secretary of commerce, echoed Douglas's argument. Patterson described the board as often out of "touch with the business it is supposed to oversee," and called on corporations to hire paid directors, "men of integrity whose voices would be authoritative, whose ideas would be pertinent, whose thinking would be done in the public interest as well as in the interests of the shareholders and employees."[277] Businesses, too, seemed to recognize the value of "outside" directors.[278]

Informed by these discussions, John Weinberg expressed deep concerns about management's control of the board, describing it as a "pathological situation."[279] To remedy this situation, Weinberg suggested focusing on "the functions, responsibilities, and limits of the authority to be reserved for the board, and those to be delegated to management." A clear definition of functions would allow executives and directors to recognize and respect the unique role of each body.[280]

According to Weinberg, the board of directors had a unique, dual role in corporate governance: directors were tasked both with the administrative role of managing the corporation and with the trusteeship duties of preserving corporate assets and protecting the shareholders. His thesis thus focused on how to balance these roles while ensuring the board's independence.

Weinberg described the board's administrative functions as "delegation and coordination." Directors were to "construct an administrative mechanism and through the medium of policies provide lubrication for its smooth and continuous operation." Accordingly, directors had to ensure that they remained informed about the corporations' affairs, and they were required to formulate corporate policy, select the chief executive, and authorize dividends. While directors could generally delegate daily administrative tasks to officers, they had to check and verify performance.[281]

As for the directors' trusteeship duties, Weinberg emphasized that the directors' duties ran to the shareholders. Referencing the famous debate between Adolf Berle and E. Merrick Dodd about the appropriate beneficiaries of directors' trusteeship duties, Weinberg echoed Berle's comments: "We cannot abandon emphasis on the view that business corporations exist for the sole purpose of making profits for their stockholders until such time as we are prepared to offer a clear, reasonable, and enforceable scheme of responsibilities to somebody else."[282]

So that the directors could perform their supervisory administrative tasks and trusteeship duties, Weinberg, like Douglas and Patterson, argued that they had to be independent. As he put it, "To have the board, which according to the law is the supreme locus of responsibility and the representative of the stockholders in top management, composed of active executives who virtually approve their own actions is a violation of a basic trusteeship principle."[283]

Cognizant also of "the importance of obtaining and maintaining high-caliber [people] on the board," Weinberg recommended having "a 50% to 75%

representation of outside, experienced [people] drawn from other fields" to "give the board a wider horizon and ... to increase the chances of preventing some of the unhealthy aspects of ... managerial domination."[284]

Weinberg's (like Douglas's and Patterson's) were strong arguments in favor of independent directors, suggesting that practitioners were rather concerned about the executives' control of the board. Why, then, didn't these calls engender a wide-ranging reform of corporate governance? As I argue below, the business and legal communities' embrace of managerialism stood in the way.

By the time Weinberg wrote his thesis, corporate managers were seen as the "strategic center" of the large corporation and, by derivation, society. In 1941, historian James Truslow Adams, for example, boldly announced that "big business ... is the function of the American congeries of resources, people, democracy ... which has given it characteristics that are unique compared with big business at other times and in other areas."[285] Using General Motors (GM) to illustrate the intricate relations between corporations and American ideals, Adams called attention to GM's "leaders" (who came "from the outside or up from the ranks"), to the multiplicity of GM stockholders, to the corporation's "decentralized operations under coordinated control," to its support of its employees (especially through high wages), and to its self-assumed "responsibility of keeping a large corporation going and giving an improved product to consumers."[286]

Adams's message resonated with many, especially business leaders. Corporate managers were deemed to possess the expertise required to lead corporations and the country, and they did not need guidance. As historian Richard Hofstadter wrote, "business structure has brought into life a managerial class of immense social and political as well as market power."[287] Business experts asserted that corporations were to be managed by multiple loyal leaders, "men of ability and initiative" capable of fighting or evading "bureaucratic ossification and bureaucratic timidity" and pursuing corporate policy, while the term free enterprise came to symbolize the free reign of managers, who in cultural imagination replaced the small producers and entrepreneurs of the 19th century.[288]

State courts wholeheartedly embraced this managerialist rhetoric, dodging concerns about excessive executive power. Their decisions described directors, insiders and outsiders alike, as representatives (not trustees) of the shareholders, who were elected to run corporations without interference from the courts (or the shareholders).[289] Such were the assumptions that legitimized the presumption of the business judgment rule as a rule of complete deference to managerial expertise. In the absence of fraud, conflict of interest, or bad faith, courts refrained from evaluating managers' actions even when their errors were gross.[290]

Managerialism substantiated the image of the corporation as a democratic institution with a social purpose. Deemed representatives, rather than trustees for the shareholders, corporate managers were free to attend to the interests of the different corporate constituencies. Significantly, beginning in the early 1940s, as the rise of totalitarianism in Europe forced American jurists to wonder whether democracy as embodied in the American form of government was ethically superior to other regimes,[291] the managerialist justification for corporate power and the actions of those who exercised it became a means of explaining the strength of American institutions and democratic ideology.

Indeed, Weinberg began his thesis with the following:

> American industry is today, in many ways, facing the most critical period in all its history. The system of free enterprise is under severe attack. Abroad it has suffered defeat in many lands, submerged by the force of totalitarian principles of economics. At home our system's right to survive is challenged by its frequent inability to maintain a stable equilibrium in the face of rapidly changing economic and political conditions.[292]

The courts' response to such challenges was simple: they described corporations as defenders of American democracy and empowered them to "contribute[] … corporate funds" to American causes.[293]

For one, by the 1950s, charitable contributions, traditionally deemed *ultra vires*, were sanctioned and left to managerial discretion. Management could choose to make certain contributions, despite shareholders' disapproval, but it was not required to make them, even if the shareholders so wished. Corporations and their directors were free to exercise their power, with or without their shareholders' consent.[294] As Adolf Berle put it in 1959, "modern directors [were] not limited to running business enterprise for maximum profit but [were] in fact and recognized in law as administrators of a community system."[295]

Social and political critics pointed to power inequities that permeated American corporations and that were reinforced by the celebration of managerialism. And corporate-law scholars noted that the rhetoric of corporate democracy was used to empower directors and executives and remove shareholders from any meaningful position in the corporation.[296] But the courts remained unwavering in their acceptance of managerialism. Worried about totalitarianism and, later, the Cold War, jurists discounted concerns about business and its potential threat to democracy and instead assumed a harmonious relationship between corporations, the corporate elite, and society.[297]

At the 1956 meeting of the American Economic Association, economist Carl Kaysen memorably explained that "[t]he modern corporation is a soulful corporation":

> No longer the agent of proprietorship seeking to maximize return on investment, management sees itself as responsible to stockholders, employees, customers, the general public, and, perhaps most important, the firm itself as an institution. ... [Moreover, its] responsibilities to the general public are widespread: leadership in local charitable enterprises, concern with factory architecture and landscaping, provision of support for higher education, and even research in pure science, to name a few.[298]

In short, Weinberg's and others' arguments did not lead to a wide-ranging reform of corporate governance because, in the mid-century, corporations and their managers were the engine that made American democracy thrive. Until, as the following section elaborates, they weren't.

Proceduralism and the Independent Director

By the 1970s, managerialism was facing growing challenges. Increased government spending, global competition, and the 1973 energy crisis led to "an unprecedented combination of high inflation and unemployment," undermining the postwar trust in Keynesian economics. "External economic shocks, compounded by a drop in productivity growth, cost-of-living adjustments built into union contracts, and an economy shifting toward services" brought about dramatic wage and profitability drops. New regulatory agencies—particularly the Environmental Protection Agency and the Occupational Safety and Health Administration—triggered businesses' ire, while the Vietnam War and the Watergate scandal created "a legitimacy crisis among major American institutions, including business."[299] Rapidly, Americans lost faith in their federal and state governments and in their industrial corporations and their ability to improve the economy.[300]

Soon, debates within the legal and business communities about the appropriate alternative to managerialism, specifically about the role of the board, ensued, and Delaware law—by then recognized as *de facto* the national corporate law—came under direct attack. In a memorable article in the *Yale Law Journal*, William Cary, a former chairman of the SEC, charged that Delaware, in seeking to create "'favorable climate' for management," has "sponsor[ed] ... a system contributing to the deterioration of corporation standard."[301]

Other jurists focused their criticism on the board of directors. Melvin Eisenberg, for example, surveyed the management potential of the board and concluded that top executives, not the board of directors, managed the affairs of the publicly held corporation.[302] Joel Seligman proclaimed that boards of directors of large and medium-sized corporations "had ceased to function as a meaningful check on the corporation's chief executive officer." Boards played little if any role in selecting executives, as management controlled the proxy machinery, while outside directors were typically chosen from the same social networks as top executives and thus were unlikely to challenge the executives.[303]

Many, layperson and professional alike, wanted to see changes to corporate governance structures. Some resuscitated the idea that firms of a certain income and employee base should be federally incorporated; the federal statute was to include specific requirements regarding board composition and the board's role.[304] Others focused on formulating a special role for the board. Harvey Goldschmid suggested requiring boards to be composed entirely of outside directors who would review the executives' decisions.[305] And Peter Drucker proposed creating boards of "professional directors," "men or women of public standing and proven competence who, as members of the board, can be truly independent of management."[306] (John Weinberg also advocated developing a profession of directors.[307])

Notably, the Business Roundtable, and the American Bar Association's Committee on Corporate Laws, Section of Corporation, Banking and Business Law, described directors as monitors of corporate executives and recommended that boards should be composed of a majority of outside directors.[308] This idea was reinforced with the 1982 publication of a tentative draft of the ALI's *Principles of Corporate Governance.* (The final version was adopted in 1992 after a decade of heated debates.)[309]

Indeed, while progressive corporate legal scholars wanted to use the monitoring model substantially to redefine the directors' duties (including to impose duties on directors toward all corporate constituencies), corporate lawyers and business groups were strongly opposed to any attempt to tinker with the very limited directorial duties. Instead, they focused on the monitoring role of non-management directors and suggested that good boards contain a majority of them. Furthermore, the business community insisted that the independent directors' only role was to monitor the conduct of the business and affairs of the corporation on behalf of the shareholders. The independent directors became the focus of the monitoring model of the board, a model that rested on the twin assumptions that the directors' actual function was to monitor the executives and that independent directors could best perform that function.[310]

Amidst a blitz of hostile takeovers that threatened to break down corporate America, the Delaware Supreme Court was quick to embrace the independent directors. Take, for one, *Unocal v. Mesa Petroleum Co.*, the seminal hostile-takeover case.[311] The Chancery Court of Delaware treated the decision of the Unocal board to engage in an exclusive self-tender in response to a hostile bid as a form of self-dealing, and concluded that it "violated the customary rules regarding equal treatment in distributions for members of the same class of stock."[312] But the Supreme Court reversed.

Weary, perhaps, of the complexities of substantive fairness analysis, which typically applied in cases involving allegations of self-dealing, the Delaware Supreme Court adopted a more lenient standard of review: directors defending against a hostile bid could enjoy the protection of the business judgment rule, provided they could demonstrate, first, that they "had reasonable grounds for believing that a danger to corporate policy and effectiveness existed" and, second, that the defensive tactic the board adopted was "reasonable in relation to the threat posed."[313] Significantly, the court noted that if a majority of the independent directors approved the defensive action, it would enhance the likelihood that the board would meet the burden of the two-prong test and be granted the protection of the business judgment rule.[314]

Trust in the independent directors ran deep, ushering a new corporate legal theory: proceduralism. Beginning with the hostile-takeover cases and trickling down to all cases involving self-dealing transactions and even allegations of breaches of the duty of care, the Delaware Supreme Court endorsed entire fairness—that is, fair dealing and fair price—as the standard of review applicable whenever a shareholder plaintiff rebutted the presumption that directors acted in good faith, due care, and the best interests of the corporation.[315] Gradually, the court substituted a concept of fair dealing, or fair process, for the traditional business-judgment standard of review.

Underlying Delaware's proceduralism was the notion that certain procedures—for example, authorization by disinterested directors or ratification by shareholders—ensured maximization of value. The courts thus focused on incentivizing corporate directors to follow these procedures by assuring them that, when they so did, their actions would not be subject to judicial review. If a majority of independent, disinterested directors, following the courts' procedural requirements, approved a corporate action (including conflict-of-interest transactions), the Delaware courts declared such actions entitled to the presumption of the business judgment rule and shielded from further judicial inquiry. It was not long before most corporate boards included a majority of outside directors and proceduralism replaced business judgment and managerialism as the legitimating principle for executive power.[316]

The turn to proceduralism was associated with a new corporate purpose: shareholder wealth maximization. Back in the 1960s, Henry G. Manne argued that a firm's stock price was an indication of managerial efficiency and the market for control—a disciplinary tool. When the price was lower "relative to what it could be with more efficient management," Manne wrote, "the more attractive the takeover becomes to those who believe that they can manage the company more efficiently."[317] In the 1980s, investment bankers similarly described hostile takeovers as a means to "unlock[] the value of 'underperforming' stock prices" to the benefit of the shareholders[318] (who, in the 1980s, were mostly institutional investors).[319]

The Delaware Supreme Court's analysis of fairness, specifically fair price, seemed to embrace a similar message. For one, in Unocal, the court stressed that the defensive mechanism the independent directors adopted "[was] consistent with the principle that 'the minority stockholder shall receive the substantial equivalent in value of what he had before.'"[320] (While the principle of fair price was derived from the merger context, the court applied it to hostile takeovers.) And in *Revlon, Inc. v. MacAndrews & Forbes Holding, Inc.*, the court stressed that when a company was for sale, "the directors' role changed from defenders of the corporate bastion to auctioneers charged with getting the best price for the stockholders at a sale of the company."[321]

If, in the mid-century, Weinberg (and others) saw the independent directors as trustees for the shareholders, in the 1980s the Delaware courts described independent directors as agents of the shareholders, responsible for maximizing their principals' wealth. Yet, while the Delaware courts used both the rhetoric of agency and that of shareholder wealth maximization, neither amounted to more than rhetoric. This rhetoric was a means to assure investors that their interests were indeed front and center of Delaware law, while proceduralism was used to reaffirm the power of corporate executives, under guidance of the independent board, to run corporations as they deemed fit—irrespective, indeed, of shareholder wealth maximization. As Justice Horsey put it in *Paramount Communications, Inc. v. Time, Inc.*:

> Delaware law confers the management of the corporate enterprise to the stockholders' duly elected board representatives. ... That [fiduciary duty to manage a corporate enterprise] may not be delegated to the stockholders. Directors are not obliged to abandon a deliberately conceived corporate plan for a short-term shareholder profit unless there is clearly no basis to sustain the corporate strategy.[322]

In the end, the Delaware courts embraced the independent directors when they could do so without undermining managerialism. While the courts did not explicitly make the connection, independent directors, presumably without other ties to the corporation, made the idea that the shareholders elected directors and thus that the directors were their agents less fictitious. At the same time, the courts' reliance on the independent directors to cleanse conflict-of-interest transactions helped limit the liability imposed on directors and executives. Unhappy shareholders were told to vote another slate of directors or sell their shares. The democratic image of the corporation, an image that helped legitimize executive power throughout the 20th century, remained intact.

Conclusion

Writing in 1992, the late Chancellor Allen noted that "two inconsistent conceptions have dominated our thinking about corporations" in the 20th century: "in the first conception, the corporation is seen as the private property of its stockholder-owners," and shareholder wealth maximization is corporate purpose. "The second conception sees the corporation ... as a social institution," and thus "tinged with a public purpose," such as "the advancement of the general welfare."[323]

The history told in this chapter enriches Allen's observation by exploring the relationship between different conceptions of corporate purpose and changing definitions of the role of the board. It reveals that, throughout the 20th century, different understandings of corporate purpose corresponded to unique corporate governance concerns. Scholars (and the courts) articulated the idea that corporations have a public purpose to counter concerns about corporate power; at the same time, they endorsed the norm of shareholder wealth maximization to counter fears that those in control would abuse their power to harm minority shareholders.

A conviction that the directors' role must be determined by reference to corporate purpose was indeed one of the themes underlying John Weinberg's thesis. During the heyday of managerialism, Weinberg described a nuanced role for independent directors; it encompassed administrative as well as trusteeship duties, suggesting that presumably inconsistent conceptions of corporate purpose can be balanced. Ultimately, to paraphrase the last sentence of Weinberg's thesis: "The key to national prosperity and welfare, perhaps national survival, may well hinge" not upon a strict adherence to one corporate purpose or another, but "upon the ability of directors to solve the intricate economic problems confronting them today."[324]

Chapter 6

Corporate Purpose at Mid-Century: Between Law and Managerialism

Harwell Wells

What role should the giant corporation play in modern society? That question, which has confronted Americans for well over a century, is the question underlying John Weinberg's extraordinary 1948 thesis, *Status and Functions of Corporate Directors*.[325] Much of the thesis, of course, focuses on its announced subject—directors of the United States's "industrial, nonregulated corporations"—and a fair amount of it is devoted to best practices for such boards, addressing such issues as a board's ideal size, compensation, structure, and membership.

But the thesis is far more than just a guidebook for would-be directors. It tackles some of the largest themes in American business and its evolution by setting the role of directors within the era's broader currents of thought about the corporation and its purpose. In this chapter, I examine the backdrop against which Weinberg wrote—the larger social, political, economic, and legal developments which shaped his world view and made the seemingly mundane role of a corporate director a pressing subject—returning at the end to Weinberg's thesis and the ways it both reflected and challenged those developments.

Managerialism

Historians label the mid-century's framework of economic and political ideas about the corporation as "managerialism," a term also popular at the time. The word is a bit misleading, inasmuch as it implies a uniformity of thought that did not always exist, but it at least serves to capture a set of shared assumptions about the economy and its operation.[326] The notion of "managerialism," a faith that corporate managers could run their corporations for the benefit of society, can be traced back to sometime after the turn of the 20th century, though the term itself was coined later.[327]

That American corporations had grown larger over the previous hundred years was obvious to observers. Along with this growth came changes in how many corporations were owned and operated. While some 19th-century corporations had hundreds or even a few thousand shareholders, the 20th century saw shareholding in many large industrial corporations spread rapidly, particularly in the 1920s, producing firms with many shareholders, none of whom actually owned much of the corporation.[328]

At the same time, legal impediments helped prevent intermediaries from acting as blockholders with the power to dictate corporate policy.[329] By the 1920s, observers both at home and abroad came to believe that, in many cases, shareholders no longer had effective control over the corporations they "owned," and that control had effectively shifted to a corporation's senior managers,[330] a development A. A. Berle, Jr., and Gardiner Means dubbed "the separation of ownership and control" in their landmark 1932 work *The Modern Corporation and Private Property*.[331]

While later studies cast doubt on some of their more sweeping conclusions,[332] Berle and Means seemed to capture and provide strong empirical support for an intuition already abroad during the 1920s: that legal and economic mechanisms were no longer sufficient to force managers to govern their corporations in the interests of shareholders. For many, this posed a problem needing to be solved by, for instance, better shareholder organization[333] or the courts imposing new limits on managerial discretion.[334] For others, though, it presented an opportunity.

Here we find the genesis of debates that continue to this day. Perhaps, a few visionary business leaders concluded, greater autonomy from shareholders made it possible to imagine a corporation run for the benefit of other groups beyond just shareholders. They were, of course, not the first business leaders to insist they were running their corporation for the benefit of groups beyond shareholders; this was a claim heard from the Lowell Associates, who claimed to look after the "mill girls" working in their Massachusetts factories in the 1830s, to George Pullman, who built a model town to house his workers in the 1890s.[335]

The version that appeared in the 1920s, however, was a new one: that the changing nature of ownership and control had so loosened the reins that corporate leaders could no longer run their firms only for shareholders' benefit but for the benefit of workers, consumers, and perhaps the general public. The best-known advocates for this view were Gerard Swope and Owen Young of General Electric (GE), pioneers of "welfare capitalist" programs that offered workers, for instance, pensions and stock ownership. Such men were not shy in insisting that their corporation was now responsible not merely to shareholders but to workers and "customers and the general public," a view they occasionally referred to as "trusteeship."

As Young said in one address, "The old notion that the heads of business are the paid attorneys of stockholders, to exploit labor and the public in the stockholders' interest, is gone—I hope forever."[336] Nor was Young's a lone voice; the idea that senior management would run a corporation to benefit constituencies beyond shareholders—"stakeholders," to borrow a later coinage—was frequently voiced by businessmen and was also prominent at business schools, as the new institutions tried to develop the idea of business as a profession oriented to societal improvement.[337] As one study noted, it "would be easy to collect quotations from the 1920s and even earlier" with similar themes.[338]

In the early 1930s, an attempt was made in the pages of the *Harvard Law Review* to give this approach a legal foundation.[339] It can be traced to 1931, when A. A. Berle, Jr., published an article entitled "Corporate Powers as Powers in Trust," which was not a managerialist manifesto at all. There, Berle, disturbed by recent judicial decisions and statutory changes that he believed gave managers greater power, particularly over a corporation's capital structure, argued that managerial powers needed to be treated in the law as "powers in trust" held for the benefit of shareholders.

Whenever those powers were exercised, he argued, they should be "twice tested, first, by the technical rules having to do with the existence and proper exercise of the power; second, by equitable rules somewhat analogous to those which apply in favor of a *cestui que trust* to the trustee's exercise of wide powers granted to him in the instrument making him a fiduciary."[340] Given that managers' powers were held in trust for shareholders, such a legal rule would be a powerful weapon to rein in managerial discretion and prevent self-dealing.

Berle must have been surprised, then, when a year later the *Harvard Law Review* published a rejoinder, "For Whom Are Corporate Managers Trustees," by Harvard Law professor Merrick Dodd. This article was a wholesale attack on the idea that "business corporations exist for the sole purpose of making money for stockholders," and the real attempt to give managerialism a legal foundation.[341]

Drawing together several recent developments, including the rhetoric of corporate leaders such as GE's Young and the rise of stockholders who "take no active part in the conduct of the business," Dodd argued that the evolving nature of business, particularly the new social role it was being called upon to play, had produced in management a new sense of its social responsibility towards groups other than shareholders. Given this, he agreed with Berle that managers should be seen as trustees, but trustees not for shareholders but solely for the corporation itself, a legal shift which would empower them to "employ its funds in a manner appropriate to a person … imbued with a sense of social responsibility without thereby being guilty of a breach of trust."[342]

Dodd agreed with Berle that managers had gained greater power in recent years, but in contrast to Berle he argued this development had not gone far enough. Unsurprisingly, Dodd's article soon drew a furious counterattack from Berle, who argued that this ignored the present realities of both managers and the law. The typical manager, Berle wrote, "does not now think of himself as a prince; he does not now assume responsibilities to the community; his bankers do not now undertake to recognize social claims; his lawyers do not advise him in terms of social responsibility."[343] Given this, Dodd's vision of a corporation run for stakeholders was a fantasy.

The debate, perhaps the first clearly articulating shareholder versus stakeholder views of the corporation, was well known enough that, 15 years later, John Weinberg would discuss it in his thesis. Yet it had a strange coda. A few months after Berle's withering reply to Dodd, he and Gardiner Means published *The Modern Corporation and Private Property*, where they not only documented the growing separation of ownership and control but presented it as a seemingly unavoidable process in which the largest 200 or so corporations would continue to grow while their shareholder bases would continue to fragment and atomize.

They then looked ahead and abandoned the advocacy for shareholder interests that marked Berle's earlier writings. In the future, they wrote, "it seems almost essential if the corporate system is to survive, that the 'control' of the great corporations should develop into a purely neutral technocracy, balancing a variety of claims by various groups in the community and assigning to each a portion of the income stream on the basis of public policy rather than private cupidity."[344] In *The Modern Corporation and Private Property*, the future was managerial.

The Berle–Dodd debate concluded, and *The Modern Corporation and Private Property* appeared, in 1932, in the depths of the Great Depression. One might have thought this would have killed any movement proposing to give corporate managers greater discretion or additional responsibilities, as the economic catastrophe of the 1930s surely demolished corporate leaders' claims to be wise statesmen who only needed to be granted broad discretion and left alone for them to produce a widely distributed economic bounty.

Quite the contrary, however, managerialism managed to survive and even thrive during the decade. Berle and Means's work likely had something to do with this; *The Modern Corporation and Private Property* was hailed as a masterwork when published, a correct diagnosis of the evolution of American business. And while the New Deal was composed of many ill-fitting parts, its policies, beginning with the National Recovery Administration in 1933, often called on business to take a broad-minded and collaborative approach with government and labor. Not the least, managerialism may have hung on as a survival mechanism for corporate leaders; while some embraced full-fledged opposition to the Roosevelt administration, others saw cooperating with the reforms as the best way to preserve some version of free-market capitalism.

We can see managerialism's persistence by looking to the work of a now-obscure organization, the Temporary National Economic Committee (TNEC), formed by President Roosevelt in 1938 in a late burst of New Deal reformism.[345] It was perhaps the last time the federal government questioned not merely how to address giant corporations and the problem of competition, but whether giant corporations—"big business"—should exist at all.[346] In the end, TNEC did very little except issue a series of monographs in 1940–41 examining aspects of American industry, studies largely ignored as World War II eclipsed the New Deal. One report, however, deserves attention here because it illustrates the way managerial thought persisted throughout the 1930s, and because it eventually fell into the hands of John Weinberg; it clearly influenced his thinking, and is one of the relatively few documents referenced in the body of his thesis.[347]

The report, "Bureaucracy and Trusteeship in Large Corporations," spent much of its time discussing the bureaucratization of large corporations, but its final chapter focused on the idea of the trusteeship of corporate managers.[348] TNEC itself had weighed whether big business was necessary for the American economy, so the discussion of managers' roles was influenced by that larger question. The vision of managerial trusteeship put forward in "Bureaucracy and Trusteeship in Large Corporations" appeared to side with large corporations in this battle, but only because, its authors insisted, managers had taken on a new role—as trustees for the corporation itself, no longer bound tightly to shareholders but with discretion to manage the corporation to serve various constituencies.

The report lay at the end of a straight line running from "business statesmanship" of the 1920s through Merrick Dodd's writings in the early 1930s.[349] It opened by declaring that "[t]he modern semipublic corporation is obviously a trusteeship, a legal-administrative relationship in which the owners, theoretically at least, entrust the managers with power to carry on the business for them so long as their mandate is complied with and the results are generally satisfactory."[350] But economic developments, it continued, had eroded outside checks on the corporation's power: "With the diffusion of ownership ... in a large sector of our economy, management is left with the responsibility for determining policies, including those affecting prices, production, and employment, within very broad limits and for all practical purposes without effective check from any source."[351]

Making a point which would become popular in the 1950s, it argued that the market, once a check on corporations, had largely lost this function: "Now we have a situation wherein society has granted certain economic liberties while relying upon the market for protection against their abuse. With this protection substantially curtailed, it is necessary that other instruments of regulation be discovered and applied."[352] One of those "other instruments of regulation" was, surprisingly, management itself.

Quoting GE's Young, the TNEC report continued by claiming that there was "increasing evidence of a vague awareness of broad responsibility on the part of corporate management," citing "examination of the annual reports of some of the large companies for the past few years [which] reveals that frequently a section deals with corporate responsibility to various groups. Those most often mentioned are the investors, labor, and consumers or the public. Sometimes government is also included. The responsibilities commonly alluded to are the provision of a fair, adequate return on investments; fair wages and working conditions, together with some mention of regularity of employment; and a good product at a fair price."[353]

As to where this new idea of corporate responsibility would find a home, the report pointed squarely to the board of directors, "[b]ecause it is commonly supposed that boards of directors are the guardians of the interests of nonmanagement groups—particularly, of course, the owners—and because boards are formally designed for that purpose."[354] It closed with a discussion of boards and board reforms, putting forward several proposals that were apparently popular among reformers and would reappear in John Weinberg's thesis, including reducing the size of boards, paying directors more, and increasing the percentage of outside directors.[355]

Nor was the new emphasis on the centrality of management limited to those studying American corporations. Some support came from unexpected quarters. In 1940, the American writer James Burnham, then a follower of Leon Trotsky, though later a conservative stalwart, published *The Managerial Revolution: What is Happening in the World*, a work that became an international bestseller.[356] Burnham was strongly influenced by Berle and Means, and he drew on their work to claim that what they had discerned was only part of a larger global process whereby "management" itself was becoming a new class on a par with capital and labor throughout industrial society. As one historian described his view: "the social divide was no longer between capitalists and proletarians but between those who control production"—for Burnham, managers—"and those who do not."[357] The successor to capitalism, in this view, would not be socialism but "a newfangled order headed by managerial elites."[358]

While Burnham's view is extreme, those who were taking a closer look at the American corporation similarly came away with a sense that the corporation had somehow come to occupy a new position in society, one placing new responsibilities on management. In 1946, the management theorist Peter Drucker published *The Concept of the Corporation*, based on an intensive two-year study of General Motors conducted in 1942 and 1943. His view of management was complex, but at the core of his remarkably influential analysis was the view that the American large corporation had become the "representative social institution" of modern society "around which crystallize our social problems and to which we look for their solutions," playing a role akin to the Catholic Church's in the Middle Ages.[359]

Drucker did not completely accept the most expansive views of corporate trusteeship—he believed management still had some responsibility to pursue profits for shareholders—but he thought the corporation must also answer deeper social needs by giving "status and function to the individual, and it must give him the justice of equal opportunities" and by recognizing that "its social function as a community is as important as its economic function as an efficient producer."[360] With a flash of hyperbole, he announced the mass-production plant, indissolubly linked to the corporation, was "our social reality, our representative institution, which has to carry the burden of our dreams."[361]

All this, however, tells us what theorists and a few corporate visionaries thought; what was the view of most business leaders? It's not an easy question to answer. One 1940 opinion poll of business leaders by *Fortune* magazine suggested that most had accepted the main New Deal statutes and reforms, some sign of a change in business thought.[362] Other studies of the corporation made at roughly the same time reached similar conclusions. In 1945, a study by managerial economist Robert Gordon—another one of the handful of works directly cited by Weinberg—concluded that "the last decade has increased the emphasis on the broader social criteria of business leadership, and ... our business leaders have gradually accepted some responsibility for the protection of the interests of labor, consumers, and the community at large."[363]

Answering the question of what managers really believed becomes even more complicated after 1945, because World War II and its immediate aftermath further changed the social and economic landscape. The war itself had helped restore the public image of businessmen. War production from the "arsenal of democracy," and the willingness of many senior corporate leaders to serve as "dollar-a-year men" in federal employment during the war, had allowed business to regain some legitimacy lost during the 1930s.[364] The war's global devastation also left the United States dominant in the world economy.

Yet management still faced challenges. Servicemen returning to factory jobs went on strike in unprecedented numbers in 1945 and 1946, demanding higher wages and, in some instances, union participation in production and investment decisions.[365] General Motors underwent a 113-day strike in the winter of 1946 before the United Auto Workers accepted a deal with significant pay raises but not the "right to manage" they had sought.[366] While the economy boomed, some suspicion of large corporations remained. When corporate profits increased 60% from 1945 to 1948, Congress held hearings on profits and a line of corporate leaders were called to testify as to why they had done so well.[367]

Perhaps the most consequential development for public and management views of the corporation was, however, the Cold War that developed between the United States and its allies and the Soviet Union in the late 1940s. The Cold War had at least two major effects. First, it led to suppression of much leftist criticism of the corporation.[368] Second, it enlisted the corporation in the larger struggle, for if the Cold War was a battle between capitalism—or the "free enterprise system"—and communism, then the corporation itself had a role to play in the battle.

Given all these developments, we return to the question: what were managers thinking in 1948, the year that John Weinberg wrote his thesis? Surprisingly, we have a source that can provide at least a partial answer. In 1947, three economists and a sociologist, including future Nobel Prize winner James Tobin, undertook a study that would be published several years later as *The American Business Creed*.[369] It's an odd work. In their research, the authors examined the public pronouncements of a large sample of American corporations and business associations, including advertisements, speeches, pamphlets and textbooks sponsored by business associations, and testimony before Congress, made from July 1948 to June 1949.[370]

From this, they distilled what they saw as a fairly coherent "creed" espoused by business leaders, albeit a creed split into two strands: "classical" and "managerial." Then, drawing on mid-century theories about the role ideology plays in social life, developed by sociologists Karl Mannheim, Theodor Adorno, and Talcott Parsons, they concluded that this ideology reflected in good part what business leaders actually believed, positing that the creed these leaders espoused played an important psychological function in "easing strains" imposed on managers trying to navigate a complicated business and social landscape.[371] Twenty-first-century readers may take a more cynical view of these pronouncements, but there is something to the idea that the public pronouncements of corporations and business associations, even if heavily polished, cannot stray too far from what those who voice them actually believe.

The American Business Creed opened by acknowledging that the "classical" strand of the creed, which saw capitalism as highly competitive and held that managers had few obligations to any but stockholders,[372] still had its adherents. However, a majority of business leaders, it continued, espoused the managerial strand of thought, which differed from the classical "chiefly in the emphasis it places on the role of professional managers in the large business firm who consciously direct economic forces for the common good."[373] Importantly, the managerial creed was rooted in a particular view of history, in which a new form of capitalism was evolving rapidly out of the old.

The authors found this view epitomized in an advertisement from General Cable Corporation:

> I am Industry.
> People were hurt when I first stirred in life;
> Then I grew and learned; ...
> With maturity I have grown, too, in social responsibility to the people—
> To America!
> And even to those beyond our shores.
> My efforts are not in selfish interest;
> Rather all my brains and brawn strain for the good of the many;
> I am the American way![374]

As the authors depicted it, such a sweeping view of history lay behind the reconceptualization of managerial responsibilities. In the managerial account, "[o]wners, particularly corporation stockholders, are deposed from their central position," they wrote. "Whereas in the classical view they are the enterprise, in the managerial view they are on a par with other groups who have stakes in, and just claims on, the organization. Managers are assigned a more important and more autonomous role than that of agents for the owners. Theirs is a statesman's function of mediating among the groups dependent on the enterprise."[375]

In one sense, there is nothing novel about this view; it differs little from the view put forward by business statesmen in the 1920s and Merrick Dodd in the 1930s. What is surprising is that by the end of the 1940s it was apparently the dominant view of corporate leaders. Perhaps because this version of managerialism was very much embraced by such leaders, it also had an important limitation. While the creed acknowledged that managers had new social responsibilities to "groups dependent on the enterprise," it was silent when it came to giving those groups any legal power over managers. "The managerial creed ... responds to the problems of the large public corporation not by calling for a legal redefinition of the social responsibility of managers but by exhorting them to assume new responsibilities voluntarily."[376]

Managers, in other words, were not changing the way they ran their firms because they were being forced to do so by any outside pressure, or because they were assuming legal obligations to those new groups, but because they had perceived social changes and were responding to them in an ethically enlightened manner. This version of managerialism almost appears as an up-to-date kind of *noblesse oblige*. This helps distinguish the managerial creed set out in *The American Business Creed* from other thinkers who held superficially similar views. The economist John Kenneth Galbraith, for instance, also believed that corporations were no longer being run solely to benefit shareholders, but in his 1952 work *American Capitalism* he attributed the change to the ability of unions and the federal government to act as a "countervailing power" to corporations.[377]

Abundant evidence shows that managerialism continued as the dominant ideology among business leaders through the 1950s and much of the 1960s. In 1951, *Fortune* magazine announced this in a special issue called "USA: The Permanent Revolution." It featured a quotation from Frank Abrams, chairman of Standard Oil, who described his role as to "conduct the affairs of the enterprise in such a way as to maintain *an equitable and working balance* among the claims of the various directly interested groups—stockholders, employees, customers, and the public at large."[378]

This view was also what was taught at Harvard and other business schools, where students learned that managers were now statesmen with an "obligation not to represent the interests of either owners or workers—much less of themselves—but to see that the corporation contributed to the general welfare."[379] So widespread was this view that one acerbic 1958 article in the *Harvard Business Review* complained that it was no longer "fashionable for the corporation to take gleeful pride in making money. What *is* fashionable is for the corporation to show that it is a great innovator; more specifically, a great public benefactor; and, very particularly, that it exists 'to serve the public'."[380] Looking back in 1970, one historian would state that "[r]ecognition of the social dimensions and responsibilities of [corporations] ... appeared, in every respect, a central feature of the evolution of modern business institutions and thought."[381]

It is tempting to conclude that, at mid-century, managerialist views had the upper hand everywhere. That would be wrong, however, because an older view of corporate managers' responsibilities still held sway in at least one important area: the law.

The Law

The question of whom managers should serve was recast in corporation law as the question of whom directors owed legally enforceable duties towards, and in the 20th-century American law provided a clear and consistent answer: shareholders. A century before, the answer might have been more complicated. In the antebellum United States (before, say, the 1830s), corporations were typically chartered by state legislatures, with each incorporation usually requiring a special act of the legislature.[382] Corporations were not chartered for general purposes, but rather for a specific purpose or purposes spelled out in the charter itself, and those purposes had a public aspect, most often to provide some piece of economic infrastructure such as a bridge or bank.[383]

In that sense, early corporations were intended to serve groups beyond shareholders, even though their investors surely sought profits.[384] In Jacksonian America, this system, however, was seen as creating monopolies and inviting corruption, and as the century progressed incorporation increasingly became available to all through general incorporation, with the public-purpose requirement being cast aside.[385] Corporate purpose as we understand it today—whether a corporation should be run for shareholders alone or to benefit other constituencies—was not an issue, because the corporation at that time almost always had managers who represented large shareholders and would act in those shareholders' interests. There was simply no way for managers to diverge from shareholder interests. The law did channel this impulse a bit; it was clear, for example, that controllers' duty of loyalty bound them to govern the corporation for the benefit of all shareholders, and not to favor controlling shareholders or appropriate corporate resources for themselves.[386]

Modern debates over which constituency a corporation's managers should serve—over "corporate purpose"—became possible only with the appearance of the giant corporation with dispersed shareholders and controlling and relatively autonomous managers charted by Berle and Means.[387] These were the preconditions for any reconceptualization of managers' roles. By the time these developments occurred, however, the law's requirement that corporations serve shareholders was already well established. The famous 1919 case that would become a touchstone for debates over corporate purpose and managers' duties was *Dodge v Ford Motor Co.*, which squarely stated that "[a] business corporation is organized and carried on primarily for the profit of its stockholders."[388]

In itself, *Dodge* merely reiterated the rules developed in the previous century to resolve disputes at closely held corporations. Ford Motor Co. was certainly a giant corporation, but it also had only a handful of shareholders,[389] and plausibly the case should be understood as one trying to prevent oppression of minority shareholders.[390] That said, the case and its holding was seen as merely restating a general assumption about the law of all corporations. It was the facts of *Dodge* that were novel—Henry Ford stubbornly insisting he would run Ford for the benefit of groups other than shareholders—not the legal assumptions underlying it.

Commentators at the time did not see *Dodge* as groundbreaking; when the case was included in corporation-law treatises and hornbooks issued soon after, it was not highlighted as announcing a new legal rule but simply accepted as a statement of well-known principles, and it is not difficult to find other cases from the time which relied on the assumption that corporations were run for shareholders.[391] A 1909 New York high-court case, for instance, barred corporations from practicing law by stating as an unsupported fact that corporations had "no guide except the sordid purpose to earn money for the stockholders."[392]

When Merrick Dodd argued in 1932 that the law should treat corporate managers as trustees not for shareholders but for the corporation as an institution, such a step would enable them to spend corporate money as though they were a person with a sense of "social responsibility." It was thus clear that Dodd, one of the leading corporate-law scholars in the nation, was arguing for a change in existing corporation law.

Nor did presumptions about what the law required of managers change much in the 1940s and 1950s, the heydays of managerialist thought. Legal scholars, to be sure, sometimes called for corporate management to be given even greater discretion to direct corporate assets as they saw fit, or for a change in corporate structure; there was, for instance, a brief movement in the 1950s when some academic commentators urged corporations to be treated as though they were governments by imposing requirements drawn from the US Constitution on them, but nothing came of it.[393]

Some areas of law also shifted in small ways to provide stronger shielding for managers' decisions; rule changes that discouraged derivative suits can be seen, in one light, as empowering managers (but also as discouraging suits aiming merely for a quick settlement), and expansion of the business judgment rule had a similar result.[394] Lest too much weight be put on these examples, it should be noted there were also many who argued for change in the other direction, advocating for increased shareholder voice in corporate affairs via "shareholder democracy" at US corporations.[395]

There is one area where managerial ideas did appear to have some impact on the law: corporate charitable giving. Since at least the late 19th century, corporations had been allowed to make charitable donations, but only if a benefit inured directly to the corporation.[396] In 1953, however, in *A. P. Smith Manufacturing Co. v Barlow*, the New Jersey Supreme Court was asked to decide whether a manufacturer's gift of $1,500 to Princeton University, a gift which promised no immediate benefit to the firm, was beyond the directors' powers.[397]

The suit may have been collusive, designed to give a court the opportunity to bless wide-ranging charitable donations, which is exactly what followed.[398] A. P. Smith Manufacturing offered some defense of its donations as ultimately benefiting the company by, for instance, earning it "good will in the community" and creating a "favorable environment for their business operations," but the court passed quickly over these justifications.[399]

Instead, it looked to the new role it believed businessmen were being called upon to play, and familiar managerial themes appeared. The opinion quoted from testimony offered by the chair of Standard Oil of New Jersey, who stated that "corporations are expected to acknowledge their public responsibilities in support of the essential elements of our free enterprise system," and from the former chair of U.S. Steel, who claimed, in a passage acknowledging a corporation's duties to multiple groups, that a corporation that did not support private, independent universities would not be "properly protecting the long-range interest of its stockholders, its employees, and its customers."[400]

The decision also cited Dodd's "For Whom Are Corporate Managers Trustees" and *The Modern Corporation and Private Property* to conclude that changed conditions required new legal approaches. In earlier times, the opinion stated, corporations were relatively small and prohibitions on charitable donations "did not significantly interfere with the public interest." In the 20th century, however, "[c]ontrol of economic wealth has passed from individual entrepreneurs to dominating corporations," requiring a different approach to a corporation's obligations.[401] In ringing words, it upheld the donation, announcing that "modern conditions require that corporations acknowledge and discharge social as well as private responsibilities as members of the communities within which they operate."[402]

Yet, for all the attention *A. P. Smith* received, its consequences were less than they appeared. What the case actually permitted was fairly small and "reasonable" donations to worthy causes, limited to 1% of surplus unless authorized by a shareholder vote.[403] Even more important, the case's soaring rhetoric did not result in any reorientation of corporation law away from its traditional attachment to shareholder benefit. In a 1959 symposium on the "Corporation in Modern Society," dominated by speakers enthusiastic for the new, managerialist view of the corporation, it was left to Eugene Rostow, Dean of the Yale Law School, to attack the "emerging ethos" that:

> corporate property [is] really that of the directors and management, to dispose of, as many suggest, in accordance with their own standards of business foresight, social statesmanship, and general good citizenship [and remind attendees that] law books have always said that the board of directors owes a single-minded duty of unswerving loyalty to the Stockholders.[404]

John L. Weinberg's Thesis

Having sketched out the main currents of managerial and legal thought about the corporation at mid-century, we can now turn back to John Weinberg's thesis. Seeing it against its historical background, we can more clearly grasp its intellectual roots, the contradictory views it sometimes appears to express, and the ways John sought to resolve them.

John's immersion in the main currents of managerial thought is obvious. The thesis directly cites a relatively small number of sources (though more are listed in the bibliography), and only a handful of those more than once. One of the top three most cited sources, however, along with two focusing on director function and compensation,[405] is TNEC's "Bureaucracy and Trusteeship in Large Corporations." The Berle–Dodd debate makes an appearance, as does Owen Young, quoted about management's duty to "administer wisely and fairly for all concerned."[406] (*The Modern Corporation and Private Property*, interestingly, appears only in the bibliography.)

Were the authors of *The American Business Creed* to evaluate the thesis, they would have little trouble placing John in the "managerial" current of business thought. John tells his readers early on that, while "[t]o make a profit is basic," that is not the extent of directors' roles; although "selected by the stockholders of the corporation, [the directors'] task is to manage the business in the interests of the investors, employees, customers, and consumers of the company's products or services and in accordance with public policy as expressed in the laws of the land."[407]

In explaining why this has become the task of directors, John relies on the evolutionary account of modern American business that appears in Dodd, is more fully set out in Berle and Means, and, according to *The American Business Creed*, was a routine feature of corporate pronouncements at the time the thesis was written. In the 19th century, John tells us, the ownership structure of firms dictated that they were run to benefit shareholders. Large corporations had a "cognizant ownership group" that named managers to "obtain maximum profits."[408]

The changing nature of ownership in the 20th century, however, sidelined shareholders, turning a shareholder into a mere "investor" making a "loan of funds."[409] As shareholders lost power over it, the corporation changed, as did the social expectations placed on it. "[T]he social conception of the corporation has gone beyond the mere protection of stockholder interests," he writes, and there has developed "social pressure demanding that the power be used for the benefit of all concerned."[410]

To this somewhat abstract explanation, that "social pressure" changed the nature of corporate leadership, John adds a more immediate driver of corporate change: the Cold War, which put the survival of the entire free-enterprise system at risk. This is announced in the thesis's opening paragraph, which warns readers that "American industry is today … facing the most critical period in all its history" and that "[t]he system of free enterprise is under severe attack" by "the force of totalitarian principles of economics."[411] Five years before the New Jersey Supreme Court would hand down *A. P. Smith*, John argues that questions of corporate governance have become entangled with the very survival of American capitalism in its struggle with communism.

In this way, John links his topic—the role of corporate directors—with the great issue of the age. He drives it home with a near-syllogism: "In our system of democratic capitalism, the business corporation holds a dominating position. In the performance of these business corporations, the board of directors assumes an especially significant role."[412] The point is made clear when he writes that "the only way boards of directors can best meet the needs of the American people, most nearly supply their wants, maintain profits, handle problems of unemployment, and face the Russian challenge, is through outstanding leadership."[413] While much of the thesis addresses questions of board governance, such as compensation of directors and board size, issues important but surely not existential, John is clear that these are vital because of the role the board is now called upon to play in a struggle for national survival.

Yet John was well aware of a major stumbling block facing his managerial view of corporate purpose, which is that it was at odds with present-day law. (Tellingly, one of the two interviews he conducted for the thesis was with a partner at a major New York law firm.)[414] The new "broad concept" of corporate responsibility put forward in his thesis, he writes, is "scarcely recognized by the courts who officially still hold the board of directors to the narrow path of securing maximum profits for the stockholders."[415] Later in the thesis, he returns to this issue, noting that "the present legal view limits [directors'] fiduciary duty to promoting the welfare of the body of stockholders,"[416] which leads him to complain about "the sluggish response of both statutory and common law to changed economic conditions and … liberal social philosophies."[417]

Again drawing on his predecessors, however, John argues this conflict will be resolved as the law changes to accommodate the new role thrust on management. Writing about the idea that directors are trustees, he first notes the traditional view, which is that whatever trusteeship directors have should involve furthering "the stockholders' interests by increasing the wealth of the corporation."[418] Alongside this, though, he finds:

> "[A] new concept emerges, conflicting in many ways with the existing legal theory, which broadens the scope of the problem to envelop the entire system of democratic capitalism. The accepted legal concept of the corporation states that the sole purpose of its existence is to provide profits for the owners. Recently, however, public opinion, which ultimately makes law, is making substantial strides in the direction of a view that the business corporation exists as an economic institution, which has a social service to perform as well as a profit-making function."[419]

In response, "[t]he courts sooner or later must recognize the interests of the general public, as well as those of the stockholders. This doctrine is gaining wider acceptance in the business community; the courts must evolve legal dogma to match it."[420] The exact nature of this new legal dogma he leaves unspecified, and he even sounds a rare note of caution that could have been borrowed directly from A. A. Berle's 1932 retort to Merrick Dodd: "We cannot abandon emphasis on the view that business corporations exist for the sole purpose of making profits for their stockholders until such time as we are prepared to offer a clear, reasonable, and enforceable scheme of responsibilities to somebody else."[421]

Conclusion

John Weinberg's 1948 thesis is not only a practical guide for corporate directors but a remarkable synthesis of the competing intellectual currents that defined mid-century American capitalism. Writing in the heyday of managerialist thought, Weinberg argued that corporate directors, in a properly organized board, could balance the interests of shareholders and other stakeholders while serving as a bulwark of democratic capitalism in its Cold War struggle. His particular contribution is his close focus on the board of directors, and the connections he draws between that body and the major events of the age. Yet the thesis also reveals the fundamental tension at managerialism's heart: the gap between aspirational corporate statesmanship and existing legal constraints that Weinberg acknowledged but could not resolve.

III. Craft: Values, Integrity, and the National Interest

Chapter 7

The Enduring Influence of the Weinbergs' Thinking
Mary K. Bush

After reading John's Princeton thesis—*Status and Functions of Corporate Directors*—along with his father's writings and speeches, an old saying resonates: "The more things change, the more they remain the same." Sidney wrote as far back as 1933. His insights into how boards should function and how they should conduct themselves, for the most part, hold true today—almost a century later. No doubt, John learned at the knee of his wise, seemingly prescient father. His thesis, quite solid in my view, reveals the excellent tutelage from his father, whether that was direct teaching or indirect—through his exposure to his father's business world.

From the practical perspective of boardroom life, the Weinbergs' thinking and counsel continue to shape the governance activities of boards today. The practices, introduced or strengthened because of their suggestions on how boards should operate, clearly influence how boards in this era carry out their responsibilities.

This is particularly true for those boards that deserve high marks for governance and for diligently carrying out their duties on behalf of the company's owners/shareholders—both large institutional investors and individual investors. Another important point both Weinbergs emphasize: governance by boards of directors is a critical component of our capitalist free-market system.

The Informed Director and the Duty of Care

Both Weinbergs devote considerable attention to the responsibility of being *informed* about the business itself and about how it is managed by the CEO and other senior management.

That responsibility is one of the most fundamentally important aspects of governing well and protecting shareholder interests. Being duly informed is also intricately intertwined with the duty of care, which is regularly cited as the gold standard for directors' commitment to their duties and responsibilities.[422] Legal cases are sometimes won or lost based on an assessment of whether directors lived up to their duty of care.

Back in 1933, Sidney saw good reason to set forth guidelines on how directors should remain informed about a company's business and management's performance. Two key events prompted him to put pen to paper and lay out 11 guiding principles to help ensure that board members would be well informed about the operations, decisions, and performance of the company.

One of those events was the passing of the federal securities laws, which imposed considerable new duties and liabilities upon directors in connection with issuing new securities. The quality of information provided to the public—and especially to prospective buyers of those securities—is of utmost importance when individuals and institutions are analyzing and evaluating the investment opportunity. That same year, a New York court allowed a case to proceed against directors of International Match, part of the Swedish Match empire, which had collapsed because of presumed fraudulent conduct by its leader, Ivar Kreuger.[423]

In deciding to allow the case against directors to go forward, the court explained:

> The law of this state is that to avoid liability for misfeasance or non-feasance, directors are bound to exercise the same degree of care in their office that men of common prudence generally show in their own affairs.[424]

Likening the care that directors should exercise in overseeing the affairs of a company to the care and prudence that one would exercise in scrutinizing one's own affairs was a practical and effective way of bringing home the point about directors' duty of care. After all, any reasonable person would gather as much data, information, and analysis as they could when managing their own affairs—particularly when it concerned their financial well-being and economic future. Therefore, the same diligence should apply to the affairs of a company where one is entrusted with the stewardship of other people's interests.

This duty of care is as fundamental to governance today as it was in 1933, when Weinberg wrote. It would be outlandish to argue that directors can fulfill their duty of care without being appropriately informed about how management is conducting the company's affairs.

Directors' responsibility to be informed relies heavily on management's cooperation in providing relevant reports, analysis, and other information that educate directors on the conduct and performance of the business, as well as the markets and competition. It is incumbent on the management team to present this information to directors in a manner that facilitates directors' education about the business and the challenges or policy matters that management wishes to address.

Sending thick tomes with hundreds of pages can be counterproductive. Briefing material must provide transparency by bringing clarity to important issues, problems, and challenges—and proposed solutions.

This is worth emphasizing because I—and many of my fellow directors—have been in situations where the briefing materials were of such volume that deciphering the critical points was a real challenge. In one case, regulatory criticism was obfuscated by excessively voluminous reporting on regulatory findings.

Transparency with the board includes informing the board of regulatory challenges or adversarial matters promptly and clearly. As the distinguished CEO of a company where I was a director imbedded in the culture of his company: "Bad news must travel fast." That includes to the board.

Upon occasion, directors have to wonder whether the obstruction of critical facts were deliberately obfuscated by voluminous materials to keep the board in the dark or to assure inattention to the issue. One would hope that this is never the case. But why raise such a question in a director's mind when information transparency—to help enable joint decisions by the board and the management team—is crucial to the success of the business?

When management is upfront about issues that matter, board members can focus on getting clarity around the facts, weighing options, and working with management to decide the best course of action. When it is necessary to provide huge quantities of information, an executive summary is essential.

The Weinbergs focused a good deal of attention on the importance of directors being well informed about the company, its business, markets, and competitors. They were right then and the point remains valid today. This responsibility of directors is of utmost importance. It is a shared responsibility—for the management team to bring information forward to the board, and for directors to question and dig deeply to be sure that they have a good grasp of the business.

It is also useful for directors to get to know and have time with colleagues who are not part of the executive team or of top management. One valuable practice is for the executive team to select colleagues from various parts of the business to provide briefings to the board apart from the executive team. Benefits abound as board members dig deeper into the business and get to know prospective successors to top management. Hearing a different perspective, whether or not it constitutes a different point of view, can also be instructive.

Some CEOs are more comfortable than others regarding such private briefing sessions for the board. Many directors find them to be quite useful. Non-executive staff who do not regularly present to the board also seem to appreciate the opportunity.

When the business is flourishing and things are calm, smart companies take advantage of that to provide directors with a deeper understanding of the business and its markets. In contrast, when a major challenge or crisis occurs, there isn't much time for learning. One needs to already have a good knowledge of the business. Being well informed lays the foundation for directors to be most able to live up to their duty of care—both in good times and in times of challenge.

A seasoned director once wisely observed, *"Being a corporate director is like being an airline pilot—hours of boredom and moments of terror."* Others might replace boredom with tedium or calm, but the phrase "moments of terror" is spot-on. Those moments make it crystal clear that doing the homework to gain deep knowledge of the company is vital.

Justice Black's opinion implied that directors were in a position to "manage" the affairs of the corporation. The Weinbergs, rightly, held a different view. They knew that there was a fine line between management and oversight. To help directors find that line and discharge their duty of care, it remains useful today for directors to return to Sidney's enduring 11 principles of boardroom service.

Sidney's 11 Principles, Selected Comments

Let's look at some of the 11 principles Sidney first stated in 1933, plus one he added in 1949.

Sidney calls for regular meetings to be held monthly at a fixed time and place. That has evolved, of course, to 4–6 times per year. Most boards can carry out their fiduciary and oversight responsibilities with this meeting cadence. CEO update letters between meetings are a good supplement. Moreover, CEO calls with individual board members are an effective way of building relationships and getting input and advice prior to a decision-making meeting. After all, board deliberations are a team sport.

During the 2008 financial crisis, at one of my boards, we instituted monthly board update calls. In a time of crisis or severe challenge to the business, such a practice is invaluable in bringing to bear the thinking and advice of all board members in real time.

Agenda and Minutes

Sidney calls for directors to receive the *agenda* in advance and to receive a copy of the minutes directly after the meeting. Because management is closest to the day-to-day business, the CEO's recommendations for the agenda are essential. Part of the value-add of board members is that they bring a different perspective. Therefore, an independent chair or lead director, on behalf of the board, necessarily contributes to agenda-setting on well-run boards. This may well be more the case nowadays as independent board chairs and lead directors have become more the norm than they were in Sidney's time.

As for the minutes, since they are the official record of the meeting, Sidney was right to advise that they be sent to the directors directly after the meeting. They can be critical in legal proceedings, so all directors should bear in mind the need to read them for accuracy and to ensure that they appropriately reflect diligence and due care and, let's not forget, who was present at the meeting.

A personal anecdote may be valuable. During a deposition, it came to light that opposing counsel believed I had not been present at a meeting of a special committee formed to advise and act on behalf of the board. We had sued a major competitor for restraint-of-trade practices. When I reviewed the minutes of that meeting, I had overlooked that I was not listed as in attendance. Luckily, this worked in my favor and in the company's favor. It could have been just the opposite.

Because opposing counsel believed that I was not present at that critical meeting, they appeared flustered and asked for a temporary adjournment of the deposition. Presumably, they were not thoroughly prepared to question me because the minutes did not show my attendance. My recollections of the meeting, our discussion, and our decision were crystal clear in my mind because that decision was a pivotal one.

We were successful in that case. But not being listed as in attendance could have hurt our case. Therefore, the first thing I check on all minutes is the attendance list.

Executive Committees

Sidney Weinberg developed the 11 principles largely because of the judge's opinion that directors had surrendered their powers to the executive committee controlled by Kreuger, an insider.

Regarding executive committees overall, the existence of executive committees declined steadily through the 1980s and 1990s. By 2014, only 34% of S&P 500 companies maintained an executive committee.[425] This should not be surprising, given that director performance as fiduciaries and overseers of management has come increasingly under the spotlight.

All directors have the same fiduciary responsibility. All are equally answerable to shareholders for decisions and actions taken by the board, and ultimately for the company's performance. Hence, direct participation in deliberations and in learning the relevant facts is best for the company and for directors in exercising the duty of care. The technology of virtual meetings has, of course, made all-director inclusion easier if there are emergency situations where gathering the board in person might have been impractical in earlier times.

In cases where an executive committee does exist, it can play a crucial role if there is an emergency or crisis situation. Should the committee deliberate or take action, it's vital that the rest of the board be made privy to the committee's decisions with due and deliberate speed. Of course, time permitting, consulting with the other board members prior to taking action is ideal. In any event, it is highly desirable to have strong, independent, and independent-thinking directors on the executive committee.

Privately held companies are different, and the considerations for maintaining an executive committee at a private company differ as well. For privately held companies, including private-equity portfolio companies, the executive committee plays a consequential role on an ongoing basis.

Investors in private companies require frequent, detailed financial reviews. After all, they invested with the goal of specific financial targets being met over specified time periods. With the executive committee keeping a sharp eye on progress, private investors are able to regularly assess their investment thesis and prompt operational or strategic shifts if needed.

Audit Committees

Sidney's advice that the audit committee be composed of independent directors only, and that all directors receive the outside auditors' reports, has become standard practice and/or required. In spite of this, things happen!

When there are suspected acts of malfeasance, the full board needs to be informed immediately, even if the audit committee is still gathering facts. All board members have responsibility and potential liability. Moreover, in such crisis situations, one should tap the thinking and input of the board as a team to arrive at the best response.

Trust and Integrity

Both Weinbergs rightfully opine that the governance work of directors is critical to the health and preservation of our capitalist system. Once again, they are spot-on. Laws, contracts, and governance processes are fundamental to the smooth working of the system. So is trust.

People tend to trust those whom they believe are people of integrity. Nowhere is that more important than on a public company board. Professional skills, accumulated experience, and the wisdom that develops over time are all important in selecting directors. However, the number one criterion, as both John and Sydney stressed, is integrity. If I can trust my fellow board members to always seek to do the right and honorable thing because of their own personal integrity, my confidence level—about serving on the board and about deliberating tough or controversial matters—rises exponentially.

Another personal anecdote illustrates. A major customer was short-changed financially because of mistakes made by the company. When the lawyers briefed the board about its obligations, they advised that under the law and SEC requirements, the company was not obliged to reimburse the customer. But while I deferred to the lawyers about what the government's laws required, I countered that we must consider moral law. That meant we were indeed obliged to: (1) inform our customers that they had suffered financial harm, and (2) reimburse them. Most of the directors eventually agreed. It's great when you don't have to fight to do the right thing.

Shareholders, Stakeholders, and Responsible Capitalism

A recurring theme of the work of both John and Sidney concerns the public interest and responsible capitalism.

John points out that public opinion, influenced by the spread of ownership of corporations to multiple small shareholders, was becoming a more prominent voice in the 1940s.[426] He goes as far as to say that "the business corporation exists as an economic institution, which has a social service to perform as well as a profit-making function."[427]

Sidney put it this way: "[T]he director must take the long view in decisions and bear in mind the public interest. He must have a social sense and must be continually aware of the human problems involved in decisions of the board."[428]

Debates today about shareholders, stakeholders, and social responsibility harken back to the 1930s and 1940s, when the Weinbergs were writing. The call today for businesses to conduct their affairs in socially responsible ways comes from many quarters, including large institutional shareholders, individual shareholders, and others.

Companies must engage in activities and make decisions that are beneficial to shareholders over the long term. Good relationships with employees, customers, and communities can be value-adding to shareholders. Companies that view social involvement through a strategic lens are more likely to discern the value that socially responsible business and responsible capitalism can bring to the company. The Delaware courts rightly hold that directors may consider the interests of non-shareholders if those interests are rationally related to stockholder interests.

In recent years, several large institutional shareholders have given voice to expectations for companies in which they invest to act in socially responsible ways. Yet, of course, they also seek an attractive return on the capital they have invested. It is not always easy to quantify the benefits of socially responsible business engagement; it is much easier to quantify the financial results of operations.

Nonetheless, a few observations. Treating customers like what they are: the lifeline to a company's thriving and longevity; treating employees, no matter their status, like true partners in making the company successful; and protecting the health of communities (which likely include both employees and customers) by preserving environmental health are all important aspects of responsible capitalism. This pays off for the company and its shareholders over the long term and pays off for stakeholders as well.

Marriott International is a stellar example. It was an honor to serve on the board of this company for about a dozen years. When the company was founded by J. Willard and Alice Marriott as an A&W root-beer stand in 1927, they believed that if they took care of their employees, the employees would take care of the customers. That belief formed the foundation of the Marriott culture, which has carried through to this day.

That culture was carried on by Bill Marriott, who succeeded his father as chairman and CEO and built Marriott into the largest—and one of the most successful and admired—hospitality companies in the world. Taking care of employees and customers, doing good things in the communities in which it operates, and recognizing that value should be assessed over the long term have been undeniable contributors to Marriott's lasting success.

For many years, a board committee called the Committee for Excellence oversaw these matters on behalf of the board. The name of the committee alone provides a strong signal about the importance of these issues to Marriott. With their advice on responsible capitalism, John and Sidney, once again, exhibited wisdom that remains applicable to our business environment today.

Some Concluding Thoughts in the Weinberg Tradition

- To properly exercise the duty of care, know well the company, its business, markets, and competition. Know well the management team. Know well your fellow board members.
- Take advantage of every opportunity to get to know colleagues who report to the executive team—those in the midst of day-to-day operations. One becomes better informed about the company and better informed for succession reviews.
- The duty of care requires continuous learning and thoroughly doing one's homework.
- If special committees or executive committees are utilized, be sure that their reports to the board are timely and thorough enough to keep all board members well informed.
- For public company boards that utilize executive committees, be sure that independent directors are well represented.
- Be sure that audit committees (and risk committees) relay information to the full board as soon as possible if a problem is brewing.
- Recognize that shareholder value and social responsibility are not necessarily at odds. They may well go hand-in-hand in preserving and growing shareholder value.
- Integrity as a criterion for board membership is at the top of the list.
- Always bear in mind that the diligence of the board in carrying out its responsibilities is fundamental to the health of our free-market, capitalist economy.

Chapter 8

Reflections on the Directors' Role: Integrity, Diligence, Profit

Simon M. Lorne

The work of a corporate director is often obscured by abstraction. Governance frameworks, legal standards, and procedural requirements fill handbooks and boardroom packets. Yet the soul of the directorship lies in judgment, character, and conscience. These qualities are tested not by hypotheticals but by the persistent, often unglamorous demands of oversight and stewardship.

This chapter offers a set of reflections—not rules—on the essential attributes of corporate directors. They are drawn from three moments in my professional life involving three individuals I have known and admired: Henry Schaeffer, Charlie Munger, and Ken Langone. Each, in his own way, illustrated a pillar of sound directorship: moral integrity, intellectual diligence, and financial purpose.

In writing these reflections, I am conscious of the setting: this volume commemorates the vision of John L. Weinberg, a man who helped shape the modern boardroom and whose 1948 thesis, prescient and plainspoken, remains among the best articulations of the director's duty. Weinberg, like the figures in the stories that follow, believed that directors must do more than occupy a seat—they must serve with fidelity, intelligence, and drive. I have tried to live by those standards and share these stories in the hope that they will affirm what we know to be true, even if it is no longer fashionable to say: the director's job is to do right, to know enough to act wisely, and to help the enterprise succeed.

That sounds simple enough. But in today's boardroom, simplicity is often elusive. Directors operate in an environment of regulation, litigation, stakeholder pressure, and mounting public scrutiny. The result, too often, is that procedural fidelity substitutes for substantive judgment. Directors are urged to follow frameworks rather than think freely; to check boxes rather than ask questions; to adhere to protocols rather than take principled stands. Against that tide, the Weinberg model stands firm.

Three Iconic Directors Worth Remembering—and John's Thesis

Henry Schaeffer

In the 1970s, as a young lawyer, I had the good fortune to fall into the role of outside counsel to a law-firm client that had no inside legal function. Consequently, I was something of a jack-of-all-trades, at least as to issues that had no need for specialized expertise that was beyond me. For example, it was I who attended all board meetings and responded to inquiries for on-the-spot legal advice.

Although small, the company had a quite complex capital structure, with exchange-listed common stock, classes of publicly traded convertible preferred stock, and publicly traded debt. Among other things, the company was in arrears in the payment of cumulative dividends on the preferred, as a result of which (as is reasonably common in such circumstances) holders of the preferred had the right to elect a majority of the directors.

At one point, a class of the company's publicly held debt was maturing, and the company's CFO noted that, for a number of the debt holders, interest payments had regularly been returned as "undeliverable." With the principal coming due, the CFO asked me if I could find a way to avoid having those funds escheat to the various states that could lay claim to them as "unclaimed property" under the relevant escheat laws. Surely, he thought, the company could make better use of those funds than the states might. After some research, I had a few ideas, none of which were certain of success, and sent the CFO a memorandum to that effect. He, in turn, circulated the memorandum to the board, and asked me to make a presentation at the next board meeting.

The board meeting came, and I made my presentation, together with my conclusions (and doubts) as to efficacy. The board was in general agreement that we should exert reasonable efforts to avoid escheat until Henry Schaeffer, one of the independent directors, said simply, but firmly, "We owe the money. We should pay it. What happens to our payment should be left up to the law." Perhaps sheepishly, the rest of the board concurred. Payments due on maturity were made, a significant part of them escheating to various states.

Lesson: Express a moral point of view when necessary.

Charlie Munger

I was also a long-time partner in the law firm that Charlie Munger and a number of his friends started in Los Angeles in 1962, now known as Munger, Tolles & Olson. I met Charlie when interviewing with the firm as a law student, and was the last lawyer in the firm to have done so. I joined the firm and eventually became a member of a rump group with Charlie and a half dozen others in the financial community, along with one other lawyer in the firm, who met for breakfast every morning at 7:30 in downtown Los Angeles. For two decades, I had the privilege of listening to Warren Buffett's partner—perhaps "the Oracle of the Oracle of Omaha"—and came to know him well.

Later in my career, I was the head of the internal audit department at Salomon Brothers, a well-known trading and investment banking firm on a par with Goldman Sachs; since 1999 it has been a part of Citigroup. Before the Citigroup acquisition, Berkshire Hathaway was Salomon's largest shareholder, and Warren Buffett and Charlie were both on its board. I was among the senior executives who attended board meetings to respond to questions that might come up. I remember well one board meeting. The day before the meeting, the CFO had mentioned to me that he was nervous about one "dicey" transaction. He'd included a brief discussion of it in the board materials—on page 138 or so—but hoped there wouldn't be any questions about it.

On the day of the meeting, Charlie's plane into New York from Los Angeles was delayed, so he arrived from the airport just about the time the board meeting started. As he sat down, Charlie said, "Before we get started, can we talk about this transaction on page 138 of the board materials?"

Lesson: Do the necessary homework and pay attention to detail.

Ken Langone

As a sideline, for some 18 years I served as co-director of Stanford Law School's "Directors' College." The program was started by Joe Grundfest, a Stanford Law professor and former SEC commissioner. Joe had recognized early that we were burdening corporate directors with increasing responsibility and associated liability, but there was little effort to educate directors as to what was expected of them. In subsequent years, with the assistance of events like the Enron, WorldCom, and similar scandals of the early 2000s, coupled with the financial crisis of 2007–2008, such programs have proliferated, although the Stanford program is still seen by many as the "gold standard."

One year at Stanford, our closing keynote address was given by Ken Langone, a billionaire financier and businessman best known for organizing the initial financing for The Home Depot and being a major supporter of New York University's medical school, which is named for him. Ken started his address by saying (more or less), "For the last couple of days, you've all been listening to a number of experts, mostly lawyers, talk about what you must do and must avoid doing as a corporate director. That's important, and you should heed their words." He then continued roughly as follows:

> But they haven't talked very much about the most important thing. That is, you should do everything in your power—and, of course, within the law—to make sure your companies make money. If you're earning good profits, most of the other things won't be too important. If you're not making money, their importance escalates disproportionately. Everything will be under a microscope, and faults will inevitably be found.

Lesson: Earn profits for your shareholders.

Integrity and Honesty—True "Independence"

For several years, "independence of directors" has been offered as a remedy for every corporate ill.[429] The problem is not in concept but in execution.

All of us, together with the Weinbergs, want directors to act as Henry Schaeffer did. (We may or may not agree with his conclusion as to accepting versus trying to circumvent escheat laws, though we have to applaud his willingness to stand up for a principle in which he believed—and, in the specific case, one that the assembled board accepted.)

As a society, we have decided to identify his stand as an indication of "independence," which is generally as good a word as any for the intangible qualities we want exhibited. But when we write it into law, and define the term, we fail to capture the essence of what we're looking for. Consider section 301 of the Sarbanes–Oxley Act, essentially mandating that corporate audit committees be comprised entirely of independent directors:

> In order to be considered to be independent … a member of an audit committee of an issuer may not, other than in his or her capacity as a member of the audit committee, the board of directors, or any other board committee—"(i) accept any consulting, advisory, or other compensatory fee from the issuer; or (ii) be an affiliated person of the issuer or any subsidiary thereof.

But do those limitations capture the qualities that we really seek? It seems unlikely. Consider three examples.

The Walt Disney Company

In the early 2000s, the Disney board included CEO Michael Eisner's personal lawyer, his architect, and the principal of the elementary school once attended by one of his children.[430] While those directorships were prior to the adoption of the Sarbanes–Oxley Act, each of them would appear to be "independent" as that term is defined in the statute. Statutorily defined independence does not eliminate cronies.

Charlie Munger

Warren Buffett's long-time partner and vice chairman at Berkshire Hathaway, Inc., was clearly *not* "independent" as defined in Sarbanes–Oxley or any similar authority. But anyone who knew him would attest to his true independence in the sense of the Henry Schaeffer model. Charlie would express his views, logically and forcefully, whenever the occasion might arise, regardless of the person or group with whom he was speaking. (Warren Buffett, for his part, would welcome any disagreement in the true spirit of their 60-year partnership.)

A Personal Instance

I spent 20 years as vice chairman and chief legal officer of a major hedge fund ("alternative investment firm," to use the polite formulation). In the first week after I joined, the CEO came into my office and declared, with some vehemence, "I'm really mad at Franklin [not the individual's real name]!"

Naturally, I asked, "What's the problem?"

He answered, "I hired him to manage risk. I like to do deals—it's in my nature. And last month he let me hire someone I never should have hired. He's supposed to fight me on things like that. If I pound the table until my hands bleed, OK, I win, but he has to fight me."

The CEO then left my office, and I knew he had explained what he expected of me. Was I independent as defined in various statutes? No. But an important part of my job was to do my best to be Henry Schaeffer or, even better, one of the Weinbergs.

By contrast, Leo Strine, then Delaware vice chancellor (and later chief justice), performed a much more nuanced consideration of "independence"—in the

Schaeffer sense—that was closer to the mark in his decision in *In re Oracle Corp. Derivative Litigation*.[431] That case involved the independence of a special litigation committee, whose independence was essential to the controlling nature of the committee's decision that certain litigation against some of Oracle's directors should be terminated.

While the vice chancellor's decision that the committee was not independent might have been erroneous (at least in this author's judgment), the nature of his inquiry—including close examination of the committee members' ties to Stanford University and the substantial contributions made and proposed to be made to Stanford from the defendants in the case—was a much more appropriate search for Schaeffer-like qualities than is possible in standard legal definitions.

Searching for Schaeffer qualities, the qualities embraced in an earlier time by Sidney Weinberg and then by John L. Weinberg, is a difficult task. Articulating those qualities in a statute is probably impossible. Nonetheless, their possession by a corporate director is essential, and it is only by close examination and thoughtful consideration that a board can ensure that the Schaeffer virtues are well represented within it. As Sidney quips, "[I]f the chief officers of the corporation do not want me to speak my mind, they should not have invited me to be a director."[432]

All that being said—and it is critically important—the relevance of collegiality among members of a board should not be underestimated. A board of directors ordinarily consists of some seven to 15 members, spending considerable—and often intense—time together discussing subjects of substantial importance to the company. That process will simply operate better if there is a high degree of mutual trust and respect among the members. It is good if they meet periodically, in twos and threes, away from the formal meetings of the board.

Indeed, a director's independent voice will be more easily exercised if she knows that level of trust and respect exists. Sidney shares this wisdom:

> I think it is a good idea for a president of a corporation, after the annual stockholders' meeting, to give a dinner for the directors and the top officers and to have at that dinner what might be called the "sub-cabinet" of officers. This gives a boost to the younger men's morale and an opportunity for the members of the board to become better acquainted with the men who, in addition to the top officers, are operating the company from day to day.[433]

By contrast, if there is not a degree of collegiality within the board, it will be that much harder for a director to express views contrary to those of management or of the board majority.

By the same token, it is incumbent on management to develop that sense of collegiality and its accompanying trust and respect. Sidney shared this further wisdom:

> If the chief executive officer bears in mind that the board is created to consult together rather than to contend with each other, he will go over new proposals with the directors individually beforehand, and in this way he may find that some modification of his original plan may be wisest and can be brought about without the embarrassment to the board which may occur if the modifications had to be made at a board meeting.[434]

Intellectual Diligence

Schaeffer independence is critically important, but it is not sufficient. Nothing, ever, replaces dedicated time and hard thinking, and companies are entitled to that from their directors. As Sidney puts it, "A conscientious director must work at it."[435]

Admittedly, it is not the level of work required by executives—a board that meets four to eight times annually, for only a day or two per meeting, cannot expect that. But with a reasonable allotment of time, diligently applied with intelligence, a director can satisfy her obligations to the company.

But for that expenditure of time and thought to be meaningful, the director must obviously have all necessary information. As Sidney trenchantly observed:

> The problem comes down to the question of the extent and quantity of information which a corporation ought to provide each director regularly and in a satisfactory manner in order to enable him to exercise the reasonable care of a prudent man in the discharge of his duties.[436]

Furthermore:

> *If* management gives a director the information he should have before decisions are made at directors' meetings, the director must then give conscientious work and take time to prepare for the meeting itself.[437]

Thus, in order to satisfy the obligations of her office, the director needs to be certain that she has unfettered access to reliable information on all matters of potential board importance. If the CEO is of the controlling sort, and all communications with the board are cleared by the CEO's office before going to directors, that is a significant warning sign.

Beyond that, the director should seek to establish and maintain relations with at least some corporate officers in control positions such that those individuals have easy access to her when and if important information needs to be shared. Sidney again: "The directors should spend time also in developing informal contacts with the executives of the company."[438]

It goes almost without saying that the single most important role of the board of directors is involuntarily replacing the CEO in those rare instances where it becomes necessary—followed closely, but much more easily, by the appointment of a successor CEO in the case of retirement or incapacity.[439] Recognizing that mandate, a question directors should ask themselves is whether the nature of the information flow is such that, if CEO replacement became an important topic for consideration, relevant information would be transmitted with relative ease. This may, in part, have been what Sidney was getting at when he wrote:

> The director should be given the opportunity to meet and talk with the younger, coming executives who are not on the board. Only in this way can he get the knowledge which is necessary in choosing top executives from within the organization and form a judgment as to the organization underneath the top management. The director should watch especially for younger men who have possibilities for development.[440]

Economic Purpose

As a practical matter, Ken Langone's view cannot be questioned. When a company is comfortably profitable, the path of its executives and directors is inevitably much, much smoother.

In recent years, however, some have called—with motives either altruistic (and more than a little naïve) or self-interested (and short-sighted)—for a different view of the purpose of the corporation.

Sidney clearly would have seen through the ruse. John, at the time he wrote his thesis—younger, with little actual experience, and more idealistic perhaps—might not have. (It is clear that the older John would not have succumbed.)

The discussion came to something of a head when, in 2019, the Business Roundtable issued a statement purporting to "redefine" the purpose of a corporation.[441] The statement, identifying other "stakeholders," in addition to shareholders, as the proper objects of a corporation's purpose reads, in pertinent part:

> While each of our individual companies [i.e., the signatories of the statement] serves its own corporate purpose, we share a fundamental commitment to all of our stakeholders. We commit to:
>
> - Delivering value to our customers. … [L]eading the way in meeting or exceeding customer expectations.
> - Investing in our employees. … [C]ompensating them fairly and providing important benefits … supporting them through training and education.
> - Dealing fairly and ethically with our suppliers. … [S]erving as good partners to the other companies, large and small, that help us meet our missions.
> - Supporting the communities in which we work. We … protect the environment by embracing sustainable practices across our businesses.
> - Generating long-term value for shareholders.
>
> Each of our stakeholders is essential. We commit to deliver value to all of them, for the future success of our companies, our communities and our country.

Each of the identified elements of so-called purpose is, of course, important. Except for the last, however, none of them qualifies as the purpose of the corporation. Beyond that, identifying them as the purpose can only serve to transfer power away from shareholders (who themselves may more fairly reflect the common interest) and toward incumbent management.

We should first instinctively view the Business Roundtable—"an association of more than 200 chief executive officers (CEOs) of America's leading companies"[442]—on a subject such as this with some skepticism. Nobody has ever suggested that competitors should be the voice of reason in considering competitive capitalism. As Adam Smith recognized early:

> As every individual, therefore, endeavours as much as he can both to employ his capital in the support of domestic industry, and so to direct that industry that its produce may be of the greatest value; every individual necessarily labours to render the annual revenue of the society as great as he can. *He generally, indeed, neither intends to promote the public interest,* nor knows how much he is promoting it. By preferring the support of domestic to that of foreign industry, *he intends only his own security*; and by directing that industry in such a manner as its produce may be of the greatest value, *he intends only his own gain*, and he is in this, as in many other cases, led by an invisible hand to promote an end which was no part of his intention.[443]

Beyond that, a statement such as that of the Business Roundtable is of little or no practical effect—perhaps contradictorily, both meaningless and unnecessary—except to the extent that it abrogates power to incumbent managements.

As to meaningless, there is no better authority, perhaps surprisingly, than Chairman Mao: "Political power grows out of the barrel of a gun."[444] Put more felicitously, identifying a "purpose" is of no value unless the beneficiaries of that purpose have the means to enforce it.

But in this context, the would-be stakeholders (other than shareholders) come to the battle without weapons. They have no vote in the election of directors. And they have no standing in litigation, except in those few instances where they might have been given standing to enforce a particular, presumably federal, statutory mandate.

It would, of course, be possible to remedy that defect, by providing other stakeholders with enforceable rights, or perhaps by allowing a federal agency to enforce the identified rights *in loco parentis*. But that would be an extensive and cumbersome process—and was emphatically *not* what the Business Roundtable intended. (Which is not to say that it won't be the ultimate result of what the Business Roundtable set in motion.)

Yet, if such legal rights, or an agency of some description, were established, how would we weigh the interests in deciding priorities? The Business Roundtable statement, were it in some fashion enforceable, would establish a variety of masters for the corporation. Have we not learned that one cannot serve two, much less multiple, masters?

But, of course, all is not lost for those other stakeholders, for here "unnecessary" comes into play. If the corporation is to serve its shareholders effectively, it *must* always consider the needs and goals of the other stakeholders. This, both Sidney and John fully recognized.

Toward the Weinberg Model

That is emphatically *not,* however, to say that constituencies other than shareholders should, or even may, be ignored. To the contrary—in the words of Sidney:

> In carrying out his functions, the director must take the long view in decisions and bear in mind the public interest. He must have a social sense and must be continually aware of the human problems involved in decisions of the board. Board decisions affect human beings.[445]

This notwithstanding, it is absolutely clear from reading Sidney's memorandum and speech that the very *purpose* of the corporation is not even a question to discuss. It is to enhance the long-term profitability of the corporation's shareholders. (In this context, it should be noted that John L. Weinberg revealed a more tentative mindset regarding this topic when, at age 23, he wrote his thesis.[446])

But the flaw in the modern conceit in some quarters that social benefit, broadly defined, should be the very purpose of the corporation suffers from more than unrealistic idealism. It promises actual harm to the corporate enterprise under some circumstances.

In today's environment, in which the law clearly recognizes that the purpose of the corporation is to enhance the long-term profitability of the enterprise for the benefit of its shareholders, liability of directors is exceedingly rare in fact.[447] That is because (after a degree of back-and-forth between the Delaware courts and the Delaware legislature), directors can be held liable only for (1) "ordinary" breaches of the duty of loyalty—in essence, acting in the face of material conflicts of interest without adequate disclosure and independent ratification or (2) such extreme breaches of the duty of care that they are tantamount to a breach of the fundamental duty of loyalty.[448]

Acceptance of some form of "stakeholder primacy"—giving the board authority to choose among constituencies which it might favor in any given decision—would free the board from virtually any responsibility at all. Every decision benefits some constituency; if directors are permitted to assert that they are paying allegiance to a constituency of their choice, they are effectively freed from any bounds. It's not constituency or stakeholder primacy; it's director primacy *über alles.* That should be a step too far for the law to go.

The various non-shareholder stakeholders are all essential to the growth and vitality of the enterprise. Even in closing a plant, if a small community is dependent on it, the corporation must, to the extent practicable, soften the blow. To do otherwise is to risk the reputation, and sooner or later the viability, of the corporation in other communities. The sole *purpose* of the corporation is properly to enhance the long-term profitability of the company. To achieve that goal, however, other constituencies must be treated with appropriate care and consideration. Indeed, for many companies, to achieve the proper purpose, "the customer must come first."

The stories above are not random. They illuminate a coherent view of corporate governance—one that John L. Weinberg lived, taught, and embodied. He believed in shareholder primacy not as dogma but as duty. He believed that the board is not a passive monitor but an active organ of the enterprise. He believed that directors must have knowledge, integrity, and focus.

In many ways, John anticipated the debates of our time. He knew the danger of boards becoming rubber stamps. He worried that too much emphasis on structure would erode substance. He believed in dialogue between board and management but insisted that directors must have backbone and judgment.

As those of us close to the world of Berkshire Hathaway know, this model is not just aspirational—it is operational. Berkshire's board, and those of companies influenced by its philosophy, reflect these principles. They are filled with directors who think like owners, who value permanence, who invest in understanding the business, and who are not distracted by ephemera.

John's original thesis remains striking in its clarity and relevance. He rejected the idea of dummy directors, derided the supine, and anticipated the call for professional, independent, but substantively engaged directors. His views are not frozen in time. They anticipate the reality that compliance is not enough and that directors must have skin in the game—intellectually, morally, and financially.

Conclusion: A Tradition Worth Keeping

The directorship is under stress. Today's boards face more regulation, scrutiny, and complexity than ever. There is temptation to retreat into process or to chase reputational trends. But the path forward is not novelty—it is fidelity.

We must preserve the tradition of the engaged, independent, responsible director. A director who, like Henry Schaeffer, can say what is right and mean it. A director who, like Charlie Munger, reads to the last page and asks the first question. A director who, like Ken Langone, never forgets that businesses are meant to succeed.

That is the director's job. That is the Weinberg model. It may not win headlines, but it will earn results—and respect. It is no coincidence that John L. Weinberg articulated this model before most of today's debates even began. His legacy remains not just relevant but necessary.

Chapter 9

Corporate Governance in the Shadow of Geopolitical Risk

Michael Montelongo

> "American industry is today, in many ways, facing the most critical period in all its history."
>
> —John L. Weinberg, *Status and Functions of Corporate Directors* (1948)

In 1948, John Weinberg, then a Princeton undergraduate, offered a prescient diagnosis of American capitalism in his senior thesis. His observation, made in the immediate aftermath of World War II, reflected a deep awareness of the interdependence between corporate leadership and national well-being. Eight decades later, his words resonate with renewed urgency. The challenges facing American industry today—ranging from geopolitical instability and technological disruption to climate risk and social fragmentation—suggest that John's call for a more responsible and nationally attuned capitalism remains not only relevant but imperative.

John argued that corporate boards bear a responsibility not merely to shareholders but to the broader public. "Upon boards of directors," he wrote, "to a certain extent, rests the responsibility for American industry and therefore the welfare of the whole country." This insight, grounded in the postwar context of industrial mobilization and national reconstruction, has enduring implications. As this chapter will argue, the evolving nature, frequency, and intensity of geopolitical risk and the increasing entanglement of economic and national security interests demand a reexamination of corporate governance through the lens of what might now be termed patriotic capitalism.

This chapter proceeds in four parts. First, it revisits John's thesis in its historical context, situating his arguments within the broader intellectual and institutional developments of mid-20th-century corporate governance. Second, it traces the evolution of board responsibilities over the subsequent decades, highlighting key inflection points in the relationship between business and the state. Third, it introduces the concept of patriotic capitalism as a contemporary framework for aligning corporate governance with national priorities. Finally, it offers practical recommendations for boards of directors, including the integration of geopolitical risk into governance structures, the cultivation of expertise in international affairs, and the importance of public–private collaboration in an era of strategic uncertainty.

By drawing on historical insight and contemporary analysis, this chapter aims to demonstrate that the future of corporate governance lies not in retreating from public responsibility but in embracing it as a strategic imperative. As John presciently noted, leadership "based not on the interest of capital or capitalism alone, but in the interest of the American people as a whole" is not merely idealistic—it is essential for long-term stability and prosperity.

A Student's Insight, a Lasting Perspective

John Weinberg's 1948 undergraduate thesis, *Status and Functions of Corporate Directors*, was written at a formative moment in American history—just after World War II, as the nation transitioned from wartime mobilization to peacetime prosperity. Though John was a student at the time, his reflections on corporate governance reveal a maturity of thought that merits attention, particularly in today's complex geopolitical environment.

John's central premise—that corporate boards bear responsibilities not only to shareholders but to the broader public—was not revolutionary, but it was unusually clear-eyed for its time. He wrote, for instance, that "upon boards of directors, to a certain extent, rests the responsibility for American industry and therefore the welfare of the whole country." This was not a sweeping claim of omnipotence but a sober recognition that corporate decisions—especially in large, strategically significant firms—can have national consequences.

Another passage worth revisiting is his assertion that "the decisions of [business leaders] are important today as never before." In 1948, this reflected the urgency of postwar reconstruction and the emerging Cold War. Today, it resonates in a different register: the interconnectedness and interdependencies of global markets, the fragility of supply chains, and the strategic importance of the technology and energy sectors all underscore the weight of boardroom decisions.

Perhaps most prescient is John's suggestion that directors should have "an understanding … in the whole field of world affairs and its potential influence upon American industry." At a time when globalization was still in its infancy, this was a forward-looking observation. In today's world—where geopolitical risk is structural, not episodic—it reads less like a recommendation and more like a necessity.

To be sure, John was not writing as a policymaker or seasoned executive, nor is this a sustainability credo as it is defined today. His thesis does not offer a blueprint for modern governance. But it does provide a useful lens through which to consider the evolving role of corporate boards. His emphasis on leadership that balances economic performance with public responsibility—particularly in the face of bad-actor threats—remains relevant, especially for multinational firms whose operations intersect with national security, international diplomacy, and global stability.

In this light, it is reasonable—not radical—to suggest that boards of major corporations should treat geopolitical awareness as part of their fiduciary and stewardship duties. This does not mean politicizing the boardroom or substituting business judgment with foreign policy. Rather, it means recognizing that in a world of strategic competition, economic interdependence, military threats, and regulatory complexity, good governance requires a broader field of vision.

John's thesis reminds us that the responsibilities of corporate leadership are not static. They evolve with the times—and the times are always changing.

History Did Not End After the First Cold War

After winning the Cold War in 1989, the West embraced the mistaken notion that it could dismiss traditional forms of great-power competition and balance-of-power diplomacy. That misguided consensus was based on two faulty assumptions: first, that the victory was absolute, ensuring America's unchallengeable supremacy for decades; and second, that the "rules-based" world order the United States was building would be both popular abroad and uncontroversial at home.[449]

That new world order also ushered in an extended era of globalization, complete with increasing economic and trade dependencies. Consequently, globalization provided significant advantages for corporate leaders, while pressing geopolitical concerns were dismissed as relics of the past.

But contrary to expectations, history did not end in 1989; rather, the decades-long illusion of a stable, globalized order was shattered by Russia's invasion of Ukraine in 2022.[450] Then, a series of geopolitical crises in Europe, the Middle

East, and East Asia brought a new and critical inflection point in geopolitics and the political economy.

Heretofore, there had been a tacit assumption that discrete flashpoints might disrupt business operations temporarily but would eventually subside. The reality today is that those flashpoints have evolved into long-term, systemic challenges that define the global business environment.

Contemporary crises are not temporary disruptions; they underscore fundamental failures of deterrence and mark a new geopolitical paradigm that businesses and governments must confront. At its core, today's geopolitical environment is driven not only by national security concerns but also by the quest for economic independence and technological leadership—forces that increasingly shape strategic competition among major powers. John's thesis goes further, suggesting a failure in the business community to recognize the importance of corporate governance in the larger context of the global threat from totalitarianism and attacks on the system of free enterprise.

Historically, military confrontation has been the primary concern when evaluating geopolitical risk. However, the concept has expanded. For example, the recent US administration's approach to tariffs as a tool for economic and diplomatic leverage demonstrates how economic policies can introduce new layers of uncertainty. Tariffs may be the current focus, but business, government, and civic leaders must recognize that multiple structural drivers—including broader geopolitics, global trade flows, technological innovation, the energy transition, and demographic shifts—are evolving simultaneously, and that the interplay among them is reshaping the strategic environment. This is making risk management more complex than ever.

This is a classic wake-up call. The business community must recognize these military and economic risks are no longer isolated and cannot be summarily dismissed as they once were; they are interconnected and systemic. For years, the default was to treat corporate governance as de facto apolitical, viewing geostrategic influences agnostically—or at best as isolated, novel events. That indulgence is over.

Today's geopolitical risk requires continuous adaptation rather than reactive crisis management. Passive monitoring of geopolitical developments is no longer sufficient; companies must actively embed agility and resilience into their operational frameworks, supply-chain strategies, investment decisions, and risk management protocols.[451] Companies that fail to integrate geopolitical considerations into their long-term strategic planning will not only face sudden and severe disruptions but may also suffer financial instability, reputational damage, and regulatory penalties.[452]

For corporate boards, these developments necessitate a reassessment of their long-term global exposure. Boards must rigorously assess vulnerabilities in supply chains, energy dependencies, and foreign investment portfolios, evaluating their exposure to potential settlement outcomes.

In Europe, for example, NATO countries are making commitments to increase defense spending and assume greater responsibility for their collective national security. This shift has significant implications for boards overseeing multinational companies. Defense contractors, cybersecurity firms, and logistics providers will likely see increased demand as European nations prioritize military readiness. Additionally, financial institutions and investors must reassess their portfolio strategies, as heightened defense spending may drive economic realignment within the European Union. Finally, companies operating in Europe must anticipate potential regulatory shifts, such as new restrictions on technology exports, changes in classifications of dual-use goods, and increased scrutiny of foreign direct investments in sectors deemed critical to national security.

Historical Context: Lessons from the Past

To be sure, the concept of geopolitical risk is not new. We've been here before and seen this movie, in a manner of speaking. Throughout history, businesses have been affected by global conflicts, economic nationalism, and shifts in power dynamics. During World War II, companies had to rapidly adjust to wartime production, while during the Cold War, businesses had to navigate restrictions on trade with the Soviet bloc. To be sure, corporate governance decisions in those eras were shaped by viewing the corporation as, in its own way, engaged in the conflicts as well.

During World War II, US corporate boards were deeply enmeshed in geopolitical strategy, albeit under the auspices of national mobilization. Companies like Ford, General Motors, and Boeing restructured their operations to support the Allied war effort, often at the direction of federal agencies. Board decisions during this period were not merely about profitability but about alignment with national security priorities—an early example of how geopolitics could override traditional corporate governance concerns.

In the Cold War era, multinational corporations faced a different kind of geopolitical calculus. Boards had to navigate the risks of operating in or near the Soviet bloc, manage exposure to nationalization in newly independent post-colonial states, and comply with US export controls and sanctions. The rise of defense contracting and the military–industrial complex also brought geopolitical considerations directly into boardrooms, especially for firms in aerospace, telecommunications, and energy.

The 1970s energy crisis marked another inflection point. The OPEC oil embargo and subsequent economic turmoil forced boards to confront the vulnerabilities of global supply chains and the strategic importance of energy diversification. Many companies began to integrate geopolitical risk into their long-term planning, recognizing that global political dynamics could have immediate and material impacts on operations and profitability.

The post-9/11 era, including increasing cyberattacks, introduced a new dimension of geopolitical risk—warfare by other means—that reshaped boardroom priorities across industries. The terrorist attacks of September 11, 2001, catalyzed a wave of regulatory, security, and operational changes that demanded board-level attention. Companies with global operations had to reassess physical and cyber vulnerabilities, while sectors such as aviation, logistics, finance, and energy faced heightened scrutiny and compliance obligations. The creation of the Department of Homeland Security and the passage of the USA PATRIOT Act introduced new legal and ethical considerations for boards, particularly around data privacy, surveillance, and international partnerships.

The 2008 financial crisis exposed vulnerabilities in global economic interdependence, leading to a renewed focus on economic sovereignty. John, writing in his *Status and Functions of Corporate Directors* in 1948, anticipated these challenges when he observed:

> American industry is today, in many ways, facing the most critical period in all its history. ... Upon boards of directors, to a certain extent, rests the responsibility for American industry and therefore the welfare of the whole country. The decisions of [business leaders] are important today as never before.[453]

Arguably, we're watching a historical sequel. History doesn't necessarily repeat itself exactly, but it does tend to rhyme.

The geopolitical risk we face now is at least as great as what we faced in World War II when we confronted and defeated Italy, Germany, and Japan. The primary difference is that World War II was a large-scale kinetic war fought between clear alliances. Today's conflicts are largely hybrid—economic, cyber, and political warfare dominate instead of direct large-scale military confrontations. However, some similarities exist in terms of economic warfare (sanctions, trade restrictions) and ideological divides.

When compared with the first Cold War, today's geopolitical risk is arguably greater because we now face aggressive economic and technological competition from multiple global adversaries, rather than a single monolithic opponent like the Soviet Union, and because we are so economically linked. While there are strong parallels between the Cold War and today's US–China rivalry—again, particularly in terms of economic and technological competition—unlike the Cold War, where the United States and Russia had little economic interdependence, the United States and China are deeply economically intertwined, making direct conflict much riskier for both sides. Additionally, today's world has more regional conflicts and non-state threats, making it more chaotic than the Cold War's structured competition.

Indeed, the clearly defined rivalries of the past have given way to multiple spheres of influence and power struggles, shaped by new dimensions of power, such as cyber warfare, economic dependencies, and non-state actors. Unlike the Cold War, which was largely a bipolar struggle between the United States and the Soviet Union, today's world is multipolar. The United States, China, Russia, the European Union, and regional players like India and Iran all exert influence in diverse ways. This makes geopolitical calculations far more complicated—there isn't a single dominant rivalry but rather a web of competing interests.

China—aligned with Russia, Iran, and North Korea, sometimes referred to collectively as the "CRINK" states—has effectively formed an axis of revisionist powers seeking to challenge the existing world system across every domain: land, sea, air, space, and cyberspace. As previously mentioned, today's threats to US security may be even more severe than those of the first Cold War: a peer competitor in China, an imperial Russia, proliferating nuclear risks, and emerging technologies that empower lesser powers while threatening the US homeland. This emerging "axis of autocracies" shows a willingness to undermine global norms and exploit asymmetries in trade, technology, and military capabilities.

At the same time, the United States has lost much of the muscle memory required to navigate a dangerously competitive world—skills once instinctive during the Cold War. Amid this mosaic, China is an interesting case study. Its ascent as a global economic superpower has redefined strategic and financial landscapes, challenging established norms in trade, security, and diplomacy.[454] Over the past two decades, many corporations have expanded operations in China, benefiting from lower production costs and access to a vast consumer market. However, increasing tensions between the United States and China have forced companies to reconsider their dependence on Chinese manufacturing. The semiconductor industry is a prime example, with major firms now shifting production to the United States, Taiwan, and other allied nations to mitigate geopolitical risks.

We are effectively operating in Donald Rumsfeld's "unknown unknowns" territory,[455] with new frontiers of conflict: cyber, space, and artificial intelligence (AI). Past geopolitical struggles were fought through military campaigns, espionage, and economic sanctions. Today, nations can wage war in cyberspace, disrupt financial systems through hacking, and use AI to manipulate narratives in other countries. This digital dimension of geopolitical risk makes it more pervasive and harder to contain. Unlike traditional warfare, cyberattacks happen instantly, and attribution is often difficult. Meanwhile, astro-politics is now a reality. The United States presently dominates in space, but China is making substantial investments to catch up.

And finally, in the post-9/11 era, the early 2000s were dominated by counterterrorism and asymmetric threats. While terrorism remains a concern, today's geopolitical risks involve more state-based conflicts and economic struggles, rather than purely ideological battles against non-state actors.

Meanwhile, the international institutions created to address these risks no longer enjoy the cachet they once did. During the Cold War, institutions like NATO, the UN, and various arms-control treaties helped mitigate the worst risks. Today, many of these institutions face declining influence, with countries like China, Russia, and even some Western nations challenging global norms. The breakdown of these diplomatic mechanisms makes risk management much harder.

The pace has only intensified. There are more frequent and overlapping crises. In past global conflicts, there were often distinct periods of tension, followed by resolution or de-escalation. Today, geopolitical crises don't seem to resolve—they evolve and multiply. The Russia–Ukraine war hasn't led to a clear settlement, Middle Eastern tensions continue to simmer, and US–China competition remains a long-term structural challenge. The persistence of multiple crises at once adds to uncertainty exacerbating the VUCA[456] and BANI[457] conditions that define today's geostrategic landscape.

Understanding these historical patterns and acknowledging that geopolitical risk today is arguably more complex, widespread, and unpredictable than at many points in modern history helps boards anticipate and prepare for future risks. Although globalization once appeared inevitable and unstoppable, recent events have shown geopolitical considerations can rapidly alter economic dynamics. Boards must learn from history and implement strategies that ensure business continuity in an unpredictable world.

Unfortunately, what makes this moment in time unique is the defining characteristic of today's geopolitical risk, which is pervasive uncertainty—there are no clear endgames to major conflicts, there is no dominant international order enforcing stability, and there is no historical precedent for managing risks that range widely from cyber warfare to global supply-chain disruptions. Today's environment is not only VUCA but also BANI on steroids, requiring boards, as in the Weinbergs' day, to adapt to these global challenges.

For businesses, investors, and governments, this means geopolitical risk isn't just a background concern—it's a central factor in decision-making. Unlike past conflicts that had clearer boundaries, today's risks spill over into markets, technology, and everyday life in ways that make resilience and adaptability more important than ever. Yet, just as worrisome is the reality that only a small fraction of US business executives and the director population have geopolitical experience. We haven't seen developments of this scale and complexity in more than 35 years, leaving many CEOs and boards without the experiential frame of reference needed to interpret and respond to this reality.

The Role of Patriotic Capitalism in the Boardroom

A new economic paradigm—patriotic capitalism—has emerged in response to these shifting global dynamics. In his time, John Weinberg characterized this as "responsible capitalism"—the notion that responsible corporate governance can contribute to national security and economic stability. He quoted Edward Stettinius, then the chair of U.S. Steel, saying, "[N]o longer can industry plow a single furrow toward a strictly economic objective; instead, it must manage its affairs with due regard to the whole field of human relations."[458]

In other words, this is a clarion call for directors to act in the national interest. This approach aligns corporate responsibility with national economic and homeland-security priorities. It reflects the growing realization that businesses and governments must align their economic strategies with geopolitical realities—more specifically, this requires strengthening the network of private-sector actors essential to advancing America's strategic objectives and expanding coordinated capital flows that safeguard national security and long-term prosperity. John summed this up quite prophetically when he said, "It seems that the only way boards of directors can best meet the needs of the American people, most nearly supply their wants, maintain profits, handle problems of unemployment, and face the Russian challenge, is through outstanding leadership, which accepts social responsibility. Such leadership will seek to frame constructive plans based not on the interest of capital or capitalism alone, but in the interest of the American people as a whole."[459]

"Patriotic" capitalism—the principle that what's good for the country is also good for the bottom line, and that the nation and its citizens are as much a key constituency as any other—is capitalism's latest incarnation and one that is arguably eclipsing, or at least supplementing, the stakeholder and ESG (environmental, social, and governance) debates. Indeed, the ultimate sustainability imperative in a volatile, uncertain, complex, and ambiguous world is the country's national security, underwritten by all the elements of national power—economic, technical, military, diplomatic, and educational. In other words, adopting a "whole-of-society" approach is essential for success, bringing together public, private, and civic actors in a coordinated effort to advance national strategic and economic security.

In that context, it's prudent for the business community to engage regularly with policymakers and regulatory bodies, and be part of a coordinated leadership effort with government leaders, both domestically and globally. Business leaders should help public officials think through the potential consequences of their decisions and create economic strategies that align with our diplomatic and national-security policies—to be on the same page, as it were. In effect, good governance at the board level supports a strong economy in the aggregate. A strong economy, of course, enables a strong America and funds a formidable defense deterrent, an ironclad insurance policy. That's important because our ability to be influential in supranational matters we care about—whether it's human rights, climate change, or many other topics—depends greatly on our total soft and hard geopolitical power.

Again, this is not a novel concept but one that has returned to prominence (the denial by some notwithstanding), and it's one John duly noted in explaining boards' responsibility in maintaining economic stability and acting in the interests of the country.[460] We saw this on full display during World War II and the Cold War, when we strategically applied our military, economic, and diplomatic might in a coordinated manner and in concert with our allies to defeat our adversaries. These historical examples exemplify patriotic capitalism in action.

Historically, coordinated public- and private-sector investment in national-security priorities has driven breakthrough innovation and economic growth. The Cold War demonstrated this clearly, yet today's capital allocation is not keeping pace with escalating geopolitical risks. Without a modern, market-aligned effort to fund assets of strategic importance, the United States and its allies face mounting strategic vulnerabilities.

In eras defined by great-power competition, this concept of patriotic capitalism recognizes the interrelationship between economic security, national security, and energy security.[461] It embodies, too, the fundamental principle that we don't have the luxury of compartmentalizing and condoning bad-actor behavior—as some governments and businesses have done in recent times, likely incentivizing more hostile acts. If we are to succeed in this post-neoliberal world, and prevail in a potential Cold War II scenario, it will require the united front we displayed decades ago.

Some contemporary policymakers frame this challenge in terms of "integrated deterrence," a strategy that combines all tools of national power, including military, economic, and political instruments, to dissuade adversaries from aggression. It emphasizes coordination across government agencies and among allies to create a more credible and comprehensive deterrent than any single tool can achieve. In many respects, patriotic capitalism can be viewed as its commercial analogue—a close cousin that mobilizes private-sector capabilities in support of national resilience and shared strategic objectives.

For US-based boards and management teams, patriotic capitalism in practice means prioritizing domestic supply-chain resilience, engaging with policymakers, and ensuring corporate strategies do not undermine national-security interests. It's about helping secure the vitality and vibrancy of the American economy—one company at a time.

These challenges also create a timely opportunity for the private sector to partner with government in defending the nation and strengthening the economy. In this moment, business leaders have a unique chance to play transformative and trusted continuity roles in shaping our collective future by helping build platforms where investors, industry leaders, and policymakers can exchange ideas and forge strategic partnerships that advance national and economic security.

Public officials and business leaders are both in the global-security and domestic-prosperity business,[462] which requires that they function as mutual force multipliers and avoid working at cross-purposes. John aptly described it this way: "An additional area where directors should have an understanding is in the whole field of world affairs and its potential influence upon American industry."[463] For example, the United States and its allies are actively working to counter economic dependencies on adversarial nations, making it imperative for companies to reassess their global footprint. This is particularly relevant in critical industries such as technology, defense, and energy, where geopolitical tensions can directly impact business viability.

Boards must now consider their role not just in terms of shareholder value but, as John Weinberg suggested, as trusted stewards of economic stability within a broader geopolitical context. This shift demands closer coordination with government agencies, increased investment in critical technologies and in secure and sustainable supply chains, and proactive engagement in shaping policies that influence international trade and security. In short, the ability to navigate the geopolitical and economic dimensions of the global system simultaneously is now a critical leadership skill. CEOs and boards must maintain closer contact with government counterparts to better anticipate—and, when appropriate, help shape—policy developments that affect their strategic environment.

Key Geopolitical Risks Boards Must Address—Both the Urgent and the Important

As outlined, the current geopolitical risk landscape is an urgent and important concern for corporate directors and boards because it directly impacts nearly every facet of business strategy, operations, and long-term growth. In past periods, geopolitical risk was often a consideration for specific industries, like defense or energy, but today it touches all sectors. No one is immune to its impact. This is an "unknown unknown," one that is extraordinarily difficult to predict or plan for—the type that is not only disruptive but destructive, the type that can be existential. So, boards must be proactive rather than reactive, integrating geopolitical risk management into their core governance responsibilities.

More specifically, key geopolitical risks for boards to monitor include:

- Supply-chain vulnerability and business continuity
    - The weaponization of supply chains,[464] as seen in semiconductor restrictions and energy shortages, requires companies to diversify suppliers and develop contingency plans. The US–China trade tensions, the war in Ukraine, and Middle East instability have all disrupted critical materials, from semiconductors to energy resources.
    - Nearshoring and "friend-shoring" have become essential strategies to reduce reliance on adversarial nations.
    - A systematic, data-driven evaluation of supply-chain dependencies is essential, allowing boards to pinpoint vulnerabilities at every stage of production, distribution, and logistics.[465]
- Regulatory and trade policy uncertainty
    - Tariff wars, sanctions, and export controls shape market access. Boards must stay ahead of shifting regulations and assess how trade policies impact their operations.

- Trade restrictions are increasingly being used as a geopolitical tool, affecting global competitiveness. Boards must implement compliance frameworks—particularly in industries like finance, technology, and manufacturing—that ensure adaptability to new regulations and access to markets.
- Emerging trade restrictions require continuous monitoring and compliance adaptation.

- Cybersecurity, technological warfare, and data-protection risks
    - Cyber warfare, increasingly weaponized by state actors,[466] has become a defining element of global conflict, threatening industries from financial services to healthcare and critical infrastructure.[467] These nation-state cyber threats are escalating, making cybersecurity a board-level concern.
    - Companies must invest in advanced defenses, including threat detection, crisis response, and workforce training against cyber espionage and infrastructure vulnerabilities.
    - As cyberattacks become more sophisticated, boards must ensure their organizations are not only reacting to threats but proactively preventing them.
- Market and investment volatility and capital risks
    - Geopolitical tensions drive market instability. Whether it's energy price fluctuations from Middle East conflicts, supply-chain issues from China, or currency volatility due to economic sanctions, companies must navigate unpredictable financial environments.
    - Economic decoupling between the United States and China is reshaping global investment patterns.
    - Boards must stress-test financial strategies against potential geopolitical shocks.
    - Boards should consider the risk of capital flight and market fluctuations when engaging in global business ventures, particularly in regions with high geopolitical tensions.
- Shareholder and stakeholder expectations and reputation risks
    - More than in previous eras, some consumers, investors, and employees expect companies to take stands on global issues such as human rights, environmental policies, and international conflicts. Boards must carefully balance these pressures while protecting shareholder value.

    - Transparency in corporate governance and political engagement is now expected, making it imperative for boards to craft clear, well-communicated strategies for handling geopolitical crises.
    - A misstep—whether through inaction or taking too strong a stance—can result in reputational damage, regulatory scrutiny, and even consumer backlash.
- Talent and workforce disruptions
    - Global instability affects talent mobility, hiring, and workforce operations. Immigration policies, regional conflicts, and regulatory changes influence companies' ability to attract and retain skilled workers.
    - Boards must anticipate and mitigate talent risks in geopolitically sensitive regions.
    - Boards should develop policies that support workforce stability, including relocation assistance and risk assessments for employees working in high-risk zones.

How Boards Should Integrate Geopolitical Risk into Strategy

To ensure resilience in this volatile landscape and reduce exposure, boards should prepare and adopt the following best practices:

- Establish geopolitical risk as a core governance priority
    - Consider assigning a dedicated committee or task force to monitor geopolitical developments. Subscribe to reputable geopolitical intelligence sources.
    - Implement structured processes for reviewing geopolitical risk data and making informed decisions in response to evolving threats. Embed geopolitical risk into the organization's enterprise risk management (ERM) framework. Treat it as a standing part of ERM and not just a headline risk.
    - Map the organization's dependencies by geography, supplier, and regulatory environment. Identify "single points of failure" and consider diversification strategies.
    - Receive regular updates on geopolitical developments relevant to operations, supply chains, and strategy.

  - Regularly update risk assessments and integrate findings into corporate strategy. Assess risk through financial, operational, reputational, and regulatory lenses.
  - Create an internal geopolitical risk dashboard, leveraging data analytics and real-time intelligence, that allows boards to stay ahead of emerging threats.
  - Ensure geopolitical risks are regularly discussed in strategy meetings and that organizations engage in stress-testing for worst-case scenarios.
- Practice robust crisis governance and develop scenario-based strategic planning
  - Set up a geopolitical nerve center or "war room"—an enterprise central hub that tracks new developments in global trade and other geopolitical matters to help business leaders navigate the uncertainty.
  - Conduct "war-gaming" exercises and tabletop exercises to anticipate potential geopolitical crises and their impact on operations.
  - Routinely stress-test supply chains, financial models,[468] and crisis-response strategies. This is imperative to ensure organizational resilience in an era of geopolitical volatility.[469] Practice, practice, then practice some more.
  - Engage external geopolitical analysts and experts to provide insights into emerging risks and global trends. Build trusted relationships with trade associations, embassies, international legal advisors, and regulators.
  - Engage in public–private partnerships or industry consortia on cross-border policy developments.
  - Ensure crisis management plans include contingencies or triggers for rapid shifts in political alliances, armed conflicts, and trade restrictions. Include clear escalation plans for geopolitical disruptions, including who within leadership handles response coordination.
- Enhance cyber resilience
  - Invest in next-generation cybersecurity infrastructure and threat intelligence to counter increasingly sophisticated state-sponsored cyber threats.
- Diversify supply chains and market exposure
  - Reevaluate supply chains for resilience. Do not be overly reliant on single-source suppliers from politically unstable regions.

  - Localize operations where feasible to meet local compliance and reduce exposure to cross-border tensions.
- Strengthen government and policy engagement
  - Build relationships with policymakers to stay informed about trade, regulatory, and security policies.
  - Advocate for policies that support long-term business stability and competitiveness.
  - Actively participate in industry coalitions to shape policy discussions and protect business interests.
  - Work with legal experts to ensure that lobbying and advocacy efforts are aligned with both domestic and international law.

Conclusion: Boards Must Engage and Be Proactive, Not Reactive

In this chapter, we have established that geopolitical risk is no longer a secondary concern—it is a dominant factor, a core business risk, a permanent strategic concern in corporate governance. We are at a pivotal point in history; the stakes have never been higher, as today's decisions will define not only corporate and national survival but also the durability of democratic capitalism itself. As global tensions rise, corporate resilience strategies must evolve to address new geopolitical uncertainties. Boards and management must institutionalize geopolitical risk management rather than treat it as an occasional disruption—take an anticipatory approach to global instability and prepare for disruptions before they materialize.

A comprehensive risk framework must integrate geopolitical forecasting with financial modeling, ensuring businesses remain adaptable in an ever-shifting global landscape. By building this kind of continuous strategic adaptation capability, corporate boards can adjust their strategies to address both historical and contemporary threats—anticipating disruptions, mitigating risks, and capitalizing on emerging global trends. This is about embracing a long-term, resilient mindset, ensuring that organizations are not only prepared for disruptions but are capable of thriving in an increasingly complex world. Indeed, a thoughtful response to these threats provides an opportunity to strengthen not only an organization's position but also the broader national-security posture of the United States and its allies.

Companies practicing sound geopolitical hygiene can safeguard their operations, protect shareholder value, and contribute to broader national and economic security goals. In a world where uncertainty is structural rather than episodic, adaptability and foresight will define the most successful organizations. Boards that fail to recognize the magnitude of these risks may face existential threats to their business models and long-term viability.

Resilience in this environment can be a competitive advantage. In practice, this means diversified supply chains, robust cybersecurity measures, and flexible operations. To further solidify resilience, boards—as John Weinberg urged—must also invest in education and training programs that enhance directors' understanding of global affairs. Having board members with backgrounds in international relations, national security, or global supply-chain management can be an invaluable asset in shaping a company's geopolitical strategy.

We have examined explicit parallels between the historical challenges corporate directors faced in the Weinbergs' era and today's modern geopolitical risks. Thankfully, we can take a page from previous geopolitical campaigns like World War II and the Cold War, and acknowledge that economic and national security (including, and especially, energy security) are increasingly intertwined.[470] We prevailed in those campaigns because industry adopted a form of patriotic capitalism fueled by a sense of shared values—principles that have evolved but remain central to effective corporate governance—and aligned their strategies with government policies and geopolitical realities.

Beyond this imperative, it is important that boards balance stakeholder pressures to take controversial positions on global issues. John suggested as much when he called for the "harmony of interests"[471]—balancing geopolitical risks with the interests of various stakeholders, ensuring long-term stability and profitability. Weigh these pressures carefully, ensuring that corporate responses align with organizational mission, vision, values, and long-term strategy, while avoiding unnecessary reputational or regulatory risks.

Finally, boards should approach geopolitical risk not just as a challenge but as an opportunity. Companies that can anticipate global trends, adjust their strategies, and adapt to new geopolitical realities will not only survive but thrive in an increasingly complex world. Proactive engagement in global markets, strategic partnerships with governments, and investments in emerging economies can provide a competitive advantage. Those that fail to act risk being caught off guard by the next major geopolitical shift.

In conclusion, boards must shift their mindset from passive observer to active strategist in geopolitical risk management. In an era defined by uncertainty, the most successful enterprises will be those that can strategically anticipate geopolitical shifts, harness intelligence-driven risk assessments, and position their organization for sustained global leadership.

IV. Aspirations and Limits: Leadership and Oversight

Chapter 10

Board Leadership

Joan MacLeod Heminway

What does it mean for a corporate board of directors—or the directors constituting it—to lead? We may be tempted to answer that question by simple reference to the managerial role of the board of directors in a corporation or the capacity of board or committee chairpersons to exercise corporate management and control. However, we would quickly realize in thinking the matter through that the answer is more nuanced and incorporates important contextual notions of audience and mission.

Father and son Sidney and John Weinberg, whose thought leadership grounds and infuses the book in which this chapter is included, both appreciated and understood the nature and value of effective board leadership. It is apparent in their writings. "I am convinced, from many years of observing boards of directors," Sidney writes, "that the influence of a director comes from his faithful, competent, and diplomatic performance of his duties and from his abilities and experience—not from his stock ownership."[472] John offers reflections on board leadership generally:

> It seems that the only way boards of directors can best meet the needs of the American people, most nearly supply their wants, maintain profits, handle problems of unemployment, and face the Russian challenge, is through outstanding leadership, which accepts social responsibility. Such leadership will seek to frame constructive plans based not on the interest of capital or capitalism alone, but in the interest of the American people as a whole.[473]

These words could as easily have been written today as in 1948, when they were originally penned. In these and other ways, both men conceptualize the leadership roles of the board of directors and its members in ways that withstand the test of time. Their writings and conduct infuse the content of this chapter and are referenced throughout.

There is some legal basis for board and director leadership in and of the corporation. By statutory fiat, corporate boards of directors are the high-level managers of the corporation. Delaware law is prototypical.[474] However, as students of leadership know well, management is not leadership;[475] and while the authority to manage can enable the exercise of leadership, a board of directors and its members must capitalize on that authority in order to most effectively lead.[476]

How do directors exercise their capacity to lead, together and individually? That is not an easy question to answer for at least two fundamental reasons. First, the concept of leadership is not well defined, generally or as a matter of board and director leadership. Second, directors are individuals, yet they act in their decision-making as a collective group. Both matters deserve consideration, and this chapter addresses each in turn.

Conceptualizing Board Leadership

Defining leadership is always a challenge. There is no single definition in or outside the academic or practical literature.[477] As former White House Advisor (to Presidents Nixon, Ford, Reagan, and Clinton) David Gergen explains, "[t]hat's because the practice of leadership draws primarily upon subjective, hard-to-measure qualities like character, compassion, empathy, and the like."[478]

Although definitions of leadership differ within a range, most focus on the ability to inspire others to action. Pulitzer Prize-winning historian and political scientist James MacGregor Burns offered that leaders motivate "followers to act for certain goals that represent the values and the motivations—the wants and needs, the aspirations and expectations—of both leaders and followers."[479] Don Polden similarly described leadership as "a process by which an individual or a group influences others to achieve positive and ethical change."[480] This chapter assumes a general definition of leadership consistent with these ideas.

Theorizing leadership in particular contexts also can be difficult. The corporate director context is, of course, rooted in the legal structure and role of the board of directors under state corporate law. An understanding of those matters and board decision-making norms is therefore critical. Key questions remain, however, even after achieving that understanding. Among other things, it would seem to be important to identify individual attributes, skills, and processes to describe and explain corporate board leadership at the institutional and individual levels.

A single statutory provision, § 141 of the General Corporation Law of the State of Delaware (the DGCL),[481] establishes the foundation for our knowledge of the configuration and mechanics of the board of directors as a constituent component of the corporation. Notably, the managerial control authorized in the statute is not absolute, and its limits have recently been altered by the introduction into the DGCL of a new statutory purpose clause that affords stockholders easier access to corporate management and control without public filing or notice.[482]

Moreover, it is important to note that the authority conveyed through DGCL § 141(a) is exercisable directly (by the board) or indirectly (under its direction). This is, as Sidney Weinberg notes, somewhat of a necessity in the age of modern business corporations.[483] The authority conferred by DGCL § 141(a) therefore allows the board to employ agents in its managerial work. Those agents can be corporate officers or other employees or individuals or entities outside the firm.

Commonly, however, we cognize the board's exercise of corporate control through delegation of routine business operational authority to the corporation's officers. Sidney Weinberg recognized the need for this delegation in his 1949 speech, *The Functions of a Corporate Director*, stating that "[t]he management of the corporation—that is, its day-by-day executive management—must be in the hands of the officers, who are elected by the directors."[484] The officers represent the individual and collective management of the corporation in the ordinary course of the firm's business. The board's association with the corporation's officers involves cautious reliance—direction, trust, and monitoring in just the right balance.

John was mindful of this tension in the board's role, identifying the board's core functions as administration and trusteeship.[485] He expressed concern that directors might overstep their appropriate and optimal administrative bounds in endeavoring to provide effective corporate leadership.[486] He advises that "[a]lthough limited by the possibility of becoming a hindrance to management and not having sufficient time from their other business obligations to devote to the company, directors should generally provide management, advise management, and supervise management."[487]

John's characterization and assessment of the board's overarching role and the important bond between the corporation's board and its officers continue to have salience (even if his analogy to political governance, offered as an illustration in making these points,[488] may not fully resonate in current times). Although the board can and does delegate managerial authority to officers (as well as other employees and agents), board leadership does not involve micromanaging the activities undertaken by those operating under the delegated authority.

Rather, board leadership involves establishing and sustaining a healthy, mutually supportive bond with the corporation's executive team.

Indeed, the relationship between directors and officers can make or break a corporation. If rapport is lacking or if the relationship between and among directors and officers is too close, the corporation may be dysfunctional. It takes leadership through strong communication skills to develop a healthy board relationship with the corporation's executive team. And it takes a compelling, brave, and honest leader to overcome natural human psychological barriers to confrontational leadership that may be needed when the executive team is failing in its day-to-day stewardship of the firm's operations.

Courage and integrity were exhibited by John, for example, when he led the board of U.S. Financial in asking for the resignation of its CEO, Robert H. Walter, in the wake of unexplained financial irregularities.[489] While his leadership could not save the firm from a bankruptcy filing, it ridded the corporation of criminal contagion that could have made matters worse if left unchecked.

Sidney also notes the importance of inquiry and outspoken action as an element of board leadership, characterizing the related leadership attribute as independence of judgment.[490] This aspect of board leadership is connected to the mutual trust needed to make director–officer relationships productive. As David Gergen notes in a political context, "Followers must trust their leaders to tell them hard truths, while, similarly, leaders must trust followers will believe in them."[491] This observation is equally applicable in the context of board leadership.

A law-oriented theoretical articulation of board and director leadership would be incomplete without addressing the focus of the board's fiduciary obligations. Board leadership is fundamentally rooted in director fiduciary duties. Under Delaware law, these fiduciary duties comprise care and loyalty, including within the latter the obligation to act in good faith.[492]

While it may be said (including in judicial opinions, especially in contested business combination transactions) that a corporation's directors owe fiduciary duties to the corporation and its stockholders, the essential beneficiary of the board's fiduciary obligations is the corporation itself.[493] Stockholders—as internal constituents of the corporation who elect the directors, enjoy voting rights on fundamental corporate changes, and may enjoy the benefits of distributions from the corporation and financial return on the sale of their stock—are a clear focus in the directors' compliance with their fiduciary duties. John recognized director fiduciary obligations as a trusteeship, noting that "[t]he director, in protecting the interests of the stockholders, checks on the operations with the fundamental belief that the stability and continuity of the enterprise are the prime considerations."[494]

Stockholders, however, are not the sole corporate constituency of concern for directors in exercising their fiduciary responsibilities. Corporate directors lead in a broader context. John recognizes this larger context of board leadership when he observes:

> [although the] accepted legal concept of the corporation states that the sole purpose of its existence is to provide profits for the owners[,] … public opinion, which ultimately makes law, is making substantial strides in the direction of a view that the business corporation exists as an economic institution, which has a social service to perform as well as a profit-making function.[495]

Sidney also recognized both the board's general stockholder orientation under fiduciary duty principles and the bigger picture of director leadership when he observed that "[t]he director has obligations to all stockholders. Beyond his legal duties, he must recognize the broad social responsibilities he has to the general public and to the country."[496] He sees board leadership in a general public context. "[A] director of a company," he writes, "must keep a broad outlook, high hopes, and believe in the future of this country. He must keep his feet on the ground but this need not keep him from looking off to the horizon."[497]

Ultimately, board leadership involves determining the best interests of the corporation and executing complex judgments to serve those interests, in good faith, with an eye to the corporation's sustainability in the greater public context in which it operates. Directors lead in their relationships with the corporation's officers and in the general execution of their fiduciary duties by mindfully structuring their work, fully informing themselves, effectively communicating internally and externally, and consistently engaging in rigorous processes designed to serve the corporation's internal and external constituencies. This leadership occurs in the execution of their activities as part of a board of directors through structures ordained by statute, regulation, and practice. However, board leadership also depends on each individual director's ability to constructively exercise their singular leadership capacity. The remainder of the chapter explores these board-level and director-level aspects of board leadership.

The Board of Directors as a Leadership Body and a Body of Leaders

Conceptualizing board leadership is challenging enough. But exercising effective board leadership is infinitely more complex. Part of the reason is that board action is collective group action: directors are not themselves, individually, managers or agents of the corporation as a matter of corporate law; DGCL § 141(a) is clear that the board itself has the authority to manage the business and affairs of the firm as a matter of internal governance.[498] John echoes this when he offers that directors are not agents or trustees but, rather, enjoy "a distinct legal relationship."[499] Directors, as members of the board of directors, act only as deliberative and voting members of a body that manages the firm at the highest level.

Another reason board leadership is complex is that effectual board action involves reaching the consensus of the individual members of that collective body—one that, if optimally constructed and operated, includes independent thinkers from different personal, academic, and experiential backgrounds. Sidney notes the value of director independence when he observes that "[c]ontroversial matters often come before a board and there are times when a director who is any good must be willing to stand up and be counted. The day of the stuffed-shirt director, elected because he is in the Blue Book, has come to an end."[500] Each board member must exercise leadership in their individual conduct for the board to be successful in its institutional leadership.

The concept of servant leadership thus emerges as important to board leadership of and for the corporation. Servant leadership has been defined in different ways since the concept was originated in an essay authored by Robert K. Greenleaf.[501] However, in general, a servant leader is a person whose leadership capacity and recognition are derived from thoughts and activities dedicated first and foremost to the constituencies they seek to benefit and inspire.[502]

Sidney alludes to this type of leadership in reference to a director's leadership role in the governance of a firm when he offers that "[a] director establishes his influence in the corporation through his service to the corporation, rather than through stock ownership. … His ability to act as a director depends on the man himself, not on his stock ownership. Every director represents all the stockholders."[503]

Also important are the corporate structures that allow for effective board leadership. Corporate constituents and stakeholders must understand and respect the leadership role of the board and its members. Bob Jerry alludes to this when he notes that institutions must create an environment in which those we need or desire to lead are primed to accept our leadership.[504] The corporate structures through which boards act can facilitate or impede the exercise of a board's servant leadership internally (within the corporation) and externally.

Important, then, to an understanding of board leadership is a deeper examination of the board's role and the structures through which boards act, as well as the responsibility of individual board members in the exercise of board leadership. The board's roles, as defined in statutory and decisional corporate law, both root and frame the directors' essential servant leadership ethos. The board's essential structures similarly establish and impact its leadership capacity. And the positions and actions of individual directors in their engagement with board activities have the capacity to enable (or, for that matter, disable) board leadership.

The Board's Roles and Leadership

On a macro level, one can categorize the responsibilities of boards of directors in many salient ways. Stephen Bainbridge offers three main categories of board activity: monitoring and disciplining senior management; providing overarching operational management (including through policymaking, advising, and guiding); and affording access to significant outside contacts useful to the corporation.[505] This is a helpful list; others also provide important insights. Within any taxonomy, however, there are more specific roles one can identify.

A full explication of the roles of a corporate board of directors is beyond the scope of this chapter. However, in illuminating board leadership, it does not suffice merely to allude to the complexity and varied nature of the board's role. With that in mind, the chapter calls out several aspects of the board's responsibilities—activities in which the board regularly engages—for attention as they relate to board leadership.

The board's role in financial affairs and operations oversight, including legal and regulatory compliance, is perhaps most familiar to corporate audiences. Although this board-level responsibility is a constant, revelations of public company financial fraud at the outset of the 21st century, followed by the 2008 global financial crisis, the COVID-19 global pandemic, and ongoing international trade wars, among other outside forces operating on corporations in the past 25 years, have placed a premium on the role of the board in monitoring the corporation's financial condition and results of operations, especially in the public company setting.[506]

In a corporation of any size, this multifaceted oversight of the firm's financial and accounting affairs is a large task. It is easy to see why some boards of directors have failed miserably in fulfilling their managerial responsibilities in this context. John notes and catalogues these failures, encouraging better director education and a great clarification of board governance.[507]

The board's role in overseeing corporate financial and operational affairs offers opportunities for leadership, as illustrated by John's actions in convincing the board of U.S. Financial to request the resignation of the corporation's CEO after financial anomalies were discovered, as earlier mentioned.[508] Sidney also alludes to board leadership in financial and operational oversight when he describes being on a board that was wrestling with how to address a business downturn.[509] These examples illustrate the capacity of the board, through director action, to act with integrity in endeavoring to ensure the corporation's sustainability financially and otherwise.

Among the other well-known roles served by boards of directors is their transactional decision-making. This role incorporates transactions involving corporate constituents and employees (e.g., dividend declarations and director and officer compensation) as well as transactions with those outside the firm (major contracts and business combinations). In their work together, Professors Sanjai Bhagat and Bernie Black note specifically the board's role in responding to takeover bids, engaging in acquisitions, engaging takeover defenses, and establishing executive compensation arrangements.[510]

John notes the limits of the board's role in this regard when he observes that "[t]he power of directors in the transaction of corporate business is limited to those actions that are necessary or proper in the carrying out of the 'purpose clause' of the corporate charter."[511] In the modern corporation, however, purpose clauses in corporate charters broadly incorporate all legal activity, offering little constraint on board authority in the transactional context.

Leadership in this context can take several forms. Directors can, for example, effectuate board leadership by voting against transactions that violate legal principles or established norms. John offers that, in exercising the board's authority to approve a dividend policy, "the veto is especially important … because the board is held legally liable that the dividends be paid only from available earnings or surplus profits and [do] not in any way impair the capital of the corporation."[512] Conflicting interest transactions also offer the opportunity for board leadership.

Human tendencies to act in self-interest must be controlled in this transactional decision-making environment, as John clearly conveys when he states that "[d]irectors must exercise the utmost honesty and fidelity in all transactions touching their duties to the corporation and its property. All their dealings with or for the corporation must show the highest degree of good faith and fair dealing."[513] This type of leadership takes on renewed importance in light of Delaware law amendments to DGCL § 144 that simplify the process for clearing conflicting interest transactions of their self-interest taint.[514] Modern mergers and acquisitions practice offers many examples of board leadership in the context of business combination deliberations.

Another important aspect of the board's role is the selection of the corporation's CEO and related C-suite (executive management) succession planning. The conclusion of this volume aptly notes that "[a] board's number one job will remain selecting an outstanding CEO, with succession planning as a close second, underscoring the Weinbergs' emphasis on strategic leadership continuity."[515] John notes the importance of ensuring that the CEO, as the principal and general positional leader of the corporation, be able to work with the board, despite "the inevitability of a dominant chief executive in our modern complex corporations."[516] Hand in hand with the CEO selection and appointment process is, of course, the CEO replacement process. In the words of Bhagat and Black, "[t]here is widespread agreement that a central board task is replacing the CEO when necessary."[517]

Optimally, a well-developed succession plan will support the identification and retention of a suitable CEO. The board of directors is charged with collaborating with the corporation's executive team to construct and periodically review the corporation's succession plan. Again, John saliently weighs in on this aspect of the board's role:

> [i]t is the duty and responsibility of the board not only to attend the management, but also to encourage development of a new generation of ability and leadership capable of maintaining the successful conduct of the business in the future. One cannot belittle the wisdom of developing a competent understudy for the chief executive within the organization.[518]

A corporate board of directors also manages internal and external communications. John refers to this board function as "cultivation of the stockholders and the investing public."[519] Clear, transparent, timely, accurate, and complete communication is critical to effective leadership—including board leadership. It establishes working facts, engenders trust, and motivates action.

Related to the board's essential role in communication is its responsibility for managing relations with the other principal internal constituents of the corporation—its officers and shareholders. This aspect of the board's activities is both foundational and interstitial. John's conception of the board as both administrators and trustees reflects the dual facets of the relational managerial role the board plays—administrators addressing (among other things) relationships between the board and other members of corporate management, and trustees addressing (among other things) relationships between the board and stockholders.[520]

Bill Ide, an expert on ethical corporate governance, forwards a similar conception, labeling John's administrators as "overseers" and his trustees as the directors' "concern for the enterprise."[521] Corporate theory also recognizes this two-part directorial responsibility, notably in the work of Margaret Blair and Lynn Stout on team production theory, which positions directors as "mediating hierarchs whose job is to balance team members' competing interests in a fashion that keeps everyone happy enough that the productive coalition stays together."[522] This balancing of interests characterizes the best leadership in and of corporate boards of directors.

Yet, in the exercise of leadership, a corporate board of directors may find achieving that balance difficult. Among other things, the board's routine managerial interactions with the corporation's officers may be disrupted in the modern corporate era by calls for directors of public company boards to interact directly with stockholders, a task historically performed by corporate officers and employees as part of the corporation's investor-relations function. "[M]any institutional shareholders with significant positions in the securities of public companies expect independent board leaders to be available for direct engagement."[523] Board leadership in this context includes ensuring that specific policies and practices are adopted and used in these interactions.[524] These policies and practices must incorporate confidentiality and selective disclosure obligations under state and federal law.[525]

Board Structure and Leadership

Governance structures vary from firm to firm, based on their unique attributes.[526] Boards of directors vary in size, for example, with the average public company board consisting of between ten and 11 directors.[527] They adopt policies geared to their many roles as those roles are executed in the corporation's overall governance and operations, and they behave in accordance with customized norms.

Boards of directors typically conduct some of their activities through committees, as authorized under the state law of their jurisdiction of incorporation. Under Delaware law, DGCL § 141(c) supplies that authority and related processes required for effective committee action.[528] Corporations often have an executive committee that handles (perhaps among other things) matters that arise in between scheduled board meetings if the board is not or cannot be summoned for a meeting. Sidney notes the potential significance of this board committee in articulating the "essentials of a code of procedure" for effective board governance.[529]

In the public company context, certain committees are expected or required by US SEC or stock exchange rules. These include the audit, compensation, and nominating/governance committees. The public-company audit committee has received particular attention over the past 25 years, eventually evolving to become a required committee consisting solely of independent directors, as Sidney suggested it should.[530] The board also may create other committees geared to the corporation's governance or operations or for specific purposes, including to address derivative litigation demands or complaints.

John addresses the import of committees to board governance and leadership. He describes the nature, general attributes, and value of board committees. Situating them within the administrative responsibilities of the board, he concludes that "the real significance of committees lies in the sum total of their contributions in developing the board policies and objectives for the corporation as a whole."[531] Indeed, the exercise of board leadership through committee action capitalizes on these contributions and the efficiency, focus, and expertise of effective committee processes, values mentioned by John in his description of committees and committee process.

The board of directors and each of its committees is led by a chair. The identity of the chair and that person's capacity to lead can make significant differences in the quality of board governance and leadership. Successful board and committee chairs are masters of group dynamics and small group communication. They embrace leadership ideals—including emotional intelligence (and, within it, effective relationship management), candor, independence, cultural awareness, and humility—as well as leadership processes.

Controversy has long existed around whether a corporation's CEO should chair its board of directors.[532] Concern also exists about successor CEOs—"where CEO-chair leaves her CEO role but remains as chair and brings on a new CEO to take her place."[533] Over time, the trend has been toward having different people serve in those separate roles. Lisa Fairfax documented the trend away from a unified CEO/chair-of-the-board position a bit more than ten years ago, noting that prominent corporations (Proctor & Gamble, Visa, Starbucks, and FedEx) were part of this trend.[534] Yet many corporate CEOs continue to chair their corporation's board of directors, either during their service as CEO or afterward.

CEOs who serve as chairs of their board of directors are challenged to lead multiple groups: management and employees as CEO, and directors as board chair. Audience can be important in leadership communications. Moreover, the skillset and leadership attributes needed to lead one group are not necessarily the same as those needed for another.

Yet, CEOs who are not also serving as the chair of their board of directors also face challenges. They must develop a special partnership with the board chair to ensure the appropriate relationship between the corporation's board and officers—especially those in the C-suite and other senior managers, who are likely to attend some or all board meetings. John recognizes the need for this partnership, advising that where there are different people in the role of CEO and board chair, "a constructive relationship between them must be established—each with his [or her] own clear-cut duties and responsibilities."[535]

Regardless, the board chair position is critical to effective board process, management, and leadership. "[I]n formal and informal ways, the chair leads the board in its decision-making, advising, and monitoring."[536] Although the role conveys clear positional leadership, defined by the board's role, effective practical leadership in the role extends beyond legal requirements, procedural responsibilities, and structural norms. The central and compelling role of the board chair in corporate governance cannot be denied or overstated. The "ongoing and effective leadership that can be provided by an active board chair"[537] deserves recognition.

Individual Directors Leading from Where They Stand

The chair of the board of directors, despite their importance, is but one board member. Each director is important to effective board leadership. For a board to provide effective leadership, it must comprise individual leaders, each of whom must fully exercise their leadership capacity in as many circumstances as possible. "The exercise of ethical leadership in organizations requires values and skills in intricate combinations."[538]

Other than the chair of the board of directors (or, in committee work, the chair of a board committee), individual directors have no independent positional leadership authority within the board. This means they must lead from where they stand. As is true for board and committee chairs, knowledge of and sensitivity to group dynamics, skillful engagement of dyad and small-group communication skills, and employment of leadership values, attributes, and processes are important to success in leading without a title. At its core, leadership in this context involves relationship management and other aspects of emotional intelligence, as well as the employment of tested skill sets and tactics.

Emotional intelligence is defined by Peter Salovey and John D. Mayer in a prescient, groundbreaking 1990 article "as the subset of social intelligence that involves the ability to monitor one's own and others' feelings and emotions, to discriminate among them and to use this information to guide one's thinking and actions."[539] Daniel Goleman popularized the concept, content, and labeling of emotional intelligence through his significant body of work on the topic, memorialized in a series of books and articles written over more than 30 years. His work evolved to identify four components of emotional intelligence: self-awareness, social awareness, self-management, and relationship management.[540] Within them are 20 listed competencies, later whittled down to 12.[541] The five competencies within relationship management are labeled: influence, coach and mentor, conflict management, teamwork, and inspirational leadership.[542] These five competencies are especially important to the role of the individual director–leader, although all 12 are relevant to the task.

The ability to influence and inspire followers, as a part of relationship management, can be approached in many ways. The concept that benevolence and integrity foster trust is, even if unremarkable, compelling.[543]

Robert Goffee and Gareth Jones take a different approach to the assessment of relationship management and overall emotional intelligence in leadership. They observe in their research that influential leaders commonly have four attributes: "They selectively show their weaknesses. … They rely heavily on intuition to gauge the appropriate timing and course of their actions. … They manage … with … tough empathy. … They reveal their differences."[544] Although these observations are made in the context of executive leadership in the workplace, these four leadership qualities—really, as the authors explain them, traits or learned personality characteristics—also may have relevance in board leadership.

A further touchpoint for individual director leadership is the concept of co-elevation. In his 2020 book *Leading without Authority*, management and team coaching consultant Keith Ferrazzi coins that term to describe a framework for use in exercising leadership in the absence of a specific conferral of leadership authority.[545] In essence, the approach involves consciously creating dyads and small groups to engage constructively.[546] The process of co-elevation is a continuous process of relationship management.

As among the individuals who serve on a board of directors, independent directors—in general, non-management directors without other loyalty-impairing relationships to the corporation or its management—have gotten particularized attention as individual directors for over 50 years. John notes the recognition that independent directors may have value in board governance.[547] In its 2024 board index, Spencer Stuart reported that 85% of US corporate directors were independent.[548] Both Sidney and John advocated for the inclusion of a majority of outside directors on public company boards.[549]

Much has been written about independent directors and their impact on firm performance and governance. The full extent of that literature need not be explored here. However, as may be obvious, the trend toward independent directors has roots in limiting the potential for conflicting interests in board deliberations and decision-making. "Directors who are also members of management have an inherent conflict of interest, and consequently, it is in this role that the independent directors must provide leadership for the interests of shareholders."[550] John wrote passionately about management domination of the board as a "pathology."[551] And on the positive side, as Sidney observed, "'outside' directors ... can bring to the discussion of a problem an 'outside' independent point of view that can be very helpful at times."[552]

The Securities Exchange Act of 1934 requires that public company audit committees comprise only independent board members.[553] Sidney advocated "that every board have a committee on audit composed entirely of outside directors and, thereby, have direct contact with the independent auditors."[554] John concurred.[555] In addition, the New York Stock Exchange and The Nasdaq Stock Market both require that the boards of directors of listed companies include a majority of independent directors.[556] Corporations with securities registered under the 1934 Act have public disclosure responsibilities regarding their independent directors.[557] Moreover, while corporations are not legally required to do so, many public company boards of directors appoint a lead independent director to represent and lead the board of directors in communications with the board chair.[558] This is common for boards of directors with a chair who is also the CEO or is otherwise not independent of management.

Independent directors, including lead independent directors, arguably have a greater burden placed on them to lead. In difficult decisions relating to CEO compensation or dismissals, for example, the need for independent directors to exercise leadership is apparent. Newsworthy examples of situations in which independent director leadership has been questioned include the Tesla, Inc., board of directors' ratification of Elon Musk's pay package in the wake of its invalidation by a Delaware Court of Chancery opinion[559] and the dismissal of Kohl's Corporation's CEO following revelations of conflicts of interest.[560]

Conclusion

Corporate board leadership, though perhaps ill defined, is grounded in the managerial authority and related duties and responsibilities of the board of directors under applicable state law.[561] However, an inspection of the board's roles and structures relative to that authority—taken together with the practical reality that the board, as a collective decision-making body, is populated with directors who bring individualized attributes and approaches to their task—reveals that board leadership is about much more. It is multifaceted, operating on different levels. The directors lead the board, and the board leads the corporation in its complex relationships with internal and external constituents.

Overall, corporate directors have vast opportunities to exercise leadership in ways that impact the board of which they are a member, the corporation they serve, and those who interact with the corporation—whether as officers, stockholders, debtholders, regulators, suppliers, distributors, customers, clients, or others, including the community and broader economy and society. Capitalizing on these opportunities involves conscious engagement in the task of board service, starting with the basics. As Sidney suggests:

> to be effective, a director must work at his job—and it is a hard job. ... The director must conscientiously do his homework to prepare himself for board meetings, and outside of board meetings he must be ready to respond, when requested, to the day-by-day calls for counsel and advice from the executives of the companies he serves.[562]

However, these basic activities are just the beginning. With a comprehensive understanding of and appreciation for the board's key roles and foundational structures, and a heightened awareness of the role of—among other things—personal leadership attributes and emotional intelligence, corporate directors can contribute to overall board leadership by leading from where they stand.

Chapter 11

Why "Discerning Questions" Are Rarely Asked—and Never Quite Answered

Amy Deen Westbrook & David A. Westbrook

For a contemporary teacher of business associations, reading Sidney and John recalls the old joke about Shakespeare: terrible writing, full of clichés. The Weinbergs, father and son, call for regular meetings of directors, provided with quantitative written information in advance.[563] They emphasize independent directors, especially with regard to executive compensation.[564] They champion the diversity of boards[565]—the list goes on. One realizes, perhaps with a start, that aspects of corporate governance that a contemporary business-associations teacher might consider obviously right and good were not ordinary for much of the 20th century. What we now view as orthodox thinking about the board of directors is not, historically speaking, very old.

The governance of large firms, generally incorporated in Delaware and publicly traded, illuminates broader fields. The development of law in this area over the last century teaches something about the limitations of law, and the ultimate dependence of law upon political institutions, in turn dependent upon some sense of community. For reasons we discuss, there is no way to use legal rules and processes to convene a group of people and ensure that they reach substantively good decisions. Rules and processes are of course important, and perpetually insufficient. But why? Realizing the insufficiency of law, depressing though it is, has profound consequences for how we think about not just corporation law, but constitutions, treaties, and the like.

The Emergence of Doctrine

Sidney's 1933 memo, his subsequent speech (1949), and John's Princeton thesis (1948) responded and furthered a then-recent tectonic shift in how corporate governance was conceived. Since the inception of the business corporation, directors were expected to direct the business of the firm. In many cases, they were also investors and employees of the firm, and in almost all cases friendly with senior management. In his 1949 speech, Sidney remarks that Standard Oil had no outside directors.[566] That is, the interests of the board of directors and the business, in effect meaning its management, were assumed to be closely aligned. Implicitly, a business was assumed to be a tight-knit affair. As Sidney put it in 1949: "A century ago, most corporations were local and dominated by one man. Corporate law required a board of directors, but one man generally controlled the board, which, as a rule, was composed of subordinates or relatives."[567]

In the years after the Civil War, however, both the American economy and individual businesses grew. And grew. While many cities had exchanges, New York's being the largest, capital was drawn from all over the country.[568] Certain large firms—for example, General Electric—embodied a new model of the large operating company: centralized management pooling the resources of vast numbers, thousands upon thousands, of widely dispersed shareholders, the nominal owners of the firm. This model continues to dominate the public imagination of "the corporation."

As is no doubt familiar to most every reader of this book, the Crash of 1929 and the ensuing Great Depression demonstrated that stockholder confidence in such corporations can evaporate quickly. Massive sell-offs resulted in plummeting prices and the widely dispersed stockholders, many of whom with no other connection to the firm in which they were invested, were badly hurt. The collapse in 1932 of Swedish Match further confirmed the vulnerability of shareholders.[569]

The law responded in three ways that bear mention. First, the Swedish Match debacle gave rise to shareholder lawsuits claiming that directors were negligent, which occasioned Sidney's 1933 memo.[570] As well as serving as senior partner of Goldman Sachs, Sidney was an outside director on several boards. Under what circumstances might he and his fellow directors be liable? Under what circumstances would directors be able to argue that, notwithstanding unfortunate events, their actions were not negligent? More generally, what do we expect of directors, particularly independent directors? How should boards be structured so that directors might fulfill society's expectations?

Second, the first New Deal Congress sought to protect shareholders through passage of the Securities Act of 1933[571] and the Securities Exchange Act of 1934.[572] The new measures imposed obligations directly upon directors: signing the registration statement, liability for misstatements or omissions of material facts, and reporting purchases and sales of the company's securities and short-swing profits.[573]

Third, in 1932, Adolph Berle and Gardner Means published *The Modern Corporation and Private Property*.[574] The corporation, Berle and Means argued, was distinguished from other forms of business organization by the separation of ownership from control. The beneficial owners, the shareholders, had no effective control over the business. On the other hand, a corporation's managers had not only control over the business but economic reasons to divert the company's profits to themselves. Berle and Means urged that the corporation be understood along the lines of the trust, with managers bearing fiduciary obligations to operate the business in the interest of the "beneficiaries," the shareholders. Failure to do so should expose managers, including directors, to legal liability.

These efforts to address the vulnerability of shareholders changed the position of the board of directors *vis-à-vis* the managers. Where the board had been expected to be supportive, perhaps occasionally offering advice, directors were now expected to take responsibility for the direction of the firm, and even to remove managers if necessary. Failure to do so meant that directors could be personally liable for the actions of managers, depending of course on the circumstances. Since directors *qua* directors do not actually run businesses, the threat of liability in effect required directors to know what managers were doing, and approve of it, or not. There was no room for "dummy directors."[575] Directors were expected to ask the "discerning question."[576]

The 1930s efforts to protect shareholders tended to separate: the board from management; "running the business" from "day-to-day operations"; and the directorial function from the managerial function, to say the same thing in three different ways. Then, as now, it would be too much to call the relationship between the board of directors and managers adversarial, except perhaps in extraordinary circumstances like takeovers.[577] But the board of directors was and still is expected to hold managers to account, to ensure that the business is run in the interest of the corporation and its shareholders. All this is familiar, the stuff of the basic course in business associations, and not that hard to state in the abstract.

The Persistent Failure of Governance

As a practical matter, how are directors to hold managers to account, and on that basis, formulate judgments about where to direct the firm? Sidney and John proposed a number of aids to institutional navigation, suggested above and discussed throughout this book: regular meetings, financial accounts, audit committees, and so forth. Sidney even set out "commandments" for boards. It is difficult to disagree with any of these. So informed, boards might be able to ask the discerning question, steer the firm around the icebergs, and see it safely into harbor.

And yet Sidney himself sometimes failed to ask the discerning question. For almost 30 years, Sidney was a director of McKesson & Robbins.[578] For some 13 years, the company was looted by Frank D. Coster, the alias (!) of Philip Musica. Sidney simply did not see it. In his 1949 speech, Sidney recounted that during the investigation of the fraud, he was asked why he and the other directors, presumably acting under the principles laid out in his memo, had not caught the fraud. Sidney reports replying "that Moses had brought down the Ten Commandments from Mount Sinai, that we all believe in them, but that unfortunately few of us live in accordance with all of them."[579] Evidently, it is not enough to know the rule, or even to have written the rule.

Frankly, Sidney's answer is not very satisfying. Without belaboring the distinction between sins of omission and commission, there is no evidence that Sidney's failure stemmed from *breaking* one of the "commandments" that he himself had laid down for corporate boards. The commandments just didn't work, not even for their author.

More generally, it is worth thinking about why, despite all our teaching, corporate governance so often fails, sometimes spectacularly. For example, Enron and the other "accounting scandals" revealed fundamental flaws in corporate accounting.[580] Congress responded rather forcefully, with the Sarbanes–Oxley Act.[581] With presumably better-informed directors, a host of financial institutions levered up their exposure to opaque investments, which ended badly just a few years later in the global financial crisis.

At the time, a few commentators tried to pin responsibility on out-of-touch boards, "dummy directors" in effect.[582] In general, however, the problem was not insufficient sophistication; it was excessive sophistication. The financial crisis was not a sudden epidemic of willfully obtuse boards. Entire industries thought, after decades of brilliant financial engineering and risk management, that great amounts of leverage could be sustained. With all these smart people involved, what could go wrong? Or, as Citigroup's former CEO, Charles O. (Chuck) Prince said, "[A]s long as the music is playing, you've got to get up and dance."[583] That said, boards did fail in the sense that the institutions they were charged with directing failed: the ships hit the icebergs.

Evidently, it is hard for directors to ask the discerning question, the question that reveals what the firm should, or should not, be doing. Which leads us to ask: What can be said about why the task set for boards by Sidney and John is so hard, even for sagacious minds, and remains hard for their presumably even better-informed successors at Goldman Sachs and elsewhere?

We argue that while corporations are often well governed in fact, the legal and intellectual problem of corporate governance is insoluble. Rocks are always in danger of rolling back down their hills. Today's good decisions are commendable, but they are no guarantee that tomorrow's decisions will also be sound. The law may guide, may even teach, but cannot solve. The problem of government is perpetual. And so directors must continue to try to govern well. Sisyphus has no choice; he must roll the rock back up the hill.[584]

Size and Complexity

As suggested above, large and complicated "private" enterprises pose problems that corporate governance seeks to address. Big ships are hard to steer. Almost all of the Weinbergs' work in these documents can be understood to contribute to the construction of boards with the information and incentives that would foster wise governance, good decisions. In concluding his thesis, however, John casts doubt on whether his project, and his father's, is even possible. Suppose a well-constructed board, with well-educated, well-informed, and even well-paid but otherwise independent directors, from a variety of backgrounds, simply isn't enough? "As a result of the increased size and complexity of corporations, we see a general inconsistency arising: the board of directors is *practically* unable to carry out the tasks it is *theoretically* supposed to."[585]

John thus concludes his thesis as countless papers since have concluded, with calls for renewed efforts. He urges more education about the proper function of boards, and exhorts industry to take up the challenge, because our very "survival" is at stake.[586] John calls for "strengthening the whole American system of economics so that it can withstand, repulse, and overcome the various attacks on it, which are in existence and are sure to increase in the future. The present-day doubts concerning not only the ability but also [the] *right* of our system to survive can only be eliminated by proper performance."[587]

In reading this passage, two points bear keeping in mind. First, obviously, the Cold War had begun. By way of reference, NATO was founded in 1949. In the wake of World War II, the emergence of the Cold War shaped American thought—and American policy—for generations. In the late 1940s, however, the opposition to a recent, if always somewhat suspect, ally was raw.

Second, and reflected in the prose, at the time he wrote *Status and Functions of Corporate Directors*, John was a college student, albeit already a World War II veteran and one raised in a household with a father deeply interested in the role of directors. Whatever the source, *Status and Functions* is a very impressive piece of work, no question. Nonetheless, there are several category mistakes here.

As important as we might believe the law of business associations to be, it is a bit much to claim that the American way of life hinges on the wisdom of corporate boards. Were that the case, this republic would have sunk beneath the waves sometime shortly after the Civil War.

More ironically, suppose that we understand the Cold War ideologically (John does) as a conflict between views on economic governance. The Soviet Union presented an intensely corporatist view of economic life, which was directed by committees. Endless committees. And John's answer, in effect, is more committees. John begins his thesis:

> In *our system* of democratic capitalism, the business corporation holds a *dominating* position. In the performance of these business corporations, the board of directors assumes an especially *significant* role. ... [P]roper operation of this corporate mechanism *will determine* in large measure the *fate* of our existing economic *way of life*.[588]

More ironically still, it is widely thought that the Soviet Union "lost" the Cold War in substantial part because the state apparatus—all those committees!—was woefully inefficient at managing the complexities of a large modern society. Managerialism has its limits.

It is not that what Sidney and then John were saying was, or is, wrong in principle. Their suggestions for the construction and operation of corporate boards are sensible, and, as noted, have become the orthodoxy. For what it is worth, we tend to agree. That said, "solving" the problem as they see it does not have, cannot have, the impacts on the governance of corporations, much less the polity, that they seek. There's an idea of Platonic governance here, but Plato is first and foremost a teller of myths: we might fully entertain what the Weinbergs are saying, just as we might entertain *The Republic*, without believing in the durability or even possibility of the ideas on the ground.

John seems to think that political necessity somehow resolves the problem of management. Management will work because it must. But the economic, political, and even moral imperative that John sees (we must solve the problem of corporate governance lest we lose our way of life to the communists) in no way addresses the epistemological problem of simply not knowing.

Risk and Uncertainty

In hiring Michael Ovitz as its president, The Walt Disney Company made a famously bad contract. Following significant rifts, Disney fired Ovitz. Ovitz's severance payment, made up of cash and the value of his options, was approximately $130,000,000.[589] Arguably, the board's Compensation Committee had not fully understood the company's potential exposure in Ovitz's employment contract. Shareholder derivative litigation alleging that board members violated their fiduciary duties dragged on for almost a decade.

In finding the Compensation Committee members not personally liable for the bad decision taken by the company, i.e., for their failure to direct wisely, Chancellor Chandler wrote:

> Delaware law does not—indeed, the common law cannot—hold fiduciaries liable for a failure to comply with the aspirational idea of best practices, any more than a common-law court deciding a medical malpractice dispute can impose a standard of liability based on ideal—rather than competent or standard—medical treatment practices, lest the average medical practitioner be found inevitably derelict.[590]

Chancellor Chandler granted that their decision-making process "fell significantly short of the best practices of ideal corporate governance," but held that they breached no duty of care.[591]

To generalize, the social purpose of the corporation was to pool capital and allow managers/entrepreneurs to take risks with that pool.[592] And risk, by definition, entails the possibility of adverse outcomes. Or, in more financial language, deviations from expected returns are part and parcel of the institution. The point of the business judgment rule, then, is to protect directors from liability for actions taken, let us un-technically say, "care-fully."

More fundamentally still, the function of limited liability is to free market actors from responsibility for the unknown consequences of their activities. Risk is a bit of a misnomer: risks can be priced because the parameters of events are known, and probabilities can be reckoned. In contrast, at issue in the management of a business moving into the future is uncertainty: What will happen? Will there be, for recent and unforeseen examples, a major financial crisis that disables the payment system and much else besides? A pandemic? A new and as yet unpredictable technology, like artificial intelligence? The sudden imposition of tariffs, worldwide? Something else unthought, and therefore not assessed probabilistically? What will such unknowns do to, say, interest rates and debt financing, to say nothing of employment and demand? And how would we begin to think about specific rules that would tell directors how to cope with the unthought as it emerges, while trying to run a profitable business?

General Understandings and Particular Judgments

When we try to address a situation, we lawyers generate processes. Risibly enough, we usually insist that we are focused on substance, not form. As our esteemed editor, Lawrence Cunningham, points out: both the Weinbergs "use the word 'Functions' in their titles. They focus on substance and purpose, not symbol or ritual."[593] This is true, but in context it may be a strawman. Who would want governance to be merely symbolic—that is, empty? (Of course, the law is symbol or ritual, or else it is not law, but business likes to see itself as pragmatic rather than mystical, so let's not shake that stance.)

The problem, of course, is there is no way to insist on "real substance." A legal rule, by its nature, cannot talk about a particular board member, in a specific context, or a business in a time or place, with all its competing interests and outright conflicts. Legal rules are not valid "for this train and this day only." While a legal text can be substantive, it is the substance of ideas that is at issue. This is obviously true for rules and regulations, but it is also true for the common law. The moment one attempts to say, for example, what "business judgment" means—in answer to a shareholder who has lost money, perhaps—one will have to do so *vis-à-vis* an understanding necessarily distinct from the particulars at hand.[594]

Cunningham continues: "John's thesis details the chairman's role and context, while today many advocate splitting the chair and CEO roles without a similar probe; the thesis focuses on functional skills, backgrounds, and traits of ideal directors (the "desiderata"), while today's governance often prioritizes skills matrices, meeting length, and recordkeeping. His partial solution was a professional cadre of directors."[595] Again, this is true. But the problem is that John is not talking about a particular chairman (a person) in a specific context (a business in a time or place, with all its competing interests and outright conflicts). The law may frame a decision, even set out a process for reaching decision, but it is not the decision itself.

Many readers will be aware of the long development ("evolution" seems too positive) of the rules of pleading shareholder derivative suits in Delaware. The same readers will be aware of the related developments of fiduciary-duty doctrine, the gradual submersion of the duty of care into the duty of loyalty. Process is critically important in most of the major Delaware corporate-law cases, from board reviews of merger agreements to oversight of central risks.[596]

The arc of Delaware corporation law bends, or has long bent, toward formality.[597] Perhaps more formality is more just. Be that as it may, Delaware's corporate jurisprudence has endeavored to "balance" society's competing interests (i) in corporations that take risks, try new things, and (ii) in protecting shareholders from abuse (not incidentally stimulating investment). The result, almost inevitably, has been an increasingly elaborate (baroque, byzantine, labyrinthine?) procedural and substantive edifice.

Sometimes buildings are torn down. Maybe that is the meaning of the migration of corporations from Delaware to Nevada or Texas: Delaware's corporate jurisprudence has long been seen as expert, and sure, which is good, but in some influential quarters it has come to be seen as bureaucratic meddling, and complicated, which is bad. One might say similar things about developments in other areas of governance.

Something else is afoot. The economic and cultural dominance of the Berle–Means corporation with which we began seems to be coming to an end. Large, publicly traded operating companies with thousands or even tens of thousands of employees and widely dispersed shareholding still exist. But the public markets are increasingly dominated by institutional investors, some of which consolidate the interests of retail investors.[598] Ownership in the public markets is becoming much more concentrated.[599]

Ownership is also concentrating in another—if anything, more significant—way. The private markets are now not only larger than the public markets;[600] they have changed nature. Private equity used to be a way to transform a business (classically a badly managed one, or a family business) with the injection of a large amount of liquidity, restructuring, and a sale, often through an initial public offering.[601] Investors locked up their cash for a time, and when that time had expired, investors needed to be paid. With the advent of resale markets, continuation funds, secondary markets in private interests, and the like, we see private equity investors rolling over their investments.[602] Moreover, private equity is an increasingly ordinary way to own swathes of industries (antitrust concerns abound), perhaps on a diversified basis.[603] That is, we may be watching the reconstruction of something like the conglomerate through private equity platforms.

From the fund's perspective, and for present purposes, the Main Street businesses (i.e., the operating companies) are portfolio companies ("portcos"), essentially annuities. Governance, therefore, is largely a meta/financial discourse. The Weinbergs' emphasis on the director, deeply educated in the firm's business, seems strangely inapposite. As Marx suggested long ago, capitalism tends to abstract concrete relations: "All that is solid melts into air."[604] Finance takes commercial relations and abstracts them again: consider the securitization of home mortgages, which made real estate itself disappear.[605] Scale, monetization, accounting, legal rights, and latterly, digitization are all intertwined. "In the cloud," we say nowadays. But where does that leave the board's grasp on business reality? What does it mean to speak of the "reality" of a truly large firm?

Although scale makes it easier to see, the problem is fundamental. In life, we don't encounter pure concepts. Nor, for that matter, do we encounter the law as such. In life, we encounter facts, events, and we try to think through what such phenomena mean, legally and otherwise. We try to use generalities to organize particulars. But what allows us to understand *this* particular phenomenon as an instantiation of *that* idea, rather than some other?

Kant strove to articulate the logical limits of conceptual thought. Hence, *The Critique of Pure Reason* (that is, the concepts with which we confront the physical world) and *The Critique of Pure Practical Reason* (the concepts with which we try to reason ethically).[606] But what about judgment, familiar from law school as the problem of "applying the rule to the facts?" What rule tells us how to judge?

In *The Critique of Judgment*, Kant argued that we know how to think about things because we feel in some sense at home, because it is common sense (Kant used the Latin *sensus communis*) to look at X in this or that way.[607] Common, that is, in this community. Judgment thus turns out to be intimately wrapped up in politics. Particular judgments are not logically necessary precisely because they are not conceptual (where logic operates), but humans reach judgments all the time, as they must, and the substance of judgments is informed not by logic but by experience, the life of the judge, which is socially engendered.

As a society, we do in fact govern corporations. Kant's intellectual problem, and the teacher's problem of how we teach corporate governance in the abstract, is resolved in practice daily. Meetings are held; matters are discussed; maybe discerning questions are asked; and a decision, a collective judgment, is reached. As Holmes said on the first page of *The Common Law*, "The life of the law has not been logic; it has been experience."[608]

Such experience is fundamentally collective rather than individual. Boards are, of course, groups. But more profoundly, things make sense in the context of some shared understanding, not least of law. So, we now turn to the understanding of the board of directors as a community.

Discerning Questions, Fluent Queries, and Trust

John implicitly understands asking the discerning question in terms of the director's role within a specific sort of conversation, held within a specific social context: "The manner of inquiry is very important. The question should be asked pleasantly, discreetly but firmly. It is definitely not a cross-examination, because the director is a participant seeking to guide and evaluate results."[609]

The discerning question is oral, asked face-to-face, part of a conversation. While the answer to the question, or the process of questioning and answering, should generate a better view of the firm's way forward, John's idea of the discerning question is not so much a specific "what to ask" but a "how to ask."

The context, of course, is a meeting of the board of directors, ordinarily a regular meeting. But what might be said about such conversations? More fundamentally, what might be said about the context, even the community, in which such conversations are held?

As Cunningham notes in the introduction to this book, John was not alone in calling for directors to ask "the discerning question." Harvard Business School Professor John Baker used the phrase.[610] Whether or not the express words are used, calls for more directors to ask more penetrating questions of managers, in the hope that corporations will be better governed, are durable parts of the corporate landscape to this day.

Corporations continue to make mistakes, sometimes big mistakes, and it is only natural to blame the governance mechanisms that failed, and to call for improved performance. At the same time, it is virtually tautological to say that a corporation that has made a big mistake has been badly governed, and since governance is the responsibility of the board, the board must have done badly, and should do better, even in cases in which board members are not held personally liable. Rephrased, the structure of corporate governance makes calls for discerning directors almost inevitable.

It would be nice to have more specific, and in that sense empirical, evidence: discerning questions that were asked and that led to better decisions. Such evidence would be difficult to gather, not only for proprietary reasons, but because what the firm would have done in the absence of the question can only be guessed. The question was asked; the firm did what it did. Still, one might imagine ethnographic accounts—oral histories, perhaps—in which the board's influence on management, through the questioning of management, were sketched in some detail.

At the same time, on the basis of experience, we may say that many firms are well run. Boards of directors often ask good questions, and get thoughtful responses. In early conversations about this project, Cunningham suggested that John's call for "discerning questions" implies an understanding of board meetings as conversations prompted by the "fluent queries" of directors. If anything, "fluent queries" is the better phrase, because it shifts the emphasis from "discernment," implicitly of a thing seen ("I discern a _____"), to the process of inquiry, to the conversation itself. From noun to verb.

And it is the verb that matters here, an inquiry from an independent, outside point of view. As John put it, this constant challenge will promote sound reasoning on the part of chief executives because, as a result of their explanations and defenses of their policies, the faults and weak spots will be exposed. "A common pitfall of directors," he notes, "is frequent failure to go beyond the initial reply to the underlying reality. Unless directors follow through on the leads opened, by utilizing and evaluating the answers, the questions become impractical intellectual exercise."[611] In other words, we cannot say "See the right thing," but we can say "Try to have the right kind of conversations."[612]

Even "Try to have the right kind of conversations" is often too much to ask. In actual boardrooms, such conversations may not happen. Or, more often, such conversations happen, but only in perfunctory fashion. Directors are supposed to direct, which is usually taken to mean: (i) set the company's overarching strategy and policies; (ii) require management to explain its running of the company; and (iii) hire and fire top management. Most of the time, however, the board only nominally does such things. Rephrased, the notion that the board stands apart from management and provides a critical outside voice is, generally, overstated. Not always. Activist board members may be truly "outside." Real conflicts emerge around mergers, or sometimes the replacement of an underperforming CEO, and no doubt in other instances.[613]

But these are dramatic situations, in which conflict focuses the mind and sides are taken. Judgment is no doubt necessary, but that does not seem to be what Sidney and John had in mind. Instead, they are asking about the role of directors in the good governance of a firm in its ordinary course of business. It is fairly easy for lawyers (and the Delaware courts) to conceive of board decisions with the clarity of a trial, e.g., a merger offer like the one at issue in *Smith v. Van Gorkom*.[614] But as Bayless Manning wrote, much of a board's work is simply paying attention.[615] It is here, in the ordinary course of a business that does not yet recognize its problems, that discernment is most valuable. How should directors have conversations about what is not yet obvious?

There are difficulties to holding such conversations. First, management calls meetings, organizes and distributes information, and largely sets the agenda. Board meetings tend to be framed *ex ante*, and in ways that align with management's desire to present itself in a good light, and to get what it wants moving forward. The "fluent queries" do not start on a blank slate: "So, tell me a little bit about your business." Instead, directors are asked to respond to information, and an agenda, set before them.

In addition, a board of directors is a somewhat self-contradictory institution. On the one hand, the board should be well informed, a concern traditionally expressed in terms of the fiduciary duty of care.[616] Deep information about the business is possessed by those who do the business, i.e., management, always well represented on boards. Indeed, in the United States, the CEO has often been chairman of the board of directors.[617]

On the other hand, board decisions should be loyal and, ideally, unbiased by anything other than concern for the firm. This concern is traditionally expressed by the duty of loyalty.[618] For this reason, Sidney and John emphasize the importance of independent directors because, while their loyalty need not be questioned, managers are inherently interested. Conversely, no outside director can devote her full time to the business. Thus, "as a structural matter, boards of directors must trust the very people, management, they are supposed to be monitoring."[619]

As Warren Buffett has noted, while the board is a legal construct, it is foremost a social institution.[620] Directors are selected for different strengths: they "bring different things to the table." So, manners matter. John touches on this:

> [Discerning questions] call for breadth of experience, tact, and sound judgment. Very often, the posing of a necessary question requires courage. It is generally agreed, however, that despite the scarcity of good questioners, and the difficulties entailed in the process, the result is well worth the efforts since the strength and vitality of the board are greatly dependent upon the amount and type of questions asked.[621]

Put more cynically, directors can feel pressure to conform to the consensus of the board (generally management-led), to let the business get on with the business.[622] What appears to some as a discerning question may well appear to others as simply being difficult, wasting time, or grandstanding.

As already suggested, like any institution, a board of directors relies on a degree of trust. It must trust, as noted above, that management has fairly presented the company's situation. Directors must trust one another to act in good faith, and often must trust in another director's very different expertise. Trust is necessary for any social group, but it also entails a weakness.

Social groups "know" certain things, but they might be wrong. The pressure to "go along" may prevent discerning questions from being asked. Going into the global financial crisis, many institutions had a great deal of trust in their own financial engineering, and governed themselves accordingly. The "wisdom of crowds" came to be revealed as the "wisdom" of a herd.

Conclusion

To reiterate and conclude, the difficulties confronting boards (and other political institutions) are in principle insoluble. The best that can be hoped is a well-functioning institution, in which a common sense, a consensus, emerges that justifies the firm's decisions and its general conduct.

While it is fairly easy for a board to manufacture superficial consensus, it is important that the consensus be challenged, tested, made to account for itself. This is the role of discerning questions, of fluent queries. But there are forces that militate against such challenges. It is difficult to maintain consensus while at the same time subjecting often strongly held positions to analytical pressure. So here, as elsewhere, sound collective judgment requires a considerable degree of trust—most simply, that management believes the questioning director is acting in the best interest of the firm, usually including its present management. And trust is hard to come by.

There's a lesson here for law: there are limits to what we can know in time, and so what we can teach with any specificity. In lieu of conceptual solutions, we must rely on the wisdom of this generation, and indeed the next, as people feel their way forward. Law ultimately cannot escape more fluid forms of association. Boards will fail, corporations will fail, occasionally spectacularly, but more often in small ways. A degree of impossibility is inescapable in corporate governance as in other human enterprises. The rock will roll down the hill, and Sisyphus will roll it back up. We are left where Sidney and John started: with hope for sound institutions, and insistence on prudence.

V. Evidence and Practice: Context, Change, and Persistence

Chapter 12

Functions and Features

David F. Larcker & Brian Tayan

The Function of Corporate Governance

The purpose of a corporation is to provide for the economic welfare of its shareholders and, in doing so, satisfy the interests of its constituents. If all corporations were owned and managed by a single individual, their oversight would be a straightforward affair. The interests of the individual as owner would be in alignment with his or her interests as CEO, and this person could generally be counted on to make decisions beneficial to the corporation.

However, corporations—especially public corporations—are not solely owned and managed by one individual, and therefore the potential arises that professional management might take actions to benefit themselves personally at the expense of the shareholders for whom they work.[623] This situation describes the well-known agency problem.

An effectively designed corporate governance system is intended to address this problem. We can define *corporate governance* as the system of control mechanisms that a corporation adopts to ensure that managers act in the interest of shareholders and, perhaps, stakeholders. At a minimum, these include a board of directors to advise and oversee management, and an external auditor to attest to the reliability of financial statements. In reality, a much larger number of constituents oversee corporate performance, including capital-market participants, investment analysts, creditors, employees, labor groups, internal auditors, regulators, the legal community, media, and public advocacy groups. If corporate managers take inappropriate action or make faulty decisions, one or more of these groups is generally positioned to identify or address the matter.

Because organizations are diverse in their size, structure, and operating environments, corporate governance systems can be structured in a vast number of ways. In the case of the modern publicly traded company, several governance features are required or shaped by regulatory authorities, listing requirements, and pressure from the capital markets. Others are advocated by self-appointed experts. For example, it is expected that a public corporation in the United States have a majority of independent directors on the board; that the board convene audit, compensation, and nominating committees to specialize in these functions; and that members of the board represent a broad array of the functional, industry, managerial, and technical knowledge required to oversee the corporation's business activities. Similarly, governance features have evolved in the areas of audit and controls, risk management, goal setting, compensation, and performance measurement.

There is no limit to the number of choices an individual firm might adopt in designing its own system. Many of the elements we observe today have been accepted as best practices because of their commonality or the logical conclusions of those who advocate their adoption. However, do we really know whether these practices are indeed "best practices"? To be more precise with the question, do we really know that adoption of a specific governance feature will lead, on average, to better financial and operating outcomes than adoption of a different governance feature or the adoption of no governance feature at all? It might very well be the case that common notions of what constitutes best practice is not best practice at all.

In this chapter, we examine a selection of governance practices and explain what common knowledge and empirical evidence have to say about them. Corporate governance practices have evolved significantly since the mid-20th century, yet many foundational principles of that era remain relevant today. John Weinberg's 1948 thesis provides a rich historical context that underscores the complexity and variability inherent in corporate governance. His insights offer a nuanced understanding that complements the empirical analysis and contemporary issues discussed in this chapter.

John emphasizes the importance of context in evaluating corporate board practices. He notes that the appraisal of board functions is complex and varies significantly across corporations, due to diverse products, competitive situations, company traditions, and individual capacities and personalities. This perspective aligns with the argument presented in this chapter that there is no one-size-fits-all approach to corporate governance. Modern governance systems must be tailored to the specific needs and circumstances of each corporation, rather than adhering strictly to so-called "best practices."

Governance Is Measurable

Corporate governance lends itself to empirical study to the extent its elements can be observed, measured, and studied. Through statistical study, we can see—on average, over time, and over a large number of organizations—whether a given feature (or combination of features) is associated with favorable or unfavorable outcomes. A study might focus on a particular board feature—such as the decision to separate the CEO and chairman roles—to see whether it is *associated* with positive or negative outcomes. The observed outcomes might be financial—such as operating profitability, share-price performance, or price-to-book ratios. Or they might be nonfinancial—such as the frequency of accounting restatements, major shareholder litigation, or bankruptcy. The researcher determines the most appropriate dependent variables. When properly constructed, the study can provide insight into whether the decision to adopt a specific feature is associated with an observable change in governance quality.

Across more than four decades, a vast library of research literature has developed that examines aspects of governance. While the interpretation of empirical studies is not always clear-cut,[624] rigorous research is vastly superior to pure theoretical guesswork or simple conjecture by governance pundits. Because of this, we can use empirical testing to gain insight into the question of whether the *features* of a governance system benefit, harm, or have no bearing on its intended *function*, and whether this is universally or only situationally the case.

John's thesis supports this empirical approach by highlighting the importance of context and the variability of governance practices. He suggests that while empirical studies provide valuable insights, they must be interpreted with an understanding of the unique circumstances of each corporation.

Features of Corporate Governance

Throughout the remainder of the chapter, we will examine specific governance features, including their purpose, the manner in which they are commonly practiced (i.e., the widely accepted "best practice"), and empirical evidence (or lack thereof) on their effectiveness.

Board Independence

Independence standards are developed and adopted to ensure that directors execute their duties with independent judgment. Listing exchanges, regulators (SEC), and courts (Delaware rulings) require corporations to have a majority of independent directors and selected committees (audit, compensation, and nominating/governance) to be comprised solely of independent directors. Listing exchanges also stipulate the criteria by which a director is deemed independent.

Nevertheless, an external rubric for measuring independence does not necessarily measure independence with accuracy. It might very well be the case that a director satisfies the regulatory definition of "independence" but still lacks independent judgment in serving in an oversight role. The New York Stock Exchange (NYSE) defines independence as having "no material relationship with the listed company either directly or as a partner, shareholder, or officer of an organization that has a relationship with the company."[625]

The exchange provides bright-line rules to determine a material relationship, including whether in the previous three years the director has been employed at the company, has received compensation in excess of $120,000 from the company, has been employed as an auditor at the company, is an executive officer where the company's present executives serve on the compensation committee, or is an officer at a company that receives more than 2% of business income from the company. Effectively, these rules draw a line in the sand for the purpose of regulatory clarity.

That said, empirical studies show these independence standards have little correlation with firm outcomes. Bhagat and Black find almost no relationship between the percentage of independent directors on a board and the long-term performance of the company's stock.[626] In contrast, Knyazeva, Knyazeva, and Masulis find that independent board members have a positive effect on firm value and operating performance.[627] The relation between independence and other governance outcomes is similarly ambiguous. Studies provide very mixed results as to whether independent directors effectively moderate CEO pay levels, negotiate better mergers and acquisitions, or improve committee performance.[628]

One reason for these results might be methodological. It very well might be the case that the independence standards fail to take into account other situational factors that affect independence and director performance. For example, some studies suggest that social ties between the CEO and board members might compromise the judgment of directors who otherwise qualify as independent under NYSE listing standards.

In a highly original study, Hwang and Kim find that independent directors with social relations to the CEO—such as having similar educational, academic, military, or employment backgrounds—are associated with higher CEO compensation, lower likelihood of CEO termination for underperformance, and higher likelihood of earnings manipulation to increase bonuses.[629] Bruynseels and Cardinaels find that social ties can similarly compromise the independence and effectiveness of audit committees.[630]

Other factors that might impair the independence of directors include the degree of CEO power over the board or whether the CEO otherwise co-opts board members.[631]

John's thesis provides a historical perspective on the debate over inside versus outside directors, emphasizing that the real criterion for a board is how it can manage the corporation with the greatest efficiency and best results. This aligns with the chapter's argument that independence standards alone do not guarantee better firm outcomes and that other factors, such as CEO power and social ties, play a significant role.

Dual Chairman/CEO

The board chair plays a central role in governance by setting the agenda (thereby controlling the timing, direction, and structure of discussion), communicating corporate priorities, and leading critical decisions involving strategy, risk management, performance evaluation, executive compensation, succession, and merger activity.

Many experts believe the chairman and CEO roles should be separated. Having an independent board chair offers several potential benefits, including: clear separation of responsibility between the board and management; eliminating conflicts in areas of performance evaluation, compensation, and director recruitment; and granting the CEO full time to focus on strategy, operations, and culture.

However, reasons exist why a company might not want to separate these roles. For example, having two leaders can create duplication of leadership and inefficient decision-making, especially to the extent that the CEO has superior information on company matters (through day-to-day management) that is not easily transferred to the chair. Separation can also make recruitment of a new CEO difficult when that individual currently holds both titles or expects to hold both titles.

Perhaps indicative of these conflicting realities, long-term studies of large publicly traded companies show that board leadership structure is hardly stable: on average, large corporations make one change to their duality structure (either separation or combination) every 12 years.[632] Nevertheless, shareholder groups and proxy advisory firms continue to oppose a combination of these roles. Each year, a few dozen shareholder-sponsored proxy proposals are put forth that would require separation of these roles, and guidelines from proxy advisory firms generally support this separation.[633]

The research literature has examined this issue extensively. For the most part, it finds no association between separation of these roles and governance quality. Baliga, Moyer, and Rao (1996) find that companies that announce a separation (or combination) of the roles do not exhibit abnormal stock-price returns around the announcement date, nor do they exhibit long-term changes in operating performance.[634]

Dey, Engel, and Liu find that forced separation due to investor pressure is associated with negative returns and lower subsequent operating performance.[635] Krause, Semadeni, and Cannella provide a meta-analysis of several papers on chairman/CEO duality and find, on average, no statistical relationship with performance or governance quality. They conclude that chairman/CEO duality is "too idiosyncratic for all firms to adopt the same structure under the guise of 'best practices.'"[636]

That is, the research literature suggests that a decision to combine or separate these boards can and should vary across companies, dependent on their situation and the leaders involved at the time.

John's thesis anticipates a nuanced view, suggesting that whether these roles are combined or separated, a constructive relationship between the CEO and the board chair is essential. This perspective supports the chapter's argument that the effectiveness of governance structures depends on the specific context and relationships within the corporation.

Diversity

Considerable demand exists to increase the gender and racial diversity of boards so that the composition of boards more closely reflects the ethnic and gender diversity of the broader population. To date, this target has not been achieved, although the composition of boards has advanced considerably toward this objective in recent years.[637] Much of this change has been purposeful, driven by pressure from institutional shareholder bases (including index fund managers) and intentional recruitment by corporations. According to data from Spencer Stuart, gender and racial diversity have, over the past decade, ranked as two of the most frequently cited attributes that boards look for when recruiting new directors.[638] Beyond voluntary recruitment, several countries have enacted policies or legislation to mandate the level of boardroom diversity.[639]

Diversity might improve boardroom decision-making by ensuring that boards have the full array of information needed to make decisions. Diversity can help boards overcome tendencies toward groupthink (in which directors reach consensus too quickly because social similarities shape their perception and decision-making), encourages healthy debate, and—from the standpoint of public policy—is an important social value consistent with equality. (Racial or gender diversity alone does not necessarily guarantee that different ways of thinking are represented on the board.) However, diversity is also associated with lower levels of communication, cooperation, teamwork, and cohesiveness.[640] Diversity can detract from the quality of decision-making if the recruitment of individuals is done without a primary focus on their qualifications.

The research literature on boardroom diversity is inconclusive. Rhode and Packel provide a literature review of the relation between diversity and corporate governance outcomes and find the results are highly mixed (positive, negative, and neutral) across studies.[641] Knyazeva, Knyazeva, and Naveen provide a more current literature review and also find no consistent relation to performance outcomes.[642] Post and Byron conduct a meta-analysis of 144 studies and find female board representation is positively associated with accounting returns but not associated with stock-price performance.[643] Ahern and Dittmar find that laws that require quotas for boardroom diversity are negative, particularly because they encourage the recruitment of inexperienced new directors.[644]

John's thesis provides a historical perspective on diversity, suggesting that while competent women should be elected to boards, the primary criterion should be the ability of the board member, regardless of gender. This aligns with the chapter's argument that diversity should be pursued for its social benefits, but its impact on governance quality requires further empirical validation.

Board Information

Board members rely on information received from management to inform their decisions. A primary mechanism for conveying this information is the quarterly board book.

Although not commonly acknowledged, board books are often deficient—potentially impairing the board's ability to oversee corporate performance. One way they are deficient is that they tend to be structured around the frameworks used for external financial reporting. While these frameworks are useful for shareholders in making stock-selection decisions, it is not clear that data presented solely under such frameworks is what directors need to make optimal decisions regarding strategy and operations. Financial reporting standards are intended to provide comparability across companies but might misrepresent unique business realities or company-specific drivers of value.

Board books are also deficient because they contain an overabundance of data (running up to 200 or 300 slides in a large corporation). The volume of data—necessary from a regulatory and compliance perspective—makes it difficult for directors to focus analysis and discussion on the most relevant issues. Furthermore, the structure of board books tends to become formulaic over time. The same slides tend to be presented in the same order, updated to include current data. If a board member asks a specific question requiring a new slide, that information is added in subsequent meetings and many times remains in future meetings even when it is no longer relevant. Board books also do not change with the marketplace, making it difficult for directors to understand how competitors, strategy, and investment need to evolve.

Fortunately, steps can be taken to overcome these deficiencies and improve the quality and relevance of board books. First, companies can improve the structure and presentation of data by providing more context around the numbers, by adjusting financial accounting conventions to reflect the true economics of business activity, by reorganizing segment data to match company-specific areas of activity and management responsibility, and by providing deeper analysis around areas of under- or overperformance.[645]

Companies might supplement these efforts by selectively granting directors access to the underlying data that feeds into presentation materials, so directors can explore for themselves the drivers of the information presented to them. Doing so allows for a more informed and substantive boardroom discussion.[646] Artificial-intelligence tools have the potential to dramatically amplify the access to and summarization of data, giving directors the ability to conduct more thoughtful analysis.[647]

Although often overlooked, board books are an important element of governance. Through thoughtful and dedicated effort, board chairs and CEOs have the ability to dramatically improve the information provided through this mechanism, with the potential to greatly enhance governance quality.

John's thesis underscores the critical role of information in enabling directors to make informed decisions. He emphasizes the need for essential facts to be presented in a readily absorbable form, which aligns with the chapter's argument for improving information mechanisms to enhance board effectiveness.

Board Evaluations

A board evaluation is the process by which the board reviews its effectiveness in carrying out its stated responsibilities. NYSE listing standards requires public company boards and their standing committees to conduct an annual evaluation; the evaluation of individual directors is not required.[648] According to The Conference Board, half of public companies evaluate individual directors, with large corporations more likely to do so.[649]

Boards have significant discretion to shape their evaluations. For example, a company might choose to compare performance against its own policies or against the practices of successful peers, evaluations might be conducted by interview or by survey, and they might be led by an internal officer (such as the general counsel), an outside law firm, or a consulting firm. Evaluations also vary in topic area and might include board composition, availability and use of skills, mechanisms for accountability, information quality, meeting effectiveness, and interpersonal relations.

Despite the requirement for an evaluation, the evidence suggests that companies are not effective in leveraging this tool to improve performance. Survey data reveals that directors do not believe board leaders ask the right questions in meetings, fellow directors do not always express their honest opinion in the presence of management, and board meetings contain a significant number of procedural and interpersonal shortcomings that impair their effectiveness. Half of directors believe one or more fellow board members should be replaced because they are ill-prepared or ineffective. Most critically, this feedback is rarely included or discussed through the board evaluation process.[650]

Board evaluations are another important feature of corporate governance that is frequently overlooked but whose proper use stands to greatly improve board effectiveness, through improvements to meeting management and, if necessary, board refreshment.

John's thesis supports the idea of self-appraisal and continuous strengthening of the board through refreshment. The focus is on function—assessing how the board is "producing for the corporation."

Succession Planning

Some observers believe the single most important decision a board can make is the selection of an individual to serve as CEO.[651] Boards recognize the importance of this responsibility, and most corporations claim to have a succession plan and disclose information about their plan.[652] Nevertheless, the research literature shows that corporations perform this function poorly.

Companies are slow to terminate an underperforming CEO. Huson, Parrino, and Starks find that large differentials in financial performance across firms (such as return on assets or stock-price returns) are associated with only small changes in the likelihood of CEO termination.[653] More current studies, such as those conducted by Hadlock and co-authors as well as Jenter and Lewellen, find greater sensitivity of termination to performance but still find only a third to half of CEO turnover events are performance-related.[654]

Boards are also often ill-equipped to name a permanent successor. Survey data suggests that only half of boards could immediately name a permanent successor if needed. Directors estimate it would take 90 days, on average, to find a permanent replacement.[655] Experience bears this out. In a comprehensive review of 1,400 succession events between 2019 and 2023, Larcker, Tayan, and Watt find interim successors are named 22% of the time. On average, 177 days elapse before a permanent replacement is found. Interim successors are associated with significantly worse stock-price performance prior to and following succession.[656]

A variety of factors explain these results. First, the evidence suggests that the labor market for CEO talent might not be very efficient. One study finds that directors of the largest publicly traded companies believe only a handful of executives (inside or outside their company) would be capable of stepping into the CEO role and performing at a high level.[657] Consistent with this, Cziraki and Jenter discover that companies recruit CEO talent from a surprisingly small pool of candidates, with over 90% of newly hired candidates being either internal talent, former executives of the firm, or external talent with a connection to the board. This suggests the "comprehensive" searches that companies engage in are not especially broad.[658]

Second, boards pay insufficient attention to the development and mentorship of internal talent. Survey data finds only two-thirds of companies rotate internal candidates to test and grow their skills as part of the grooming process.[659] Boards are also surprisingly uninformed of the strengths and weaknesses of the senior executive team below the C-suite level, with only a small minority formally participating in their internal review, serving as professional mentors to them, or developing professional relations with them.[660] Significant evidence suggests that boards are overly deferential to the CEO in letting them lead the process, advocate for chosen successors, and control their access to candidates.[661]

As such, succession planning is a prime example of a governance process that many companies claim to prioritize but fail to implement in a substantive manner.

John's thesis emphasizes the duty of the board to develop future leadership and ensure continuity. This perspective supports the chapter's argument that boards need to terminate underperforming CEOs promptly and be prepared to name a permanent successor. The story in this book about John's decisive termination of an obfuscating CEO at U.S. Financial attests to his commitment to this point of view.

Executive Compensation

Executive compensation programs are designed to attract, retain, and motivate qualified talent to pursue corporate objectives. While most scrutiny, and criticism, of CEO pay is focused on the expected level of pay, the form in which compensation is granted and the performance conditions under which it is earned are equally if not more important to understanding how pay might influence behavior and whether the pay program is appropriate.

CEO compensation is a widespread source of controversy in the United States, with most members of the public believing CEO pay is excessive. Some further contend the high levels of CEO pay that we observe are indicative of widespread failure of corporate governance.[662] According to an argument put forth by Bebchuk and Fried, "Flawed compensation arrangements have not been limited to a small number of 'bad apples'; they have been widespread, persistent, and systemic."[663]

While CEO compensation in the United States is certainly high, the level of pay only conveys part of the information stakeholders need to determine whether it is appropriate. Only a small portion of compensation consists of a fixed (cash) value. An analysis of compensation awarded to the CEOs of the 3,000 largest public companies shows a median value of $6.6 million, only 19% of which is salary. An additional 18% is offered through the annual bonus, subject to minimum, target, and maximum levels based on the achievement of performance metrics.

Almost all of the remainder—over half of pay—is offered as equity (in the form of restricted stock or stock options) and long-term incentive plans (LTIPs), whose final amounts depend heavily on stock-price and operating performance. The mix of CEO pay therefore indicates that even though the promised level of compensation might be high, its ultimate value can vary considerably based on performance.

Compensation mix is also important for the behaviors it encourages, including its influence on an executive's risk appetite. Research tends to show that equity incentives are associated with improved financial performance.[664] They represent a form of wealth sharing and encourage executives to pursue shareholder value by offering the opportunity to participate in this value creation.[665] Equity incentives also impose risk on executives that counteracts a natural tendency to become risk-averse over time.[666] Research shows that stock-option incentives encourage executives to take actions to increase the value of those options by increasing the risk profile (volatility) of their firms.[667]

At the same time, excessive risk incentives (i.e., too much stock-option exposure) can also encourage inappropriate behavior, such as workplace misconduct (underinvestment in safety or noncompliance with regulations) or the manipulation of earnings to increase the value of equity awards.[668] Some research suggests that excessive risk incentives contributed to the financial crisis of 2008, although this conclusion is contended.[669]

Boards must be thoughtful in determining the right level and mix of awards (including the appropriate level of risk-based incentives) and monitor actions to ensure they are compatible with corporate objectives. As such, CEO compensation is a prime example of a governance mechanism that is only superficially understood by many experts and requires thoughtful analysis.

John's thesis highlights the need for equitable and rational compensation plans to maintain a high caliber of executives. This aligns with the chapter's argument that the structure of compensation is as important as the level of pay in influencing executive behavior.

Voting Rights

Most public companies grant shareholders voting rights in proportion to their economic ownership in the firm (so-called "one share, one vote"). Nevertheless, a minority of companies (10%) issue share classes with disproportionate voting rights (for example, ten votes per share) that allow the holder of this class of stock the ability to exert voting control beyond their economic interest.[670] This share structure is generally called "dual-class shares" (or multiple share classes, if three classes are offered). The class with favorable voting rights typically does not trade in the public market but is held by an insider, founding family, or other shareholder friendly to management. Most institutional investors oppose dual-class shares, not least because these are the investors who tend to hold the shares with inferior voting rights.

In some circumstances, it might make sense to create dual-class stock. For example, a high-growth firm might want to raise capital to pursue its strategy but not issue straight common stock for fear of giving up voting control to new investors or expose itself to a takeover. Many venture-backed startups issue dual-class shares prior to initial public offering (IPO). At the same time, a dual-class share structure insulates those in a control position from the pressures of capital markets and minority owners.

The evidence on dual-class shares is mixed and can support both positive and negative interpretations. Gompers, Ishii, and Metrick find unequal voting rights are associated with lower market-to-book values.[671] Smart, Thirumalai, and Zutter find companies with a dual-class structure trade at lower values following IPO and this valuation discount persists.[672] Lauterbach and Pajuste find a positive stock-price reaction to the voluntary removal of dual-class shares.[673]

On the other hand, Cremers, Lauterbach, and Pajuste find shareholders are not harmed by a dual-class structure; these companies have similar long-term performance to single-class companies.[674] Anderson, Ottolenghi, and Reeb determine that the governance quality of companies with dual-class shares depends on factors beyond share structure (such as who holds the shares with disproportionate voting rights), rather than on the existence of multiple classes themselves.[675]

While controversial, dual-class shares can be viewed as a mini "case study" on governance factors in general. Whether a multiple-class share structure is positive or negative will depend on situational factors—the composition, skill, diligence, and moral compass of insiders (the executive team, board, and controlling shareholders), as well as the willingness of directors to provide active oversight to ensure performance.

Conclusion

In corporate governance, context matters. The structural features of a governance system are intended to protect the economic interests of all shareholders. In this chapter, we have reviewed a handful of these features, including board independence, the chairman/CEO role, diversity, CEO succession planning, executive compensation, and dual-class shares. In all of these cases, the debate over "best practices" is skewed by biases regarding what "should" be done, without regard to the quality of the company's choices or the context in which they are adopted. Just because a corporation has adopted a practice does not mean that it performs it well—or poorly.

Although the function of corporate governance has evolved significantly since the mid-20th century, many foundational principles remain relevant today. John Weinberg's 1948 thesis provides a rich historical context that underscores the complexity and variability inherent in corporate governance. His insights offer a nuanced understanding that complements the empirical analysis and contemporary issues discussed in this chapter.

John emphasizes the importance of context in evaluating the functions of corporate boards. He notes that the appraisal of board functions is complex and varies significantly across different corporations due to diverse products, competitive situations, company traditions, and individual capacities and personalities. This perspective aligns with the argument presented in the chapter that there is no one-size-fits-all approach to corporate governance.

Modern governance systems must be tailored to the specific needs and circumstances of each corporation, rather than adhering strictly to so-called "best practices." John's assertion that "no two corporations handle their top-management problems alike" highlights the necessity for a contextual understanding of governance practices. The thesis, like this chapter, illustrates this on numerous governance topics, including director independence, board leadership, board composition, information flows, board evaluations, and succession planning.

In conclusion, John Weinberg's 1948 thesis provides valuable historical insights that align with the contemporary issues and empirical analysis presented in this chapter. His emphasis on context, variability, and the nuanced understanding of governance practices supports the argument that effective corporate governance must be tailored to the specific needs and circumstances of each corporation. By integrating John's insights with current empirical research, we can appreciate the enduring relevance of these foundational principles in shaping modern governance systems.

Chapter 13

Board Practices from John Weinberg's Thesis to Today

Andrew Jones

Corporate boards have long served as both a mirror and a mechanism of American capitalism. They reflect prevailing assumptions about corporate purpose, accountability, and power—and they help shape those norms through decisions on composition, leadership, structure, and oversight. In 1948, John L. Weinberg, then a Princeton undergraduate and later a senior partner in Goldman Sachs, authored a thesis titled *Status and Functions of Corporate Directors*.

Drawing on extensive data from the National Industrial Conference Board (NICB), his thesis offered an early empirically informed analysis of board practices in the United States.[676] John's legacy is institutionalized in the John L. Weinberg Center for Corporate Governance at the University of Delaware, established in 2000 to advance corporate governance in the legal home of most US public companies.

The NICB was founded in 1916 to promote cooperation between business and labor at a time of widespread industrial unrest. Conceived as a nonpartisan, research-driven institution, it sought to improve economic decision-making by providing objective data and analysis. In 1970, the NICB was renamed The Conference Board, reflecting its broadened global scope and its continued evolution into a leading independent, business-oriented, nonprofit think tank.

Today, it serves companies, investors, policymakers, and academics through nonpartisan research and practical benchmarking.[677] Its ongoing studies of US public company boards—undertaken by its Governance & Sustainability Center, in partnership with ESGAUGE, the KPMG Board Leadership Center, Russell Reynolds Associates, and the Weinberg Center—offer a unique longitudinal view into how governance practices have responded to regulatory reform, economic shifts, and stakeholder demands.[678]

This chapter draws on The Conference Board's historical and contemporary research to revisit six key themes from John's 1948 thesis that remain relevant today: board composition, board size, board leadership, committee structure, director stock ownership, and director education. Using current benchmarking data from Russell 3000 and S&P 500 companies, it examines how board governance has evolved in response to regulatory reform, investor expectations, social change, and rising complexity.

These are not merely structural or technical considerations—they speak to deeper concerns about power, oversight, legitimacy, and the changing nature of corporate leadership. By placing John's mid-20th-century insights in dialogue with 21st-century data, the chapter offers a long view of where progress has been made, where challenges remain, and how directors can govern more effectively in today's environment.

Board Composition and Diversity: Who Serves and Why

The composition of a corporate board is both a reflection of and a mechanism for implementing a company's governance philosophy, risk tolerance, and long-term strategic priorities. It is therefore unsurprising that board composition—who is on the board, the skills and experience they bring, what perspectives and backgrounds they represent, and how they are selected—has remained one of the most scrutinized and evolving areas of corporate governance in both academic literature and reform practice.[679]

John Weinberg's 1948 thesis included an extended analysis of the distinction between "inside" (direct ties) and "outside" (independent) directors and the implications of board composition for corporate effectiveness. He noted that while inside directors—typically senior executives—bring deep operational knowledge and a strong connection to the business, they may lack independence and risk creating a system in which management effectively supervises itself. Outside directors, by contrast, offer broader perspectives, policy experience, and the ability to assess corporate strategy from a distance. John acknowledged growing recognition of their value, particularly in larger corporations, where outside directors had already become more common.[680]

John's discussion foreshadowed many modern governance debates. He also stressed that a board's effectiveness depends not just on insider status or stature, but on the mix of experiences, perspectives, and motivations. In particular, he observed that a diversity of occupational backgrounds—spanning industry, banking, law, and beyond—could strengthen oversight and decision-making. "The wider the variety of occupations and experience, the greater will be the benefit to the corporation," he wrote, anticipating later arguments for professional diversity on boards long before contemporary standards on board diversity were formalized.[681]

Despite such early insights, US boards remained largely homogenous for decades, particularly in demographic terms. Through the 1960s and 1970s, director pipelines were dominated by internal promotions or appointments from affiliated institutions such as law firms and financial entities. Board refreshment was sporadic, tenures long, and accountability mechanisms weak. Governance expectations began to shift in the late 1970s and 1980s as legal, market, and investor dynamics began to reshape the corporate landscape. The emergence of institutional investors, early shareholder activism, and mounting concerns about management entrenchment prompted growing calls for greater independence and external perspectives on boards.[682] Yet "diversity" in the modern sense—relating to gender, race, and lived experience—remained a secondary consideration.

It was not until the 1990s and early 2000s, especially in the wake of high-profile corporate failures like Enron and WorldCom, that board composition received sharper regulatory attention. The Sarbanes–Oxley Act of 2002, along with enhanced listing requirements, introduced stricter standards on independence, audit-committee membership, and financial expertise.[683] While these reforms indirectly encouraged board turnover, efforts to improve demographic diversity remained largely voluntary and unregulated, relying instead on reputational pressure, advocacy, and evolving investor expectations.

By the 2010s, board refreshment and diversity had become increasingly intertwined in governance discourse. Influential investor-stewardship codes (e.g., the UK Stewardship Code, Japan's Corporate Governance Code), along with US-based proxy-voting policies by asset managers like BlackRock, Vanguard, and State Street, placed greater emphasis on board diversity as both a business imperative and a risk governance issue.[684] Voluntary initiatives such as the 30% Club and the Board Diversity Action Alliance gained traction, and leading companies began disclosing targets for gender and racial/ethnic representation on boards.

After 2020, board diversity efforts gained new momentum. Catalyzed by broader societal movements (notably Black Lives Matter), heightened investor engagement, and regulatory actions, US public companies increased the representation of women, racially and ethnically diverse individuals, and directors with nontraditional career paths. According to contemporary analysis by The Conference Board of disclosures by publicly traded US companies, the share of women on S&P 500 boards increased from 27% in 2020 to 34%

in 2025 (Figure 1), while the corresponding share for Russell 3000 boards rose from 21% to 30%.

The share of racially and ethnically diverse (non-white) directors also rose—from 20% to 25% in the S&P 500, and from 21% to 24% in the Russell 3000—marking record highs for both gender and racial diversity on US public company boards.[685] Gains were strongest between 2020 and 2023, when investor attention and state legislative action spurred a wave of new appointments.

Figure 13.1: Women board directors, lead directors, and board chairs, S&P 500, 2020–2025

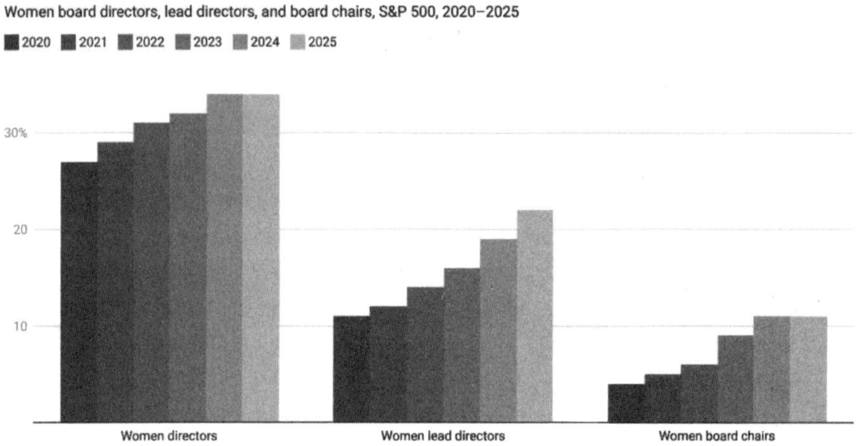

Source: The Conference Board/ESGAUGE, 2025.

By 2025, however, there were signs of this momentum slowing, with a more challenging legal and political climate influencing the invalidation of several state and regulatory initiatives. California's board-diversity mandates (SB 826 for women and AB 979 for underrepresented minorities) were struck down on equal-protection grounds, with appellate decisions in 2023 upholding those rulings.[686] In late 2024, the US Court of Appeals for the Fifth Circuit vacated the SEC-approved Nasdaq board-diversity disclosure rule, deeming it unconstitutional under the First Amendment.[687] These developments reflected a broader shift in the political, legal, and regulatory landscape, raising new legal risks for companies that explicitly consider demographic characteristics in board selection.

Appointment trends reflect this shift. According to data from The Conference Board, the share of newly appointed independent directors from historically-minority groups peaked in 2022 but declined by 2025 in both the S&P 500 and Russell 3000 (Figure 2). In 2022, only 50% of new S&P 500 directors and 52% in the Russell 3000 identified as "White." By 2025, that figure had risen to 75%

in both indexes, reflecting a broad decline in appointments from certain other racial and ethnic groups.[688]

Figure 13.2: Newly appointed board director demographics, S&P 500, 2020–2025

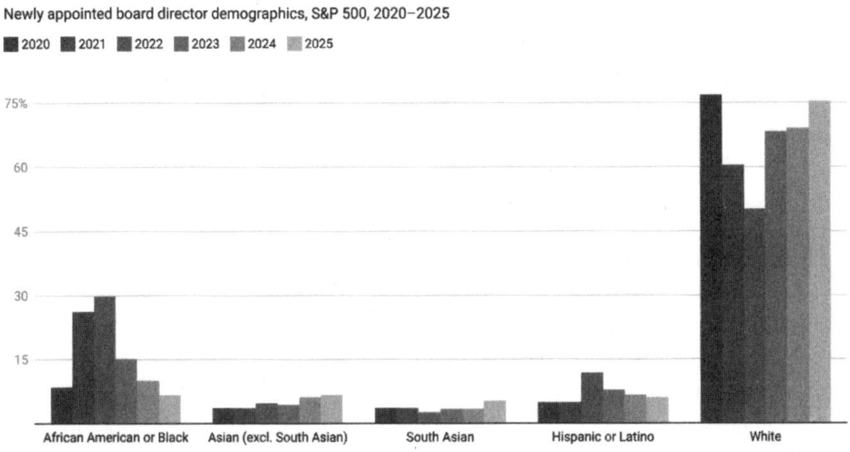

Source: The Conference Board/ESGAUGE, 2025.

The drop was especially sharp for "African American or Black" directors: in the Russell 3000, their share fell from 26% in 2022 to 8% in 2025; in the S&P 500, from 30% to 7%. "Hispanic or Latino" representation among newly elected directors also declined, falling from its 2022 peak (9% in the Russell 3000 and 12% in the S&P 500) to 6% in both indexes in 2025.[689]

This pullback may reflect a natural plateau—particularly among large companies that had already met diversity targets—but it also likely points to heightened legal risks, political scrutiny, talent pipeline constraints, and a shift from recruitment to integration. Year-over-year benchmarking has also become more difficult due to a marked retreat in director racial and ethnic diversity disclosure in 2025, amid sustained scrutiny of corporate diversity commitments. From 2024 to 2025, the share of S&P 500 companies providing any such disclosure dropped from 98% to 66%; in the Russell 3000, it fell from 86% to 45%.[690] In this context, board diversity remains a nuanced challenge, requiring balance between representation, qualifications, group dynamics, and governance needs.

At the same time, attention has shifted toward functional diversity—the range of directors' professional skills and backgrounds. Boards are adapting to new oversight demands, especially in areas like technology, human capital, and ESG (environmental, social, and governance). These shifts reflect a gradual move away from traditional profiles—former CEOs, CFOs, and general counsel—

and toward a more adaptive, stakeholder-facing mix of competencies suited to today's complex risk environment.[691] For example, from 2020 to 2025:

- S&P 500 directors with cybersecurity experience rose from 13% to 27%; in the Russell 3000, from 7% to 17%.
- Human-capital expertise increased from 23% to 40% in the S&P 500, and from 14% to 28% in the Russell 3000.
- International experience rose from 41% to 52% in the S&P 500, and from 23% to 31% in the Russell 3000.
- ESG expertise increased from 2% to 15% in the S&P 500, and from 1% to 10% in the Russell 3000.

Looking ahead, the trajectory of board composition will be shaped by the interplay of legal constraints, investor priorities, and changing business demands. While the rollback of regulatory mandates may limit prescriptive approaches, the underlying rationale for diversity—both demographic and functional—remains intact: it enhances board deliberations, strengthens oversight, and contributes to long-term value creation. Weinberg's early advocacy for occupational diversity continues to resonate today. It reminds us that board composition is not just about who sits at the table, but whether the collective group is equipped to govern wisely and decisively in an era of constant change.

Board Size: Finding the Right Balance

In addition to who serves on the board, it is equally important to consider how many directors should serve. An effective board must be large enough to offer a breadth of expertise, perspectives, and stakeholder representation, yet small enough to remain cohesive, decisive, and actively engaged. Striking this balance is central to the effectiveness of governance, particularly as the scope of board responsibilities expands to include emerging areas such as climate, cybersecurity, and talent strategy.

In his 1948 thesis, Weinberg cited NICB data to observe that board size varied by company scale: larger corporations typically had nine to 15 directors, while smaller firms often had boards of five to seven. Weinberg emphasized the importance of limiting board membership to "those able to visualize the needs and able to make major contributions toward the success of the company as a whole." He cautioned that oversized boards risked becoming symbolic, with real authority concentrated in a smaller executive committee—diminishing the deliberative function of the full board.[692]

This concern remains valid today. Academic and practitioner research consistently finds that larger boards can dilute individual accountability, hinder engagement, and complicate group dynamics. Coordination challenges may suppress open dialogue, reduce participation, and delay decision-making. Conversely, boards that are too small may lack the functional expertise, independence, and diversity necessary to address increasingly complex oversight demands across risk, strategy, compliance, and stakeholder expectations.[693]

According to current data from The Conference Board, the average board size for Russell 3000 companies is nine directors, with a median also of nine. In the S&P 500, the average rises to 10.7 and the median to 11. Roughly 16% of Russell 3000 boards and 23% of S&P 500 boards have exactly ten directors, a figure often cited as a practical equilibrium between diversity of thought and board cohesion. At the extremes, only 3% of S&P 500 companies report boards with fewer than eight members, while over 14% have more than 12—predominantly in highly regulated industries or firms with global operations.[694]

The Conference Board data also show that the optimal board size varies across sectors or organizational structures. In industries such as financial services, energy, and healthcare—where regulatory scrutiny is intense and risk exposure is high—boards tend to be larger to accommodate a wider range of expertise and committee responsibilities. By contrast, companies in fast-moving sectors like technology or consumer goods often favor smaller boards to promote speed, flexibility, and more informal interaction.[695]

Board expansion, when it occurs, tends to be incremental. Companies rarely add multiple new seats simultaneously. Instead, they phase in directors as part of refreshment cycles or succession plans. Increasingly, companies use temporary size expansions to accommodate mentoring, facilitate knowledge transfer, or prepare for future retirements. In some cases, growth in board size is also used strategically to broaden representation or enhance committee functionality without displacing current directors.

Ultimately, there is no one-size-fits-all formula. While data point to common thresholds—typically between nine and 11 directors for large US public companies—board size should reflect the complexity of the enterprise, its regulatory context, ownership structure, and strategic priorities. Research continues to support the view that size alone is not a predictor of performance. What matters more is how effectively the board uses its structure to deliberate, challenge, and act in service of the company and its stakeholders.

Board Leadership: Chair, CEO, and Independent Oversight

Beyond composition and size, the role of board leadership is pivotal in shaping how effectively a board functions. Who sets the agenda, facilitates dialogue, and holds management accountable can determine whether the board acts as an independent governing body or merely endorses executive decisions.

In his 1948 thesis, John noted, "The office of chairman of the board, because of its potential leadership over the directorate, is an extremely important position in the corporation. Its utilization for the benefit of the corporation has only been partially recognized."[696] He cited NICB data that showed only about half of the corporations studied had chairmen of the board, with the larger corporations using the office more frequently.

John also highlighted "the differences between the chairman, the chief executive, and the president" as a persistent source of confusion, adding that "[t]his perplexity may be very harmful." He cautioned that when one individual holds both the CEO and chair roles, it creates a "dual responsibility," whereas when the roles are split, a constructive relationship with clearly defined duties is critical. He concluded that "there is a definite need in a specific place in the corporate structure for someone to handle board leadership."

Since John's time, one of the most enduring debates in global corporate governance has been whether the board chair should be independent of management or whether the CEO may also serve as chair. In the United States, the traditional model has been combined leadership, reflecting the view that a unified voice can enhance authority and accountability. However, this model has faced increasing scrutiny from institutional investors, proxy advisors, and governance practitioners. Academics have also explored whether separating these roles has a measurable effect on firm performance.[697]

Proponents of separating the CEO and chair roles argue that it enhances board independence, avoids excessive concentration of power, and facilitates more objective oversight—especially regarding CEO evaluation, compensation, and succession. A non-executive chair can also focus on the board's effectiveness and provide a stronger counterweight to management. Opponents of mandated separation counter that combining the roles can lead to more streamlined leadership and communication. In this view, a strong lead independent director (LID), robust committees, and engaged board culture can mitigate the risks of concentration—particularly in founder-led firms or organizations that prioritize agility and innovation.[698]

There is no US regulatory requirement to separate the CEO and chair roles. Instead, both New York Stock Exchange (NYSE) and Nasdaq listing standards require companies to disclose their board leadership structure and explain why it is appropriate. This "disclose and explain" framework reflects a principles-based approach, allowing flexibility while recognizing that leadership structure is a material governance consideration. Proxy advisors such as Institutional Shareholder Services (ISS) also include board leadership structure in their voting analyses, especially when performance concerns are present.[699]

Outside the United States, norms differ. In the United Kingdom, Australia, and much of Europe, governance codes explicitly recommend the separation of chair and CEO roles, often linking this separation to board independence and shareholder trust. These recommendations are typically enforced through "comply or explain" provisions, under which companies must justify deviations. In civil-law countries like France and Germany, the structure of corporate law often mandates role separation by default.[700]

Where companies in the United States have not adopted a fully independent chair structure, many designate a LID. While not equivalent to a non-executive chair, the LID often performs many of the same functions: presiding over executive sessions, reviewing board materials, liaising between independent directors and the CEO, and engaging with shareholders. A strong LID can help reinforce discipline and independence even in a combined CEO–chair model.

According to current data from The Conference Board, 33.5% of Russell 3000 companies reported that the current CEO served as chair in 2025, down slightly from 37% in 2018. In the S&P 500, the figure was 42.8% in 2025, down from 48.7% in 2018. However, the presence of LIDs remains widespread: 45.3% of Russell 3000 companies and 62% of S&P 500 companies designated a LID in 2025.[701]

These patterns reflect a broader, incremental shift toward reinforcing the independence of board leadership—even where full role separation is not in place. Sectoral differences remain notable, with independent board chairs most common at Russell 3000 companies in the industrials, energy, information technology, materials, and healthcare sectors. They are least common in consumer staples and financial services companies. These differences often reflect variations in business models, governance norms, and investor expectations—particularly where capital intensity, innovation cycles, or global operations place a premium on independent oversight.[702]

In recent years, shareholder pressure has increasingly targeted board leadership structure, particularly during contested elections or periods of underperformance.

Notably, shareholder proposals calling for an independent board chair remain a consistent feature of US proxy seasons. While these proposals rarely win majority support, they can still influence board deliberations. From 2020 to 2025, Russell 3000 companies faced between 35 and 91 such proposals annually, with average shareholder support ranging from 29.5% to 34.4%. Notably, 2023 saw a spike in volume—91 proposals—despite no corresponding increase in support levels, which have hovered just below 30% in recent years.[703]

Ultimately, the question of whether the chair should be independent is secondary to whether the board is effectively led. The qualities that matter most—integrity, sound judgment, facilitation skill, and commitment to governance excellence—apply regardless of title. Whether through an independent chair or a capable lead director, high-performing boards ensure that leadership structures support robust oversight, effective challenge, and strategic foresight.

Board Structure: Committees and the Architecture of Oversight

Governance is also shaped by how boards organize their work: through leadership roles, standing committees, and specialized oversight bodies. In his 1948 thesis, John provided a detailed examination of board committees, emphasizing their growing role in facilitating effective administration and informed oversight. Drawing on data from the NICB, he noted that executive committees were the most significant of the top-management committees at the time, especially among large corporations. Over 60% of companies with assets exceeding $50 million had such committees, compared with just 7% of those with under $1 million in assets. These committees, often composed primarily of senior executives, were empowered to act on behalf of the board between meetings, formulate policy, and filter key issues—raising concerns about the concentration of authority and the need for clearly defined limits and accountability.

John also traced the emergence of more specialized oversight bodies, notably salary (now compensation) and audit committees.[704] He highlighted the 1938 McKesson & Robbins scandal as a turning point that prompted the US SEC to advocate for audit committees composed exclusively of non-officer directors.[705] These reforms, he argued, were critical to restoring trust in the board's trusteeship function. He called for audit committees to be independent, permanent, and empowered to select and oversee external auditors. Similarly, he emphasized that salary committees should be led by outside directors to ensure objective oversight of executive compensation.[706] In both cases, he underscored the need for clear mandates, regular engagement, and independence from management—anticipating many of the committee structures and principles that define modern board governance.

Since John's time, board committees have expanded dramatically in number, scope, and regulatory significance. The Sarbanes–Oxley Act of 2002 made fully independent audit committees a legal requirement for US public companies, mandated that they oversee external auditors directly, and required at least one member to be a financial expert. The Dodd–Frank Wall Street Reform and Consumer Protection Act of 2010 added further momentum to compensation-committee reform, introducing nonbinding shareholder "say-on-pay" votes, enhanced disclosure rules, and requirements for committee independence. These developments codified the accountability mechanisms that John had only begun to envision.[707]

Nominating and governance committees—once limited to selecting board members—have taken on wider mandates, including oversight of ESG matters, director performance evaluations, and engagement with investors. These shifts are partly driven by expectations from institutional investors and proxy advisory firms, as well as NYSE and Nasdaq listing rules requiring independent directors and formal committee charters.[708]

Internationally, similar trends have unfolded: the United Kingdom's Corporate Governance Code mandates independent audit, nomination, and remuneration committees, while the European Union's Shareholder Rights Directive II requires transparency in director pay and reinforces board accountability. Regulatory frameworks in Canada, Australia, and Singapore similarly promote committee independence, robust disclosure, and regular performance evaluation.[709]

Current data from The Conference Board underscore how board structures continue to adapt to a more complex oversight environment (Figure 3). Core committees—audit, compensation, and nominating/governance—are now ubiquitous due to exchange rules, but their mandates have expanded. Audit committees often oversee enterprise risk management, beyond traditional financial reporting. Compensation committees have extended their remit to include human capital and workforce oversight, with many companies renaming the committee to "Compensation and Talent."[710] Nominating/governance committees now frequently monitor ESG risks, succession planning, and shareholder relations.

Figure 13.3: Share of companies with selected board committees, S&P 500 and Russell 3000, 2026

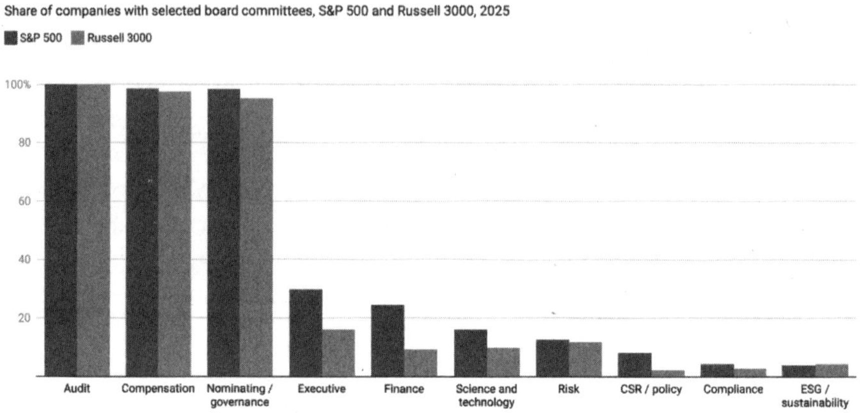

Source: The Conference Board/ESGAUGE, 2025.

At the same time, new committee types have emerged. Risk committees are common in sectors such as financial services and energy, and companies in the S&P 500 have introduced technology, cybersecurity, and science-focused committees. However, only 4% of S&P 500 companies have dedicated ESG committees, reflecting a broader trend of integrating ESG oversight into nominating/governance or audit committees instead.[711]

The executive committee—dominant when Weinberg authored his thesis—is now in retreat. Just 30% of S&P 500 companies and 16% of Russell 3000 companies maintained one in 2025, a decline from earlier decades.[712] This shift reflects the increasing preference for full-board deliberation on major strategic, financial, and reputational matters, including mergers, capital allocation, and stakeholder concerns. While specialized committees allow for focus and flexibility, boards increasingly reserve core decisions for plenary discussion.

John's enduring insight—that structure matters only insofar as it enables effective oversight—remains relevant. Titles and charters are necessary but insufficient. What ultimately distinguishes high-performing boards is their ability to use structures as tools for ensuring that directors receive the right information, engage in rigorous deliberation, and act independently in service of the company and its stakeholders.

Director Stock Ownership: Aligning Interests and Accountability

Structural design and formal roles matter, but so too does alignment of interests between directors and shareholders. Director stock ownership can represent a key mechanism for fostering this alignment, and has long been a debated aspect of director effectiveness. John's 1948 thesis included analysis of this issue, drawing on NICB data. He noted that while most state laws at the time technically required directors to hold a nominal number of qualifying shares, many corporations had begun to relax this standard. "[T]he revisions of the laws," he wrote, "show a tendency to eliminate this requirement, and leave the decision in the hands of the corporation itself."[713]

John described two dominant schools of thought: one held that directors need not hold shares to serve effectively, while the other believed a financial stake was necessary to ensure alignment with shareholder interests. Citing the NICB's *Compensation and Duties of Corporate Directors* (1946), he highlighted survey results showing that while most executives viewed stock ownership as desirable, they did not consider it essential. "Only two [of 97 respondents] felt that a large equity was indispensable for a good board member; on the other hand, only nine answers felt that it made no difference." His conclusion was pragmatic: while share ownership may strengthen engagement, "[c]orporations either with or without large personal stock ownership by directors may succeed or fail—no general rule is applicable."[714]

In the decades that followed, stock ownership emerged as a key plank in the architecture of director accountability. Particularly after the corporate scandals of the early 2000s—Enron, WorldCom, and others—investors, regulators, and proxy advisors increasingly pressed for clear director ownership policies. Many companies went beyond recommending share ownership to mandating it, and introduced retention requirements to ensure directors remained meaningfully invested.[715]

Today, stock ownership and retention guidelines are a key feature of board governance frameworks. Analysis of public disclosure data by The Conference Board shows that, as of 2025, 44.1% of Russell 3000 companies had adopted stock-ownership guidelines for directors, while an additional 28.6% combined ownership guidelines with retention policies. However, more than one in four companies (26.4%) still reported having no such requirements in place. Among S&P 500 companies, uptake is significantly higher: by 2025, 97.3% had adopted some form of stock-ownership or retention policy, with only 2.7% having none.[716]

Ownership guidelines are typically tied to a multiple of the director's annual cash retainer—often five times or more—and are expected to be met within a specified timeframe, such as five years. Retention policies, while less prevalent, require directors to hold a portion of shares received as compensation until after their board service ends. These measures are intended to promote long-term alignment between directors and shareholders.[717]

They also reflect a broader shift toward equity-based compensation in director pay structures. In 2025, 85.8% of Russell 3000 companies provided stock awards to directors, up from 79.4% in 2020. The use of stock options continued to decline, falling to just 13.8% in 2025. Among S&P 500 companies, 97.1% granted stock awards in 2025, with a median value of $195,000—significantly higher than the median $105,000 cash retainer.[718]

John's warning about perfunctory directors who lacked a stake in the enterprise remains relevant. Yet the modern emphasis on ownership guidelines, combined with enhanced equity-based pay structures, reflects how governance practices have evolved to institutionalize what was once only encouraged.

The Informed Director: Education, Information, and Engagement

No matter how well a board is structured or how skilled its members may be, its effectiveness depends on whether directors are well informed and actively engaged. In his thesis, John emphasized that directors must not only be willing to direct but must "*know enough* to direct." Drawing extensively on NICB research, he described a wide array of formal and informal mechanisms for keeping directors informed, including board meetings, advance agendas, committee reports, financial summaries, budgets, management briefings, plant visits, newsletters, luncheons, and informal personal contacts. He stressed that effective information flow requires coordination, judgment, and mutual understanding between directors and management—particularly the chief executive, whose role in shaping the information environment is paramount. John warned that directors who arrive unprepared, fail to engage, or lack confidence in interacting with full-time executives diminish the board's contribution. To support meaningful oversight, he argued, boards must integrate both structured data and informal dialogue into a coherent process that enables directors to analyze, question, and participate substantively in decisions.[719]

This concern remains foundational in modern governance. While legal structures grant boards oversight powers, the exercise of those powers depends on directors having access to relevant, timely, and accurate information—and the capacity to interpret it thoughtfully. Following John's 1948 thesis, boards gradually professionalized, and directors were increasingly expected to possess, or develop, subject-matter expertise. Yet for much of the 20th century, education practices remained ad hoc. Information often flowed through informal channels or management-controlled filters, offering little assurance of completeness or independence. The practices John described—such as site visits, briefings, and social gatherings—persisted but were rarely structured or systematized to ensure all directors were equally informed or engaged.[720]

By the 1980s and 1990s, legal and regulatory developments had begun to impose clearer standards on board conduct and information practices. Landmark cases such as *Smith v. Van Gorkom* (1985) and *In re Caremark International Inc. Derivative Litigation* (1996) transformed the legal landscape, making it clear that directors could be held personally liable if they failed to properly inform themselves.[721] These decisions elevated the legal expectation that directors exercise not only care but also informed judgment.

In response, many companies introduced formal onboarding processes and began to offer regular briefings on emerging risks and compliance matters. As globalization and digital transformation accelerated, boards faced new demands to understand areas beyond traditional financial oversight, including cyber threats, international regulatory regimes, and environmental sustainability—catalyzing a shift from passive information reception to proactive, continuous learning.[722]

Today, director education has evolved into a structured and ongoing process, particularly among larger US public companies. As of 2025, data from The Conference Board show that 58% of Russell 3000 and 52% of S&P 500 companies conduct in-house director orientation and continuing education programs. An additional 28% of Russell 3000 and 47% of S&P 500 companies supplement in-house efforts with external resources, while fewer than 1% in either index fully outsource education. Evaluations are also becoming more comprehensive: 54% of S&P 500 companies conduct full-board, committee, and individual director evaluations, compared with 37% of Russell 3000 companies, a notable rise from 43% and 24% respectively in 2020.

Furthermore, 40% of S&P 500 companies now employ independent facilitators to conduct board assessments, up from 21% in 2020; Russell 3000 adoption of this practice increased from 10% to 18% over the same period. Skills matrices have also become a staple: in 2025, 80% of S&P 500 companies and 48% of Russell 3000 companies disclosed the use of such matrices to help identify gaps in expertise. These developments reflect a growing recognition that director learning is not ancillary but central to effective board governance in today's high-stakes environment.[723]

As regulatory complexity increases and stakeholder expectations rise, the demand for truly informed and engaged directors has never been higher. Directors must be capable not only of absorbing information but of probing it—asking the right questions, identifying omissions, and understanding long-term implications. John's foundational insights remain pertinent, and high-quality information flow and director education are no longer peripheral responsibilities; they are core elements of fiduciary duty in an era defined by complexity, scrutiny, and accelerating change.

Conclusion

While authored in a very different business and societal landscape, John Weinberg's 1948 thesis offers a valuable lens through which to examine enduring questions in US corporate governance. Rather than focusing solely on legal structures, John examined the director as a participant in a system shaped by evolving norms, responsibilities, and relationships—capturing governance as a dynamic, living practice.

This chapter has revisited six central themes from his thesis—board composition, board size, leadership structure, committee design, director stock ownership, and director education—drawing on contemporary data and insights from The Conference Board. It shows how governance has responded to regulatory changes, investor scrutiny, social expectations, and increasing complexity, while also illustrating how many of the questions John raised—about independence, engagement, and access to information—remain relevant in 2025 and beyond.

Today's directors operate in a more global, transparent, and high-stakes environment. Boards are expected to oversee not just financial performance but also climate strategy, human capital, cybersecurity, political risk, and social impact. As corporate governance enters a new era defined by expanded responsibilities and greater scrutiny, the core challenge persists: ensuring that directors have the judgment, independence, and courage to ask the right questions—and act on them. John's thesis provides a useful reminder that many of today's governance challenges are rooted in long-standing tensions—and that effectiveness depends as much on discernment and adaptability as on structure.

Chapter 14

Board Practices in Context: Evidence from a Society for Corporate Governance Survey

Paul F. Washington

The Society for Corporate Governance appreciates the opportunity to contribute to this book featuring certain works of John L. Weinberg and Sidney J. Weinberg. A distinctive feature of the Society's contributions to corporate governance research is the original data generated through benchmarking surveys of our members, covering a wide range of topics. Unlike academic studies or proxy-advisor surveys, the Society's data reflect the practical experiences and judgments of governance professionals working directly with boards.

This chapter presents the results of a survey designed for this book.[724] The topics were selected to reflect on and respond to distinctive features of the Weinberg works. The survey was conducted in August–September 2025, in time to be presented at the Weinberg Center's symposium on October 9, 2025, while still providing fresh data for inclusion in this volume.

First, we explore board composition, including the concepts of director independence and of a professional director—those who serve on multiple boards without holding executive positions. The concept of the professional director is of special interest because it was John's main normative prescription in his thesis. The related concept of director independence is also timely as it continues to be a subject of active discussion and debate by policymakers.

Second, we address policies and practices regarding the number of directorships board members hold. This topic is of interest given the large number of boards on which Sidney Weinberg served, the smaller but still large number on which John Weinberg served, and the growing practice in recent years—driven in part by demands of the role and investor and proxy-advisor expectations and policies—of imposing limits on public company directorships.

Third, we examine board leadership structures, which have evolved significantly over time. This includes the separation of the CEO and board-chair roles, a practice that has gained some traction in recent years. John's thesis discusses board leadership in a section entitled "The Status of the Chairman of the Board," highlighting the longstanding importance of this topic in corporate governance.

Finally, we address the topic of director compensation, which has implications for several of the topics listed above—including board composition, independence, and the number of boards on which an individual director may serve. The Society did not conduct a survey on this topic; instead, this chapter draws on recent third-party market data.

The Society's survey results and other data indicate that: (1) there is a prevalent (but not dominant) cohort of "professional directors" in corporate America; (2) both public and private companies enthusiastically embrace the practice of having independent directors constitute a majority of their boards; (3) a majority of public firms limit the number of boards on which their independent directors may serve; (4) a large percentage of public and private firms embrace separating the board chair and CEO roles; and (5) director compensation is lagging in terms of growth and, perhaps, effectiveness.

This chapter's analysis of, and reflection on, these survey results and other data offer some suggestions for further consideration by corporate boards. These include the benefits of: (1) having directors who are "still in the trenches" and do not qualify as professional directors; (2) evaluating director independence not just under the rules but *in practice* when assessing board performance; (3) private companies considering limiting the number of boards on which their directors serve (and for *all* companies, considering private company board service when assessing a director's time commitments); (4) making a non-ideological, company-specific analysis of board leadership structures; and (5) without placing undue focus on director compensation, ensuring that the company has a compensation program tailored to advance the effectiveness of its particular board.

Board Composition: Professional Directors

There is a class of "professional directors" in US boardrooms. As our survey of public, private, and non-profit corporations indicated, two-thirds of companies represented by respondents have at least one independent director who (a) serves on other boards and (b) does not currently hold an executive position. The percentage was somewhat higher for private companies (71%) than for public companies (67%).

Figure 14.1: Do you have any directors who are "professional directors" (i.e., independent board members serving several non-competing organizations holding no executive position and representing no particular group)?

Answer Choices	Responses	
Yes	66%	107
No	29%	46
Unsure	5%	8
Other (please specify)	0%	0
	Answered	**161**
	Skipped	**16**

While these data suggest that professional directors are pervasive, they do not indicate that they are a numerically dominant force in corporate boardrooms. As noted in the chart below, at only 38% of the respondent companies do directors who serve on multiple boards represent more than half the board members.

Figure 14.2: Approximately what percentage of your directors (including the CEO or other executive directors) serve on multiple public company boards (i.e., public company boards in addition to your organization's board)?

Answer Choices	Responses	
None	9%	15
Under 10%	7%	12
10% up to 25%	17%	29
25% up to 50%	29%	49
50% up to 75%	22%	38
At least 75%	15%	26
Unsure	1%	2
	Answered	**171**
	Skipped	**6**

By virtue of their experience on multiple boards, as well as their presumed previous tenure as an executive, professional directors can undoubtedly bring value to both the deliberations and cultural dynamics of boards and committees. At the same time, it can be valuable to have directors who are still active either as

CEOs or as executives a level or two below the CEO. Indeed, senior executives outside the C-suite may not only bring valuable substantive knowledge, but also a perspective of what it means to lead a business unit or department outside the sometimes-rarefied air of the boardroom or C-suite.

Board Composition: Director Independence

The survey results indicate that director independence continues to be a focus. As a threshold matter, the survey respondents were, by key measures, in line with the broader market. For example, about two-thirds (61%) have between nine and 12 directors on their board, consistent with the broader market of public companies.[725]

Figure 14.3: How many members currently serve on your board?

Answer Choices	Responses	
Fewer than 5 members	1%	1
5 to 8 members	18%	31
9 to 12 members	61%	106
13 to 16 members	17%	30
More than 16 members	3%	6
	Answered	**174**
	Skipped	**3**

Public, private, and non-profit corporations strongly embrace the practice of having a super-majority of independent directors. Overall, survey respondents noted that 82% of their directors were independent.

Based on the survey results, the average percentage of independent directors at *public* companies was 83%, exceeding the majority-independent requirement of stock exchange listing standards. The 83% also exceeds the companies' own policies—70% of public companies have policies requiring that a simple majority of the board be independent, and just 8% require that three-quarters of directors be independent.

The story was similar for private companies, where the percentage of independent directors was lower—but still dramatically higher than external or internal requirements. Based on our survey, an average of 64% of the board members at each *private* company were independent, far above any regulatory standards (which are either non-existent or sometimes require just one-third

Figure 14.4: What is the current composition of your board in terms of inside, outside, and independent directors?

Answer Choices	Average Percentage	Responses	
% of Inside Directors	12%		154
% of Outside Directors	69%		125
% of Independent Directors	82%		157
		Answered	**161**
		Skipped	**16**

Note: Inside Directors: executive directors, including CEO and other senior executives. Outside Directors: non-executive directors, not involved in day-to-day management. Independent Directors: directors with no material relationship with the company.

of the board be independent) or company policy (where only 46% require a majority of independent directors, none require three-quarters independence, and 23% have no independence requirement at all).

While the survey results did not speak to when and how boards conduct their independence analyses, it may be worth spending a moment on the topic. Boards may be naturally inclined to make a binary determination as to independence once a year, when it comes time to nominate directors for re-election, driven largely by the objective criteria set forth in stock exchange listing standards. In our view, however, boards may be well served by considering the *multifaceted concept* of independence and the *nuanced context* in which it is manifested as part of *both* the renomination and self-evaluation processes.

As for the *concept* of independence, the New York Stock Exchange (NYSE) listing standards define independence largely as the absence of a "material relationship with the company."[726] By comparison, courts have adopted more holistic, if varying, approaches to defining independence.[727] As the Chancery Court held in the context of a special litigation committee, "the question of independence 'turns on whether a director is, *for any substantial reason*, incapable of making a decision with only the best interests of the corporation in mind.'"[728] The concept of independence is therefore not limited to ties to management or to the company, but to any relationships that may interfere with the exercise of independent judgment.

As for context, as the *Oracle* court noted, independent judgment must be exercised in the context of fiduciary duties of care and loyalty. Thus, independence must be consistent with the duty of loyalty; and judgment must be carried out in accordance with the duty of care. Moreover, while each director is held accountable for their own judgment, they inherently exercise it as part of a group—and thus their independent judgment must coexist with collective decision-making. Further, directors exercise their individual judgment, and boards their collective judgment, often in reliance on management.

This suggests that even if boards are required to engage in a binary exercise in defining *whether* a director is independent, they can undertake—as part of the annual board nomination and self-evaluation processes—a more nuanced evaluation of *how* a director has exercised their independent judgment. In this regard, a board may wish to consider whether the director has exercised their independent judgment in the broader context of their fiduciary duties, the collective decision-making process, and an appropriately constructive relationship with management.

Limits on Overboarding

The Society's survey data relating to director "overboarding" are illuminating and suggest a number of areas for further board attention and consideration. As shown in the charts below, about two-thirds of respondent companies impose limits on the number of boards on which an independent director can serve, with the most common limit being a total of four boards.

Figure 14.5: Does your organization impose any formal limits on the number of directorships an independent director can hold across organizations?

No	24%	40
Not applicable or unsure	3%	5
Other (please specify)	1%	2
	Answered	**166**
	Skipped	**11**

Note: This question excludes limits that may be imposed on board leadership (e.g., board chair or lead director) and/or particular committee chairs or committee members (e.g., audit committee).

But unlike with director independence, here there is a sharp division between public and private companies. Nearly 90% of public companies impose some limit on multiple directorships, while only 13% of private companies do so. Further, the limitations that are imposed currently apply almost exclusively

Figure 14.6: What is the limit on the number of public company directorships an independent director can hold in total, including your organization?

Answer Choices	Responses	
1	0%	0
2	3%	3
3	18%	22
4	61%	73
More than 4	9%	11
Not applicable or unsure	3%	4
Other (please specify)	6%	7
	Answered	**120**
	Skipped	**57**

Note: This question excludes limits that may be imposed on board leadership (e.g., board chair or lead director) and/or particular committee chairs or committee members (e.g., audit committee).

to public company boards, not to either private company boards or non-profit boards.

While serving on a private company board may require a lesser time commitment than a public company directorship, the commitment can still be substantial. One survey from 2024 indicated that private company directorships require an average of 150 hours per year, versus 200 hours for a public company.[729] Thus, private companies may want to consider adopting some form of overboarding policy, and all companies may want to consider non-public-company board service—even if it is not subject to the same numerical limit as public company boards.

The survey indicated that there has not been much movement recently in limits on the number of boards on which an independent director may serve. Two-thirds of respondents reported no change in the past five years, while one-fifth reported a tightening of the limits.

Notably, the companies (all public) that made changes were driven by perceptions of "best" or industry practices, rather than by board workload or board effectiveness. It is entirely understandable that boards may wish to draw a line in the sand about the total number of boards on which their directors

Figure 14.7: Has this limit changed in the past five years?

Answer Choices	Responses	
Yes, the limit has increased	3%	3
Yes, the limit has decreased	20%	23
No	67%	78
Not applicable or unsure	5%	6
Other (please specify)	5%	6
	Answered	**116**
	Skipped	**61**

Note: This question excludes limits that may be imposed on board leadership (e.g., board chair or lead director) and/or particular committee chairs or committee members (e.g., audit committee).

can serve—and then leave it alone. After all, boards will not want to constantly revisit the question of lowering the limit, which could force directors to step off their board or another one. Having said that, if boards do consider changing the limits, they may want to focus on the specific circumstances facing the company, board, and director, not just perceptions of industry practice.

Apart from any numerical limits, boards may want to revisit each director's other commitments—and ability to devote sufficient time to the board—on a

Figure 14.8: What was/were the reason(s) for changing the limit? Select all that apply.

Answer Choices	Responses	
Increasing director responsibilities	25%	8
Investor pressure	34%	11
Changes in corporate governance best practices	66%	21
Shift in peer/industry standards and practices	44%	14
Enhanced focus on board effectiveness	19%	6
Requests or preferences from directors	13%	4
Other (please specify)	0%	0
	Answered	**32**
	Skipped	**145**

more frequent (i.e., annual) basis. As noted below, boards most often consider the impact of multiple directorships only during the board recruitment or onboarding process, or as part of a pre-clearance process when a director joins another board. A minority (43%) consider it as part of the performance evaluation process. While it may lead to some uncomfortable conversations, it can be better to address an overboarding situation head-on, rather than wait for a director's performance to lag or an activist investor to raise the issue.

Figure 14.9: How does your organization evaluate the impact of directors holding multiple public company directorships on their effectiveness and availability? Select all that apply.

Answer Choices	Responses	
As part of the regular performance evaluation (e.g., annual performance reviews)	43%	72
Evaluation and pre-clearance by Nom/Gov Committee or other board committee or director(s) in advance of the director joining another board	57%	96
Focused review during the board nomination process for newly nominated directors	51%	86
Notification to Nom/Gov Committee or other board committee or director(s) in advance of the director joining another board	59%	99
No formal evaluation	10%	17
Not applicable or unsure	6%	10
Other (please specify)	10%	17
	Answered	**168**
	Skipped	**9**

Board Leadership

The Society's survey respondents were less inclined than public companies in general to have one individual serve as both board chair and CEO. Approximately 26% of all respondents have what is commonly referred to as a "combined chair/CEO": 30% at public companies and 13% at private companies. This compares with a range from about 34% of the Russell 3000 to 62% of the S&P 100 and 70% of the Dow 30 with such a combination.[730]

Figure 14.10: What is the leadership structure of your board? Select all that apply.

Answer Choices	Responses	
Combined CEO and board chair	26%	43
Separate CEO and independent board chair	57%	94
Separate CEO and non-independent board chair	12%	19
Lead independent director	27%	44
Other (please specify)	2%	4
	Answered	**165**
	Skipped	**12**

Even taking that divergence into account, the Society's survey data provide insights into industry practices that cannot be derived from public company disclosures. First, over half (56%) of the private companies that responded to the survey question indicated that they have an independent board chair, which is in line with the 54% of public company survey respondents that have an independent board chair. The relatively high percentage of private companies choosing to have an independent chair is notable because they typically have a high degree of flexibility in choosing their board leadership structure and do not face pressures from shareholders and proxy advisors to appoint an independent chair.

Figure 14.11: What is the leadership structure of your board? Select all that apply.

Answer Choices	Responses	
Combined CEO and board chair	12.50%	2
Separate CEO and independent board chair	56.25%	9
Separate CEO and non-independent board chair	12.50%	2
Lead independent director	25.00%	4
Other (please specify)	6.25%	1
	Answered	**16**
	Skipped	**5**

Also noteworthy is how boards—public and private alike—approach the subject. As shown in the chart below, just half (49%) of the companies surveyed have a policy that allows the board to choose the appropriate leadership structure, while 16% require a separation of the chair and CEO roles.

Figure 14.12: Does your organization have a formal policy regarding the separation or combination of the CEO and board chair roles?

Answer Choices	Responses	
Yes, policy requires separate CEO and independent board chair	16%	27
Yes, policy requires combined CEO and board chair	0%	0
Yes, policy allows board to determine whether to combine or separate CEO and board chair and whether board chair should be independent	49%	81
No	28%	46
Other (please specify)	6%	10
	Answered	**164**
	Skipped	**13**

Of the companies that require a separation of the roles, most cite board independence and governance as a reason (96%), followed by industry practices (44%) and the different responsibilities of the roles (37%).

Figure 14.13: Please specify the rationale for your policy regarding the separation of these roles. Select all that apply.

Answer Choices	Responses	
The roles have different responsibilities	37%	10
To enhance board independence and governance	96%	26
Based on industry best practices	44%	12
Other (please specify)	7%	2
	Answered	**27**
	Skipped	**150**

Given the longstanding lack of empirical evidence that separating the chair and CEO roles correlates with improved corporate governance,[731] and given the significance of board leadership as a governance matter, it is notable that only about half the companies surveyed explicitly allow the board to make a case-by-case determination as to the appropriate leadership structure (while 28% do not have a policy at all). Further, given the company-specific factors that could support either combining *or* separating the two positions, it is concerning that nearly half the companies that require separation of the roles are relying on industry practices as a reason to do so.

Director Compensation

A recent analysis by FW Cook of compensation at 300 US public companies found that non-employee director compensation is lagging growth in market capitalization, especially at large-cap companies.[732] In addition, as compared with CEO pay, there is much less of a difference between non-employee director compensation based on company size. These trends are understandable.

Companies are naturally reluctant to draw too much investor or public attention to director compensation, so significant increases in line with market capitalization could raise concerns. In addition, the fact that company size has less of an impact on director compensation than CEO compensation likely reflects that small- and mid-cap companies need to compete with their larger brethren to retain and attract directors—and that company size may have less of an impact on a non-employee director's role than on a CEO's role.

More notable—and potentially concerning—is that company performance has less of an impact on director compensation than in the past. In 2015, higher-performing companies (those in the 75th percentile) paid 15–26% more than the median. In 2025, that range was reduced to 8–14%. Similarly, directors at lower-performing mid- and large-cap firms (those in the 25th percentile) experience less of a relative hit to compensation than they did ten years ago.

In recent years, directors have sought to be more engaged in developing and overseeing implementation of corporate strategy. When doing so, it may make sense for boards to take a closer look at how they can better link director compensation to the particular company's size, complexity, and performance. At the same time, boards might consider how to adjust director compensation both (1) to attract and retain directors outside of the professional director class *and* (2) to pay enough to reduce financial incentives for professional directors to become overboarded.

To be sure, these considerations may lead to an increase in the level, and greater diversity in the structure, of director compensation. But those trends may be beneficial—as long as director compensation does not become a distraction for investors or too much of a focus for directors. On the latter point, a board likely does not want to lose a qualified director because of compensation; at the same time, it probably does not want a director for whom compensation is a deciding factor, as that may affect their ability to exercise independent judgment.

Conclusion

The Society's survey results may not be a surprise to those who closely follow corporate governance trends, but they do indicate that additional work lies ahead for corporate boards in these areas: the extent to which they want "professional directors" on their boards; what director independence means in practice; how to consider service on the boards of private and non-profit corporations when assessing a director's outside time commitments; evaluating board leadership structures on an ongoing, company-specific basis; and tailoring director compensation to reflect the evolving role of directors and the board's contribution to corporate performance. In each case, there is an opportunity for boards to focus not on truisms or received wisdom, but on what leads to the most effective governance in their own company's particular circumstances.

Consistent with the Weinbergs' emphasis on judgment rather than formula, the survey results suggest that effective board practices cannot be reduced to uniform rules, but instead require company-specific assessments informed by context, experience, and the board's evolving role.

Afterword

What Are We Missing?

Leo E. Strine, Jr.

In his incisive, remarkable thesis, John Weinberg identified many enduring issues and best practices relevant to good corporate governance today.[733] What is the line between an engaged, effective board and one that undermines the dynamism and efficiency of management? What skills and experience are most important to being an effective director? How large should a board be? To what extent should a board be comprised of outside directors?

How can boards of directors best receive the information they need to fulfill their role? Are the incentives for outside directors sufficient to ensure that they demand the information needed to do their job and to oversee management in an active and effective way?

Do corporate boards have a duty to govern their corporations in a manner that puts stockholders first, or may or must they consider the best interests of the corporation's other stakeholders and society as a whole? How to balance society's interest in having the large corporations whose growth and power they have facilitated conduct themselves in a socially responsible manner and the risk of government overreach impairing private freedom?

John's prescience and common sense demonstrate the value of listening—not just literally, when someone else speaks, but in reading pertinent writings. Reading his well-researched thesis should humble any of us who might think that our own musings on corporate governance are novel or that we have identified genuinely unprecedented issues for consideration.

Pervading the thesis is a consideration of the already-ongoing struggle to balance the efficiency of centralized management against its potential for abuse and self-interest, and how to use tools like litigation and threat of liability, removal at the ballot box, and requirements for stockholder approval to ensure that the dynamism of strong corporate leadership is better aligned with the interests of not just public stockholders but the public as a whole.

A student of corporate law or governance in the last few decades of the 20th century would find that, with a few adjustments to discuss developments like corporate takeovers and the reaggregation of capital and rise of institutional investor power, John's thesis grounds them in much of the same thinking and debates within the boundaries of corporate law and business-school scholarship about corporate governance. The stakeholder-versus-stockholder debate. The basic questions of the proper boundaries between the role of the board of directors and the day-to-day managers of the corporation's other stakeholders. The question of how accountable boards should be to the stockholder electorate.

But the thesis is also remarkable for what it does not address, mirroring much of later 20th-century scholarship in the area. As prescient as the thesis is in many ways, and as thoughtful, reasoned, and other-regarding as the author's voice is about the need for corporate leaders to avoid selfish conduct and to channel corporate behavior in a manner consistent with society's legitimate expectations, the thesis illustrates the blinkers that have long characterized corporate governance thinking.

How?

Consider the reality that the thesis was written in the wake of a world war where the United States and its allies had confronted adversaries with explicitly racist ideologies, and that black Americans had given their lives to help win that war. But black American veterans had come home to a society where Jim Crow was the de jure or de facto reality in every region of the nation, and where many of them were subject to racial violence on their way home.

When John wrote his thesis, American corporations were operating in a society that was racially segregated and where black people were denied an equal opportunity at employment with corporations at all, much less the chance to climb the corporate ladder, and were denied the wealth necessary to become stockholders themselves. The absence of any consideration of this ongoing reality, by a commentator with an evident capacity for empathy and compassion, is a telling reminder that we all live within a social context and that we all bear a responsibility for what we choose not to see and, even more, for failing to address what we see.

The thesis recognized that our society had chartered corporations and facilitated their growth into hugely important societal institutions, and that corporate boards thus had a duty to govern themselves in the best interests of society or expect government action to make them do so. Coming out of a world war and facing the ideological challenge of communism, the thesis understandably focused on the question of whether the American balanced approach to responding to the Great Depression—think the New Deal and its support for market dynamism within a construct providing more fairness and protection to the many exposed to the risks of corporate conduct—would yield sufficiently widespread prosperity to defeat calls for more radical change.

But the thesis also implicitly embraced the idea that society meant white Americans, and that our nation's historical subordination of black people was a given that corporate boards had no responsibility to address. To this point, that the nearly coincident speech of John's father, Sidney, gave some enlightened consideration of the possibility of engaging more women in the role of directors underscores this reality, as the women being talked about were white women, who had gained ground in obtaining voting rights, and more access to different professions, and had proven themselves vital to the war effort in many ways.[734] The speech could see a role for corporations in gains in equality for women, making its blindness to racial inequality more obvious.

Likewise, during the period when John was writing his thesis, American corporations were engaging in environmentally and humanly harmful behavior whose deleterious effects are still being felt now. Leaded gasoline. Tobacco. Chemicals of many kinds.

We now know that in many of these areas, large corporations that were American icons knew that their products and operations posed huge environmental and human risks but continued to engage in harmful conduct in order to secure continued profits. Their stockholders made good returns and have never been asked to make society whole. Left to bear the residual harm were not the so-called residual claimants, but injured consumers, breathers of fouled air and drinkers of dirty water, other species, and taxpayers who had to bear the costs of trying to ameliorate and remedy that harm. Much of the second wave of the New Deal—i.e., the Great Society—involved regulatory laws to address the failure of American corporations to conduct themselves in a way that was safe for consumers, their communities of operation, and the environment.

Recognizing that Lake Erie caught on fire more than a generation after John's thesis because of the accumulation of industrial pollution and at a time when the federal Clean Air and Water Acts were just being passed underscores the hazards of blinkered thinking about corporate governance and its implications for society. When a fair and incisive young person like John comprehensively reviews the corporate governance literature and does not mention issues like this, we should not judge him but ask whether we ourselves are learning from history.

Most of the serious and harmful warming of the climate that has occurred to date is the result of human conduct of previous generations, including the generation in which John wrote. And as with issues like leaded gasoline and tobacco, there is overwhelming evidence that corporations knew that their continued production of carbon-based energy would have seriously dangerous implications for the planet, other species, and humanity itself, but failed to make that knowledge public, much less change their behavior.[735] The human and environmental harm caused by so-called forever chemicals, or PFAS, and by the irresponsible sale of opioids are other examples of why corporate governance matters to us all, and not just to stockholders.

That such a caring, intelligent commentator did not address issues like these reminds us of the importance of good practices that encourage deep and wide-lensed thinking by those charged with the important and difficult job of running high-integrity, profitable companies. To what extent must they bear personal responsibility for running their companies in a way that does not cause lasting harm? And for those with a view on corporate governance, what is your responsibility for advocating for a framework for corporate competition that takes into account the demonstrated propensity of for-profit corporations to operate in ways that put profit first and subordinate safety for workers, consumers, communities of operation, and the environment?

With billions and billions of us living now, and with the ability of current-day corporations to act with greater impact and velocity, we cannot afford to relearn the hard lessons of history. Instead, we must apply them with full vigor and ensure that corporations operate within a strong set of boundaries that channel their behavior in a socially responsible manner. The challenges of doing so in a global economy where corporate power extends across borders, and where technologies that affect human beings cross regulatory lines with ease (think artificial intelligence—AI), are formidable. The huge increase in both the power of mobilized capital demanding outsized profits and in corporate political spending only compounds those challenges.

Unless we think there has been a Darwinian evolution of unprecedented rapidity in the moral capacities of corporate leaders, reason and modesty suggest that the need to consider how corporations affect us all is more urgent than ever. The historical evidence for accepting the words "just trust us" satisfies no fairly applied standard of persuasion.

Power without responsibility is dangerous. That is not a new concept. And it is one that young John embraced.

Can we learn from him by facing reality? When corporations invent and deploy AI and other transformative technologies, that will affect others for generations to come. When corporations continue to sell more carbon-based energy, or to use it to develop and sell products like AI, that will affect others forever. How do we shape regulatory and corporate governance policies that facilitate greater human wealth and technological improvement, while not creating far more harm than good to humanity, other species, and the planet?

This short essay is not the place to propose my own tentative answers to those difficult questions. Rather, my intention is simpler. Let John's good work inspire us—and especially corporate leaders—to face the mirror test and see the world: wrinkles, blemishes, and all.

To what are American corporate leaders now blind? How do they best seek the light? What is their obligation to do so? And what responsibility do they bear if they know that the corporation's conduct poses serious dangers and they do not disclose that, or responsibly address the harm? What might they be missing?

And what might we, as citizens, be missing?

Even more troublingly, what might we all know to be true, unjust, and harmful to others—including future generations—but be ignoring because our own self-interest trumps our moral conscience? Put simply, what do we see but refuse to acknowledge? And what did we acknowledge to be true and right in the recent past but now obfuscate, elide, deny, or renounce because the political wind has changed direction?

What trust can be placed in corporate leadership if it bends to governmental pressure on issues of ethical principle and empirical fact? It is easy to critique the blind spots and failures of prior generations. Much harder is the true intellectual and moral challenge for any current generation of citizens of a democratic republic: doing better ourselves.

Conclusion

Where to from Here?

Lawrence A. Cunningham

The Weinbergs of Goldman Sachs left a distinctive legacy to corporate governance—ineffably through their board service and investment counsel, and indelibly through John's thesis and Sidney's memorandum and speech. Their belief that corporations must balance their economic mandate with social responsibilities, exemplified in the Berle–Dodd debate, continues to resonate today.

If the lessons of 1948–49 remain durable despite substantial contextual evolution, and the fundamentals endure over change, what do those lessons portend for the future? What does a firsthand account of the board of directors from 75 years ago suggest we can forecast about that future 75 years from now?[736]

We could start by filling in the familiar historical landmarks in corporate governance. They tend to reinforce a sense that, while radical change may seem afoot, enduring realities mean that some things are constant. Throughout modern corporate history, change tends to be incremental, not extreme. For instance, the Weinbergs' insights during the 1940s reflected the ongoing debate about whether corporations are primarily economic or social institutions—a debate still relevant today.

As we traverse through the decades, we see that the 1960s and 1970s were marked by a tussle over markets versus regulation, with figures like Milton Friedman and Ralph Nader representing polar positions. The Weinbergs would likely advocate for a balanced perspective, recognizing the merits and pitfalls of both approaches. In the 1970s and 1980s, as scholars debated whether corporations should be chartered at the state level or under federal authority, the Weinbergs' emphasis on the specific needs of diverse companies would have clearly counseled in favor of states.

One major change in corporate boardrooms in recent times has been demographic, shifting from predominantly inside directors who were mostly white and male to a more demographically diverse composition today. The Weinbergs' perspective on the necessity of varied experiences and backgrounds for effective governance supports this evolution. While boards have diversified demographically, they rightly retain a shared business acumen, a hallmark of effective governance emphasized by the Weinbergs.

Moreover, we can anticipate that certain gold standards of governance will persist, as practices such as regular meeting attendance and board independence remain essential. However, the Weinbergs would remind us that the essence of effective governance lies in the intangible qualities of respect, trust, and candor among directors and executives—traits that facilitate productive debate and decision-making whether they adhere to an externally ordained "gold standard" or set of "best practices."

Another salient difference between the eras—between the thesis and what a contemporary student might write—is the distinction between functions and structures. In the thesis, the focus is on the functions of the board—its substance, purpose, and the essential roles it plays in governance. The thesis explores how boards should engage in policy formulation, decision-making, and oversight based on a clear understanding of their responsibilities. It emphasizes the need for boards to actively engage with management, ensure policies are aligned with organizational goals, and regularly review them to ensure their continued relevance.

In contrast, today's corporate governance discussions are more concerned with structures—the processes and procedures that surround governance. While structures such as formalized committees, compliance frameworks, and reporting mechanisms have become more prominent, the fundamental functions of the board, as articulated in this thesis, remain unchanged. This is one reason why publishing this work now is so timely; it returns the focus to the essential purpose of governance, at a time when the broader discourse has become preoccupied with processes, without always addressing the underlying substance of director responsibilities.

* * * * *

Every era presents boards with novel challenges on many fronts—bribery and terrorism in the recent past, climate and cyber issues today, and who knows what tomorrow will bring. Yet, in each era, the board's fundamental role remains the same: to appoint, support, and monitor corporate executives while helping to define and pursue corporate strategic objectives. The practical implications of these fundamentals will persist:

- Boards will balance the contending interests of multiple claimants, from shareholders to employees and social activists, echoing the Weinbergs' sense of practical governance.
- Boards will continue to be diverse in race and gender but will share a common foundation of business experience, necessitating consensus-building.
- Directors' personal qualities—respect, trust, and candor—will prove more significant than merely adhering to traditional governance standards.
- A board's number one job will remain selecting an outstanding CEO, with succession planning as a close second, underscoring the Weinbergs' emphasis on strategic leadership continuity.
- While boards may be financially and technologically savvy, they will still rely on management for expertise and information, reflecting the asymmetries highlighted by the Weinbergs.
- Boards will face changing circumstances, needing to be agile and responsive, while recognizing that each board and every company is unique.

The pressing issues of the day will likely differ from ours—unpredictable possibilities ranging from episodic crises to chronic discontent. But then, as now, core constraints, aspirations, realities, roles, and duties will endure. To adapt a French phrase that captures this phenomenon, *plus ça change, plus c'est la même chose*, or the more the board changes, the more it stays the same.

Endnotes | Annotations

PREFACE

1 John L. Weinberg, "Status and Functions of Corporate Directors" (senior thesis, Princeton University, 1948), in *Boardroom Legacy: The Weinbergs of Goldman Sachs and the Evolution of Corporate Governance*, ed. Lawrence A. Cunningham (Harriman House, 2026), chap. III.A.1.

2 Ibid., chap. II.F.

3 Ibid., chap. VI.A.1.

4 Ibid., chap. III.A.3.

5 Ibid., chap. I.D.

INTRODUCTION

6 The Weinbergs whose work is featured in this project led Goldman Sachs for a majority of the 20th century. Sidney holds the record for longest-serving head of the storied investment bank (39 years). John's tenure, counting a period as co-head with John Whitehead, was second only to Sidney's and those of Marcus Goldman (chair from 1869–94) and Samuel Sachs (1894–1928).

7 See Garry Evans, "The Weinberg Interview," *Euromoney*, June 1, 1990.

8 See Lisa Endlich, *Goldman Sachs: The Culture of Success* (Touchstone, 1999), 45–49; Charles D. Ellis, *The Partnership: The Making of Goldman Sachs* (Penguin Books, 2008).

9 Weinberg Center for Corporate Governance, https://weinberg.udel.edu.

10 Sidney J. Weinberg, "The Functions of a Corporate Director" (speech, 1949), in *Boardroom Legacy: The Weinbergs of Goldman Sachs and the Evolution of Corporate Governance*, ed. Lawrence A. Cunningham (Harriman House, 2026). The speech was published as Sidney J. Weinberg, "A Corporation Director Looks at His Job," *Harvard Business Review* 27 (1949): 585, and later reprinted as Sidney J. Weinberg, "The Functions of a Corporate Director," *Directors & Boards* (Summer 2003): 18.

11 See Alden Whitman, "Sidney J. Weinberg Dies at 77; 'Mr. Wall Street' of Finance," *New York Times*, July 24, 1969, A1.

12 See Note, "With Men in Service," *Scarsdale Inquirer*, January 8, 1943; Landon Thomas, Jr., "John L. Weinberg, 81, Former Leader of Goldman, Dies," *New York Times*, August 9, 2006, C12.

13 See Tom Brokaw, *The Greatest Generation* (Random House, 1998).

14 See John C. Whitehead, *A Life in Leadership* (Basic Books, 2005), 116.

15 Weinberg Center for Corporate Governance, https://weinberg.udel.edu.

16 Other examples: John Calhoun Baker, "The Board of Directors," *Dun's Review* (February 1946): 11–15; George E. Bates, "The Board of Directors," *Harvard Business Review* (1940): 72–87; William H. Mylander, "Management by Executive Committee," *Harvard Business Review* (1955): 51–58 (case study of DuPont Company); National Industrial Conference Board, *The Corporate Directorship* (1953).

17 See Frank Partnoy, *The Match King: Ivar Kreuger, The Financial Genius Behind a Century of Wall Street Scandals* (PublicAffairs, 2010).

18 See Geoffrey Jones and Ingrid Vargas, "Ivar Kreuger and the Swedish Match Empire," *Harvard Business School Case Collection* (November 2003).

19 See Endlich, *Goldman Sachs*, 55–56.

20 Weinberg, "Status and Functions," chap. IV.C.2.

21 Stephanie Cuba, "Women Pioneers of Corporate America," *Financial History* 155 (Fall 2025): 8.

22 488 A.2d 858 (Del. 1985).

23 John C. Baker, *Directors and Their Functions* (Harvard Business School, Division of Research, 1945), 19.

24 Myles L. Mace, *Directors: Myth and Reality* (Harvard Business School Publications, 1971): 43.

25 Robert W. Hamilton, "Corporate Governance in America 1950–2000: Major Changes but Uncertain Benefits," *Journal of Corporation Law* (2000): 349.

26 See Stephen M. Bainbridge, "Director Primacy: The Means and Ends of Corporate Governance," *Northwestern University Law Review* 97 (2003): 547.

27 See Stephen G. Mandis, *What Happened to Goldman Sachs: An Insider's Story of Organizational Drift and Its Unintended Consequences* (Harvard Business Review Press, 2013).

28 Interviews with Bill Williams, retired partner, Sullivan & Cromwell (January 6 and 14, 2025).

29 "U.S. Financial Asks for Halt in Trading," *New York Times*, November 28, 1972; James Carberry, "U.S. Financial Misses Interest Payments," *Wall Street Journal*, April 9, 1973.

30 SEC Litigation Release 6258 (February 25, 1974).

31 Interviews with Bill Williams.

32 Ellis, *The Partnership*, 300.

33 Robert H. Rock and James Kristie, "Ed Woolard: A Life in Governance," *Directors & Boards* (Fall 2000): 40.

CHAPTER 1

34 Justice William Harman Black, a trial court judge on the New York Supreme Court from 1923 to 1938, was a prominent figure in corporate law and finance. See "Southern Society Elects Justice Black," *New York Times* (April 18, 1937).

35 The case was decided on June 4, 1933. Sidney's memorandum, dated June 21, 1933, leads with a reference to and extensive quotes from the opinion. See *Match Corp. v. Allen*, 89 *New York Law Journal* 3375 (June 5, 1933); "Court Denies Ban on $100,000,000 Suit," *New York Times* (June 4, 1933).

CHAPTER 2

36 Pleasantries in the opening paragraphs are omitted. Sidney's speech as published in *Harvard Business Review* has been influential and cited often. See Weinberg Center for Corporate Governance, https://weinberg.udel.edu.

37 Over ensuing decades, considerable debate has contended with whether the board's role is primarily an advisory one or a monitoring one.

38 An advocacy movement on behalf of women on boards gained considerable influence in the late 1940s and early 1950s, using a combination of shareholder proposals and nominations at annual shareholders' meetings.

39 Cumulative voting became widespread in the 1940s, in part due to corporate laws in many states mandating this approach.

40 Sidney's use of the word "enlightened" in this context may be a playful reference to legal controversies surrounding General Electric's lightbulb patents during this period. See Lea Shaver, "Illuminating Innovation," *Washington & Lee Law Review* 69 (2012): 1891.

41 The reference is certainly to the Match International judicial opinion Sidney noted in his memorandum, which cited earlier judicial opinions. The phrase is associated with Justice William O. Douglas, who, six years before joining the Supreme Court, wrote a critique of the board mocking the opposite practice. William O. Douglas, "Directors Who Do Not Direct," *Harvard Law Review* 47 (1934): 1305.

42 At the time of this speech, Sidney Weinberg served on multiple boards and plant closings were common in the US economy in the immediate aftermath of World War II. In 1949, Sidney was most likely referring to Cluett, Peabody, a New England textile manufacturer which lost much of its military-uniform business and faced early challenges from foreign imports.

CHAPTER 3: ANNOTATIONS ON JOHN'S THESIS

43 *Adam Smith on directors.* Smith's observation remains foundational in modern corporate governance, particularly with the development of principal–agent theory. Today, this challenge is addressed through mechanisms like performance-based executive compensation, independent boards, and governance aimed at aligning the interests of management and shareholders. Apropos of Adam Smith and Sidney Weinberg, see William O. Douglas, *Go East Young Man* (Random House, 1974), 292 (referring to Sidney: having "served for years together as members of the Visiting Committee of the Harvard Business School," Sidney "was bright, amiable, and as conservative as Adam Smith").

Stockholder participation. Today, shareholder involvement has shifted dramatically. The vast number of shareholders in modern corporations makes direct participation in governance virtually impossible for most. Instead, shareholder influence is largely exercised through voting mechanisms at annual meetings, often mediated by proxy advisors and institutional investors.

Legal devices concentrating control. Although certain practices, such as pyramiding, have largely fallen into desuetude, other mechanisms that concentrate control—like dual-class share structures—remain common in modern corporate governance. The use of non-voting shares, for example, is a significant point of contention in current debates over corporate governance, with some arguing that such structures undermine shareholder democracy.

Expansion of corporate size and influence. The growth of corporations has continued, with multinational corporations playing an even more dominant role in the global economy. Modern corporate governance debates frequently center around how to balance the enormous power wielded by large corporations with the interests of shareholders, employees, and society at large.

44 The common phrase for this concept came to be the separation of ownership from control. The rise of institutional investors (e.g., BlackRock, Vanguard, and State Street) since the late 20th century has created a different kind of concentrated ownership. These institutions collectively own a significant portion of many large companies, enabling them to exert considerable influence over management decisions, especially through proxy votes. However, the individual small shareholder John describes still lacks much influence, reinforcing his observations.

Concentration of control. The prominence of a relatively small group of individuals in corporate governance persists. Moreover, today's corporate governance trends, such as the increasing focus on board independence and the rise of "overboarding" concerns (where directors serve on too many boards), continue to resonate with John's observations from the 1940s. Modern corporate governance codes, such as those from the New York Stock Exchange (NYSE) and Nasdaq, have rules limiting overboarding to ensure directors can dedicate adequate time and attention to their responsibilities. It's also interesting to compare the figures the thesis cited as "ridiculous extremes," those serving on 70 to 80 boards at once, with Sidney's service on about 30 at once. Today, 30 would be a "ridiculous extreme," underscoring differences between the demands on directors in the 1940s and today.

Shift from entrepreneur to investor. This shift is most pronounced with the rise of passive investing, where shareholders are often entirely disengaged from company management, and decisions are left to asset managers. Index funds now control large percentages of many major corporations, further distancing shareholders from active participation in governance.

Stockholder disengagement and proxy voting. The rise of shareholder activism, particularly through proxy battles led by institutional investors and activist hedge funds, has changed the landscape. Though individual shareholders may remain passive, institutional investors frequently use their voting power to influence corporate strategy, governance practices, and executive compensation. Tools like proxy voting have empowered these large investors to drive changes in governance, though the average retail shareholder remains relatively disengaged. In recent years, there has been a push toward making proxy voting more accessible and transparent to individual investors.

Corporate mergers and concentration post-World War II. Corporate concentration remains a key issue today. In fact, we've seen even greater consolidation in industries such as technology, telecommunications, and financial services, where a handful of companies dominate the market. Antitrust discussions, particularly in sectors like tech (e.g., Amazon, Google), mirror the concerns John noted about corporate power and its implications for governance and competition.

45 *Stockholder apathy in times of prosperity*. This phenomenon persists in modern markets, where prolonged bull markets often lead to reduced shareholder scrutiny. However, during downturns, as in the wake of the 2008 financial crisis or the COVID-19 pandemic, corporate governance issues come into sharper focus. Shareholders then demand more accountability from directors and executives, leading to reforms, some of which are on point while others overshoot.

"Rubber stamp" directors and multiple directorships. These issues have persisted into the present, with reforms aimed at increasing board independence and limiting the number of directorships any one person can hold. Today, corporate governance codes, as well as the Sarbanes–Oxley Act of 2002 and Dodd–Frank Act of 2010, place greater emphasis on the independence of directors, particularly those serving on audit committees. Additionally, institutional investors and proxy advisors often advocate for limits on the number of boards a director may serve on simultaneously.

Management domination and self-dealing. Modern governance principles emphasize the importance of independent directors who can act as a counterbalance to powerful management teams. The rise of activist investors and institutional shareholders has also shifted the power dynamics between management and boards.

Education and role definition of directors. Today, director education is a critical part of corporate governance. Organizations like the National Association of Corporate Directors (NACD) provide training programs and resources to help directors understand their roles, responsibilities, and best practices. Additionally, governance frameworks, such as the Delaware corporation law, have further clarified director functions, emphasizing their obligation to act in the best interest of shareholders.

Refraining from general condemnation of boards. This perspective is mirrored in contemporary debates about corporate governance. While scandals like those at Enron, WorldCom, and, more recently, companies like Theranos and WeWork have led to calls for systemic reform, many experts agree that the solution lies in better governance practices, not in discarding the board model entirely. Efforts to improve board accountability, diversity, and performance evaluations continue to evolve in response to these challenges.

46 The concept of corporate social responsibility, including the contending interests of stakeholders and stockholders, appears and reappears throughout economic history, dating at least to the debate over the Bank of North America in the 1780s. See Robert E. Wright, "Corporate Social Responsibility and the Rise of the Non-profit Sector in America," in Will Pettigrew and David Smith, eds., *A History of Socially Responsible Business, c. 1600–1950* (Palgrave Macmillan, 2017), 117–36. The account in the thesis reflects heightened interest during the 1940s that has recurred periodically since. In recent years, concepts such as

environmental sustainability, ethical labor practices, and corporate philanthropy have been included in many business strategies.

Stockholder primacy. Stockholder primacy remains a guiding principle, though the broader legal landscape has evolved. Landmark legal frameworks, such as the Benefit Corporation model, now allow companies to prioritize social and environmental goals alongside profit. Additionally, corporate law in Delaware—where many US companies are incorporated—acknowledges how a director focus on shareholder interests may require directors to consider the interests of other constituents, particularly customers and employees.

Role of the board in balancing interests. The board of directors is still seen as the linchpin in managing competing stakeholder interests. The rise of ESG (environmental, social, and governance) considerations in corporate governance added new complexities to board oversight.

47 The corporate form continues to dominate, with corporations accounting for the overwhelming majority of business activity in the US and globally. The importance of directors has only increased, as they are responsible for navigating complex regulatory environments, globalization, and technological disruption. Their role in setting strategic direction and ensuring good governance is critical to maintaining both corporate success and public trust.

Inactivity of large stockholders. The trend of passive ownership continues in today's market, with institutional investors like pension funds, mutual funds, and ETFs owning significant portions of publicly traded companies but not directly participating in day-to-day governance.

Director education. The need for director education remains an issue in corporate governance today. Modern governance standards emphasize the importance of board diversity, not just in terms of demographics but in terms of skills and expertise. Many companies offer or require directors to undergo regular training on governance practices, obligations, and trends. Organizations like the NACD and academic institutions have developed programs to ensure that directors are well prepared to meet the challenges of a complex business environment.

48 Federal law has encroached incrementally into this area, highlighted by the Sarbanes–Oxley Act's imposition of independence requirements for members of board audit committees. Concerning interlocking directorates, in a 1953 case, the US government won an order against two companies where Sidney Weinberg served as a director—B.F. Goodrich and Sears, Roebuck. A court determined that the two companies were competitors (both were retail sellers of home appliances, automotive supplies, tires, sporting goods, and other merchandise), so that Section 8 applied and the dual service was prohibited. *United States v. Sears, Roebuck & Co.*, 111 F. Supp. 614 (S.D.N.Y. 1953).

The government's victory in its interlocking directorate lawsuit was a modest win compared with more ambitious claims it made against the investment-banking industry. In a lawsuit against the 17 largest investment banks, including Goldman Sachs, the government alleged numerous violations of federal law, including the Sherman Act. *United States v. Morgan*, 118 F. Supp. 621 (S.D.N.Y. 1953). It said the firms coordinated and conspired to use various anti-competitive techniques to produce a functional cartel, including through such director seats. After extensive proceedings, however, the federal district court in a 225-page opinion rejected the government's arguments to find in favor of all the banks. Its detailed discussion of the board service and corporate practices of the period made it clear that such service was legitimate.

49 The thesis highlights issues of stockholders' limited power in director elections, which remain relevant, though the shareholder landscape has transformed considerably. In 1948, shareholders were predominantly individual investors with minimal influence over corporate governance. Today, however, institutional investors—index funds, mutual funds, pension funds, and other large entities—hold significant stakes and wield considerable influence. This shift has led to a stronger push for governance reforms, such as proxy access, majority voting for director elections, and other board accountability measures. Despite these changes, concerns persist regarding CEO influence and self-perpetuating boards, as well as whether such institutions face frictions that may cause their interests to differ from those of individual shareholders.

50 The debate continues, although director ownership is common today. The theory is to align director and shareholder interests. That would be more accurate if the director bought shares with personal funds, rather than the common practice of the company paying the director in shares. The penultimate section of Sidney Weinberg's speech is entitled "Re Stock Ownership."

51 The emphasis on corporate diversity, implying diverse director functions, remains valid and helpful to counter the recurring tendency in contemporary corporate governance to one-size-fits-all practices. The emphasis on boards as overseers and decision-makers on discrete issues likewise continues. The line between oversight and management remains both fine and vital.

52 Sally Rand was a burlesque dancer of the era who was famous for her ostrich-feather fan dance.

53 All three of these dilemmas persist in varying degrees, making this one of the most interesting passages in the thesis for contemporary audiences. The administrative–fiduciary balance is less of an issue with greater emphasis on independent directors providing oversight without encroaching on management's operational domain. Only later came the mantra popularized by the NACD and coined by John Nash: "Nose in, fingers out" (NIFO). See NACD, "The Role of the Board vs. the Role of Management," *NACD Directorship*, February 28, 2022. The line between oversight and management still matters and risks of directorial overstep persist, as do the risks of rubber stamps. Director recruiting is much different today—a cottage industry has replaced a simple network method—but some of the problems are simply "new wine in old bottles."

54 In the early 21st century, the increasing importance of information technology, including cybersecurity, stimulated increased interest in promoting directors with technological expertise. However, the related research reveals mixed results. See David Larcker and Brian Tayan, *Corporate Governance Matters*, 2nd ed. (Pearson Education, 2016), 83. The challenges noted in this section remain

central to modern corporate governance. While expertise is valued, the focus remains one of strategic direction rather than operational second-guessing. More than ever, the lanes in which directors and managers travel are different and need respected boundaries.

55 Information flow into the board remains imperative. Modern readers could substitute a reference to Enron for McKesson & Robbins. The principles remain the same, but technological advancements have made information sharing faster and more dynamic.

56 John is articulating the function of policy formulation. In contemporary corporate governance, this is an area with an undue emphasis on features, where the focus is on the formalized structures for policy review and oversight, rather than the grubby details.

57 This remains the board's most important job. John's assessment of Justin Dart proved true over the next 35 years as he built a drug-store powerhouse that he diversified over the years into operations that included Tupperware containers, Duracell batteries, and West Bend appliances. See James Barron, "Justin Dart, The Industrialist and Friend of Reagan, Dies," *New York Times*, January 27, 1984, B4. Mr. Dart's son, Justin Dart, Jr., a victim of polio, was a prominent champion of the rights of the disabled, credited with crafting the Americans with Disabilities Act enacted during the presidency of George Herbert Walker Bush. See Louie Estrada, "Justin Dart Jr. Dies: Activist Battled for Rights of Disabled," *Washington Post*, June 23, 2002.

58 John's discussion of committees noted the "danger of overemphasizing committees," something many 21st-century audit-committee members would recognize as a familiar problem. Today's committee categories remain analogous to those stated in John's thesis, though their roles and scope have changed.

Audit. The audit function was gradually strengthened over the years, most intensively and conspicuously in the Sarbanes–Oxley Act of 2002, whose philosophy is very much aligned with the philosophy John articulated in his thesis. The Sarbanes–Oxley Act imposed independence requirements on public company audit committees.

Salary/compensation. From about the 1980s, this committee became known as the compensation committee, reflecting the evolution of corporate governance as a field and the increasing complexity of methods participants believed were appropriate to incentivize and monitor executives. The Dodd–Frank Act of 2010 imposed independence and other requirements on public company compensation committees.

Nom/gov. The third primary committee today did not exist when the Weinbergs wrote, reflecting the inchoate state of the field of corporate governance at the time. Nevertheless, the thesis does aptly discuss some of its functions, including director succession, throughout.

Executive committee. These are less common today and have been criticized by some as too cozy, but they can and often do contribute value.

59 This remains one of the most enduring and intense debates in corporate governance. The debate reaches into many aspects of corporate governance,

including fundamental topics such as board composition and goals. Conceptions of board roles also figure in discussions of corporate strategy. This section of John's thesis contains prescient statements of Delaware corporate law famously stated in 1971: "[I]nequitable action does not become permissible simply because it is legally possible." *Schnell v. Chris-Craft Indus., Inc.*, 285 A.2d 437, 439 (Del. 1971). The notion is cited repeatedly and taught in corporate-law classrooms to stress that business planners must comply with both the statutory law and the equitable principles found in case law.

60 These insights on the "discerning question" are among the wisest and most valuable the thesis offers and seem to reflect not only the maturity of the young writer but the strength of his relationship with his father, the "director's director." See discussion and citations in this book's introduction.

61 The thesis footnote cites the W. O. Douglas speech given in Fort Worth on January 9, 1939. The thesis bibliography cites William O. Douglas, "Decline of American Directorates," *Management Review*, February 1939, 43–44. We found a copy of the speech, as well as references to it, which fulminate over the decline of the American directorate. We could not find a copy of the article but, given the content of the speech, it is quite likely that the themes and ideas presented were adapted into the article titled "Decline of American Directorates."

62 Warren Buffett famously made the same point in slightly different terms, saying: "The biggest problem is not the terrible manager. The biggest problem is the mediocre manager—and that's true everywhere. That is a very difficult thing [and] my most difficult problem." See Lawrence A. Cunningham, "Conversations from the Buffett Symposium," *Cardozo Law Review* 19 (1997): 719, 727 (transcript quoting Buffett in a colloquy with corporate governance legend Ira Millstein).

63 These are enduring challenges. Today, the mantra coined by John Nash of the NACD is routinely cited in accounts of the relationship between boards and management: "Nose in, fingers out" (NIFO). See NACD, "The Role of the Board vs. the Role of Management," February 28, 2022.

64 The board chair continues to be a uniquely powerful role. The chairman's role has driven one of the most contentious topics in contemporary corporate governance: whether to split or combine the roles of chair and CEO.

65 Today, at the largest companies, the overwhelming tendency is to have all outside directors other than the CEO. Yet the relative value of outside directors is disputed.

66 The concept of the "dummy board" is anachronistic by today's standards of corporate governance. See "The Fiduciary Character of a Promoter," *Harvard Law Review* 22, no. 1 (1908): 48–50. True, the underlying legal principles persist—specifically, the duty of promoters to disclose or account for secret profits. But expectations for corporate boards are so much more rigorous that while the term "dummy board" may have once been a shorthand for corporate malfeasance, today words like "supine" or "torpid" are bad enough.

67 John several times references a "serious shortage of capable directors." He notes the demands of the job and considerable disincentives to serve, including a lack

of pay and liability risks, which are echoed periodically in subsequent history, most notably in the D&O insurance crisis following *Smith v. Van Gorkom*, 488 A.2d 858 (Del. 1985). See "Corporate Liability Crisis," *Wall Street Journal*, August 21, 1986; "The D&O Crisis: Corporate Boardroom Woes Grow," *National Law Journal*, August 4, 1986.

68 The state tendencies John identified continued for many decades. Compare *Diamond v. Oreamuno*, 248 N.E.2d 910 (N.Y. 1969) (imposing a duty and liability) with *Freeman v. Decio*, 584 F.2d 186 (7th Cir. 1978) (applying Indiana law and refusing to follow *Diamond*); see also *Brophy v. Cities Service Co.*, 70 A.2d 5 (Del. Ch. 1949). Since then, however, the law of insider trading has become increasingly federalized, largely under the Securities Exchange Act of 1934.

69 The fundamental fiduciary principles John outlined remain. But the doctrinal landscape has evolved to map onto a much broader and more intricate pattern of corporate activities and board conduct.

70 *Ultra vires* is an ancient doctrine. It fell into desuetude but remains a staple of corporate-law doctrine.

71 The passage offers useful insights about the state of the law through the date of the thesis. The law has, of course, developed. The three cited cases are not the most prominent, but they are notable. In hindsight, among prominent cases of the period likewise supporting observations in this section, one stands out: *Barnes v. Andrews*, 298 F. 614 (S.D.N.Y. 1924) (by Learned Hand).

72 The major developments concerning information duties of directors are *Smith v. Van Gorkom* and *Caremark*, about which vast volumes have been written.

73 From the 1960s, the historical common-law restrictions against interested director transactions began to be modernized and relaxed by state statute. A prominent example is the 1967 amendments to the Delaware General Corporation Law which authorize certain interested transactions. Del. Code Ann. tit. 8, § 144.

74 In the ensuing decades, federal securities class-action lawsuits became a dominant form of litigation risk for companies that added many challenges to the directors' role.

75 John's discussion of the era's concern about director liability and the expansion of indemnification was echoed in the 1980s, when a similar concern stimulated the authorization and widespread adoption and endorsement of exculpation provisions such as DGCL section 102(b)(7).

76 This section appears to be original and personal, suggested by the reference to the demands of multiple directorships that John would have observed firsthand with his father Sidney as well as the third-person reference to the writer. John allows himself this personal perspective in eight occasions in the thesis. See Section IV.A.2 (twice, concerning CEOs); IV.C.4 (criteria for quality directors); Section I.C (not letting specific board problems inculpate all boards); and Section II.C (the appeal of "useful safeguards" like cumulative voting).

Overboarding. Today, the term overboarding is used to describe a director serving on an excessive number of boards, neither a new nor novel problem. See entry above on "Concentration of control."

Two-tiered boards. Two-tiered boards are a longstanding feature of Germanic corporations, including those of Austria, Germany, and The Netherlands, but they never caught on in the United States for a variety of cultural, business, and legal reasons.

77 Directors have become increasingly well compensated in the past several decades, especially in the period after the Sarbanes–Oxley Act of 2002, which contributed to an increase in director compensation.

78 What John describes is called networking today.

79 John's normative proposal suggested the creation of a professional directorship, an idea that was formally presented decades later by two corporate law professors. See Ronald Gilson and Reinier Kraakman, "Reinventing the Outside Director: An Agenda for Institutional Investors," *Stanford Law Review* 43 (1991): 836. Today's cohort of so-called professional directors is quite different from the professionalized college of directors John contemplated. Today's "professional directors" include celebrity directors—distinguished military, political, legal, or other institutional figures—and others chosen for reasons other than strategic and business insight, which may not help a company advance.

80 The bibliography obviously includes many sources that are not cited in the footnotes to the thesis. Notable among these, however, may be that of his interview with Edward Green, Law Partner, Sullivan & Cromwell, the law firm that has long been chief outside counsel for Goldman Sachs. A few sources cited in footnotes are not repeated in the bibliography: (1) chap. I.B: Hon. Wright Patman, *Congressional Record*, 75th Cong., First Sess., Vol. 81, p. 5777; (2) chap. I.D: Address by Edward R Stettinius, Jr., Chairman of the Board of the U.S. Steel Corporation at the Annual Convention of the Association of Life Insurance Presidents 1939; and (3) chap. II.H: Moody's Investors' Service, *Moody's Manual of Investments—Industrial Securities* (1947), pp. 2732, 2811.

CHAPTER 4

81 Weinberg, "Status and Functions."

82 Sidney J. Weinberg, "The Responsibility of Directors" (memorandum, 1933), in *Boardroom Legacy: The Weinbergs of Goldman Sachs and the Evolution of Corporate Governance*, ed. Lawrence A. Cunningham (Harriman House, 2026).

83 Weinberg, "The Functions."

84 Henry G. Manne, "Mergers and the Market for Corporate Control," *Journal of Political Economy* 73, no. 2 (1965): 110–20.

85 Brian R. Cheffins, *Advanced Introduction to Corporate Governance Law and Regulation* (Edward Elgar, 2024), 230.

86 Ibid., 21, 231.

87 Ibid., 177.

88 Leo E. Strine, Jr., "Can We Do Better by Ordinary Investors? A Pragmatic Reaction to the Dueling Ideological Mythologists of Corporate Law," *Columbia Law Review* 114, no. 2 (2014): 453.

89 Christopher M. Bruner, "Conceptions of Corporate Purpose in Post-Crisis Financial Firms," *Seattle University Law Review* 36, no. 2 (2013): 532.

90 Leo E. Strine, Jr., "The Dangers of Denial: The Need for a Clear-Eyed Understanding of the Power and Accountability Structure Established by the Delaware General Corporation Law," *Wake Forest Law Review* 50, no. 3 (2015): 776–77.

91 Weinberg, "The Functions," Introduction.

92 Weinberg, "Status and Functions," chap. I.A.

93 Ibid.

94 Weinberg, "The Functions," Introduction.

95 Ibid.

96 Weinberg, "Status and Functions," chap. I.B.

97 Ibid., chap. I.E.

98 Ibid., chap. I.B.

99 Ibid.

100 Ibid.

101 Ibid.

102 Ibid., chap. II.C.

103 Lynn A. Stout, "On the Rise of Shareholder Primacy, Signs of Its Fall, and the Return of Managerialism (in the Closet)," *Seattle University Law Review* 36, no. 2 (2013): 1173.

104 Weinberg, "The Functions," *heading* Language of the Law.

105 Ibid., *heading* Composition of the Board.

106 Weinberg, "Status and Functions," chap. IV.A.1.

107 Ibid., chap. III (introduction).

108 Ibid., chap. II.H.

109 Ibid., chap. II.F.

110 Weinberg, "The Functions," *heading* Language of the Law.

111 Weinberg, "Status and Functions," chap. I.D.

112 Ibid., chap. III.B.

113 Ibid., chap. V.E.

114 Ibid. See also chap. VII.

115 Ibid., chap. I.B.

116 Stefano Zamagni, "It Is Time to Move on From Milton Friedman's View of the Corporation," in *Milton Friedman 50 Years Later*, eds. Luigi Zingales, Jana Kasperkevic, and Asher Schechter (Stigler Center, 2020), 48, https://www.promarket.org/wp-content/uploads/2020/11/Milton-Friedman-50-years-later-ebook.pdf.

117 Weinberg, "Status and Functions," chap. III.B.2.

118 A. A. Berle, Jr., "Corporate Powers as Powers in Trust," *Harvard Law Review* 44, no. 7 (1931): 1049–74.

119 Weinberg, "Status and Functions," chap. III.B.2.

120 E. Merrick Dodd, Jr., "For Whom Are Corporate Managers Trustees?" *Harvard Law Review* 45, no. 7 (1932): 1145–63.

121 Weinberg, "Status and Functions," chap. III.B.2.

122 Ibid., chap. III.B.

123 A. A. Berle, Jr., "For Whom Corporate Managers are Trustees: A Note," *Harvard*

Law Review 45, no. 8 (1932): 1365–72; Weinberg, "Status and Functions," chap. III.B.2.

124 Berle, "For Whom," 1366.

125 Ibid., 1367, 1368.

126 Weinberg, "Status and Functions," chap. III.B.

127 Ibid., chap. III.B.2.

128 Weinberg, "The Functions," *heading* Language of the Law.

129 Dodd, "For Whom," 1163.

130 E. Merrick Dodd, Jr., "Is Effective Enforcement of the Fiduciary Duties of Corporate Managers Practicable?" *University of Chicago Law Review* 2, no. 2 (1935): 206.

131 Ibid.

132 David Ciepley, "How America's Corporations Lost Their Public Purpose, and How It Might be (Partially) Restored," *Accounting, Economics, and Law: A Convivium* 10, no. 3 (2020): *13*.

133 Weinberg, "Status and Functions," chap. V.A., citing W. M. Fletcher, *Cyclopedia of the Law of Private Corporations*, perm. ed., vol. 3 (Callaghan, 1931), § 838.

134 *Dodge v. Ford Motor Co.*, 170 N.W. 668 (Mich. 1919).

135 Dodd, "For Whom," 1146, n. 3.

136 *Dodge*, 170 N.W. 668, 684.

137 David G. Yosifon, "The Law of Corporate Purpose," *Berkeley Business Law Journal* 10, no. 2 (2013): 188.

138 Jonathan R. Macey, "Corporate Law as Myth," *Southern California Law Review* 93, no. 5 (2020): 948.

139 Yosifon, "Law of Corporate," 188.

140 Lynn A. Stout, "Why We Should Stop Teaching Dodge v. Ford," *Virginia Law and Business Review* 3, no. 1 (2008): 166.

141 Ibid., 165.

142 Jeffrey M. Lipshaw, "The False Dichotomy of Corporate Governance Platitudes," *Journal of Corporation Law* 46, no. 2 (2021): 367.

143 Carroll R. Wetzel and James L. Winokur, "Corporations and the Public Interest—A Review of the Corporate Purpose and Business Judgment Rules," *Business Lawyer* 27, no. 1 (1971): 235.

144 *Kavanaugh v. Kavanaugh Knitting Co.*, 123 N.E. 148 (N.Y. 1919).

145 William J. Grange, *Corporation Law for Officers and Directors: A Guide to Correct Procedure* (Ronald Press, 1940), 404.

146 Henry W. Ballantine, *Ballantine on Corporations: Revised Edition* (Callaghan, 1946), 228.

147 Ibid., 228, n. 26.

148 Donald C. Langevoort, "The Effects of Shareholder Primacy, Publicness, and Privateness on Corporate Cultures," *Seattle University Law Review* 43, no. 2 (2020): 382.

149 Editors of *Fortune, U.S.A.: The Permanent Revolution* (Prentice Hall, 1951), 80, 81, 85.

150 Peter F. Drucker, "The Responsibilities of Management," *Harper's*, November 1954, 67.
151 "Directors Peer into the Mirror," *Business Week*, December 21, 1957, 57.
152 Adolf A. Berle, Jr., *The 20th Century Capitalist Revolution* (Harcourt, Brace, 1954), 169.
153 Dodd, "Is Effective Enforcement," 206.
154 Ronald Chen and Jon Hanson, "The Illusion of Law: The Legitimating Schemas of Modern Policy and Corporate Law," *Michigan Law Review* 103, no. 1 (2004): 37.
155 William W. Bratton and Michael L. Wachter, "Shareholder Primacy's Corporatist Origins: Adolf Berle and the Modern Corporation," *Journal of Corporation Law 34 (2008): 99, 134.*
156 Weinberg, "Status and Functions," chap. V.E; see also Ibid., chap. III.B.
157 Harwell Wells, "'Corporation Law is Dead': Heroic Managerialism, Legal Change, and the Puzzle of Corporation Law at the Height of the American Century," *University of Pennsylvania Journal of Business Law* 15 no. 2 (2013): 348.
158 Joseph L. Weiner, "The Berle–Dodd Dialogue on the Concept of the Corporation," *Columbia Law Review* 64, no. 8 (1964): 1466. See also Frederick G. Kempin, "The Public Interest in the Corporation," *Dickinson Law Review* 64, no. 4 (1959): 361; Theodore S. Farfaglia, "The Business Judgement Rule: A Guide to Corporate Directors' Liability," *St. Louis University Law Journal* 7, no. 2 (1962): 152.
159 J. A. Livingston, *The American Stockholder* (J.B. Lippincott, 1958): 217; Adam Winkler, "Corporate Law or the Law of Business: Stakeholders and Corporate Governance at the End of History," *Law and Contemporary Problems* 67, no. 4 (2004): 117.
160 Livingston, *American Stockholder*, 217; J. A. C. Hetherington, "Fact and Legal Theory: Shareholders, Managers, and Corporate Social Responsibility," *Stanford Law Review* 21, no. 2 (1969): 278–79.
161 *Casey v. Woodruff*, 49 N.Y.S. 2d 625, 643 (Sup. Ct. 1944) (Shientag J.), discussed in this context by George D. Hornstein, *Corporation Law and Practice* (West Publishing, 1959), 538–39.
162 David S. Ruder, "Public Obligations of Private Corporations," *University of Pennsylvania Law Review* 114, no. 2 (1965): 223.
163 Farfaglia, "Business Judgement Rule," 151; Charles D. Lewis, "The Business Judgment Rule and Corporate Directors' Liability for Mismanagement," *Baylor Law Review* 22, no. 2 (1970): 157.
164 Lewis, "Business Judgment Rule," 157–58; J. Gordon Arbuckle, "Continuing Viability of the Business Judgment Rule as a Guide for Judicial Restraint," *George Washington Law Review* 35, no. 3 (1967): 565.
165 Einer Elhauge, "Sacrificing Corporate Profits in the Public Interest," *New York University Law Review* 80, no. 3 (2005): 775; Jill E. Fisch, "Measuring Efficiency in Corporate Law: The Role of Shareholder Primacy," *Journal of Corporation Law* 31, no. 3 (2006): 651.
166 Wetzel and Winokur, "Corporations and the Public Interest," 239.

167 Brian R. Cheffins, *The Public Company Transformed* (Oxford University Press, 2018), 69–70, 126, 367.
168 Ibid., 194–96.
169 Ibid., 314–18.
170 Grange, *Corporation Law*, 268.
171 "The Stockholder—Forgotten Man," *Business Week*, November 8, 1941, 76.
172 "Executives, Directors, Wake Up!", *Forbes*, August 1, 1944, 34.
173 Ballantine, *Ballantine on Corporations*, 390–91.
174 Weinberg, "Status and Functions," chap. III.A.4.
175 "Women Heckle," *Forbes*, June 15, 1949, 14.
176 Fredrick Lewis Allen, *The Big Change: America Transforms Itself 1900–1950* (Hamish Hamilton, 1952), 236.
177 Grange, *Corporation Law*, 268.
178 "The Stockholder—Forgotten Man," *Business Week*, November 8, 1941.
179 "Dear Stockholder—," *Forbes*, December 1, 1940, 14.
180 Larry E. Ribstein, "Imagining Wall Street," *Virginia Law & Business Review* 1, no. 2 (2006): 170.
181 Robert A. Gordon, *Business Leadership in the Large Corporation* (University of California Press, 1945), 164.
182 "Stockholder–Management Relations," *Forbes*, February 1, 1947, 40.
183 "Rough Ride for Bosses," *Forbes*, July 15, 1949, 12.
184 "Battle by Proxy," *Barron's*, May 22, 1950, 9.
185 "Mokan Elects Seven Directors After Meeting Lasting Till Early Morn," *Wall Street Journal*, December 5, 1940, 3.
186 "Bond & Share Wins Five Hour Contest," *New York Times*, October 15, 1942, 33.
187 "Railroad Election Becomes a Brawl," *New York Times*, July 19, 1947, 29.
188 "Annual Meetings Draw Record Attendance and Pointed Questioning," *Wall Street Journal*, April 27, 1949, 1.
189 John H. Armour and Brian R. Cheffins, "Origins of 'Offensive' Shareholder Activism in the United States" in *Origins of Shareholder Advocacy*, ed. Jonathan G. S. Koppell (Palgrave, 2011), 253.
190 The search terms are those employed in Michael J. Fleming, "New Evidence on the Effectiveness of the Proxy Mechanism," Federal Reserve Bank of New York Research Paper no. 9503 (1995), 3.
191 Pub. L. No. 73-291, 48 Stat. 881, § 14.
192 Sheldon E. Bernstein and Henry G. Fischer, "The Regulation of the Solicitation of Proxies: Some Reflections on Corporate Democracy," *University of Chicago Law Review* 7, no. 2 (1940): 244.
193 Douglas V. Austin, *Proxy Contests and Corporate Reform* (University of Michigan Press, 1965), 7.
194 Securities and Exchange Commission, *Thirteenth Annual Report of the Securities and Exchange Commission Fiscal Year Ended June 30, 1947* (US Government Printing Office, 1948), 42.
195 Mary O'Sullivan, "The Expansion of the US Stock Market, 1885–1930: Historical Facts and Theoretical Fashions," *Enterprise & Society* 8, no. 3 (2015): 523.

196 Brian R. Cheffins, Steven A. Bank, and Harwell Wells, "Questioning 'Law and Finance': US Stock Market Development, 1930–70," *Business History* 55, no. 4 (2013): 603.
197 Ronald J. Gilson and Alan Schwartz, "Sales and Elections as Methods for Transferring Control," *Theoretical Inquiries in Law* 2, no. 2 (2001): 790.
198 John Armour and Brian Cheffins, "The Origins of the Market for Corporate Control," *University of Illinois Law Review* no. 5 (2014): 1838, 1850–55.
199 Ibid., 1839.
200 In comparison with the 159 proxy contests where board control was sought between 1900 and 1949, there were, based on newspaper archive searches, 82 open-market bids. See Armour and Cheffins, "Origins of 'Offensive' Shareholder Activism," 269; Armour and Cheffins, "Origins of the Market," 1839.
201 Armour and Cheffins, "Origins of the Market," 1840 (Figure 1), 1841 (Figure 2).
202 17 C.F.R. § 240.14a-8.
203 Paul H. Edelman, Randall S. Thomas, and Robert B. Thompson, "Shareholder Voting in an Age of Intermediary Capitalism," *Southern California Law Review* 87, no. 6 (2014): 1396.
204 Daniel M. Friedman, "SEC Regulation of Corporate Proxies," *Harvard Law Review* 63, no. 5 (1950): 802.
205 Frank D. Emerson and Franklin C. Latcham, "SEC Proxy Regulation: Steps Toward More Effective Stockholder Participation," *Yale Law Journal* 59, no. 4 (1950): 667.
206 Emerson and Latcham, "SEC Proxy Regulation," 655 (nearly 90% in 1947).
207 Frank D. Emerson, and Franklin C. Latcham, "The SEC Proxy Proposal Rule: The Corporate Gadfly," *University of Chicago Law Review* 19, no. 4 (1952): 812, tables accompanying footnotes 28, 29.
208 Ibid., 829 table accompanying n. 131.
209 Ibid., 830.
210 Ibid.
211 Ibid., 831.
212 "Bethlehem Steel Defeats 4 Rules," *New York Times*, April 13, 1949, 47.
213 Quoted in Emerson and Latcham. "The SEC Proxy Proposal," 831.
214 Armour and Cheffins, "Origins of 'Offensive' Shareholder Activism," 257.
215 Diana B. Henriques, *The White Sharks of Wall Street: Thomas Mellon Evans and the Original Corporate Raiders* (New York, 2000), 93.
216 Armour and Cheffins, "Origins of 'Offensive' Shareholder Activism," 257.
217 Alan M. Weinberger, "What's in a Name—The Tale of Louis Wolfson's Affirmed," *Hofstra Law Review* 39, no. 3 (2011): 645.
218 Ibid., 653. On the Montgomery Ward proxy contest, see David Karr, *Fight for Control* (New York, 1956), 145–68.
219 Henriques, *The White Sharks of Wall Street*, 79.
220 "Dissenters Prevail in Proxy Contest," *New York Times*, May 5, 1949, 43.
221 "Merritt–Chapman Elects L. E. Wolfson Chair to Succeed T.A. Scott," *Wall Street Journal*, April 5, 1951, 6.
222 On the description of Green, see Frank D. Emerson and Franklin C. Latcham,

"Proxy Contests: A Study in Shareholder Sovereignty," *California Law Review* 41, no. 3 (1953): 427.

223 Henriques, *The White Sharks of Wall Street*, 81–82. See also "Twin City Rapid Transit President Retained in Compromise of Factions," *Wall Street Journal*, March 16, 1949, 2.

224 Henriques, *The White Sharks of Wall Street*, 82–88.

225 Ibid., 114; "Charles Green, 71; Headed Drug Chain," *New York Times*, January 31, 1980, D17.

226 "Battle by Proxy," *Barron's*, May 22, 1950.

227 Ibid.

228 Brian R. Cheffins, Steven A. Bank, and Harwell Wells, "Questioning 'Law and Finance': U.S. Corporate Governance in the Twentieth Century," *Business History Review* 83, no. 3 (2009): 587.

CHAPTER 5

229 Dalia T. Mitchell, "Status Bound: The Twentieth Century Evolution of Directors' Liability," *New York University Journal of Law and Business* 5 (2009): 137–38. Portions of this chapter draw on certain of the author's previously published works, all of which are cited herein. Assertions from the earlier works are incorporated here, sometimes verbatim and sometimes with revisions, without separate quotation marks or pinpoint citations.

230 Jeffrey N. Gordon, "The Rise of Independent Directors in the United States, 1950–2005: Of Shareholder Value and Stock Market Prices," *Stanford Law Review* 59 (2007): 1468.

231 See Faith Stevelman and Sarah C. Haan, "Boards in Information Governance," *University of Pennsylvania Journal of Business Law* 23 (2020): 180.

232 Dalia T. Mitchell, "Proceduralism: Delaware's Legacy," *The University of Chicago Business Law Review* 2 (2023): 333.

233 Harwell Wells, "The Rise of the Close Corporation and the Making of Corporation Law," *Berkeley Business Law Journal* 5 (2008): 284.

234 Stephen J. Lubben and Alana J. Darnell, "Delaware's Duty of Care," *Delaware Journal of Corporate Law* 31 (2006): 595.

235 Marcia M. McMurray, "An Historical Perspective on the Duty of Care, the Duty of Loyalty, and the Business Judgment Rule," *Vanderbilt Law Review* 40 (1987): 606–7.

236 James A. Ward, "Power and Accountability on the Pennsylvania Railroad, 1846–1878," *Business History Review* 49 (1975): 56.

237 Hearings before the Committee on Interstate and Foreign Commerce, House of Representatives, 78th Congress, H.R. 1493, H.R. 1821, and H.R. 2019. See also Miguel Cantillo Simon, "The Rise and Fall of Bank Control in the United States: 1890–1939," *American Economic Review* 88 (1998): 1080.

238 Julia C. Ott, *When Wall Street Met Main Street: The Quest for an Investors' Democracy* (Harvard University Press, 2011), 127.

239 William Lazonick and Mary O'Sullivan, "American Corporate Finance: From Organizational to Market Control," in *Competitiveness Matters: Industry*

and Economic Performance in the U.S., eds. Candace Howes and Ajit Singh (University of Michigan Press, 2000), 109.

240 Mitchell, "Status Bound," 85–86.

241 Scott R. Bowman, *The Modern Corporation and American Political Thought: Law, Power, and Ideology* (Penn State University Press, 1996), 60.

242 See Morton J. Horwitz, *The Transformation of American Law, 1870–1960: The Crisis of Legal Orthodoxy* (Oxford University Press, 1992), 65–107.

243 Ibid, 80–90.

244 Joel Seligman, "A Brief History of Delaware's General Corporation Law of 1899," *Delaware Journal of Corporate Law* 1 (1976): 273.

245 Ibid., 273–75.

246 Wells, "The Rise of the Close Corporation," 284–85.

247 See, e.g., Thomas M. Cooley, *Treatise on the Constitutional Limitations which Rest upon the Legislative Power of the States of the American Union* (3rd ed., 1874), 279–80 n.2; J. Newton Baker, "The Evil of Special Privilege," *Yale Law Journal* 22 (1913): 220.

248 L. S. Zacharias, "Repaving the Brandeis Way: The Decline of Developmental Property," *Northwestern University Law Review* 82 (1988), 618–19.

249 Michael J. Sandel, *Democracy's Discontent: America in Search of a Public Philosophy* (The Belknap Press, 1996), 211–21.

250 Adolf A. Berle, Jr., and Gardiner C. Means, *The Modern Corporation and Private Property* (Macmillan, 1932), 356.

251 Weinberg, "Status and Functions," chap. I.B.

252 Edward S. Herman, *Corporate Control, Corporate Power* (Cambridge University Press, 1981), 11.

253 Horwitz, *The Transformation*, 77–78, 99 (quoting *Manson v. Curtis*, 119 N.E. 559, 562 (N.Y. 1918)). See also *Hoyt v. Thompson*, 19 N.Y. 207 (N.Y. 1859).

254 "Donations by a Business Corporation as Intra Vires," *Columbia Law Review* 31 (1931): 136.

255 Ibid., 137–38; *People ex rel. Metropolitan Life Insurance Co. v. Hotchkiss*, 120 N.Y.S.2d 651 (N.Y. App. Div. 1909).

256 "Donations by a Business Corporation as Intra Vires," 136.

257 Raynal C. Bolling, "The United States Steel Corporation and Labor Conditions," *Annals of the American Academy of Political and Social Science* 42 (1912): 38.

258 Allen Kaufman and Lawrence Zacharias, "From Trust to Contract: The Legal Language of Managerial Ideology, 1920–1980," *Business History Review* 66 (1992): 527. John Weinberg's thesis also quotes Young. Weinberg, "Status and Functions," chap. III.B.2.

259 Roland Marchand, *Creating the Corporate Soul: The Rise of Public Relations and Corporate Imagery in American Big Business* (University of California Press, 2000), 15.

260 Berle and Means, *The Modern Corporation*, 312.

261 Adolf A. Berle, Jr., "Corporate Powers as Powers in Trust," *Harvard Law Review* 44 (1931): 1049.

262 Mitchell, "Status Bound," 99–103.

263 "Business v. the Public," *Accounting Review* 8 (1933): 162.
264 Ibid., 163.
265 Eric Hilt, "History of American Corporate Governance: Law, Institutions, and Politics," *Annual Review of Financial Economics* 6 (2014): 16.
266 Mark Roe, "Political Theory of American Corporate Finance," *Columbia Law Review* 91 (1991): 17.
267 Ibid., 19–20.
268 William O. Douglas, "Directors Who Do Not Direct," *Harvard Law Review* 47 (1934): 1306–14.
269 Ibid., 1307, 1313.
270 Ibid., 1314.
271 Ibid., 1322.
272 Ibid., 1328.
273 William O. Douglas, "Corporation Directors," in *Democracy and Finance: The Addresses and Public Statements of William O. Douglas*, ed. James Allen (Yale University Press, 1940), 53.
274 Douglas, "Directors Who Do Not Direct," 1328.
275 Herbert Hovenkamp, "The Classical Corporation in American Legal Thought," *Georgetown Law Journal* 76 (1988): 1688. See also E. Merrick Dodd, Jr., "The Modern Corporation, Private Property, and Recent Federal Legislation," *Harvard Law Review* 54 (1941): 917.
276 Mitchell, "Status Bound," 113–23.
277 Richard C. Patterson, Jr., "Wanted: Directors Who Direct," *New York Times*, January 21, 1940, 97.
278 Howard W. Calkins, "Concerns Ponder 'Work' Directors," *New York Times*, December 23, 1939, 83.
279 Weinberg, "Status and Functions," chap. IV.A.2.
280 Ibid., chap. III.A.
281 Ibid., chap. III.B.2.
282 Ibid., chap. IV.A.1.
283 Ibid., chap. IV.C.4.
284 Ibid., chap. II.A.
285 Harold Williamson, "Book Review," (reviewing James Truslow Adams, *Big Business in a Democracy* (C. Scribner's sons, 1941)), *Annals of the American Academy of Political and Social Sciences* 244 (1946): 196.
286 Ibid.
287 Richard Hofstadter, "What Happened to the Antitrust Movement?" in *The Paranoid Style in American Politics and Other Essays* (Harper's Magazine, 1965), 236.
288 Peter F. Drucker, *Concept of the Corporation* (Routledge, 1946), 33, 36.
289 Jack Jacobs, "Fifty Years of Corporate Law Evolution: A Delaware Judge's Retrospective," *Harvard Business Law Review* 5 (2015): 143.
290 Mitchell, "Status Bound," 118.
291 Edward A. Purcell, *The Crisis of Democratic Theory: Scientific Naturalism and the Problem of Value* (The University Press of Kentucky, 1973), 138.

292 Weinberg, "Status and Functions," chap. I.
293 *A. P. Smith Mfg. Co. v. Barlow*, 13 N.J. 145, 153 (1953).
294 Ibid., 153–54.
295 Adolf A. Berle, "Foreword," in Edward S. Mason, ed., *The Corporation in Modern Society* (Harvard University Press, 1959), xii.
296 See, e.g., C. Wright Mills, *The Power Elite* (1956), 28–29; Gabriel Kolko, *The Triumph of Conservatism: A Reinterpretation of American History, 1900–1916* (1963) 3, 8, 286.
297 Karen Ho, *Liquidated: An Ethnography of Wall Street* (Duke University Press, 2009), 195; Gerald F. Davis, "The Twilight of the Berle and Means Corporation," *Seattle University Law Review* 34 (2011): 1125.
298 Carl Kaysen, "The Social Significance of the Modern Corporation," *American Economic Review* 47 (1957): 314.
299 Mark Mizruchi, *The Fracturing of the American Corporate Elite* (University of Michigan Press, 2013), 8.
300 Rakesh Khurana, *From Higher Aims to Hired Hands: The Social Transformation of American Business Schools and the Unfulfilled Promise of Management as a Profession* (Princeton University Press, 2007), 298–99.
301 William L. Cary, "Federalism and Corporate Law: Reflections upon Delaware," *Yale Law Journal* 83 (1974): 668–69.
302 Melvin A. Eisenberg, "Legal Models of Management Structure in the Modern Corporation: Officers, Directors, and Accountants," *California Law Review* 63 (1975): 376.
303 Joel Seligman, "A Sheep in Wolf's Clothing: The American Law Institute Principles of Corporate Governance Project," *George Washington Law Review* 55 (1987): 330–32.
304 Ralph Nader et al, *Taming the Giant Corporation* (W.W. Norton, 1976).
305 Harvey J. Goldschmid, "The Greening of the Board Room: Reflections on Corporate Responsibility," *Columbia Journal of Law and Social Problems* 10 (1973): 15.
306 Henry Ridgely Horsey, "The Duty of Care Component of the Delaware Business Judgment Rule," *Delaware Journal of Corporation Law* 19 (1994): 991 (quoting Peter F. Drucker, *The Unseen Revolution: How Pension Fund Socialism Came to America* [Harper & Row, 1976], 91).
307 Weinberg, "Status and Functions," chap. VI.C.1.
308 "Corporate Director's Guidebook," *Business Lawyer* 32 (1976): 5, as revised in *Business Lawyer* 33 (1978): 1591; Seligman, "A Sheep in Wolf's Clothing," 341–42.
309 Mitchell, "Status Bound," 135–36.
310 Ibid., 135–40.
311 *Unocal v. Mesa Petroleum, Co.*, 493 A.2d 946 (Del. 1985).
312 Jeffrey N. Gordon, "The Story of Unocal v. Mesa Petroleum: The Core of Takeover Law," in *Corporate Law Stories*, ed. Mark Ramseyer (West Academic, 2009), 227.
313 *Unocal*, 954.
314 Ibid., 955.

315 See, e.g., *Cede & Co. v. Technicolor, Inc.*, 634 A.2d 345, 361 (Del. 1993).
316 Mitchell, "Proceduralism."
317 Henry G. Manne, "Mergers and the Market for Corporate Control," *Journal of Political Economy* 73 (1965): 113.
318 Ho, *Liquidated*, 130.
319 Ronald J. Gilson & Jeffrey N. Gordon, "The Agency Costs of Agency Capitalism: Activist Investors and the Reevaluation of Governance Rights," *Columbia Law Review* 113 (2013): 874–84.
320 *Unocal.*, 956–57.
321 *Revlon, Inc. v. MacAndrews & Forbes Holding, Inc.*, 506 A.2d 173, 182 (Del. 1986).
322 *Paramount Communications, Inc. v. Time, Inc.*, 571 A.2d 1140, 1154 (Del. 1989) (citations omitted).
323 William T. Allen, "Our Schizophrenic Conception of the Business Corporation," *Cardozo Law Review* 14 (1992): 264–66.
324 Weinberg, "Status and Functions," chap. VII (Conclusion).

CHAPTER 6

325 Weinberg, "Status and Functions." Portions of this chapter draw on certain of the author's previously published works, all of which are cited herein. Assertions from the earlier works are incorporated here, sometimes verbatim and sometimes with revisions, without separate quotation marks or pinpoint citations.
326 Kyle Edward Williams, *Taming the Octopus: The Long Battle for the Soul of the Corporation* (W.W. Norton, 2024), 69.
327 Gregory Mark, "The Corporate Economy: Ideologies of Regulation and Antitrust, 1920–2000," in *The Cambridge History of Law in America*, vol. 3, ed. Michael Grossberg and Christopher Tomlins (Cambridge University Press, 2008), 642.
328 Gardiner Means, "The Diffusion of Stock Ownership in the United States," *Quarterly Journal of Economics* 44, no. 4 (August 1930): 594; Ott, *When Wall Street Met Main Street.*
329 Marco Becht and J. Bradford DeLong, "Why Has There Been So Little Blockholding in America?" in *A History of Corporate Governance Around the World: Family Business Groups to Professional Managers*, ed. Randall K. Morck (University of Chicago Press, 2005).
330 Harwell Wells, "The Birth of Corporate Governance," *Seattle University Law Review* 33, no. 4 (January 2010): 1253.
331 Berle and Means, *The Modern Corporation.*
332 Brian Cheffins and Steven Bank, "Is Berle and Means Really a Myth?", *Business History Review* 83, no. 3 (Autumn 2009): 443.
333 William Z. Ripley, *Main Street and Wall Street* (Little, Brown, 1927).
334 Berle, "Corporate Power as Powers in Trust," 1049.
335 Stanley Buder, *Capitalizing on Change: A Social History of American Business* (University of North Carolina Press, 2009), 87–88, 165–170.
336 Williams, *Taming the Octopus*, 14.

337 Khurana, *From Higher Aims to Hired Hands*, 148.
338 Francis X. Sutton, Seymour E. Harris, Carl Kaysen, and James Tobin, *The American Business Creed* (Harvard University Press, 1955), 387.
339 Harwell Wells, "The Cycles of Corporate Social Responsibility," *University of Kansas Law Review* 51, no. 1 (November 2002): 87.
340 Berle, "Corporate Powers as Powers in Trust," 1049.
341 Dodd, "For Whom," 1148.
342 Dodd, "For Whom," 1161.
343 Berle, "For Whom," 1367.
344 Berle and Means, *The Modern Corporation*, 312–13.
345 Ellis Hawley, *The New Deal and the Problem of Monopoly* (Princeton University Press, 1966), 403–10, 462–65; Alan Brinkley, "The New Deal and the Idea of the State," in *The Rise and Fall of the New Deal Order 1930–1980*, eds. Steve Fraser and Gary Gerstle (Princeton University Press, 1989), 87.
346 Hawley, *New Deal*, 460–65.
347 Weinberg, "Status and Functions," chaps. IV.A and IV.C.4.
348 US Temporary National Economic Committee, "Bureaucracy and Trusteeship in Large Corporations," *Investigation of Concentration of Economic Power*, Monograph No. 11 (US Government Printing Office, 1939).
349 Dodd thought so. E. Merrick Dodd, Jr., Book Review, "Bureaucracy and Trusteeship in Large Corporations, Temporary National Economic Committee, Monograph No. 11 by Marshall E. Dimock," *University of Chicago Law Review* 9, no. 3 (April 1942): 538.
350 US TNEC, "Bureaucracy and Trusteeship in Large Corporations," 3.
351 Ibid., 22.
352 Ibid., 108.
353 Ibid., 108–9.
354 Ibid., 124.
355 Ibid., 130.
356 James Burnham, *The Managerial Revolution: What is Happening in the World* (John Day, 1941); Ferdinand Mount, "Orwell and the Oligarchs," *Political Quarterly* 82, no. 2 (April 2011): 147.
357 Francesco Boldizzoni, *Foretelling the End of Capitalism* (Harvard University Press, 2020), 89–91.
358 Howard Brick, *Transcending Capitalism: Visions of a New Society in Modern American Thought* (Cornell University Press, 2006), 158.
359 Drucker, *Concept of the Corporation*, 5, 6, 142.
360 Ibid., 140.
361 Ibid., 142.
362 *Fortune* 21 (March 1940): 39, quoted in US TNEC, "Bureaucracy and Trusteeship in Large Corporations," 120–21.
363 Gordon, *Business Leadership*, 341–42.
364 Nelson Lichtenstein, *A Contest of Ideas: Capital, Politics, and Labor* (University of Illinois Press, 2013), 53.
365 Jonathan Levy, *Ages of American Capitalism* (Random House, 2021), 472–73.

366 Ibid., 475.
367 Williams, *Taming the Octopus*, 71.
368 Levy, *Ages of American Capitalism*, 479.
369 Sutton et al., *The American Business Creed.*
370 Ibid., 2, 10.
371 Ibid., 308 n. 8.
372 Ibid., 33, 121.
373 Ibid., 34.
374 Ibid., 36.
375 Ibid., 58.
376 Ibid., 263.
377 John Kenneth Galbraith, *American Capitalism: The Concept of Countervailing Power* (Houghton Mifflin, 1952).
378 Jennifer Delton, *Rethinking the 1950s: How Anticommunism and the Cold War Made America Liberal* (Cambridge University Press, 2013), 68.
379 Khurana, *From Higher Aims to Hired Hands*, 324.
380 Theodore Levitt, "The Dangers of Social Responsibility," *Harvard Business Review* 36 (September–October 1958): 42.
381 Morrell Heald, *The Social Responsibility of Business: Company and Community 1900–1960* (Case Western Reserve University Press, 1970), 299.
382 Robert E. Wright, *Corporation Nation* (University of Pennsylvania Press, 2014), 15–16.
383 Elizabeth Pollman, "The History and Revival of the Corporate Purpose Clause," *Texas Law Review* 99, no. 7 (June 2021): 1433–34.
384 Joseph K. Angell and Samuel Ames, *A Treatise on the Law of Private Corporations Aggregate* (Hillard, Gray, Little & Wilkins, 1832), 7.
385 Wright, *Corporation Nation*, 47–48.
386 William Wilson Cook, *A Treatise on the Law of Corporations Having a Capital Stock*, vol. 2 (Callaghan, 1898), 1256–58; D. Gordon Smith, "The Shareholder Primacy Norm," *Journal of Corporation Law* 23, no. 2 (Winter 1998): 296–97, 305–7.
387 Harwell Wells, "Corporate Purpose in the United States 1800–2000," in *Corporate Purpose, CSR, and ESG*, eds. Binder, Hopt & Kuntz (Oxford University Press, 2024), 173.
388 *Dodge v. Ford Motor Co.*, 170 N.W. 668, 684 (Mich. 1919).
389 M. Todd Henderson, "The Story of Ford Motor Co.," in *Corporate Law Stories*, ed. J. Mark Ramseyer (Foundation Press, 2009).
390 Smith, "Shareholder Primacy Norm," 315–20.
391 Henry W. Ballantine, *Ballantine on Corporations* (Callaghan, 1927), 207, 501.
392 *Matter of Cooperative Law Company*, 93 N.E. 15 (N.Y. 1909).
393 Harwell Wells, "'Corporation Law is Dead': Heroic Managerialism, Legal Change, and the Puzzle of Corporation Law at the Height of the American Century," *University of Pennsylvania Journal of Business Law* 15, no. 2 (Winter 2013): 336–39.
394 Mitchell, "Status Bound," 116–20.

395 Harwell Wells, "A Long View of Shareholder Power: From the Antebellum Corporation to the Twenty-First Century," *Florida Law Review* 67, no. 3 (May 2015): 1074–83.

396 *Steinway v. Steinway & Sons*, 40 N.Y.S. 718 (1896); *Davis v Old Colony R.R. Co.*, 131 Mass. 258 (1881).

397 *A. P. Smith Mfg. Co. v. Barlow*, 98 A.2d 581 (N.J. 1953).

398 Geoffrey Miller, "Narrative and Truth in Judicial Opinions: Corporate Charitable Giving Cases," *Michigan State Law Review* 2009, no. 4 (Winter 2009): 840.

399 *A. P. Smith*, 583.

400 Ibid.

401 Ibid., 584.

402 Ibid., 586.

403 Ibid., 587.

404 Eugene V. Rostow, "To Whom and For What Ends if Corporate Management Responsible?" in *The Corporation in Modern Society*, ed. Edward S. Mason (Cambridge University Press, 1959), 63.

405 National Industrial Conference Board, "Compensation and Duties of Corporate Directors," *Studies in Business Policy 16* (1946); Melvin Copeland and Andrew R. Towl, *The Board of Directors and Business Management* (Harvard University, 1947).

406 Weinberg, "Status and Functions," chap. III.B.2.

407 Ibid., chap. I.D.

408 Ibid., chap. I.B.

409 Ibid., chap. I.B.

410 Ibid., chap. I.D.

411 Ibid., chap. I.

412 Ibid.

413 Ibid., chap. I.D.

414 Ibid., Bibliography.

415 Ibid., chap. I.D.

416 Ibid., chap. III.B.

417 Ibid., chap. V.E.

418 Ibid., chap. III.B.

419 Ibid.

420 Ibid., chap. V.E.

421 Ibid., chap. III.B.2.

CHAPTER 7

422 *Smith v. Van Gorkom*, 488 A.2d 858 (Del. 1985); *In re Caremark International Inc. Derivative Litigation*, 698 A.2d 959 (Del. Ch. 1996).

423 Lawrence A. Cunningham, "Introduction: From Thesis to Testament," in *Boardroom Legacy: The Weinbergs of Goldman Sachs and the Evolution of Corporate Governance*, ed. Lawrence A. Cunningham (Harriman House, 2026).

424 *Match Corp. v. Allen*, 89 *New York Law Journal* 3375 (June 5, 1933); see "Court Denies Ban on $100,000,000 Suit," *New York Times* (June 4, 1933).

425 *Spencer Stuart U.S. Board Index 2014.*
426 Weinberg, "Status and Functions," chap. III.B.
427 Ibid.
428 Weinberg, "The Functions," *heading* The Business of Directing.

CHAPTER 8

429 See Simon Lorne, "Have We Taken Independence a Step Too Far?", *Directors & Boards* (February 23, 2016): 16.
430 *Brehm v. Eisner*, 906 A.2d 27, 57 (Del. 2006).
431 824 A.2d 917 (Del. Ch. 2003).
432 Weinberg, "The Functions," *heading* The Business of Directing.
433 Ibid., *heading* Tools for the Director.
434 Ibid.
435 Ibid., *heading* The Most Important Function.
436 Weinberg, "The Responsibility."
437 Weinberg, "The Functions," *heading* Do Your Homework (emphasis added).
438 Ibid.
439 Ibid., *heading* The Most Important Function.
440 Ibid., *heading* Tools for the Director.
441 "Business Roundtable Redefines the Purpose of a Corporation to Promote 'An Economy That Serves All Americans'," Business Roundtable, August 19, 2019.
442 See https://opportunity.businessroundtable.org/about-us.
443 Adam Smith, *An Inquiry into the Nature and Causes of the Wealth of Nations*, ed. R. H. Campbell and A. S. Skinner (Clarendon Press, 1976 [1776]), Book IV, chap. II, para. 9 (emphasis added).
444 *Quotations from Chairman Mao Tse-Tung*, 2nd ed. (1966), quoting "Problems of War and Strategy," *Selected Works*, vol. II, 224 (November 6, 1938).
445 Weinberg, "The Functions," *heading* The Business of Directing.
446 Weinberg, "Status and Functions," chap. I.D (citing Edward R. Stettinius, Jr., *Address to the Annual Convention of the Association of Life Insurance Presidents*, 1939). The chapters in Part II of this volume explore how the thesis reflects related debates of the day.
447 See, e.g., Bernard S. Black, Brian R. Cheffins, and L. Michael Klausner, "Outside Director Liability," *Stanford Law Review 58 (2005): 1055.*
448 *In re Caremark International Inc. Derivative Litigation*, 698 A.2d 959 (Del. Ch. 1996); *Stone v. Ritter*, 911 A.2d 362 (Del. 2006).

CHAPTER 9

449 Hal Brands, "The Dangerous Myth of American Decline," *Foreign Affairs* (July/August 2021).
450 Jeffrey Mankoff, *Empires of Eurasia: How Imperial Legacies Shape International Security* (Yale University Press, 2022).
451 Martin Reeves, Annelies O'Dea, and Philipp Carlsson-Szlezak, "How Boards Can Build Long-Term Resilience," *Harvard Business Review* (October 2022).

452 National Association of Corporate Directors, *Geopolitical and Cyber Hot Spots* (2022).

453 Weinberg, "Status and Functions," chap. I.E.

454 Susan L. Shirk, *Overreach: How China Derailed Its Peaceful Rise* (Oxford University Press, 2022).

455 US Department of Defense, "DoD News Briefing—Secretary Rumsfeld and Gen. Myers," February 12, 2002.

456 Warren Bennis and Burt Nanus, *Leaders: Strategies for Taking Charge* (Harper & Row, 1985). VUCA stands for *Volatility, Uncertainty, Complexity, and Ambiguity*. The term was introduced by the US Army War College in 1987 to describe the complex and rapidly changing post-Cold War world. It was influenced by leadership theories from Bennis and Nanus.

457 Jamais Cascio, "Human Responses to a BANI World," *Medium*, April 18, 2018. BANI stands for Brittle, Anxious, Nonlinear, and Incomprehensible. The term was coined by Cascio in 2018 as a framework to describe the increasingly chaotic and unpredictable nature of the modern world, offering an update to the VUCA model.

458 Edward R. Stettinius, Jr., quoted in Weinberg, "Status and Functions," chap. I.D.

459 Weinberg, "Status and Functions," chap. I.D.

460 Ibid., chaps. I.D and I.E.

461 Joel Slawotsky, "U.S. Corporate Director Responsibilities to Oversee National Security Threats in an Era of Great Power Rivalry," *Journal of Corporation Law* 49 (2024): 875; Harry G. Broadman, "Inducing U.S. 'Economic Patriotism' Through Outbound Investment National Security Screening," *Forbes*, February 28, 2023.

462 James Stavridis and Evelyn N. Farkas, "The 21st Century Force Multiplier: Public–Private Collaboration," *The Washington Quarterly* 35, no. 2 (2012): 7–20; David H. McCormick, Charles E. Luftig, and James M. Cunningham, *Economic Might, National Security, and the Future of American Statecraft* (Atlantic Council, July 9, 2020); Robert G. Eccles, interview with Roy Swan, "Roy Swan Explains His Concept of 'Patriotic Capitalism,'" *Interviews* (RobertEccles.com), accessed February 21, 2026, https://interviews.roberteccles.com/roy-swan-explains-his-concept-of-patriotic-capitalism.

463 Weinberg, "Status and Functions," chap. VI.A.2.

464 Susan Lund et al., *Risk, Resilience, and Rebalancing in Global Value Chains* (McKinsey Global Institute, August 2020).

465 Ibid.

466 David E. Sanger, Nicole Perlroth, and Eric Schmitt, "Scope of Russian Hack Becomes Clear: Multiple U.S. Agencies Were Hit," *New York Times*, December 15, 2020.

467 US Cybersecurity and Infrastructure Security Agency (CISA), "Defending Against Nation-State Cyber Threats," 2023.

468 Controllers Council, "Best Practices for Conducting Financial Stress Testing," 2024.

469 Reeves, O'Dea, and Carlsson-Szlezak, "How Boards Can Build Long-Term Resilience."
470 Robert D. Blackwill and Jennifer M. Harris, *War by Other Means: Geoeconomics and Statecraft* (Harvard University Press, 2016).
471 Weinberg, "Status and Functions," chap. I.D.

CHAPTER 10

472 Weinberg, "The Functions," *heading* The Effective Director.
473 Weinberg, "Status and Functions," chap. I.D.
474 Del. Code Ann. tit. 8, § 141.
475 Abraham Zaleznik, "Managers and Leaders: Are they Different?", *Harvard Business Review* (January 2024).
476 John P. Kotter, Vanessa Akhtar, and Gaurav Gupta, *Change* (John Wiley & Sons, 2021), 26–29, 203–4.
477 April Mara Barton, "Teaching Lawyers to Think Like Leaders: The Next Big Shift in Legal Education," *Baylor Law Review* 73, no. 1 (2021): 119.
478 David Gergen, *Hearts Touched with Fire* (Simon & Schuster, 2022), 22; Barton, "Teaching Lawyers," 118.
479 James MacGregor Burns, *Leadership* (Harper & Row, 1978), 19.
480 Donald J. Polden, "Leadership Matters: Lawyers' Leadership Skills and Competencies," *Santa Clara Law Review* 52, no. 3 (2012): 902–3.
481 Del. Code Ann. tit. 8, § 141.
482 Ibid., § 122(18) (2025).
483 Weinberg, "The Functions," *heading* The Language of the Law.
484 Ibid.
485 Weinberg, "Status and Functions," chap. III (introduction).
486 Ibid., chap. III.A.
487 Ibid., chap. III (introduction).
488 Ibid., chap. III.A.
489 Cunningham, "Introduction."
490 Weinberg, "The Functions," *heading* The Business of Directing; Weinberg, "The Responsibility," *point 6.*
491 Gergen, *Hearts Touched with Fire*, 195.
492 *Stone v. Ritter*, 911 A.2d 362, 370 (Del. 2006).
493 Joan MacLeod Heminway, "Shareholder Wealth Maximization as a Function of Statutes, Decisional Law, and Organic Documents," *Washington & Lee Law Review* 74, no. 2 (2017): 952–54.
494 Weinberg, "Status and Functions," chap. III.B.3.
495 Ibid., chap. III.B.
496 Weinberg, "The Functions," *heading* Language of the Law.
497 Ibid., *heading* The Effective Director.
498 Del. Code Ann. tit. 8, § 141.
499 Weinberg, "Status and Functions," chap. II.A.
500 Weinberg, "The Functions," *heading* The Business of Directing.
501 Robert K. Greenleaf, *Servant as Leader* (Robert K. Greenleaf Center, 1973).
502 Ibid., 7.

503 Weinberg, "The Functions," *heading* Re Stock Ownership.
504 Robert H. Jerry, II, "Leadership and Followership," *University of Toledo Law Review* 44, no. 2 (2013): 34.
505 Stephen M. Bainbridge, "Why a Board? Group Decisionmaking in Corporate Governance," *Vanderbilt Law Review* 55, no. 1 (2002): 8.
506 Gordon, "The Rise of Independent Directors," 1539–40.
507 Weinberg, "Status and Functions," chaps. I.C, IV.E, VI.C.
508 Cunningham, "Introduction."
509 Weinberg, "The Functions," *heading* Composition of the Board.
510 Sanjai Bhagat and Bernard Black, "The Uncertain Relationship Between Board Composition and Firm Performance," *The Business Lawyer* 54 (May 1999): 921.
511 Weinberg, "Status and Functions," chap. V.B.1.
512 Ibid., chap. III.A.4.
513 Ibid., chap. V.B.4.
514 Del. Code Ann. tit. 8, § 144.
515 Lawrence A. Cunningham, "Conclusion: Where to from Here," in *Boardroom Legacy: The Weinbergs of Goldman Sachs and the Evolution of Corporate Governance*, ed. Lawrence A. Cunningham (Harriman House, 2026).
516 Weinberg, "Status and Functions," chap. IV.A.2.
517 Bhagat and Black, "The Uncertain Relationship," 924.
518 Weinberg, "Status and Functions," chap. III.A.3.
519 Ibid., chap. III.A.4.
520 Ibid., chap. III (introduction).
521 R. William Ide, "Post-Enron Corporate Governance Opportunities: Creating a Culture of Greater Board Collaboration and Oversight," *Mercer Law Review* 54, no. 2 (2003): 836.
522 Margaret M. Blair and Lynn A. Stout, "A Team Production Theory of Corporate Law," *Virginia Law Review* 85, no. 2 (1999): 281.
523 Corporate Laws Committee, ABA Business Law Section, "Corporate Director's Guidebook—Seventh Edition," *The Business Lawyer* 75 (Fall 2020): 2818–19.
524 Ibid., 2757, 2825.
525 Ibid., 2757.
526 Houman B. Shadab, "Innovation and Corporate Governance: The Impact of Sarbanes–Oxley," *University of Pennsylvania Journal of Business & Employment Law* 10, no. 4 (2008): 972–73.
527 Ted Sikora, "2025 Inside the Public Company Boardroom," National Association of Corporate Directors (April 1, 2025).
528 Del. Code Ann. tit. 8, § 141(c).
529 Weinberg, "The Responsibility."
530 Weinberg, "The Functions," *heading* A Basis of Cooperation.
531 Weinberg, "Status and Functions," chap. III.A.5.
532 Lisa M. Fairfax, "Separation Anxiety: A Cautious Endorsement of the Independent Board Chair," *Indiana Law Review* 47, no. 4 (2014): 237; Thuy-Nga T. Vo, "To Be or Not to Be Both CEO and Board Chair," *Brooklyn Law Review* 76, no. 1 (2010): 65.

533 Yaron Nili, "Successor CEOs," *Boston University Law Review* 99, no. 3 (2019): 792.
534 Fairfax, "Separation Anxiety," 244.
535 Weinberg, "Status and Functions," chap. IV.B.
536 Nili, "Successor CEOs," 798.
537 Michael E. Murphy, "Restoring Trust in Corporate America: Toward A Republican Theory of Corporate Legitimacy," *New York University Journal of Law & Business* 5, no. 2 (2009): 473.
538 Kenneth R. Andrews, "Corporate Governance Eludes the Legal Mind," *University of Miami Law Review* 37, no. 2 (1983): 215.
539 Peter Salovey and John D. Mayer, "Emotional Intelligence," *Imagination, Cognition and Personality* 9, no. 3 (1990): 189.
540 Daniel Goleman, "An EI-Based Theory of Performance," in *The Emotionally Intelligent Workplace: How to Select for, Measure, and Improve Emotional Intelligence in Individuals, Groups, and Organizations*, ed. Cary Cherniss and Daniel Goleman (Jossey–Bass, 2001), 28–29.
541 Ibid.; Hay Group, *Emotional and Social Competency Inventory (ESCI): A User Guide for Accredited Practitioners* (June 2011), 4–6.
542 Hay Group, *Emotional and Social Competence Inventory*, 4.
543 Kelli Alces Williams, "Leaders Are Not Fiduciaries," *Alabama Law Review* 72, no. 2 (2020): 405.
544 Robert Goffee and Gareth Jones, "Why Should Anyone Be Led by You?", *Harvard Business Review*, September–October 2000, 64.
545 Keith Ferrazzi, *Leading without Authority* (Currency, 2020), 9.
546 Ibid., 200.
547 Weinberg, "Status and Functions," chap. IV.C.2.
548 *Spencer Stuart U.S. Board Index 2024*, 33.
549 Weinberg, "Status and Functions," chap. IV.C.4; Weinberg, "The Functions."
550 Ide, "Post-Enron Corporate Governance," 836.
551 Weinberg, "Status and Functions," chap. IV.A.1.
552 Weinberg, "The Responsibility."
553 15 U.S.C. § 78j-1(m)(3).
554 Weinberg, "The Functions," *heading* A Basis of Cooperation.
555 Weinberg, "Status and Functions," chap. III.A.5.
556 The Nasdaq Stock Market LLC Rules, § 5605(b)(1); New York Stock Exchange, *Listed Company Manual*, § 303A.01.
557 17 C.F.R. § 229.407(a).
558 Corporate Laws Committee, "Corporate Director's Guidebook," 2820.
559 *Tornetta v. Musk*, 310 A.3d 430, 509 (Del. Ch. 2024), *rev'd sub nom. In re Tesla, Inc. Derivative Litigation*, 2025 Westlaw 3689114 (Del. Dec. 19, 2025).
560 Press Release, Kohl's Announces CEO Transition Process (May 1, 2025).
561 Andrews, "Corporate Governance Eludes," 215.
562 Weinberg, "The Functions," *heading* The Effective Director.

CHAPTER 11

563 Weinberg, "Status and Functions," chaps. II.G and III.A.1; Weinberg, "The Responsibility," *point* 6; Weinberg, "The Functions," *heading* A Basis of Cooperation.
564 Weinberg, "The Responsibility," *point* 11; Weinberg, "The Functions," *heading* A Basis of Cooperation, *point* 11; Weinberg, "Status and Functions," chap. III.A.5.
565 Weinberg, "The Responsibility," *heading* Composition of the Board; Weinberg, "Status and Functions," chap. IV.C.4.
566 Weinberg, "The Functions," *heading* Composition of the Board.
567 Ibid., Introduction.
568 Mary O'Sullivan, "The Expansion of the U.S. Stock Market, 1885–1930: Historical Facts and Theoretical Fashions," *Enterprise and Society* 8, no. 3 (September 2007): 489.
569 Partnoy, *The Match King*.
570 Cunningham, "Introduction."
571 15 U.S.C. § 77b.
572 15 U.S.C. § 78m.
573 Weinberg, "Status and Functions," chap. I.C; Weinberg, "The Responsibility."
574 Adolf A. Berle and Gardiner C. Means, *The Modern Corporation and Private Property*, rev. ed. (Transaction Publishers, 1991).
575 Weinberg, "The Responsibility;" Weinberg, "Status and Functions," chap. IV.C.3.
576 Weinberg, "Status and Functions," chap. III.A.2.
577 *Revlon, Inc. v. MacAndrews & Forbes Holdings, Inc.*, 506 A.2d 173 (Del. 1986).
578 Cunningham, "Introduction."
579 Weinberg, "The Functions," *heading* A Basis of Cooperation.
580 See David A. Westbrook, "Corporation Law After Enron: The Possibility of a Capitalist Reimagination," *Georgetown Law Journal* 92 (2003): 61.
581 Public Law No. 107-204, 116 Stat. 745 (July 30, 2002).
582 *In re Citigroup Inc. Shareholder Derivative Litigation*, 964 A.2d 106 (Del. Ch. 2009). But see David A. Westbrook, *Out of Crisis: Rethinking Our Financial Markets* (Paradigm Publishers, 2010).
583 "Dumbest Business Moments of the Decade," *CNNMoney*, July 8, 2007.
584 Albert Camus, *The Myth of Sisyphus and Other Essays*, trans. Justin O'Brien (Alfred A. Knopf, 1942), 119.
585 Weinberg, "Status and Functions," chap. VII (emphasis in original).
586 Ibid.
587 Ibid. (emphasis in original).
588 Ibid., chap. I (emphasis added).
589 *Brehm v. Eisner*, 906 A.2d 27, 57 (Del. 2006).
590 *In re Walt Disney Company Derivative Litigation*, 907 A.2d 693, 697 (Del. Ch. 2005).
591 Ibid.
592 See, e.g., Margaret M. Blair, "Locking in Capital: What Corporate Law Achieved for Business Organizers in the Nineteenth Century," *UCLA Law Review* 51 (2003): 387.

593 Cunningham, "Introduction."

594 *Tornetta v. Musk*, 310 A.3d 430, 509 (Del. Ch. 2024) (scrutinizing fairness of Elon Musk's compensation plan due to his status as a controlling shareholder accompanied by flawed processes). rev'd sub nom. In re Tesla, Inc. Derivative Litigation, ___ A.3d ___, 2025 WL 3689114 (Del. Dec. 19, 2025).

595 Cunningham, "Introduction."

596 See, e.g., *Smith v. Van Gorkom*, 488 A.2d 858 (Del. 1985); *In re Caremark International*, 698 A.2d 959 (Del. Ch. 1996); *Stone v. Ritter*, 911 A.2d 362 (Del. 2006); *Marchand v. Barnhill*, 212 A.3d 805 (Del. 2019).

597 See David A. Westbrook, *Between Citizen and State: An Introduction to the Corporation* (Paradigm Publishers 2008), 80–83.

598 Lucian A. Bebchuk and Scott Hirst, "The Specter of the Giant Three," *Boston University Law Review* 99 (2019): 721.

599 Amy Deen Westbrook and David A. Westbrook, "Unicorns, Guardians, and the Concentration of the U.S. Equity Markets," *Nebraska Law Review* 96 (2018): 688.

600 Ibid.

601 Stephen Fraidin and Meredith Foster, "The Evolution of Private Equity and the Change in General Partner Compensation Terms in the 1980s," *Fordham Journal of Corporate and Financial Law* 16 (2019): 327.

602 See generally Kobi Kastiel and Yaron Nili, "The Rise of Private Equity Continuation Funds," *Harvard Law School Forum on Corporate Governance*, June 18, 2024.

603 Dan Primack, "Private Equity's Antitrust Future," *Axios*, October 31, 2022.

604 Karl Marx and Friedrich Engels, *The Communist Manifesto*, trans. Samuel Moore (Verso, 1998 [1848]), 16.

605 See Westbrook, *Out of Crisis*.

606 Immanuel Kant, *Critique of Pure Reason*, trans. Paul Guyer and Allen W. Wood (Cambridge University Press, 1998 [1781]).

607 Ibid.

608 O.W. Holmes, Jr., *The Common Law* 1 (Little, Brown, 1881), 1.

609 Weinberg, "Status and Functions," chap. III.B.3

610 Cunningham, "Introduction."

611 Weinberg, "Status and Functions," chap. III.B.3.

612 See David A. Westbrook, *Social Thought from the Ruins: Quixote's Dinner Party* (Routledge, 2025); David A. Westbrook, *Navigators of the Contemporary: Why Ethnography Matters* (University of Chicago Press, 2009).

613 See Gordon, "The Rise of Independent Directors," 1540.

614 488 A.2d 858, 863 (Del. 1985).

615 Bayless Manning, "The Business Judgment Rule and the Director's Duty of Attention: Time for Reality," *Business Lawyer* 39 (1984): 1477, 1499.

616 See *Smith v. Van Gorkom*.

617 Fairfax, "Separation Anxiety," 248.

618 See, e.g., *Benihana of Tokyo, Inc. v. Benihana, Inc.*, 906 A.2d 114 (Del. 2006); *In re Walt Disney Company Derivative Litigation*.

619 See Westbrook, *Between Citizen and State*, 80.
620 Cunningham, "Conversations from the Buffett Symposium," 719, 738.
621 Weinberg, "Status and Functions," chap. III.B.3.
622 See Lisa M. Fairfax, "Sarbanes–Oxley, Corporate Federalism, and the Declining Significance of Federal Reforms on State Director Independence," *Ohio Northern University Law Review* 31 (2005): 410.

CHAPTER 12

623 For example, executives might manipulate financial results to increase the size of their bonuses.
624 Interpreting empirical studies can be a challenge due to a variety of issues. Still, competently generated empirical results are superior to guesswork or intuition.
625 New York Stock Exchange, *Listed Company Manual*, § 303A.02.
626 Sanjai Bhagat and Bernard Black, "The Noncorrelation Between Board Independence and Long-Term Firm Performance," *Journal of Corporation Law* 27 (2002): 231.
627 Anzhela Knyazeva, Diana Knyazeva, and Ronald W. Masulis, "The Supply of Corporate Directors and Board Independence," *Review of Financial Studies* 26 (2013): 1561.
628 Michelle L. Zorn, Christine Shopshire, John A. Martin, James G. Combs, and David J. Ketchen, "Home Alone: The Effect of Lone-Insider Boards on CEO Pay, Financial Misconduct, and Firm Performance," *Strategic Management Journal* 38 (2017): 2623; Sydney Finkelstein and Donald C. Hambrick, "Chief Executive Compensation: A Study of the Intersection of Markets and Political Processes," *Strategic Management Journal* 10 (1989): 121; Seil Kim and April Klein, "Did the 1999 NYSE and NASDAQ Listing Standard Changes on Audit Committee Composition Benefit Investors?" *Accounting Review* 92 (2017): 187.
629 Byoung-Hyoun Hwang and Seoyoung Kim, "It Pays to Have Friends," *Journal of Financial Economics* 93 (2009): 138.
630 Liesbeth Bruynseels and Eddy Cardinaels, "The Audit Committee: Management Watchdog or Personal Friend of the CEO?" *Accounting Review* 89 (2014):113.
631 Jeffrey L. Coles, Naveen D. Daniel, and Lalitha Naveen, "Co-opted Boards," *Review of Financial Studies* 27 (June 2014): 1751.
632 David F. Larcker and Brian Tayan, "Chairman and CEO: The Controversy over Board Leadership Structure," *Stanford Closer Look Series*, June 24, 2016.
633 See Subodh Mishra, "Investors Press U.S. Boards To Separate Chair, CEO Roles," *Harvard Law School Forum on Corporate Governance*, October 12, 2023; ISS, *US Proxy Voting Guidelines* (2025), 22; Glass Lewis, *US Proxy Paper Guidelines* (2024), 15–16.
634 B. Ram Baliga, R. Charles Moyer, and Ramesh S. Rao, "CEO Duality and Firm Performance: What's the Fuss?" *Strategic Management Journal* 17 (1996): 41.
635 Aiyesha Dey, Ellen Engel, and Xiaohui Liu, "CEO and Board Chair Roles: To Split or Not to Split?", *Journal of Corporate Finance* 17 (2011): 1595.
636 Ryan Krause, Matthew Semadeni, and Albert A. Cannella, "CEO Duality: A Review and Research Agenda," *Journal of Management* 40 (2014): 256.

637 The Conference Board, "US Corporate Board Diversity: Boards Are More Diverse Than Ever, But the Pace of Growth is Slowing," November 9, 2023; Subodh Mishra, "U.S. Board Diversity Trends in 2019," *Harvard Law School Forum on Corporate Governance*, June 18, 2019.

638 Spencer Stuart Board Indexes.

639 Altrata, *Global Gender Diversity* (2024).

640 Charles A. O'Reilly III, Katherine Y. Williams, and Sigal Barsade, "The Impact of Relational Demography on Teamwork: When Differences Make a Difference," *Academy of Management Proceedings & Membership Directory* (1999): G1.

641 Deborah L. Rhode and Amanda K. Packel, "Diversity on Corporate Boards: How Much Difference Does 'Difference' Make?" *Delaware Journal of Corporate Law* 39 (2014): 377.

642 Anzhela Knyazeva, Diana Knyazeva, and Lalitha Naveen, "Diversity on Corporate Boards," *Annual Review of Financial Economics* 13 (2021): 301.

643 Corinne Post and Kris Byron, "Women on Boards and Firm Financial Performance: A Meta-Analysis," *Academy of Management Journal* 58 (2015): 1546.

644 Kenneth R. Ahern and Amy K. Dittmar, "The Changing of the Boards: The Impact on Firm Valuation of Mandated Female Board Representation," *Quarterly Journal of Economics* (2012): 137.

645 Alex Baum, David F. Larcker, Brian Tayan, and Jacob Welch, "Building a Better Board Book," *Stanford Closer Look Series* (October 2017).

646 David F. Larcker and Brian Tayan, "Netflix Approach to Governance: Genuine Transparency with the Board," *Stanford Closer Look Series* (May 2018).

647 See David F. Larcker, Amit Seru, Brian Tayan, and Laurie Yoler, "The Artificially Intelligent Boardroom," *Stanford Closer Look Series* (March 2025).

648 New York Stock Exchange, *Corporate Governance Standards.*

649 The Conference Board and ESGauge, *Driving Board Excellence* (November 2023).

650 Rock Center for Corporate Governance at Stanford University and The Miles Group, *2016 Survey: Board of Director Evaluation and Effectiveness* (November 2016); PwC, *How Effective is the Board? It Depends on Who You Ask* (July 2024).

651 Corporate Board Member and Diligent Institute, *What Directors Think: Still Taking Care of Business* (2023), https://www.diligentinstitute.com/report/what-directors-think-2023.

652 James Crowe, *Management Succession Planning Disclosure in 2023 Proxy Statements* (CII Research and Education Fund, December 2023).

653 Mark R. Huson, Robert Parrino, and Laura T. Starks, "Internal Monitoring Mechanisms and CEO Turnover: A Long-Term Perspective," *Journal of Finance* 56 (2001): 2265.

654 C. Edward Fee, Charles J. Hadlock, Jing Huang, and Joshua R. Pierce, "Robust Models of CEO Turnover: New Evidence on Relative Performance Evaluation," *The Review of Corporate Finance Studies* 7 (2018): 70; Dirk Jenter and Katharina Lewellen, "Performance-Induced CEO Turnover," *The Review of Financial Studies* 34 (2021) 569.

655 Heidrick & Struggles and the Rock Center for Corporate Governance at Stanford University, *2010 CEO Succession Planning Survey* (June 2010).

656 David F. Larcker, Brian Tayan, and Edward M. Watts, "Firing and Hiring the CEO: What Does CEO Turnover Data Tell Us about Succession Planning?", *Stanford Closer Look Series (April 7, 2022).*

657 Stanford Rock Center for Corporate Governance at Stanford University, *CEO Talent: America's Scarcest Resource? 2017 CEO Talent Survey.*

658 Peter Cziraki and Dirk Jenter, *The Market for CEOs* (working paper, 2020), https://ssrn.com/abstract=3644496.

659 Heidrick & Struggles and the Rock Center for Corporate Governance at Stanford University (2010).

660 The Conference Board, the Institute of Executive Development, and the Rock Center for Corporate Governance at Stanford University, *How Well Do Corporate Directors Know Senior Management?* (2014).

661 A. J. Galainena, David F. Larcker, Mason Morfit, Bloor Redding, Amit Seru, and Brian Tayan, "The CEO Scorecard: How Directors Select a CEO When They Have Real Skin in the Game," *Stanford Closer Look Series* (December 2024).

662 Harwell Wells, "No Man Can Be Worth $1,000,000 a Year: The Fight over Executive Compensation in 1930s America," *University of Richmond Law Review* 44 (January 2010): 689; David F. Larcker and Brian Tayan, "Pay for Performance—But Not Too Much Pay: The American Public's View of CEO Pay," *Stanford Closer Look Series* (November 25, 2019).

663 Lucian A. Bebchuk and Jesse M. Fried, "Pay without Performance: Overview of the Issues," *Academy of Management Perspectives* 20 (2006): 5; Lucian A. Bebchuk and Jesse M. Fried, *Pay Without Performance: The Unfulfilled Promise of Executive Compensation* (Harvard University Press, 2006).

664 Randall Morck, Andrei Shleifer, and Robert W. Vishny, "Management Ownership and Market Valuation: An Empirical Analysis," *Journal of Financial Economics* 20 (1988): 293; John J. McConnell and Henri Servaes, "Additional Evidence on Equity Ownership and Corporate Values," *Journal of Financial Economics* 27 (1990): 595; Ulf von Lilienfeld-Toal and Stefan Ruenzi, "CEO Ownership, Stock Market Performance, and Managerial Discretion," *Journal of Finance* 69 (2014): 1013.

665 Nicholas E. Donatiello, David F. Larcker, and Brian Tayan, "CEO Pay, Performance, and Value Sharing," *Stanford Closer Look Series* (March 2016).

666 Executives with a concentrated equity portfolio in company stock might become risk-averse because a decrease in the price of their stock would significantly reduce their personal wealth. To offset this tendency, the board can award stock options that encourage investment in promising, but uncertain, new projects.

667 Jeff L. Coles, Naveen D. Daniel, and Lalitha Naveen, "Managerial Incentives and Risk-Taking," *Journal of Financial Economics* 79 (2006): 431; Todd A. Gormley, David A. Matsa, and Todd Milbourn, "CEO Compensation and Corporate Risk: Evidence from a Natural Experiment," *Journal of Accounting and Economics* 56 (2013): 79; Christopher S. Armstrong and Rahul Vashishtha,

"Executive Stock Options, Differential Risk-Taking Incentives, and Firm Value," *Journal of Financial Economics* 104 (2012): 70.

668 Justin Chircop, Monika Tarsalewska, and Agnieszka Trzeciakiewicz, "CEO Risk Taking Equity Incentives and Workplace Misconduct," *The Accounting Review* 100 (2025): 139; Christopher S. Armstrong, David F. Larcker, Gaizka Ormazabal, and Daniel J. Taylor, "The Relation Between Equity Incentives and Misreporting: The Role of Risk-Taking Incentives," *Journal of Financial Economics* 109 (2013): 327; Robert H. Davidson, "Who Did It Matters: Executive Equity Compensation and Financial Reporting Fraud," *Journal of Accounting and Economics* 73 (2022).

669 Robert DeYoung, Emma Y. Peng, and Meng Yan, "Executive Compensation and Business Policy Choices at U.S. Commercial Banks," *Journal of Financial and Quantitative Analysis* 48 (2013): 165; Rüdiger Fahlenbrach and René M. Stulz, "Bank CEO Incentives and the Credit Crisis," *Journal of Financial Economics* 99 (2011): 11.

670 Based on 2023 data for 2,856 companies in the Russell 2000 Index, SharkRepellent, FactSet Research Systems, Inc.

671 Paul A. Gompers, Joy Ishii, and Andrew Metrick, "Extreme Governance: An Analysis of Dual-Class Firms in the United States," *Review of Financial Studies* 23 (2010): 1051.

672 Scott B. Smart, Ramabhadran S. Thirumalai, and Chad J. Zutter, "What's in a Vote? The Short- and Long-Run Impact of Dual-Class Equity on IPO Firm Values," *Journal of Accounting and Economics* 45 (March 2008): 94.

673 Beni Lauterbach, and Anete Pajuste, "The Long-Term Valuation Effects of Voluntary Dual-Class Share Unifications," *Journal of Corporate Finance* 31 (April 2015): 171.

674 Martijn Cremers, Beni Lauterbach, and Anete Pajuste, "The Life-Cycle of Dual Class Firms," *Review of Corporate Finance Studies* 13 (2024): 459.

675 Ronald Anderson, Ezgi Ottolenghi, and David Reeb, *The Dual Class Premium: A Family Affair* (working paper, 2017), https://ssrn.com/abstract=3006669.

CHAPTER 13

676 Weinberg, "Status and Functions."

677 The Conference Board, "Timeline," accessed May 2, 2025, https://www.conference-board.org/timeline.

678 For more, visit TCB Benchmarking at: https://www.conference-board.org/topics/tcb-benchmarking.

679 Thomas Clarke, *International Corporate Governance: A Comparative Approach* (Routledge, 2007).

680 Weinberg, "Status and Functions," chap. IV.C.

681 Ibid., chap. IV.C.2.

682 Gordon, "The Rise of Independent Directors," 1465.

683 Roberta Romano, "The Sarbanes–Oxley Act and the Making of Quack Corporate Governance," *Yale Law Journal* 114, no. 7 (2005): 1521.

684 Lucian A. Bebchuk and Scott Hirst, "Index Funds and the Future of Corporate

Governance: Theory, Evidence, and Policy," *Columbia Law Review* 119, no. 8 (2019): 2029.

685 Andrew Jones and Ariane Marchis-Mouren, *Corporate Board Practices in the Russell 3000 and S&P 500: 2025 Edition* (The Conference Board, 2025), 7–9.

686 *Crest v. Padilla, Nos. 19STCV27561 and 20STCV37513* (Cal. Super. Ct., L.A. County, 2022); *Crest v. Padilla*, No. B321726 (Cal. Ct. App., 2d Dist. 2023).

687 *Alliance for Fair Board Recruitment v. Securities and Exchange Commission*, 71 F.4th 218 (5th Cir. 2024).

688 Jones and Marchis-Mouren, *Corporate Board Practices*, 9.

689 The Conference Board and ESGAUGE, *Public Disclosure Data on Corporate Board Practices* (2025).

690 Ibid.

691 Jones and Marchis-Mouren, *Corporate Board Practices*, 11–13.

692 Weinberg, "Status and Functions," chap. II.G.

693 Jeffrey Sonnenfeld, "What Makes Great Boards Great," *Harvard Business Review* (September 2002); Morten Huse, *Boards, Governance and Value Creation* (Cambridge University Press, 2007), 131–36.

694 Jones and Marchis-Mouren, *Corporate Board Practices*, 2–3.

695 Ibid.

696 Weinberg, "Status and Functions," chap. IV.B. All ensuing quotations in this and the next paragraph are from this chapter.

697 Ryan Krause, Michael C. Withers, and Matthew A. Semadeni, "Do Board Chairs Matter? The Influence of Board Chairs on Firm Performance," *Strategic Management Journal* 38, no. 3 (March 2017): 697–713.

698 David Larcker and Brian Tayan, *Corporate Governance Matters*, 2nd ed. (Pearson Education, 2016), 112–16.

699 See, e.g., Institutional Shareholder Services, *US Proxy Voting Guidelines Benchmark Policy Recommendations* (2024).

700 Financial Reporting Council, *UK Corporate Governance Code* (2018); ASX Corporate Governance Council, *Corporate Governance Principles and Recommendations*, 4th ed. (2019); European Commission, *Study on Directors' Duties and Sustainable Corporate Governance* (2020).

701 Conference Board and ESGAUGE, *Public Disclosure Data.*

702 Ibid.

703 Ibid.

704 Weinberg, "Status and Functions," chap. III.A.5.

705 Ibid., chap. III.A.1.

706 Ibid., chap. III.A.5.

707 Sarbanes–Oxley Act of 2002, Pub. L. No. 107-204; Dodd–Frank Wall Street Reform and Consumer Protection Act of 2010, Pub. L. No. 111-203

708 New York Stock Exchange, *Listed Company Manual*, § 303A.09; Nasdaq Listing Rule 5605.

709 Financial Reporting Council, *UK Corporate Governance Code*; European Parliament, "Directive (EU) 2017/828," *Official Journal of the European Union*, May 17, 2017.

710 Rita Meyerson, Andrew Jones, Marion Devine, Matt Rosenbaum, and Christine Guinessey, *The Evolving Role of the CHRO in the Boardroom* (The Conference Board, 2025).
711 Jones and Marchis-Mouren, *Corporate Board Practices*, 4–5.
712 Ibid.
713 Weinberg, "Status and Functions," chap. II.D.
714 Ibid.
715 Stephen M. Bainbridge, *Corporate Governance After the Financial Crisis* (Oxford University Press, 2012), 88–92.
716 Conference Board and ESGAUGE, *Public Disclosure Data.*
717 Ibid.
718 Paul Hodgson, Andrew Jones, and Ariane Marchis-Mouren, *Board Director Compensation Practices in the Russell 3000 and S&P 500: 2025 Edition* (The Conference Board, 2025).
719 Weinberg, "Status and Functions," chap. III.A.1.
720 Jay W. Lorsch and Elizabeth MacIver, *Pawns or Potentates: The Reality of America's Corporate Boards* (Harvard Business School Press, 1989), 68–70.
721 *Smith v. Van Gorkom*, 488 A.2d 858 (Del. 1985); *In re Caremark International Inc. Derivative Litigation*, 698 A.2d 959 (Del. Ch. 1996).
722 Stephen M. Bainbridge, *Corporate Law and Economics* (Foundation Press, 2002), 303–6.
723 Jones and Marchis-Mouren, *Corporate Board Practices*, 11–13.

CHAPTER 14

724 Data in this chapter are derived from a benchmarking survey conducted by the Society for Corporate Governance among its members in August and September 2025. Respondents—177 primarily corporate secretaries, in-house counsel, and other in-house governance professionals—represent a diverse range of public and private companies and nonprofit organizations across various sizes and industries. The analysis also includes an examination of similarities and differences in policies and practices employed by public companies (n=142) and private companies (n=21).
725 See *Spencer Stuart U.S. Board Index 2025*, 42.
726 See New York Stock Exchange, *Listed Company Manual*, § 303A.02.
727 See, e.g., HSF Kramer, "A Delayed Look at the Delaware Supreme Court Decision in *In re Match Derivative Litigation*," client alert, October 2024.
728 *In re Oracle Corp. Derivative Litigation*, 824 A.2d 917, 938–39 (Del. Ch. 2003).
729 Spencer Stuart, *Director Pulse Survey: Time Commitment* (2024).
730 MyLogIQ, *A Look at Combined CEO–Chairs* (2021).
731 See, e.g., Stephen M. Bainbridge, "The Case for the CEO as Chair," *Harvard Law School Forum on Corporate Governance*, September 1, 2011.
732 FW Cook, *2025 Director Compensation Report.*

AFTERWORD

733 Weinberg, "Status and Functions."

734 Weinberg, "The Functions."

735 See Leo E. Strine, Jr., "Ignorance is Strength: Climate Change, Corporate Governance, Politics, and the English Language," *Journal of Law and Political Economy* 5 (2025): 170; Leo E. Strine, Jr., "Using Experience Smartly to Ensure a Better Future: How the Hard-Earned Lessons of History Should Shape the External and Internal Governance of Corporate Use of Artificial Intelligence," *Journal of Corporation Law* 50 (2025): 1265.

CONCLUSION

736 See Lawrence A. Cunningham, "Imagining the Public Company Board of 2053," *Corporate Board* (2024).

Index

C

D

E

F

G

M

N

Y

Z

About the Author

Lawrence A. Cunningham is a widely published author, public company director, and advocate of long-term, shareholder-oriented corporate governance. A Professor Emeritus at George Washington University and Director of the John L. Weinberg Center for Corporate Governance at the University of Delaware, he serves on the boards of Markel Group and Constellation Software. In 2018, the National Association of Corporate Directors honored him with its Lifetime Achievement Award for advancing effective board leadership and governance. He is the author of twenty books, including *The Essays of Warren Buffett* and *Boardroom Legacy*.